The American Experience in World War II

Edited with introductions by

Walter L. Hixson
University of Akron, Ohio

A ROUTLEDGE SERIES

Contents of the Collection

The American Experience in World War II

Volume 11

Remembering and Representing the Second World War

Edited with introductions by

Walter L. Hixson
University of Akron, Ohio

Routledge
New York and London

Published in 2003 by
Routledge
29 West 35th Street
New York, NY 10001
www.routledge-ny.com

Published in Great Britain by
Routledge
11 New Fetter Lane
London EC4P 4EE
www.routledge.co.uk

Routledge is an imprint of the Taylor & Francis Group.
Copyright © 2003 by Taylor & Francis Books, Inc.

10 9 8 7 6 5 4 3 2 1

Library of Congress Cataloging-in-Publication Data

The American experience in World War II / edited with introductions by Walter Hixson.
    p. cm.
    Contents: v. 1. The United States and the road to war in Europe—v. 2. Isolationists and internationalists : the battle over intervention—v. 3. The United States and the road to war in the Pacific—v. 4. Pearl Harbor in history and memory—v. 5. The United States in the European theater—v. 6. The United States in the Pacific war—v. 7. The atomic bomb in history and memory—v. 8. American diplomacy in the Second World War—v. 9. American culture at war : the homefront—v. 10. The American people at war : minorities and women in the Second World War—v. 11. Remembering and representing the Second World War—v. 12. The United States transformed : the lessons and legacies of the Second World War.
    ISBN 0-415-94028-1 (set)—ISBN 0-415-94029-X (v. 1: alk. paper)—ISBN 0-415-94030-3 (v. 2: alk. paper)—ISBN 0-415-94031-1 (v. 3: alk. paper)—ISBN 0-415-94032-X (v. 4: alk. paper)—ISBN 0-415-94033-8 (v. 5: alk. paper)—ISBN 0-415-94034-6 (v. 6: alk. paper)—ISBN 0-415-94035-4 (v. 7: alk. paper)—ISBN 0-415-94036-2 (v. 8: alk. paper)—ISBN 0-415-94037-0 (v. 9: alk. paper)—ISBN 0-415-94038-9 (v. 10: alk. paper)—ISBN 0-415-94039-7 (v. 11: alk. paper)—ISBN 0-415-94040-0 (v. 12: alk. paper).
    1. World War, 1939–1945—United States. 2. United States—History—1933–1945.
I. Title: American experience in World War Two. II. Title: American experience in World War 2. III. Hixson, Walter L.
B769.(title entry)
940.53'73—dc21   2002031849

Contents

Series Introduction

World War II overshadows the twentieth century. The conflict, truly global in scope, transformed the world. While less *directly* affected than most nations, the United States underwent fundamental change as a result of its participation in the Second World War. The volumes in this collection reflect the profound changes in American military history, foreign policy, domestic politics, social relations, and its memory and representation of the war over succeeding generations.

World War II evolved in Europe primarily as a result of the aggression built into the national socialist German regime under the dictatorship of Adolf Hitler. The Nazi leader's brutal racialist expansionism made war virtually inevitable. After a series of aggressive acts in central Europe, Britain, France, and allied nations declared war on Germany. In the United States, President Franklin D. Roosevelt monitored these events with increasing concern but neither he nor the vast majority of the American public, imbued with bitter memories of World War I, wished to get involved in the early stages of the war. By the summer of 1940, however, with Germany in the course of bombing Britain and having sacked the Low Countries and France, the United States began to move toward intervention. The articles in volume 1, "The United States and the Road to War in Europe," analyze these developments.

The path toward intervention precipitated a bitter battle between so-called "isolationists"—really non-interventionists—and proponents of U.S. involvement in the European war. The two sides waged a political struggle over the direction and character of U.S. foreign policy between 1939 and December 7, 1941. By that date the Roosevelt administration had orchestrated a series of steps that found the United States directly aiding the Allies and determined to play a key role in preventing German domination of Europe. The articles in volume 2, "Isolationists and Internationalists: The Battle over Intervention," address the history and the historical debate over the struggle for the soul of the nation's foreign policy on the eve of World War II.

The United States ultimately became a belligerent as a result of events in Asia. Japanese intervention in China, Indochina, and other regions clashed with European imperialism and the rising American empire in Asia. The articles in volume 3, "The United States and the Road to War in the

Pacific," chronicle the coming of the Pacific War between the United States and Japan. War came with the Japanese assault on Pearl Harbor on December 7, followed by Hitler's declaration of war on the United States. The world thus became embroiled in a deadly struggle, with monumental implications, between the Axis powers led by Germany and Japan, and the United Nations under the stewardship of the United States, Great Britain, and the Soviet Union.

In the more than sixty years that have passed since the outbreak of the war, Americans have been drawn back to its origins at Pearl Harbor. Articles in volume 4, "Pearl Harbor in History and Memory," analyze the origins of the Japanese surprise attack, the American response, the groundless conspiracy theories focusing on the Roosevelt administration, the lasting imprint of Pearl Harbor on American memories, and its influence on U.S.-Japanese relations throughout the postwar era.

Well before the outbreak of war, the Roosevelt administration and military planners had already agreed on a "Europe-first" strategy. The articles in volume 5, "The United States in the European Theater," examine U.S. military strategy and engagements from the outbreak of war, through the D-Day invasion, the Battle of the Bulge, and the ultimate defeat of the Nazi regime in May 1945. Volume 6, "The United States in the Pacific War" analyzes American strategy to defeat Japan, "island hopping," key battles such as Midway, and the ultimate defeat of Japan in August 1945.

In volume 7, "The Atomic Bomb in History and Memory," scholars probe the origins and evolution of the American decision to drop atomic bombs on Hiroshima and Nagasaki on August 6 and 9, 1945. No shortage of controversy prevails over issues such as Japan's readiness to surrender, American non-nuclear options, and other paths not taken at the end of the Pacific war. Debate, implications, lessons, memories, and cultural resonances all receive attention from the contributors to the volume, a chronicle on the fiery birth of the nuclear age.

The American victory on both fronts in World War II would have been impossible without the careful cultivation of allies. The articles in volume 8 focus on American diplomacy in the Second World War. Despite the close affinity between the United States and Great Britain, tension over strategy and war aims surfaced throughout the war. Similarly, the United States and the Soviet Union, while able to cooperate militarily, held the other's ideology in contempt and distrusted the rival state's political aims. Volume 8 analyzes these and other diplomatic relationships throughout the war.

While statesmen conducted diplomacy and soldiers waged war, the American people found their lives dramatically affected on the homefront. The articles in volume 9, "American Culture at War: The Homefront," reflect the transformations wrought by the war effort, including rationing, unprecedented mobility, attitudes about war, and the experiences of individual communities and regions of the country. The lives of women, African-Americans, and other minorities were so dramatically affected by the war as to merit separate treatment, which they receive in volume 10, "The American People at War: Women and Minorities in the Second World War." These articles explore issues such as the new role of women as industrial workers, as frontline nurses, and in combat. Other essays analyze the "Double V" campaign of African-Americans and the impetus the war gave to the modern civil rights movement. The internment of Japanese-Americans and the effects of the war on other ethnic groups are also addressed in this volume.

As a result of the war's pervasive impact on American life and its obvious significance to history, it is no surprise that the conflict has been the subject of countless memoirs, novels, films, and other representations in the popular culture. Volume 11 explores "Remembering and Representing the Second World War," with particular emphasis on filmic representations. Articles in the volume range from analyses of wartime propaganda to popular films of the postwar era, including two Steven Spielberg epics, "Schindler's List" and "Saving Private Ryan."

The final volume of the twelve-part series addresses "The United States Transformed: Lessons and Legacies of the Second World War." Having emerged relatively unscathed and as the most powerful nation in the world, the United States faced a host of issues ranging from economic adjustments at home to foreign policy challenges—notably decolonization and the Cold War—abroad. The nation's ability to respond to these and other challenges would characterize the postwar years, an era forever changed by World War II and its many legacies.

Walter L. Hixson

The editor would like to extend special appreciation to Brian Himebaugh.

Volume Introduction

Scholars study not only what happened in the past but also how that past is represented within various cultural settings. Cultural representations, including popular culture, inform us as to the reception and collective memory of events. In the first entry, Chad Berry focuses on the complex construction of American collective memory of World War II.

Film has been an especially significant medium for representation of the history of World War II. Historian Michael Todd Bennett analyzes the propagandistic character of pro-British American cinema on the eve of U.S. intervention in World War II. Frederic Krome addresses the same subject in his reconstruction of the history of the award-winning documentary *The True Glory*, which despite its commercial success was actually a blow to Anglo-American relations.

As Gregory D. Black and Clayton R. Koppes demonstrate, the U.S. government well understood that American film could promote the war effort. Thus, the mobilization of American society for war included government collusion with Hollywood to produce patriotic films designed to demonize the nation's enemies and ensure unity at home. Ralph R. Donald explains how film representations of the Pearl Harbor attack played on the theme of Japanese treachery in order to help promote outrage and to galvanize the American "sleeping giant" into decisive military action. Susan D. Moeller analyzes American media representations of Japan, arguing that they changed to conform to dominant American attitudes rather than objective reality. Peter L. Valenti argues that the World War II fantasy films *A Guy Named Joe* and *The Enchanted Cottage* offered "cultural sustenance" to audiences weary of the grinding war effort.

Throughout the postwar years, Hollywood continued to mold consensus with scores of film representations of the conflict. Philip D. Beidler analyzes the role of the wildly popular musical *South Pacific* in creating American remembrances of World War II. Leonard J. Leff argues that the novel and film *The Pawnbroker* laid the groundwork for later and more popularly successful representations of the Holocaust. In his article on Steven Spielberg and *Schindler's List*, Frank Manchel explores the complexity of Hollywood filmmaking and the role of the filmmaker as mediator between the audience and the reality that films depict. Eliot Cohen seeks explanations for the divergent reception between public audiences and critics of Spielberg's epic film *Saving Private Ryan.*

Thomas Cripps and David Culbert explore the ironies of the path-breaking government film, *The Negro Solider,* which they credit with helping to ignite the postwar civil rights movement. Greg Garrett argues, however, that the overwhelming majority of wartime films extolled the virtues of white society to the exclusion of people of color. Leonard Leff explores the complex legacy of World War II's impact on American women as represented in the film *Johnny Belinda.* In "Saving Private Property," Catherine Gunther Kodat argues that the celebrated Spielberg film *Saving Private Ryan* memorialized World War II as a means to reinforce neoconservative values of the 1990s. Todd Bennett analyzes the integral role that an American propaganda film on the Soviet Union—*Mission to Moscow*—played in the wartime strategy of Franklin D. Roosevelt. Alvin H. Rosenfield analyzes the role of television programming in educating American audiences about the Nazi holocaust of World War II. Michael Mandelbaum explores the significance of Herman Wouk's two volumes of historical fiction on World War II in celebrating the legacy of the conflict.

Public, Private, and Popular: The United States Remembers World War II

*Chad Berry**

One hundred years before fighting broke out in World War II, Carl von Clausewitz, the European military theorist, wrote that war was a "true chameleon" whose color changes to match its background. He continued,

> As a total phenomenon, its dominant tendencies always make war a paradoxical trinity—composed of primordial violence, hatred, and enmity, which are to be regarded as a blind natural force; of the play of chance and probability within which the creative spirit is free to roam; and of its elements of subordination, as an instrument of policy, which makes it subject to reason alone.[1]

Thus, according to Clausewitz, policy makers, soldiers, and artists all contribute to the paradoxical trinity that constitutes the totality of war. Put differently, Clausewitz speaks of public, private, and popular, and I would like to focus on the place where the elements of this trinity intersect—memory—as I describe the ways in which the people of the United States have remembered World War II, a memory that has been complex and at odds throughout much of the last fifty years.

A few words of clarification: World War II involved a mobilization such as the people of the United States had never experienced, and the mobilization, of course, involved not only getting soldiers and supply personnel across oceans but also countless changes within the country,

* I would like to thank John Bodnar, David Thelen, and Patrick Ettinger for their help in writing this essay.

particularly to produce the staggering amount of war matériel. Although I am concentrating on the memory of soldiers (or private memory) and how this memory compares with public and popular memory, I want to point out that during these past few years of commemoration of the fiftieth anniversary of the war, home front memories have often been ignored (especially publicly) in favor of GI commemoration, primarily, I believe, because women were so much a part of the home front, while men were so much a part of the battle front.[2] If World War II was "everybody's war," commemoration in the 1990s has seemed to be only for those who fought on the front lines.

Public Memory

I will begin with public memory, for no better reason other than this view of the war has been in many ways the most pervasive, or at least the one that many assume is the "true" memory of U.S. involvement in the war. According to public memory and accompanying public ideology, World War II was a *good war*, one in which the United States entered the conflict valiantly and heroically (and even arrogantly) to save the world from the evil associated with the Third Reich and Imperial Japan. The good war thesis became a powerfully seductive and intoxicating view of an idealized past and a golden age.[3]

According to the good war thesis, and in true cowboy-and-Indian fashion, the Allies, and particularly the Americans, were *good,* and the Axis, particularly the Japanese, who had embarrassed the country with the attack on Pearl Harbor, were *bad,* even to the point of being subhuman. The noted wartime correspondent Ernie Pyle described his thoughts of the Pacific enemy: "In Europe," he wrote, "we felt our enemies, horrible and deadly as they were, were still people. But out here I gathered that the Japanese were looked upon as something subhuman and repulsive; the way some people feel about cockroaches or mice." Seeing a group of prisoners, he wrote, "gave me the creeps, and I wanted to take a mental bath after looking at them." This is quite a justification of the good war.[4]

But historians have pointed out how specific myths and images of war, after being stripped of their context and molded into abstractions, have, in the words of Craig M. Cameron, "been appropriated to create a historical narrative...that has in turn served a variety of uses in...American society."[5] Throughout the last fifty years, veterans' groups, the military, and the federal government have shaped wartime memories to serve their own needs. For example, Cameron shows how heroic myths of "uncommon valor" among the United States Marine Corps in the Pacific War (liberation there was always seen as due primarily if not exclusively to the United States) were used repeatedly by the Marines in later years to protect their institution against government cuts and to solidify their past as an invaluable part of the country's defense arsenal. The myth of a good war and, by implication, good fighting, Cameron argues, not only perpetuated the uncritical acceptance of the good war thesis, it papered over questions about responsibility and ramifications of violence in the Pacific War, such as Marines so angry at the enemy that they tortured and killed prisoners of war and violated Japanese war dead, including shooting off the genitals of dead Japanese soldiers.[6]

For its part, the U.S. government had an enormous role in creating and sustaining the image of the good war and was aided greatly by a press that was expected to temper the violence. Because fighting never took place within the country, it was relatively easy for the government to create stories of the good war for the folks back home. And the press generally cooperated: *Life* magazine, for example, refrained from publishing graphic photographs that contained dead or injured soldiers. Because of the reporting of Ernie Pyle and other correspondents, soldiers were "boyish" and happy—indeed, eager—about marching off to fight. GIs were always kind to children, civilians, and prisoners of war abroad. The military, historian Michael C. C. Adams has argued, was a "surrogate father" that watched over its boys' morals.[7] But what the military as a surrogate father told American parents about their boys was sanitized. Paul Fussell, for example, disdains the "optimistic publicity" of public memory.[8] He says that soldiers knew that their experience was not only repeatedly "sanitized" but also "Norman Rockwellized" and even "Disneyfied."[9] A good example of sanitation was the GI phrase "snafu" (situation normal all fucked up), which became translated as "fouled up" here at home, because the *U.S. Infantry Journal* condemned profanity. Other examples from the war, including war crimes, rampant sexuality, alcohol abuse, homosexuality, and war psychoses, discount the image of the good war fostered by the government and the media.[10]

After the war, the government continued to perpetuate the good war in public commemoration. Valiant and "good" soldiers dominate the interpretation of two national war memorials, the United States Marine

3

Corps Memorial in Washington, D.C., and the memorial over the USS
Arizona in Pearl Harbor, Hawaii. Indeed, interpretation at the two
memorials has made them sacred U.S. Valhallas that house the souls of
the brave and heroic. The Marine Corps memorial is taken from a
staged photograph of Marines struggling to raise the American flag on
Mount Surabachi on Iwo Jima in 1945. The image, which became
emblazoned in the minds of most Americans, evokes the democratic
ethos cultivated throughout U.S. involvement in the war: across an
ocean brave soldiers were raising the flag together as citizens back
home were doing their part: it was everybody's war.[11]

Unlike the interpretation at the Marine Corps memorial, the
Arizona memorial does not completely mask the brutality of war.
Because the memorial is built over the sunken wreckage of the
battleship in which sailors are interred, the visitor is eerily able to
watch air bubbles rise from the murky wreckage below the water. Any
tinges of death, however, are eventually overwhelmed by the theme of
a strong and ultimately triumphant United States rising from the Pearl
Harbor attack: the monument is built of concrete and white marble in
an elongated shape that sags in the middle, indicating that the country
took a blow during the attack on Pearl Harbor but bounced back. Even
in the *Arizona,* victory wins out over violence.[12]

Finally, it is easier to describe public memory by listening to voices
trying to defend it. This was certainly true in 1995 as many voices
clamored over a planned exhibition at the Smithsonian Institution's
National Air and Space Museum that would include the *Enola Gay,* the
B-29 bomber that dropped the first atomic bomb on Hiroshima. The experience of the *Enola Gay* exhibition shows the extent to which groups
will fight to preserve public memory. Martin Harwit, then director of
the museum, is reported to have wanted the exhibition to show an
alternative to the good war, in his words, "a counterpoint to the World
War II gallery we now have, which portrays the heroism of the airmen
but neglects to mention in any real sense the misery of the war. I think
we just can't afford to make war a heroic event where people could
prove their manliness and then come home to woo the fair damsel."[13]

The Air Force Association (AFA) was one of the first groups to
raise objections to the exhibition, arguing that instead of the heroic
interpretation that was deserved, the "U.S. conduct of the war was
depicted as brutal, vindictive, and racially motivated." Gen. Monroe W.
Hatch, Jr., president of the AFA, said the plan "treats Japan and the

United States as if their participation in the war were morally equivalent."[14] Voices howled over casting doubt on the accepted justification of dropping the bomb, that close to a quarter of a million U.S. casualties would result (some said at least a million) by invading Japan. In reality, historians have obtained declassified estimates of 69,000.[15] Veterans were appalled. George R. Caron, a tail gunner on the *Enola Gay*, wrote, "We didn't start the war, and it had to be won by any possible means....Japan lost the war about a year before the atom bombs were dropped but wouldn't give up. I believe the Japanese would have fought on with the last man, woman, and child."[16]

Soon, the American Legion was involved in fighting the exhibition, and in May 1994 it passed a resolution that strongly objected to

> the use of the *Enola Gay* and the heroic men who flew her in an exhibit [that] questions the moral and political wisdom involved in the dropping of the atomic bomb and [implies] that America was somehow in the wrong and her loyal airmen somehow criminal in carrying out this last act of the war, which, in fact, hastened the war's end and preserved the lives of countless Americans and Japanese alike.[17]

Defenders of a heroic memory of World War II prevailed. On 30 January 1995, Smithsonian Secretary I. Michael Heyman announced that the original exhibition would be scrapped, as historians cried foul and leveled charges of historical cleansing and McCarthyism. It quickly became apparent that defenders of the good war would accept nothing but heroic victory. The pilot of the *Enola Gay*, Paul Tibbets, said that "those of us who gained that victory have nothing to be ashamed of.... The million of us remaining will die believing that we made the world a better place because of our efforts to secure peace that has held for almost fifty years." His is certainly a well-argued defense of the good war.[18]

Private Memory

The *Enola Gay* controversy proves that the effort to legitimize public memory can become a battle in and of itself. But what is not so clear until one begins exploring the *private* memories of actual soldiers is the often vast discord between public and private memory of World War II. Even though the Air Force Association and the American Legion would have one believe that every soldier who fought shares their heroic memory of World War II, private memories are much darker and more ambivalent. If public memory of World War II is highlighted by what some have called a conservative memory, including leitmotifs of valor, heroism, comradeship, release, and higher cause, private memory is often typified by a liberal experience, including themes of death, suffering, stupidity, and futility, themes that have never been easily communicable to the public.[19] According to Craig Cameron, private memory has been "preserved in quiet ways…in scrapbooks and personal memories," ways that have not captured much public attention.[20]

Reading the private memories of soldiers collected in oral histories quickly tempers the notion of a good war. The recollections of Dwayne Burns, then eighteen years old, on the eve of D-Day incorporate much of both the conservative and liberal experiences of war; he takes pride in comradeship but is also deeply fearful of imminent death. Dwayne Burns was ambivalent:

> We didn't know just what was ahead, but we were honed to a fine edge. We were as trained and ready as we'll ever be. We were tired of waiting and ready for the next step. Now here we sat, each man alone in the dark with his own thoughts and fears. These men around me were the best friends I will ever know. Four months is a long time when you live and work together, day and night. I wondered how many will die before the sun comes up tomorrow. "Lord," I pray, "please let me do everything right. Don't let me get anybody killed and don't let me get killed, either. I really think I'm too young for this. I should be home having a good time. Whoever told me I was a fighter anyway?"[21]

Other soldiers, however, were far less ambivalent, and their memories and opinions of their experience have little in common with the good war thesis. According to historian Michael Adams, combat was not glamorous for those engaged in it, nor were U.S. soldiers "happy warriors"; many soldiers, he argues, felt they put in more than their fair share of suffering and dying, and the memories of soldiers perfectly echo his point. Infantryman Charles Brummett, for example, remembered feeling like an animal while sleeping in the mud and snow and even resenting other soldiers who did not have to endure the harsh conditions. "It wasn't like some of the other service, you know," he said, "You didn't have a place to go inside to a good warm meal."[22] According to Adams,

Some resented those who were home enjoying prosperity, and some have continued to suffer psychological or physical pain as a result of their wartime experience. Dealing with the experience of combat takes more than a parade. Death was normally not romantic, particularly when the victim was blown apart: many Americans fail to understand that most MIAs simply ceased to exist.[23]

Soldiers were often preoccupied with worry, as Dwayne Burns was; infrequently were they the proud, confident men marching forward in the good war. While on Okinawa, William Manchester remembered that his "throat was thick with fear."[24] According to Joe D. Reilly of the 501st Parachute Infantry Regiment, "Not much conversation took place in the plane. Each man had his own thoughts, anxiety, and fear. You wouldn't be human if you didn't. My thoughts were dominated by hoping the pilot would not get scared and would bring our plane into the drop zone area."[25] While in the plane over the English Channel, reality quickly dawned on Ken Cordry, a Screaming Eagle from the 101st Airborne. "After getting my seat in the plane," he said, "it finally struck me that this was it; that in a few minutes I'd be behind the German lines—that is, if we made it to our drop zone, and if I made the landing without being hit, and if I was able to find some of our men after landing. It was a terrible sinking feeling, realizing that within a few minutes I might not even be around on this old earth anymore."[26] Richard Scudder, from Oklahoma, remembers the tremendous anxiety he had as he was about to jump out of his plane and into the enemy territory of occupied France. "For the ride across the Channel," he said, "nothing seemed real. It seemed to me like the world was coming to an end. When our plane taxied down around on the runway, a real sick feeling came over us." Over France, he said, "all hell broke loose. The bullets hitting our planes sounded like someone was throwing gravel on a tin roof." His worry came to a head when it was his time to jump:

As I got to the door, a burst of flak exploded right above my head. I don't know how this could ever happen but it did: A piece of that flak got under my helmet and hit me in the eyebrow, and the blood streamed down across my face, and I remember frantically feeling for a hole, thinking that I had been shot with one of those tracer bullets that I had witnessed coming up toward us. Thank God it was only a scratch in my eyebrow. That was a relief to find that I hadn't picked up a bullet. [27]

Ultimately, Ken Cordry's and Richard Scudder's fear and anxiety concerned death, and much of private memory is preoccupied with dying, either worrying that one's number might be up next or seeing the grotesque sight of bodies everywhere whose numbers had already been called. Harold Baumgarten knew what war was like, and before he shoved off for Europe he took steps to insure that things would be covered in the event that he died:

> I had a good background in American history and wartime battles and realized that it was not going to be easy, and I did not expect to come back alive, and wrote such to my sister—that she was to get the mail before my parents and break the news gently to them when she received the telegram that I was no longer alive. [28]

Elliott Johnson, who had landed in France on D-Day, 6 June 1944 and was able to take off his shoes and socks and change clothes on 4 July 1944 was later fighting in the Hürtgen Forest, and he recalled the horrific memory of a forward observer who had gone out with his crew. "White phosphorus was thrown at them," Johnson explained. "Two of the men burned before his eyes. He came running to where I was in another part of Hürtgen Forest. I went down the road to meet him. He was sobbing and falling into my arms. He kept saying, 'No more killing, no more killing, no more killing.'" [29] One soldier whose arm was blown off in Italy looked down on his injured self and cursed God and the United States because he suffered "for something I never did or know anything about." [30] Even somewhat ambivalent about his combat experience, William Manchester was obsessed with his dead comrades:

> Inside, though, I was still scared. I felt the growing reserve which is the veteran's shield against grief. I wondered, as I had wondered before, what had become of our dead, where they were now. And in a way which I cannot explain I felt responsible for the lost Raggedy Asses, guilty because I was here and they weren't, frustrated because I was unable to purge my shock by loathing the enemy...I was in the midst of satanic madness: I knew it. I wanted to return to sanity: I couldn't. [31]

Memories associated with D-Day in particular are peppered with haunting stories of death and the dead, and these memories impart a far different impression of a "good war's" invasion. Robert Flory, a paratrooper, remembered landing "in water up to my chest. I saw one plane take a direct hit and explode in mid-air. Every man in that plane died a quick and merciful death."[32] Others died far less mercifully. John Fitzgerald, another paratrooper, landed safely but soon began to see those who didn't:

> We passed the church where a trooper had landed direct on its steeple. His chute was still swaying slowly in the breeze with no one in it. Many of the troopers were killed before they hit the ground or shortly after they landed, and some were still hanging in trees looking like rag dolls shot full of holes. Their blood was dripping on this place they came to free. Seeing these first Americans dead and the way they had died had a chilling effect on us.[33]

On his way to fill his canteen at a well near a farmhouse, one sight in particular has never left John's mind:

> It was a picture story of the death of one 82nd Airborne trooper. He had occupied a German foxhole and made it his personal Alamo. In a half circle around the hole lay the bodies of nine German soldiers, the body closest to the hole only three feet away, a "potato masher" [German hand grenade] clutched in its fist. The other distorted forms lay where they fell, testimony to the ferocity of the fight. His ammunition bandoleers were still on his shoulders, but empty of all the M-1 clips. Cartridge cases littered the ground. His rifle stock was broken in two, its splinters adding to the debris. He had fought alone, and like many others that night, he had died alone. I looked at his dog tags. The name read Martin V. Hersh. I wrote the name down in a small prayer book I carried, hoping someday I would meet someone who knew him. I never did.[34]

Warner Hamlett, an infantryman with the 116th Regiment, remembered a moment when a fellow GI almost sensed that his death was imminent just as they landed on Omaha beach:

> While resting in between the obstacles, Private Gillingham fell beside me, white with fear. He seemed to be begging for help with his eyes. His look was that of a child asking what to do. I said, "Gillingham, let's stay separated as much as we can, because the Germans will fire at two quicker than one." He remained silent and then I heard a shell coming and dove into the sand facedown. Shrapnel rose over my head and hit all

around me. It took Gillingham's chin off, including the bone, except for a small piece of flesh. He tried to hold his chin in place as he ran towards the seawall. He made it to the wall, where Will Hawks and I gave him his morphine shot. He stayed with me for approximately thirty minutes until he died. The entire time, he remained conscious and aware that he was dying.[35]

Finally, William R. Cubbins, a bomber pilot, always worried about dying in the night while in his plane. "To me," he has written in his memoirs, "death in the lonesomeness of night-blackened skies is so impersonal it violates the rules of dying. Death should never be without meaning or purpose, or dignity. To disappear suddenly in the faceless void of night is to lose one's very existence, to become as an incomplete sentence."[36]

Memories of war that included terrible death also include the bungling and botched plans of warfare, hardly a testimony to the theme of omnipotence of the good war. Harry Bare, a member of the 116th Infantry Regiment, found himself in charge of the remaining men in his squadron because so many had not made it from the landing craft:

As ranking noncom I tried to get my men off the boat and make it somehow to the cliff, but it was horrible—men frozen in the sand, unable to move. My radio man had his head blown off three yards from me. The beach was covered with bodies—men with no legs, no arms—God, it was awful. It was absolutely terrible.[37]

Sims Gauthier, landing at Utah Beach, said there was mass confusion because so many officers were killed. "It was just like geese flying in the flock when the leader is killed," he recalled. Struggling to navigate the craft to its beach landing, Sims heard a tremendous explosion next to his craft that lifted it out of the water and sent a shock wave through it:

Then I saw what had happened. An LCT with the four DD tanks had just been blown sky high and everything just disappeared in a matter of seconds. It was another mine, and I said, "Well Howard [Vander Beek], it looks like the stuff has hit the fan!" First wave, and still seven thousand yards from shore, and no control vessels for Red Beach, and four tanks and an LCT and crew on the bottom.[38]

Things were little better at Omaha Beach. Thomas Valence of the 116th infantry division quickly abandoned his instructions and, later, his equipment, as he struggled to stay alive while fighting the water and the German fire and trying to make it to the beach:

It was then that he was first shot in the left hand: I floundered in the water and had my hand up in the air, trying to get my balance. I made my way forward as best I could. My rifle jammed, so I picked up a carbine and got off a couple of rounds. We were shooting at something that seemed inconsequential. There was no way I was going to knock out a German concrete emplacement with a .30-caliber rifle. I was hit again, once in the left thigh, which broke my hip bone, and a couple of times in my pack, and then my chin strap on my helmet was severed by a bullet. I worked my way up onto the beach, and staggered up against a wall, and collapsed there. The bodies of the other guys washed ashore, and I was one live body amongst many of my friends who were dead and, in many cases, blown to pieces.[39]

Other soldiers fifty years later still remembered the destruction of the war and could still see the human toll, particularly on children, who were fighting to remain alive even after their community had been liberated, as James Etter told me in an interview:

I went to Fort Harrison, Indiana, and then from there to El Paso, Texas. And to basic training there. And then I went to Germany just outside of Nuremberg, the war was just over at that time. I got there in time to be a replacement troop and of course we landed in Le Havre, France. To see how, oh, the terrible destruction of war was unbelievable, really. I mean, Le Havre had been bombed both ways, you know. The Germans had took it from the French and the Germans had such a strong hold there then that the Allies had just bombed and bombed them then to get the Germans out. And to land there and see [the] destruction of Le Havre was not a pretty sight. And even though we had been real poor on the farm here and many times it was cornbread and beans or something like that, I don't think we ever went to bed hungry, not really. Not real hungry. I mean, we might have been hungry for something besides what we had or something but really not. And it was there that I [first] saw real poverty.

Well, when we landed in Le Havre, you know, I saw
children for the first time that, you know, they had given us
stuff that I didn't think was very good to eat. It didn't look like
it was anyway. And to throw that out and just see little kids
running and grabbing it, dirt and all, and sticking it in their
mouths, I had never saw that. You know, you flip a cigarette
butt and three or four little fellows just diving for that. You
know, and knocking the fire out and saving that butt. I had
never saw that.[40]

Other soldiers, in elegant simplicity, remembered the war as among
the most stupid of humankind's actions. Admiral Gene LaRocque, for
example, was particularly virulent about World War II, and his memory
and opinions would make one believe he was talking about the Vietnam
War, not the supposedly "good war" of World War II:

In that four years, I thought, what a hell of a waste of a man's
life. I lost a lot of friends. I had the task of telling my
roommate's parents about our last days together. You lose
limbs, sight, part of your life—for what? Old men send young
men to war. Flags, banners, and patriotic sayings.[41]

LaRocque was particularly critical of the consequences of the good
war thesis, pointing out how he believed that the United States has been
unique in its postwar legacy of always "fighting a war since 1940."
"Count the wars—Korea, Vietnam—count the years. We have built up
in our body politic," he continued, "a group of old men," mainly, he
implies, those who served in World War II, "who look upon military
service as a noble adventure. It was the big excitement of their lives and
they'd like to see young people come along and share that excitement."
The good war myth, he adds, is easy to sustain because "we've always
gone somewhere else to fight our wars, so we've not really learned
about its horror. Seventy percent of our military budget is to fight
somewhere else."[42]

Overall, the hundreds of oral histories that have been collected of
soldiers' memories of World War II impart quite a different viewpoint
than the good war notion of public memory. The violence and stress
associated with wartime combat made some ex-GIs unable to discuss
their experience, which is quite different from the stereotypical veteran
who is all too eager to discuss his heroic war stories. In 1993, for
example, I interviewed Jesse Martin, who served with distinction in the
Pacific War, earning a host of medals, including the Purple Heart and

the Congressional Medal of Honor. But when his life history came to World War II, with tears in his eyes, he was absolutely unable to discuss his four years. The experience was too painful even fifty years later, and a significant part of his life history was left untold.[43]

Popular Memory

The third part of Clausewitz's trinity is artistic, or popular memory of war. Many have uncritically assumed that popular culture, particularly Hollywood movies, echoed the good war myth by sanitizing the experience for American viewers. Admiral LaRocque said that

for about twenty years after the war, I couldn't look at any film on World War II. It brought back memories that I didn't want to keep around. I hated to see how they glorified war. In all those films, people get blown up with their clothes and fall gracefully to the ground. You don't see anybody blown apart. You don't see arms and legs and mutilated bodies. You see only an antiseptic, clean, neat way to die gloriously.[44]

Historian Craig Cameron has also been critical of Hollywood attempts to recreate the war experience for viewers, arguing that Hollywood, a major force in the sanitation of memory, has been interested first and foremost in profits, and the liberal view, he writes, would not be profitable until the 1970s.[45]

But a more critical viewing of Hollywood movies and even a reading of novels about the war leaves one to conclude that popular memory is not necessarily public memory, nor is it like private memory. In 1981, for example, Frank Capra, the famed director who produced *Why We Fight* for the government during World War II, a series designed to bolster support for the war, said that he lost interest in making optimistic movies about the war after directing *It's a Wonderful Life* in 1946, because he was demoralized by the incredible brutality witnessed on all sides in the war.[46]

What I want to suggest is that popular memory of the war, represented primarily in movies and novels, bridges the often discordant public and private memories. As historian John Bodnar notes, "Americans did most of their reflecting about the memory and meaning of the war...not when they viewed public memorials but when they went to the movies."[47] Popular memory of the war was a democratic middle ground that allowed debate between the public memory of victory and the private memory of violence.

13

I want to reconsider what has been hailed as one of the most "heroic" movies of World War II, *The Sands of Iwo Jima*, released in 1949 and starring John Wayne as Sergeant Stryker, a character, it is argued, responsible through the years for sending thousands of young men into military service. Sergeant Stryker is brave, good looking, tough, courageous, heroic, and even ruthless in his pursuit of victory in the Pacific. These traits were publicly cultivated in young men of fighting age during the war. Made with the help of the Marine Corps, the film shows actual footage of the fighting on the islands of Tarawa and Iwo Jima. Craig Cameron argues that *Sands* is the "single most important and lasting movie for the Marines' image."[48]

But one cannot watch the film without being amazed by the extent to which the valiant masculinity of the good war was challenged. Sergeant Stryker is criticized throughout the war for the man he has become, particularly by young Marine Pete Conway, played by John Agar, who hates Stryker because Stryker is just like Conway's own overly masculine father who has just been killed in action. "I'm a civilian, not a Marine," Conway barks to Stryker. The story line, then, becomes centered on the ability of war to unleash dangerously violent natures in men, represented in Stryker, versus the compassionate and sensitive man (presumably associated with peacetime), represented by Conway. Stryker's wife and ten-year-old son have abandoned him because he has chosen the Corps over his family, and when he gets no mail from his wife and son he gets "blind, staggering, stinking, falling down drunk" on liberty. Meanwhile, on his time off Conway meets the woman of his dreams; back on duty he begins talking about wanting to marry her, because maybe his number will come up on Tarawa Island. Stryker overhears Conway in the next tent and the following day warns him against getting serious with a woman under such circumstances. Eventually, Conway marries the woman, and they have a son nine months later. Conway tells Stryker he wants his son to read Shakespeare, not the Marine Manual. He wants his son "to be intelligent, considerate, cultured, and a gentleman," by implication, everything that Stryker is not. During the battle for Iwo Jima, Conway asks "Aren't you human at all?" when Stryker ignores a dying Marine's call for help because they might be spotted by the enemy. The conflict between Conway and Stryker is settled as the Marines are ascending Mount Surabachi, the last Japanese stronghold on Iwo Jima and, by the way, the setting for the photograph that became the Marine Corps

14

Memorial in Washington. Just as Stryker orders that the flag be raised on top of the volcano, he is fatally shot, and Conway finds a letter Stryker has written to his son, instructing him never to "hurt her [his mother] or anyone as I did" and asking him to be like him in some ways but not in others. The symbolic message cannot be ignored: men must abandon the overly masculine and violent behavior of war and return to loving relationships with women of peacetime.[49]

Other movies that have been criticized for cultivating the image of the good war are in fact, like *The Sands of Iwo Jima*, ambivalent about World II, particularly regarding male violence and male-female relationships. These include *The Best Years of Our Lives* and *To Hell and Back*. In the latter movie, Audie Murphy, hailed as the country's most decorated and heroic soldier, ultimately cares more about getting back home to care for his orphaned younger siblings. Although heroic publicly, privately he writes that "my eyeballs burn; my bones ache; and my muscles twitch from exhaustion. Oh, to sleep and never awaken. The war is without beginning, without end. It goes on forever."[50] He tells a woman he meets in Naples that he hopes his younger brother, who is boyishly obsessed with guns, never has to use them. *To Hell and Back* balances heroics with concerns about violence and responsibility.[51]

Even literature contained themes that reflected the dangerous tendency of men toward violence, as manifest in the war. Norman Mailer's *The Naked and the Dead*, published in 1949, is one such example. Sergeant Sam Croft, a significant character in the novel, is similar to Stryker: he lives for battle, he abhors weakness, and he has chosen fighting over women. Mailer also discusses the inequality of life in the military; his characters, like Charles Brummett, tire of the perquisites that officers have over GIs.[52]

These are only two examples of popular memory of World War II, but they reflect, according to John Bodnar, popular memory's enigmatic rather than doctrinaire character,[53] hence functioning as the borderland between the much different landscapes of public and private memories. As such, popular memory includes elements of victory from public memory and violence from the private, and popular memory seems to allow Americans themselves to arrive at their own conclusion about the war. Popular memory, as a part of popular culture, seems to sustain the cultural contradictions between public and private memory, and it is likely one of the reasons for the *Enola Gay* controversy.[54]

How, then, is the U.S. memory of World War II different from memory in other countries? One result of the good war thesis in the United States is that of declension; this thesis has often resulted in hopelessness in later decades because some Americans assume that the good war was part of a golden age and not a result of unique circumstances. Some Americans therefore believe that in order to reverse the postwar (particularly the post-Vietnam) decline, the country must return to that golden age. The problem, of course, as historians often point out, is that those who think things were better in the past or who want to return to the past know too little about it.[55]

This observation may suggest that such controversy over the *Enola Gay* is healthy, because it represents an attempt not only to challenge public memory but also to educate people about the past. Furthermore, it may indicate a key difference in U.S. memory of World War II, because unlike Austria, Germany, Japan, and perhaps even France, U.S. memory has been (at least until very recently) less forgetful. Adherents of the good war thesis were attracted to a past golden age, while in other countries, memory entailed escaping the past. But this attraction to the past should not be assumed to mean that U.S. memory of World War II is less complex or even one-sided. One haunting and troubling concern that many Americans have over the *Enola Gay* is the effort to censor memory (and particularly interpretation) about the past; if other countries are becoming more democratic in their memories of World War II, some Americans, particularly historians, believe the recent controversy indicates an undemocratic drift among the cultivators of United States public memory. Nevertheless, only by examining private and popular memory along with public memory can one come to terms with remembering the war in the United States and, by implication, other countries touched by the global conflict.[56]

NOTES

1. Carl von Clausewitz, *On War*, ed. and trans., Michael Howard and Peter Paret (Princeton: Princeton University Press, 1984), 89; cited in Craig M. Cameron, *American Samurai: Myth, Imagination, and the Conduct of Battle in the First Marine Division, 1941-1951* (New York: 1994), 2.

2. For a good collection of homefront oral histories, see Louis Fairchild, *They Called it the War Effort: Oral Histories from World War II Orange, Texas* (Austin: 1993).

3. The good war thesis is evident in such veterans' magazines as *American Legion* and *Air Force Magazine*. For use of the thesis by historians, see John Morton Blum, *V Was for Victory: Politics and Culture during World War II* (San Diego: 1976).

4. Ernie Pyle, *Last Chapter* (New York: 1945), 5.

5. Cameron, *American Samurai*, 20.

6. Ibid., 20; James J. Weingartner, "Trophies of War: U.S. Troops and the Mutilation of Japanese War Dead, 1941-1945," *Pacific Historical Review* 61 (Feb. 1992): 53-67.

7. Michael C. C. Adams, *The Best War Ever: America and World War II* (Baltimore: Johns Hopkins University Press, 1994), 12.

8. Paul Fussell, *Thank God for the Atom Bomb and Other Essays* (New York: 1989), 9.

9. Paul Fussell, *Wartime* (New York: Oxford University Press, 1989), 268.

10. Ibid.; Ernie Pyle, *Brave Men* (New York: 1944).

11. See Karal Ann Marling and John Wetenhall, *Iwo Jima: Monuments, Memories, and the American Hero* (Cambridge: 1991), 2-40.

12. Edward T. Linenthal, *Sacred Ground: Americans and Their Battlefields* (Urbana: 1991), 179-81.

13. Quoted in John T. Correll, "War Stories at Air and Space," *Air Force Magazine* 77 (April 1994): 26. For recent comments by historians on the controversy, see "History and the Public: What Can We Handle?" a special issue of the *Journal of American History* 82 (Dec. 1995): 1029-1144; see especially Martin Harwit, "Academic Freedom" in 'The Last Act,'" *Journal of American History* 82 (Dec. 1995): 1064-84.

14. See "Letters to the Editor," *Air Force Magazine* 77 (Nov. 1994): 6.

15. Martin J. Sherwin, "Hiroshima as Politics and History," *Journal of American History* 82 (Dec. 1995): 1085-93.

16. Letters to the Editor, *Air Force Magazine* 77 (Nov. 1994): 6.

17. Quoted in John T. Correll, "'The Last Act' at Air and Space," *Air Force Magazine* 77 (Sept. 1994): 64.

18. See John R. Dichtl, "A Chronology of the Smithsonian's Last Act," *OAH Newsletter* 22 (Nov. 1994): 1, 12; "Enola Gay Controversy Continues," *OAH Newsletter* 23 (Feb. 1995): 3; *Washington Post*, 30 Jan. 1995, D1, D8; *New York Times* 31 Jan. 1995; Brian D. Smith, *American Legion* (Nov. 1994): 26-29, 64-70; John Bodnar, "The Enola Gay and the Problem of Remembering World War II in America," unpub. ms. (in the author's possession); lecture by Martin Sherwin and Edward Linenthal, "Roundtable: Hiroshima and the Politics of History: The Enola Gay Controversy at the Smithsonian's National Air and Space Museum," OAH Annual Meeting, 30 March 1995, Washington, D.C.

19. See, for example, the very honest memoir by Leon C. Standifer, *Not in Vain: A Rifleman Remembers World War II* (Baton Rouge: Louisiana State University Press, 1992).

20. Cameron, *American Samurai*, 246; cf. James Jones, *WWII* (New York: 1975), 16. See also Eric J. Leed, *No Man's Land* (Cambridge: 1979).

21. Quoted in Ronald J. Drez, ed., *Voices of D-Day: The Story of the Allied Invasion Told by Those Who Were There* in *Eisenhower Center Studies of War and Peace*, ed. Stephen E. Ambrose and Günter Bischof (Baton Rouge: Louisiana State University Press, 1994), 131.

22. Tape-recorded interview with Charles Brummett by Chad Berry, Whiting, Ind., 9 April 1992 (Indiana University Oral History Research Center), 16.

23. Adams, *Best War Ever*, 157. See also Samuel A. Stouffer, *The American Soldier: Combat and its Aftermath* (Washington: 1949).

24. William Manchester, *Goodbye, Darkness: A Memoir of the Pacific War* (Boston: 1979), 358. Once combat grew more severe, Manchester noted that "a structured account of events is impossible. Continuity disappears; the timepiece in the attic of memory ticks erratically" (365).

25. Quoted in Drez, *Voices of D-Day*, 92.

26. Ibid., 71.

27. Ibid., 80.

28. Ibid., 29.

29. Quoted in Studs Terkel, *"The Good War": An Oral History of World War Two* (New York: 1984), 263.

30. Fussell, *Thank God for the Atom Bomb*, 33.

31. Manchester, *Goodbye, Darkness*, 374.

32. Quoted in Drez, *Voices of D-Day*, 87.

33. Ibid., 89.

34. Ibid., 89-90.

35. Ibid., 208-9.

36. William R. Cubbins, *The War of the Cottontails: Memoirs of a WWII Bomber Pilot* (Chapel Hill, NC: 1989), 189.

37. Quoted in Drez, *Voices of D-Day*, 207.

38. Ibid., 174.

39. Ibid., 202.

40. Tape-recorded interview with James and Sally Etter by Chad Berry, Hartford, Ky., 25 June 1992 (Indiana University Oral History Research Center), 15, 17.

41. Quoted in Terkel, *"The Good War,"* 190.

42. Ibid., 190-91.

43. See also Fairchild, *They Called it the War Effort*. See tape-recorded interview with Jesse and Emma Martin by Chad Berry, Indianapolis, Ind., 7 Dec. 1993 (tape is in the author's possession).

44. Quoted in Terkel, *The Good War*, 193.

45. Cameron, *American Samurai*, 262.

46. Walter Karp, "The Patriotism of Frank Capra," *Esquire*, Feb. 1981, 32.

47. Bodnar, "Enola Gay and the Problem of Remembering," 5.

19

48. Cameron, *American Samurai*, 260.

49. Jeanine Basinger, *The World War II Combat Film: Anatomy of a Genre* (New York: 1986), 169-70.

50. Audie Murphy, *To Hell and Back* (New York: 1949), 46.

51. See Bodnar, "Enola Gay and the Problem of Remembering," 8.

52. Norman Mailer, *The Naked and the Dead* (New York: 1981); see Bodnar, "Enola Gay and the Problem of Remembering," 10.

53. Bodnar, "Enola Gay and the Problem of Remembering," 10.

54. See Richard H. Kohn, "History and the Culture Wars: The Case of the Smithsonian Institution's *Enola Gay* Exhibition," *Journal of American History* 82 (Dec. 1995): 1036-63.

55. See Adams, *The Best War Ever*, 158.

56. H. Taya Cook and Theodore Cook, *Japan at War: An Oral History* (New York: 1992); Henry Rousso, *The Vichy Syndrome: History and Memory in France Since 1944* (Cambridge: 1991).

Michael Todd Bennett
University of Georgia

Anglophilia on Film: Creating an Atmosphere for Alliance, 1935-1941

A host of movies appearing in American theaters from 1935 to 1941 projected a pro-British

bias onto the screen. These productions both mirrored and informed the increasingly close Anglo-American

relations at both the popular and official levels before World War II. Films mirrored these trends because

Hollywood, hungry for profit, followed public opinion. But the American motion picture industry also played a

diplomatic role by reinforcing public support for President Franklin D. Roosevelt's interventionist policies.

Those policies culminated in an Anglo-American military alliance after Pearl Harbor. In creating an atmosphere

in which this alliance could flourish, movies drew upon deep cultural, geographical, historical, and political ties.

But these ties guaranteed a partnership neither in reality nor on the screen. On the screen that partnership was

contingent upon international events, market forces, official policies, and individual acts. As a result, the U.S.

motion picture industry, first unintentionally and only by 1941 consciously, strengthened these unofficial ties,

softened the malevolent images of monarchy and imperialism, and stressed to American viewers that Britain—

democratic, freedom-loving, and triumphant—was inhabited by people just like themselves.

As Americans confronted (or ignored) the world in 1935, an "unneutral" affinity for Britain emerged in the nation's foreign policy. In August of that year the United States Congress, inspired in particular by the Italian invasion of Ethiopia—but also by growing German and Japanese threats—passed the Neutrality Act of 1935. Designed to limit the possibility of either enemy attacks on American shipping or financial ties dragging the nation into war, the act prohibited supplying belligerent nations with implements of war. Although the act committed the nation to isolation, that isolation was in fact not neutral. Roosevelt, seeking to preserve executive power, lobbied for "flexible neutrality" from Congress in the final version of the act. Flexible neutrality allowed the president to declare embargoes and to define what war materials were to be regarded as contraband.[1] Thus, if Britain, which controlled the Atlantic with her navy, became embroiled in a conflict, Roosevelt could choose to remain isolated and yet simultaneously aid that beleaguered nation.

Extant Non-Neutrality: Shakespeare, Robin Hood, and Empire

American films fell short of impartiality as well. Cinema served as one medium of a unifying cultural exchange, perhaps the most popular tie drawing the two nations together during the "great rapprochement." Common language, origins, and demo-cratic institutions all helped solidify Anglo-American relations throughout the twentieth century.[2] In

1935 Warner Bros. Pictures' *A Midsummer Night's Dream* provided a prime example of the cultural ties uniting England and the U.S. Film critic Richard Sheridan Ames, although bemoaning the film's vulgarization of William Shakespeare's work, recognized that it helped expose American moviegoers to the play. Starring a young James Cagney, *A Midsummer Night's Dream* appeared for 163 days at Warner's first-run theaters in New York and Los Angeles, longer than any of the studio's other productions that year. The National Board of Review voted the film one of 1935's ten best in terms of popular appeal.[3] Following *Mutiny on the Bounty* and *Captain Blood, The Adventures of Robin Hood* reinforced the close Anglo-American cultural relationship. In director Michael Curtiz's version of the Robin Hood legend, Prince John conquered Anglo-Saxon England in the absence of the crusading King Richard the Lionhearted. In a "swashbuckling defense of human rights," Errol Flynn as Robin Hood rose to defeat John and his henchmen in vivid technicolor.[4] Flynn's Robin entered upon this revolu-tionary course after having witnessed "the beatings, the blindings with hot irons, the burning of our barns and homes, [and] the mistreatment of our women," perpetrated by the tyrannical John.[5] All of this heroism added up to a "Merrie England" film which championed Albion as a land of individualism, liberty, and morality. Along with rich technicolor and a sense of romantic adventure, this portrayal of English ideals helped to make the film immensely profitable and popular.[6]

Meeting with similar success, a series of imperial pictures produced by Hollywood after 1935 asserted a more direct link of a common imperial heritage. Although both nations had long-since reached the end of physical imperialism, popular support for it remained strong even into the 1930s.[7] This "popular imperialism" made its way onto American screens via a London-to- Hollywood cultural exchange. British filmmakers, such as Alexander Korda, proved that the genre could be profitable. Hollywood, always looking for new topics to satisfy the insatiable demand for adventure films, simply adapted imperial pictures to the western genre. Dodge City became Calcutta. Asians and Arabs replaced Native Americans. But British officers also displaced cowboys, a shift that exposed a shared imperial tradition and strong cultural ties. As a result, the "thirties were pre-eminently Hollywood's imperial decade, when the ethos and rituals of British imperialism were given glamorous celluloid life."[8]

The first in a long line of Hollywood films to deal with empire in the 1930s was *The Lives of a Bengal Lancer*. Based upon a novel by Francis Yeats-Brown, the Paramount production starred Gary Cooper as McGregor, a Scotch Canadian serving in the 41st Bengal Lancers stationed in India.[9] In India, McGregor and his fellow imper-ialists met the intrigue of Mohammed Khan, who, with Russian assistance, sought to capture a supply train in order to equip his army for an attack on the British Raj. However, McGregor subjugated the mutinous Khan in a climactic frontier battle. If these visual images of British triumph were not enough, Cooper's McGregor expressed imperial hubris when he speculated "how for generation after generation a handful of men have ordered the lives of 300 million people ...."[10]

Critics recognized and applauded *The Lives of a Bengal Lancer's* resounding support for England and its empire. Critic Otis Ferguson announced himself "taken by the show, imperialism and all."[11] The *New York Times'* Andre Sennwald, who named the picture the fourth best of the first half of 1935, maintained that it glorified the British empire better than any film produced in Britain for that purpose. Recognizing that London was currying international favor, Sennwald declared that Paramount's "Kiplingesque" work "ought to prove a great blessing to Downing Street."[12] The film's glorification of Britain and its empire threatened to be such a propaganda blessing that several countries resisted its exhibition. After much delay on account of the feature's "English theme," the censor board in Mussolini's Italy, for instance, reluctantly accepted *The Lives of a Bengal Lancer*.[13] In the Third World, the film's portrayal of the triumph of British imperialists stirred an even more vociferous reaction.[14] Conversely, *The Lives of a Bengal Lancer* proved so popular in the United States that it spurred a series of imperial films that continued throughout the decade and into the next.[15]

Always keen to shifts in the marketplace, the Warner brothers began production of their own imperial saga. That strategy proved successful as *The Charge of the Light Brigade* earned over $1.5 million, more than any of the studio's 1936 productions. In addition, the film received recognition as the best film released in November 1936 by the National Screen Council and honorable mention as one of the year's best by *Film Daily*.[16] Starring Errol Flynn as Captain Geoffrey Vickers, the production, again told from the British perspective, chronicled the activities of the 27th Lancers in India before the Crimean War. The lancers again faced a treacherous native leader, this time the Surat Khan, who, backed by Russia, rebelled against British might. Vickers and his colleagues largely ignored the Khan's bothersome raids

23

belled against British might. Vickers and his colleagues largely ignored the Khan's bothersome raids until he attacked the lancers' outpost at Chukoti, murdering not only soldiers—but women and children. Vowing revenge, Vickers surreptitiously ordered the 27th to the Crimea, whence the Khan had repaired with his Russian benefactors. There Vickers indeed had his revenge. But he suffered a martyr's death at the hands of the Tsar's forces as the lines of Alfred Lord Tennyson's elegiac poem scrolled over the famous cavalry charge.[17] The film's emphasis upon the lancers' martyrdom in the Crimea provided a prime example of Hollywood's Anglophilia to at least one critic. Although in reality the charge was a massive blunder, Frank S. Nugent of the *New York Times* wrote that, because of the studio's efforts to "strike another blow for Queen Victoria and the empire on whose dominions the sun never sets, ... it was no blunder." But this example was only one of many as "Hollywood, ignoring the ... stains ...on the British tunic, has found only glory and rattling good melodrama in its imperialist sagas." In particular, the film capital juxtaposed this glorious image of British imperialism with one in which "every sheik, mullah,

amir, princeling and khan is a treacherous, lecherous, bloodthirsty, cruel and cowardly mad dog who, like as not, is hand in glove with a crafty Russian ...." In summary, Nugent concluded that

> England need have no fears for its empire so long as Hollywood insists upon being the Kipling of the Pacific. The film city's pious regard for the sacrosanct bearers of the white man's burden continues to be one of the most amusing manifestations of Hollywood's anglophilia. In its veneration of British colonial policy, in its respect for the omniscience and high moral purposes of His, or Her, Majesty's diplomatic represen-tatives and in its adulation of the courage, the virtue and the manly beauty of English soldiery abroad, Hollywood yields to no one—not even to the British filmmakers themselves.[18]

The poetry of Rudyard Kipling, mentioned by Nugent, directly inspired the Radio-Keith-Orpheum (RKO) production of *Gunga Din*. Cary Grant, Douglas Fairbanks, Jr., and Victor McLaglen starred as members of a lancer unit stationed in India which confronted the machinations of the Thugee, the "Thugs," a Hindu sect which worshipped the goddess of blood Kali and which actually existed in India from the twelfth until the early nineteenth century. As the Thugs' influence spread, Cutter (Grant), Ballantine (Fairbanks, Jr.), and MacChesney (McLaglen) set out in pursuit. Their counterpart, the Thugee Guru, nevertheless increased his power and threatened to "roll on, from village to town, from town to mighty city, ever mounting, ever widening, until at last my wave engulfs all India."[19] At the moment that the Guru seemed poised at the gates of London, Gunga Din (portrayed by Sam Jaffe) sounded a bugle from the top of the Thugee temple to warn the British army of its impending entrapment. Forewarned, the soldiers routed the Thugs and con-

The Film Archive

British crowds at *Dawn Patrol* opening, 1938.

vincingly ended their challenge to the Raj. Following this exhibition of British might, a fictional Kipling arrived to extol the virtues of the hero Gunga Din as the words of his poem—in a convention now becoming quite popular—scrolled over the scene.[20]

Although appearing only briefly in the film, Kipling and his prose played key roles in Gunga Din's unique expression of pro-British sentiment.[21] Critic B.R. Crisler noted that "Kipling's contribution to" Gunga Din was "more than just the title," but "also a mood, an atmosphere, even ... an 'inspiration.'"[22] The poet's "inspiration" included a sense of racial patriarchy that undergirded the visual imperialism of the 1930s no less than it had the physical imperialism of the nineteenth century. In Gunga Din, for example, the appearance of two kinds of Indians justified this Kiplingesque vision: one non-white type in the George Stevens film was Gunga Dint—he acquiescent native amenable to white rule; the other was the treacherous native, the Thugee Guru, who stood at the end of a line of perfidious natives first seen in The Lives of a Bengal Lancer's Mohammed Khan and then The Charge of the Light Brigade's Surat Khan. The British officers expressed disdain for both of these characters. When the Guru tortured Cutter to obtain information about the movements of the British army, the latter stated "See here, mate, I'm a soldier of Her Majesty the Queen. I don't grovel before any heathen."[23] Cutter and his British colleagues had a much different, but no less powerful, relationship with Gunga Din, a water boy who addressed his European masters as "sahib."[24] In this manner Gunga Din, always smiling and servile, occupied a position on screen not unlike the shuffling and deferential African American so common in the era's pictures. As with the black stereotype, American audiences largely accepted the racism of Hollywood's imperial productions.[25]

Enter International Relations: Analogies and War

For all their popular successes, Gunga Din and other imperial films were largely isolated from the contemporary European political scene. All of the film capital's productions—whether cultural or imperial—were biased simply because of an unconscious, close relationship with Great Britain, engendered by culture, geography, history, and common political structures and interests. As early as 1937, however, some films became politically conscious, although not yet propagandistic, as they commented upon the increasingly tense international situation. Pictures dealing with Britain

became politically conscious in wake of the Spanish Civil War, which opened in July 1936 and which helped to awaken the American public, and thus the film industry, to the threat of world war.[26]

The first film shown in America that commented upon the Spanish Civil War was a British production, Alexander Korda's Fire Over England. Using the metaphor of the sixteenth century tensions between Spain and England, the film instructed the audience that Spain's King Philip II, like the contemporary leaders Francisco Franco or Adolph Hitler, ruled "by force and fear." Only "the free people of a little island—England" stood in the way of fascist "tyranny." On screen, however, the people of England remained divided over what course to take to challenge that tyranny. Fire Over England's aged Lord Treasurer advocated appeasing the Spanish because of the great disparity in power between that nation's navy and England's. Pointing to a globe, the Treasurer illustrated his point and stated "See, here lies England. But half an island. Not 300 miles long, Not 200 miles broad. How small we are. How wretched and defenseless. Now turn to Spain ...."[27]

Advocating preparedness instead, the film's protagonist Michael Ingolby convinced Queen Elizabeth to match the Spanish Armada with an enhanced Royal Navy. Played by Laurence Olivier, Michael first countered Spanish Fifth Column activity by supplying King Philip with disinformation about the English fleet. The protagonist then returned to defend En-

Gunga Din (1939) Kipling's Vision.

gland, newly equipped with a modern navy, against the Armada's impending attack. As the Armada approached, the queen, sounding much like Prime Minister Winston Churchill in June 1940, advised her people that neither "Spain nor any Prince of Europe shall invade us! Pluck up your hearts: by your peace in camp and your valor in the field we shall shortly have a famous victory."[28] Thus encouraged, Michael and his fellow Englishmen supplied that victory. Afterwards, scenes of freedom-loving and victorious England flooded the screen. These scenes, which included shots of St. Paul's Cathedral and of English entrepreneurs, coupled with Elizabeth's "stump speeches about old England," were so blatantly pro-British that they proved rather "tiresome" to film-maker and critic Pare Lorentz.[29]

Although far ahead of opinion in both the U.S. and the United Kingdom (UK) regarding a strong stance in Spain, *Fire Over England* did parallel "unneutral" American foreign policy. In 1937 Congress added the cash-and-carry provisions to the neutrality law allowing non-military trade with belligerents if they paid for goods and transported them on their own vessels. Although mainly a response to renewed Japanese expansion in the Pacific, cash-and-carry represented a step towards aid to Britain in U.S. foreign policy as it provided the UK, whose Navy controlled the Atlantic, with access to U.S. manufactures and foodstuffs.[30]

Hollywood, following—and at the same time reinforcing—public opinion, clearly expressed its support for an "unneutral" but non-interventionist foreign policy in *The Dawn Patrol*. Warner Bros. produced the picture to take advantage of the strained world political scene of 1938, which included Hitler's annexation of Austria, his claims to Czechoslovakia, and the subsequent (and ignominious) Munich Agreement. Warner Bros. executive producer Hal B. Wallis wrote Jack Warner that "we could knock out a very great picture in a very short time, and one that I think would bring us a fortune now when the whole world is talking and thinking war and re-armament."[31]

The Film Archive

The Dawn Patrol (1930/38) and the horrors of war.

The resulting film reflected the isolationism and pacifism that lingered among Americans. Starring Errol Flynn as Courtney, David Niven as Scott, and Basil Rathbone as Brand, the remake of a 1930 film of the same title focused upon a unit of the Royal Air Force warring on the Western Front during World War I. Flynn, Niven, and the remainder of the patrol regularly went out on morning missions to perform reconnaissance work or drop bombs behind enemy lines. Each time that the patrol sortied, several aviators did not return. The unit commander, first Brand and then Courtney, waited like expectant fathers for their flyers. Inevitably, at least one did not return, leading Brand to exclaim that the war was "a slaughter-house—that's what it is. And I'm the butcher!" To replace the downed aviators, ever younger recruits, some with only a few weeks training, arrived in camp. One of these recruits was Scott's younger brother, whom the dutiful Courtney sent on a fatal mission.[32] Scenes such as these led moviegoer Mary Jane Fulton to tell Warner Bros. studios that its film "could make every one work harder to keep peace."[33]

Although the related themes of pacifism and isolationism permeated the film, *The Dawn Patrol* represented something else. The film marked the rebirth of the war film, a genre not prevalent since the first third of the decade. The final moments of the film provided a heroic image. In that scene, Courtney, not wanting to subject Scott to the sure death of an impossible dawn attack, took his place in the mission. In this action-filled climax, Courtney battled German planes and bombed an all-important ammunition cache before triumphantly returning to camp. This and other scenes revived the genre so well that reviewer John Alden labeled it as a piece of pro-war propaganda. Alden wrote that, although there was in the picture an effort to include anti-war sentiment, when a viewer left "the theater, you aren't remembering those sidelights. You're remembering only the heroic deeds of the fliers who died helping to kill off the Germans."[34] Censor boards in New Zealand, the Balkans, Egypt, France, and Hungary rejected *The Dawn Patrol* due to its martial theme.[35]

Just as *The Dawn Patrol* marked a transition away from isolation in Hollywood's productions, it foreshadowed rising cinematic Anglophilia. The picture was told from the British perspective, a point of view quite unlike the German one of *All Quiet on the Western Front*. This British outlook colored the characterization of Germans. Although the film, in the spirit of Munich, briefly hinted at an Anglo-German agreement, Courtney, Scott, and others consistently referred to their enemies as "Jerries," "Huns," and "Heinies."[36] In its analysis of the film, the Production Code Administration (PCA) noted these references to Germans and recognized that, in contrast, all of the prominent English characters received a "sympathetic" portrayal.[37] In publicizing the film, Warner Bros. keyed upon this portrayal by emphasizing the production's all-British cast led by Flynn, who, according to Warner's marketers, starred in such pic- tures as *Captain Blood* and *The Dawn Patrol* because of his patriotism.[38] The studio's efforts worked. English critic C.A. LeJeune noted that the *Dawn Patrol* was "a Hollywood picture about English people that is as English as a Sussex morning."[39]

Yet, Hollywood, because it produced films for an American public unwilling to intervene in Europe's affairs, remained reluctant to overtly enlist on London's behalf. The film capital's engagement remained contingent upon several factors. The outbreak of war in Europe on 1 September 1939 fulfilled the first of these requirements.

Even before the war's commencement, however, British officials and diplomats had sought to remove any contingencies that might obstruct trans-Atlantic cooperation. To encourage the United States to emerge from its isolationist shell, English diplomats such as Sir Ronald Lindsay and Anthony Eden courted America. Foreign Secretary Eden wrote in March 1937 that "the crucial importance of retaining the goodwill of the United States Government and public opinion. . .is a matter which is keenly engaging my attention."[40] He instructed Lindsay (ambassador to the U.S. since 1930) to prepare a report on how to best enlist American sympathies. Lindsay replied that "in major questions of foreign policy, America always moves very slowly; for it is an axiom of American political leaders not to take any decided step of importance until every part of the country is more or less in line."[41] Before trying to secure official American-goodwill, then, Lindsay encouraged the British government to court the American public. Instead of the blatant propaganda of the First World War, the ambassador advocated more subtle forms of psychological manipulation through such cultural tools as broadcasts, plays, and films. Americans, Lindsay concluded, could "be worked on through their emotions."[42] Although Eden resigned less than a year later in protest of Chamberlain's policy of appeasement, the ambassador's recommendation for a psychological offensive was followed.[43]

Film provided one weapon in that offensive and Alexander Korda wielded it effectively.[44] A member of the Conservative Party Film Association, Korda utilized Chancellor of the Exchequer Winston Churchill as a script writer and as a historical advisor on his 1937 film *Lawrence of Arabia*. Resulting partly from this relationship, Korda, by official request, relocated to Hollywood in 1939 to produce films that projected a favorable image of Britain. This arrangement had two advantages: first, Britain assured itself of maintaining a wellspring of favorable publicity safe from invading armies; second, this celluloid source of publicity "would not emanate from official sources" and would have no overt affiliations with the state.[45]

Soon after his arrival, Korda produced *That Hamilton Woman* starring Vivien Leigh and Laurence Olivier. Just as his earlier *Fire Over England* chronicled a defining event in English history, *That Hamilton Woman* depicted Lord Horatio Nelson's naval victories over the French fleet during the Napoleonic Wars (1792-1815). Through Nelson's triumphs, Korda hoped to produce "a historical film with parallels to the present."[46] The film's most obvious attempt to corroborate the past with the present occurred when Nelson (portrayed by Olivier) addressed a number of British officials regarding peace negotiations with Napoleon. Nelson objected to such negotiations because Napoleon, he claimed, was not a peaceful man. He then directly equated Napoleon with Hitler. The former, Nelson stated,

That Hamilton Woman (1941).

"can never be master of the world until he has smashed us up. And believe me, gentlemen, he means to be master of the world." Smashing his fist upon the table, Nelson declared that "You cannot make peace with dictators. You have to destroy them, wipe them out."[47] Olivier's didacticism led critics to comment upon the propagandist goals of Korda's film. The *Motion Picture Daily*'s Roscoe Williams noted that the picture "refers to Napoleon as 'dictator' and contains dialogue lines which are, of course, pertinent to the

27

present world situation. If this be propaganda, then it is to that extent a propaganda picture."[48] *Variety* agreed that the "situation in Europe at the time when Nelson was rising to glory as a fighting admiral has obvious parallels to the present contest across the English Channel."[49] In response to *That Hamilton Woman*, the United States Senate—as part of an investigation into movie propaganda—summoned Korda to testify before the Committee on Interstate Commerce in 1941. That request, however, went unfulfilled due to the interruption of Pearl Harbor.[50]

Korda composed a part of what isolationist Senator Gerald P. Nye called Hollywood's "British Army of Occupation." English actors, actresses, directors, and executives—including Olivier, Leigh, Leslie Howard, Ronald Coleman, Cedric Hardwicke, Merle Oberon, Basil Rathbone, Alfred Hitchcock, C. Aubrey Smith, Niven, Donald Crisp, and RKO executive Lord Lothian—"held a commanding place in Hollywood."[51] Although residing far from the raging European war, these artists attempted to perform services for their homeland. Useful service included the staging of Allied war relief benefits under the auspices of such Hollywood-based organizations as Bundles for Britain or the British War Relief Association of Southern California. (At one such benefit Korda presented his film *Thief of Baghdad*.)[52] Britain's fight against fascism thus maintained a high profile in the movie capital.

Many of Hollywood's industry leaders sympathized with Britain's fight. Several of the motion picture industry's most influential executives were Jewish and inclined to present anti-Nazi images to American viewers by 1939. These executives included Adolph Zukor of Paramount, Carl Laemmle of Universal, Louis B. Mayer and Samuel Goldwyn of Metro-Goldwyn-Mayer (MGM), David O. Selznick, and the Warner brothers. Leaders of the most political studio of the age, Harry and Jack Warner were the sons of Polish Jews who had earlier fled their homeland to escape persecution. Their heritage led the brothers to play a militant role in anti-Nazi politics of the 1930s through such organizations as the Hollywood Anti-Nazi League.[53] The Warners naturally drifted into pro-British political activities as the island nation began to fight against Nazi expansion. In December 1940, Harry Warner donated twenty-two ambulances to the British Red Cross. In 1941, the brothers, members of the pro-Allied and interventionist Fight for Freedom organization, announced that proceeds from *London Can Take It*, a documentary which chronicled that city's heroic endurance of

Nazi air attacks, would be donated to the British Spitfire Fund for the purchase of American-made aircraft.[54] By September of that year, after his studio had produced such Anglophilic films as *The Sea Hawk*, Harry Warner openly declared his support for England during questioning by the Senate committee investigating film propaganda.[55]

No matter how sympathetic they were, the Warner brothers and other industry executives were not willing to produce films colored with pro-Allied and anti-fascist hues until the foreign and domestic markets permitted. For most films during the thirties, domestic receipts roughly equalled production costs. Thus, the European market provided a critical margin of profit for American feature films. Initially the studios resisted producing either anti-fascist or pro-Allied pictures that might alienate viewers in Germany or Italy. Finally, Nazi officials relieved the studios' dilemma when, on 17 August 1940, they banned American films from German-controlled areas due to supposed Jewish influence on American films.. When Italy followed suit, the English market, which had been about equal in importance to the German market for Hollywood producers, became nearly the sole source of foreign revenue. As a result, Hollywood "took its gloves off" in the fight for England and against Nazi Germany.[56] Soon after Germany's invasion of Poland in September 1939 Hollywood produced its first anti-Nazi film, Warner Bros.' *Confessions of a Nazi Spy.*[57]

Hollywood Takes Sides: Anglophilia on Film

Emboldened by this initial step and spurred by the influence of the British Army of Occupation and unique market conditions, the American film industry set out on a path to support the western democracies, particularly Great Britain. This cinematic course both followed and led American public opinion and paralleled the increasingly pro-British and interventionist diplomacy of President Roosevelt from 1939 to 1941. And during those years Anglophilia on film helped to reinforce the presidential policies which finally led to an Anglo-American alliance after Pearl Harbor.

Before then, Americans looked upon the outbreak of European hostilities in 1939 with a combination of fear and hope. Most Americans feared that the European war threatened to draw in the United States. But a majority also recognized that Nazi aggression, so evident in Poland, had to be stopped before it reached American shores. Thus, many hoped that the western democracies could halt Hitler's march.[58] President Roosevelt shaped his foreign policies towards this goal. After the outbreak of war, Roosevelt, although he expressed a strong desire to keep the country out of war, also expressed an "unneutral" wish to aid Britain and France. On 3 September, in a Fireside Chat, he issued a Proclamation of Neutrality, which officially committed the U.S. to neutral status. But the president went on to reject a strict definition by stating "I cannot ask that every American remain neutral in thought as well. Even a neutral has a right to take account of facts. Even a neutral cannot be asked to close his mind or his conscience."[59]

Support for the Allies was one foreign policy view which a majority of Americans already held in 1939. After the invasion of Poland, a "strong wave of sympathy for the western allies swept over the United States."[60] Of those Americans then polled, 84 percent wanted Britain and France to win the war against Germany. Further, the public, recognizing that Britain and France provided a first line of defense for the U.S., was willing to entertain the idea of intervention. Only 5 percent advo-cated intervention, but that figure rose to 29 percent if it looked as if Germany had the upper-hand on Britain and France.[61]

Recognizing this public support for the Allies, both Congress and the motion picture industry enrolled on their behalf. Congress, with the president's support, extended cash-and-carry to cover armaments and munitions. The industry similarly responded with Universal's *The Sun Never Sets*. The final edition in the series of imperial pictures that began in 1935, *The Sun Never Sets* took that support for imperial Britain to new heights, producing a film that, according to *New York Times* critic Frank S. Nugent, was "absurdly Anglophile."[62] The film seemed so because of its portrayals of British colonial officers and their families—which the PCA's reviewer described as "sympathetic."[63] The opening text of the film, starring Basil Rathbone and Douglas Fairbanks, Jr. as Clive and John Randolph, dedicated the picture to the countless millions bred in the British Isles who, through the past four centuries, have gone forth to the far corners of the earth to find new countries, to establish laws and the ethics of government, [and] who have kept high the standard of civilization ...."[64] As upholders of this standard, Clive and John faced something new in this imperial film set within the contemporary world. Instead of the traditional rebellious natives, these colonial officers faced the threat of European competition. Clive ventured to the Gold Coast to monitor the actions of Zurof, a scientist who used his occupation as a cover to broadcast propaganda from a secret radio transmitter.[65] Frustrated in

his efforts, Clive returned to London. Taking his brother's place, John then discovered Zurof's camp and revealed the transmitter's location. With Colonial Office approval, Clive then flew from London to Africa and led a bombing mission to silence the obnoxious broadcasts.[66]

In the realm of reality, 1940 brought closer Anglo-American relations. Hitler did little throughout the winter of 1939-40. Most believed that the Fuhrer would launch an attack upon either France or Britain in the spring of 1940. In expectation of that attack, Roosevelt further aligned the United States with Hitler's foes in a commencement speech at the University of Virginia. The president stated that

> we, as a nation, are convinced that military and naval victory for the gods of force and hate would endanger the institutions of democracy in the Western World, and that equally therefore, the whole of our sympathies lies with those nations that are giving their life blood in combat against those forces.[67]

Later, however, the American diplomatic emphasis on aid to the Allies changed to aid to Britain only. Hitler forced this shift by overrunning France and forcing an armistice on 21 June. France's capitulation left Britain as Hitler's lone remaining European foe. And Britain's defensive position looked none too promising. On 4 June German troops pushed the British army off the European continent at Dunkirk.

Foreign Correspondent (1940): Broadcasting the Blitz.

29

To buttress London, Roosevelt sent $5 million of surplus war materials of World War I vintage to London. In so doing, the president launched a new phase in American foreign policy, aid to Britain, which lasted until 1941.[68]

Foreign Correspondent, a British film directed by Alfred Hitchcock, paralleled and encouraged Roosevelt's attempts to aid the beleaguered island. Set in a contem-porary England endangered by Germany, the film detailed the fictional kidnapping of a European diplomat attempting to maintain peace. Members of the "peace party" in England, a party populated by German spies, abducted the diplomat in order to obtain the provisions of a secret treaty clause that maintained the tenuous European peace. These German fifth columnists hoped to break the provisions of that treaty in order to begin a European war which might enable them to gain political power in England itself. Huntley Haverstock (played by Joel McCrea), a foreign correspondent for a New York newspaper, arrived in London originally to investigate the disappearance of the diplomat. The reporter, however, soon became involved in the British war effort. After the cinematic German spies had broken the treaty's provisions and initiated war, Haverstock tried to facilitate American aid to relieve Britain's desperate plight with a radio broadcast not unlike those conducted by Edward R. Murrow. As German bombs burst overhead and the lights of the London studio dimmed, Haverstock encouraged Americans to keep the light of democracy burning by sending materiel to Britain.[69] Haverstock's call for

The Sea Hawk (1940): Resisting tyranny.

American intervention mirrored the new prime minister's policies. As his forces retreated from Dunkirk, Churchill buttressed domestic spirit and called for American assistance. In a famous radio address, the prime minister declared that Britain would never surrender and instead "would carry on the struggle, until, in God's good time, the New World, with all its power and might, steps forth to the rescue and liberation of the Old."[70]

One month after Churchill spoke these words, *The Sea Hawk*, a Warner Bros. production, appeared on America's screens. The film chronicled English naval victory over a continental aggressor—in this case, again sixteenth century Spain. King Philip II, as he had in Korda's *Fire Over England*, served as a metaphorical Hitler. Nowhere was this relationship better established than in the film's opening scenes, in which Philip appeared "as an earlier Hitler, thumping his fist over the map of the world."[71] These scenes were not part of the original 1924 film and were added by screenwriter Seton I. Miller in 1939 to link the remake with current events. In the scenes, the camera focused upon a map of Spain. Tracking backwards, the camera revealed that the map of Spain was part of a large map of the world. Over that scene, Philip said to his assistant in a "low tense voice" that the only thing standing between Spain and world domination was England.[72]

The scene, filmed by director Michael Curtiz, then emphasized the threat to the United States posed by Philip's (or Hitler's) aggression. The king, his voice becoming mystical, moved slowly towards the map. His shadow crept upon it, blended "with the dark grey of Spain," and spread over the rest of world as he called each area by name. He spoke of Spanish expansion into northern Africa, Europe to the Ural Mountains, and "then to the New World. To the North. To the South. West to the Pacific." As Philip's shadow darkened the entire world map, and particularly that of North America, he declared that "One day before my death we shall sit here and gaze upon this map upon the wall. It will have ceased to be a map of the world. It will be Spain."[73]

If Philip's expansionism was not enough of an anti-Nazi message for American viewers, *The Sea Hawk* depicted that expansion as being driven by cruelty. English captives, enslaved below deck, powered the Armada. "Chained to the benches," the prisoners appeared "naked, except for loin cloths, ... bearded, unkempt, scarred, ... their faces drawn and haggard." However, they were "not criminal types," who belonged in slavery. Instead, the slaves powering the Spanish empire from below deck were "nearly all fine types, ... the majority of them English middle-class, with good strong faces .... Here and there a patrician, intellectual type, ... all of them ground down to the tortured status of animals."[74] Sir Geoffrey Thorpe (portrayed by Errol Flynn) was among the oarsmen who provided an English antithesis to The Sea Hawk's imagery of Nazi cruelty. Even in captivity the Englishmen served their freedom-loving country and resisted tyranny. When the slaves realized, for instance, that the Spanish ship upon which they labored had drifted into the English Channel, they held back on their oars to assure success by the queen's navy.[75] This stark contrast was exactly the one intended by screenwriters Miller and Howard Koch. Miller claimed that the "unifying theme of the story is that the gods favor those that sail by the wind (the free) against those propelled by the galley-oar."[76] The theme of English enslavement by continental aggressors was hyped by studio publicists. Warner advertisers claimed that in this way the film paralleled "current events with the sixteenth century—England as the foe of the aggressor, then as now."[77]

Led by the recently escaped Thorpe and Queen Elizabeth, the English survived this potential enslavement and triumphed over the continental aggressors by film's end. Just before the queen sent her charges to fight Philip's naval version of blitzkrieg, she uttered the words that most directly linked the film with the early stages of World War II:

> A great duty confronts us all. To prepare our nation for a war that none of us wants .... We have tried by all means in our power to avert this war. We have no quarrel with the people of Spain or of any other country. But when the ruthless ambition of a man threatens to engulf the world, it becomes the solemn obligation of all free men, to affirm that earth does not belong to any one man, but to all·men .... We shall now make ready to meet the great Armada which Philip sends against us. To this end I pledge you ships worthy of our seamen, ... a sturdy fleet hewn out of the forests of England. A navy foremost in the world—not only in our time, but in generations to come.[78]

As Queen Elizabeth spoke these final words, Curtiz's cameras showed the strength of the Royal Navy, the pillar of British military might—in the sixteenth, as well as in the twentieth, century. Panning from the queen to the wooded shore behind her, the camera showed each tall pine change into "a ship"s

lofty spar ... row upon row of them ... a forest of mast-heads, each flying the British flag." Directly linking the navy of the past with the navy of the present, those masts then dissolved to "the steel superstructure of modern warships," as martial anthems swelled and the camera showed "Britain's battle fleet in majestic parade ...."[79] In adopting this closing montage, Warner Bros. clearly had the contemporary European situation in mind. Directly pitting the England of 1940 against Hitler's Germany, the scene was neither a part of the original 1924 film nor included in Miller's temporary script of May 1939. Only in desperate days of early 1940 did Howard Koch add it.[80]

Errol Flynn as hero in The Sea Hawk.

The Sea Hawk generated a wealth of reaction among critics, all of whom noted the connections between scenes such as these and the European war. Newsweek wrote that the production blurred the distinction between the glory days of Queen Elizabeth's and Churchill's England. And, in that nebulous world, Flynn's Thorpe stood "between England and blitzkrieg."[81] The Daily Film Renter, an industry publication intended for exhibitors, claimed that the picture made "the best of two worlds, the old and new, by treating of Spain's threatened attack upon England with her secretly built Armada along the lines of Hitler's promised invasion of to-day."[82] According to Kenneth McCaleb, film critic for the New York Mirror, "history repeats—in England and in Hollywood" as The Sea Hawk "reminds us that back in the days of Good Queen Bess, the British island kingdom withstood a Spanish blitzkrieg just as it is standing off the Nazis in this day of George VI."[83] In that latter day the film enjoyed wide popular acceptance. After its world premiere at the Hollywood Theatre on 17 July 1940, Film Daily named The Sea Hawk to its honor roll of the year's best films. The studio's most popular production of 1940, The Sea Hawk played for 47 days at Warner's first-run theaters in New York and Los

31

Angeles, a number matched by only one other Warner feature.[84]

Armed with such pro-British images, the American public favored measures to help the island keep the Nazis at arm's length. Just two days after *The Sea Hawk*'s release, 53 percent of American citizens polled wanted to give England more help short of war in its struggle against Hitler. By late September over half of the American people, recognizing the importance of that land to U.S. security, thought that helping Britain was more important than staying out of war.[85]

Emboldened by this growing public support for aid to Britain and even intervention, Roosevelt, who kept a close watch upon such polls, became more assertive in his policies. In September the president announced that he and Churchill had reached a destroyers-for-bases deal. The agreement, in which the United States traded fifty overage destroyers in exchange for leases to eight naval and air bases, "marked the end of American neutrality. In giving 50 destroyers to Great Britain, the United States was openly declaring its support of England in the war against Germany."[86] Nearly two-thirds of the American public approved of the understanding between the president and the prime minister and the former's newly assertive stance. The deal and other pro-British policies received further support in November 1940 when Roosevelt's bid for re-election succeeded in part because of his policies of "intervention on the side of the Allies."[87] After the election, Roosevelt announced his lend-lease plan. Under lend-lease, the United States would lend or lease war materials primarily to Britain for the duration of the war. After the war, the English would then compensate the U.S. for the borrowed goods. Intended to avoid the acrimonious war debts issue that still lingered from World War I, Roosevelt's program, which Congress approved in March 1941, allowed "Britain unrestricted access to American industrial resources."[88] The enactment of lend-lease served as yet another stepping stone in American foreign policy away from isolation and towards both intervention and an Anglo-American alliance.

The oligopoly held by the major studios helped the president gain support for his increasingly interventionist and pro-British foreign policies.[89] Five major studios—Paramount, MGM, RKO, Warner Bros., and Twentieth-Century Fox—dominated the motion picture industry. In July 1938 the Justice Department, at the behest of the remaining independent producers and theater owners, charged the major stu-

dios with violation of the Sherman Anti-Trust Act. Coupled with the economic downturn of the Roosevelt recession and the competition of radio, major studio executives feared this action. The industry lobbied the White House for relief through Secretary of Commerce Harry Hopkins. Pressured by Hopkins, the Department of Justice and the studios reached an agreement in November 1940 that averted—at least for eight years—the dismantling of the status quo. This compromise resulted from an industry pledge to serve the Roosevelt administration's propaganda needs in exchange for temporary exemption from anti-trust litigation.[90] By 1941 this exchange began to bear fruit. In February of that year, Roosevelt publicly thanked the industry for its cooperation in America's rearmament efforts in a message read at the Academy Awards banquet. In March, Lowell Mellett, head of the administration's publicity arm, the Office of Government Reports, wrote to the president that in its production of propagandistic films the picture industry was "pretty well living up to its offers of cooperation." Mellett ascribed this new spirit of partnership to the industry's fear of Justice Department litigation.[91]

This *quid pro quo* led isolationist Senator Gerald P. Nye (R-North Dakota) to call for an investigation by the Senate's Committee on Interstate Commerce. Nye turned his attention towards the motion picture industry because, in his opinion, films had "become the most gigantic engines of propaganda in existence to rouse the war fever in America ...." He believed that they had become "engines of propaganda" due to the influence of the English market, the many British in Hollywood, the industry's monopoly that allowed it to control content, and Roosevelt's benevolent intervention on behalf of the industry against federal anti-trust litigation. Directly equating films with the then-raging foreign policy debate between isolationists and interventionists, Nye claimed that anti-Nazi and pro-British films confused the reasoning of the American people. In a radio address, the senator illustrated his point:

> When you go to the movies, you go there to be entertained .... And then the picture starts—goes to work on you, all done by trained actors, full of drama, cunningly devised .... Before you know where you are you have actually listened to a speech designed to make you believe that Hitler is going to get you.[92]

Begun in September of 1941, Nye's investigation, unlike his earlier inquiry into the "merchants of death," accomplished little due to counterattacks by the industry and interventionists and the interruption of the Japanese attack on Pearl Harbor just over two months later.

Regardless of Nye's efforts, American films, public opinion, and foreign policy all became more pro-British and interventionist in 1941. By January of that year, 68 percent of responding Americans believed that the United States' future safety depended upon a British victory. To insure that occurrence, for which more than two-thirds of the public hoped, Roosevelt committed the nation even more fully.

In March the U.S. and Great Britain took the unprecedented peacetime step of coordinating military objectives. With the crafting of ABC-1, an agreement to concentrate on the defeat of Germany first if the U.S. entered the war, the two nations marched closer to a formal alliance.[93]

American films followed the same path. In the wake of the deal struck between Hollywood and Washington, Warner Bros. executives saw in the story of Sergeant Alvin C. York, a Tennessee mountaineer who achieved hero status after initially resisting World War I, an opportunity to explain the need for American mobilization. The line separating entertainment from propaganda, a line blurred by The Sea Hawk, was crossed. Warner Bros. executive Robert Buckner, in a memo to Wallis, claimed that the picture both entertained and provided the nation with "a good, timely message."[94] In the film, York, a conscientious objector, reluctantly reported to training camp. Impressed by his skills but concerned with his objector status, the camp's commanding officer provided York with an American history book as a counterweight to the Bible and instructed him to consider the two carefully. Ambivalent, York retreated with the books to a Tennessee mountaintop to chose either personal isolation from, or intervention in, the European conflict. A miraculous breeze turned the pages of his Bible to the verse "Render therefore unto Caesar the things which are Caesar's; and unto God the things that are God's."[95] In that passage both York and American viewers found a religious justification for war. The moral repugnance of war so prominent a decade earlier in All Quiet on the Western Front had turned full circle into justification for it in Sergeant York.[96]

Morally fortified, Cooper's York entered the Great War against Germany on behalf of Britain. Upon their arrival at the front, York and his colleagues jumped into a trench with a handful of British soldiers. Noting the doughboys' inexperience, a veteran Englishman instructed the amateurs when to

"flop" in the trench to avoid a shell. After this instruction, the British infantryman requested a cigarette from his new American allies. Receiving it, he said "you Yanks just got here in the nick of time. We were running shy of these. Besides, we could do with some help." The cinematic York provided help as he almost singlehandedly killed twenty German soldiers while taking 132 others prisoner in director Howard Hawks' version of the 1918 Meuse-Argonne offensive.[97] The real York lent his assistance in 1941 as well. In publicizing the film, Warner Bros. sent York on a nation-wide tour. On the tour, the hero met with President Roosevelt, who told reporters that the picture came "at a good time," at the White House and urged his fellow Americans to "give all our aid to England."[98] The film's mixture of pro-British sentiment and interventionism struck a responsive chord among many viewers. The National Board of Review's Motion Picture Council voted Sergeant York, which grossed almost $4 million in less than a year, as 1941's best film in terms of popular appeal, beating out Gone With the Wind.[99] In addition, the famed self help author, Dr. Norman Vincent Peale, wrote to Jack Warner that the picture rendered a very great service to our country in this crisis for it gives a sensible solution to a problem facing many young men—that is the problem of war. In fact, this picture may actually help to save this country. It will show them that there is something worth giving everything for, namely, liberty and freedom.[100]

One month after Warner's release of Sergeant York, Roosevelt and Churchill signed the Atlantic Charter, an agreement which outlined the Anglo-American wartime and post-war objectives. These objectives for the post-war world included the Four Freedoms the president had enunciated the previous January, liberal trade, disarmament, and the creation of an international organization. Then, with an Anglo-American agreement on the shape of the post-war world in hand, Roosevelt declared an American naval convoy of ships—both American and British—in the North Atlantic. Announced in response to a German U-boat attack upon the Greer, the convoy "marked a decisive step toward war."[101]

American films soon took that decisive step as well. Premiering in late September 1941, Twentieth Century-Fox's A Yank in the R.A.F. was among the first of Hollywood's films to portray American belligerence. Filmed partly in England, the movie was "supercharged with propaganda."[102] Tyrone Power's character, Tim Baker, opened the film by flying supplies to London. After this parallel to the U.S.'s efforts to supply Britain through such measures as lend-lease, Baker, arriving in London during one such mission, decided to enroll in the Royal Air Force. Flying a Spitfire, he provided soldiers at Dunkirk with air cover and later took part in the R.A.F.'s attempts to counter the *Luftwaffe* in aerial combat over the English Channel.[103]

With Tyrone Power, in *A Yank in the R.A.F.*, intervening on behalf of Britain upon America's screens, the nation had a role model for what was soon reality. The United States had moved closer and closer to that reality throughout the period 1939-41. U.S. involvement in the war and the conclusion of a military alliance was, like pro-British movies, contingent upon external factors. Cinematic Anglophilia required the influence of the British, Nazi anti-Semitism, the emergence of a unique market—and official interference. Both cinematic and diplomatic developments depended upon international events. On the latter front, the nation received its final justification for intervention when Japan attacked Pearl Harbor and Hitler inexplicably followed with his own declaration of war upon the U.S. Washington subsequently concluded an informal Anglo-American military alliance, the first such move by the U.S. in more than 150 years. In a partnership (which also included the Soviet Union) founded in part upon culture and fueled by motion picture messages, the U.S. and Britain followed the dictates of ABC-1 and directed their initial military attentions toward the defeat of Nazi Germany.

Conclusions

But the road to intervention and alliance was a tortuous one. Roosevelt, at least after 1939 when eventual involvement appeared unavoidable, faced the task of moving a reluctant nation. The American public remained unwilling to become embroiled in a second continental war. Constrained by that opinion, the president, in part through motion pictures, attempted to lead the nation towards intervention. By nullifying the Department of Justice's anti-trust efforts, Roosevelt gained Hollywood's aid in selling his ideas. This action served as an important step towards what followed. Once hostilities began, the president formally drafted the film capital through the creation of the Office of War Information (OWI).[104]

Motion pictures shown in American theaters closely paralleled both the president's and the nation's moves towards that war. In 1935, when the United States first looked at the world in the inter-war period it did so through British eyes. Just as that year's Neutrality Act rejected strict neutrality, so too

did films such as *The Lives of a Bengal Lancer*, *Mutiny on the Bounty*, and *Captain Blood*. When World War II began in 1939 and Roosevelt encouraged the nation to embrace the Allies over the nation's radio airwaves, Hollywood turned out *The Sun Never Sets*, *Wuthering Heights*, *Gunga Din*, and *Goodbye, Mr. Chips*. Finally, in 1940-41 when the United Kingdom emerged as the last barrier standing between Nazi Germany and the U.S., American audiences demanded and received *Foreign Correspondent*, *The Sea Hawk*, and *A Yank in the R.A.F.* As these pictures played in theaters nationwide, the U.S. strengthened trans-Atlantic ties. America's affinity for Great Britain provided a shade of grey between the black and white of isolation or intervention.

Films, by reinforcing the dominant public opinion favorable to Great Britain, helped to create an atmosphere—the grey area—in which this political alliance could flourish. The contribution of cinema to the "second rapprochement," which has been followed by cordial Anglo-American relations up to the present day, suggests that the political fusion drew heavily upon culture. Films shown in America from 1935 to 1941, then, both drew upon and strengthened the trans-Atlantic cultural exchange. Inter-war film served as one ingredient of a cultural additive to diplomacy, an additive which has become a recent focus of historians studying unofficial relations.[105]

Within this milieu of unofficial, cultural relations, Hollywood produced films with pro-British, or anti-Nazi, messages to satisfy demand from both above and below. Pluralistic in composition, intent, and effect, motion pictures both manipulated and reflected their audiences. Foremost, Hollywood executives were businesspeople who gave the viewing public what it wanted. But they were also willing to inject their own views and bend to official desires. Driven by the marketplace, the shifting interna-tional situation, their own desires, and Washington, Hollywood added ever-increasing doses of Anglophilia to productions from 1935 to 1941. It began simply enough with adaptations of Shakespearean plays and trips to the colonies with British empire- builders. But commencing with *The Dawn Patrol*, Hollywood reluctantly began to choose sides. By 1940 and 1941, with the releases of *The Sea Hawk* and *Sergeant York*, the film capital placed itself firmly in the British camp. Popular cinema did not generate an alliance on its own. But Anglophilia on film helped to reinforce evolving public opinion and thus to lay the groundwork for the popular acceptance of FDR's foreign policies.

Notes

1 Robert Dallek, *Franklin D. Roosevelt and American Foreign Policy, 1932-1945* (New York: Oxford University Press), 102-9.

2 For a full discussion of the Anglo-American rapprochement see Bradford Perkins, *The Great Rapprochement: England and the United States, 1895-1914* (New York: Atheneum, 1968). An analysis of culture in the creation of an amicable relationship is provided in H.C. Allen, *Great Britain and the United States: A History of Anglo-American Relations, 1783-1952* (New York: St. Martin's, 1955), 17-29, 133-40, 150 and 153. Other factors, of course, such as a common interest in preventing German expansion and a joint effort to capture oil supplies contributed to better relations in the years before World War II. See David Reynolds, *The Creation of the Anglo-American Alliance, 1937-1941: A Study in Competitive Co-operation* (Chapel Hill: The University of North Carolina Press, 1982), 1-3 and 286-94; Daniel Yergin, *The Prize: The Epic Quest for Oil, Money, and Power* (New York: Simon and Schuster, 1992), 260-8 and 368-75. The cinematic affinity for British subjects did not happen overnight, but instead drew from a long tradition. See, for instance, *Disraeli*, directed by Alfred E. Green, with George Arliss, Doris Lloyd, David Torrence, Jan Bennett, and Florence Arliss, Warner Bros. Pictures, 1929; *Cavalcade*, directed by Frank Lloyd, with Diana Wynyard, Clive Brook, Una O'Connor, and Herbert Mundin, Twentieth Century-Fox, 1933; *The Private Life of Henry VIII*, directed by Alexander Korda, with Charles Laughton, Robert Donat, and Franklin Dyald, London Film Productions/United Artists, 1933.

3 *A Midsummer Night's Dream*, directed by Max Reinhardt and William Dieterle, with James Cagney, Joe E. Brown, Dick Powell, Mickey Rooney, and Victor Jory, Warner Bros. Pictures, 1935; Richard Sheridan Ames, *Rob Wagner's Script*, 19 October 1935, 10, cited in Anthony Slide, ed., *Selected Film Criticism, 1931-40* (Metuchen, N.J.: Scarecrow Press, 1983), 153; Nick Roddick, *A New Deal in Entertainment: Warner Brothers in the 1930s* (London: British Film Institute), 265-6. English critics gave the film a lukewarm reception because they felt it was a poor adaptation. For the English critical reaction see Ernest Marshall, "The Word From London: Reaction to the Shakespeare-Reinhardt 'Dream' Is Not Entirely Favorable," *New York Times*, 1 December 1935, sec. XI, p. 8.

4 "The New Pictures," *Time*, 16 May 1938, 57.

5 *The Adventures of Robin Hood*, directed by Michael Curtiz and William Keighley, with Errol Flynn, Olivia de Havilland, Basil Rathbone, and Claude Rains, Warner Bros. Pictures, 1938.

6 Earning profits of nearly $2 million, *Robin Hood*, voted 1938's seventh best film by *Film Daily*, emerged as Warner Brothers' biggest moneymaker of the year. After playing for forty-two days, the second most of any 1938 Hollywood production, at the studio's first-run theaters, the feature received an Academy Award nomination for Best Picture. Roddick, *New Deal Entertainment*, 179, 235-6, 267 and 279; James C. Robertson, *The Casablanca Man: The Cinema of Michael Curtiz* (London: Routledge, 1993), 44; *Mutiny on the Bounty*, directed by Frank Lloyd, with Charles Laughton, Clark Gable, and Franchot Tone, Metro-Goldwyn-Mayer, 1935; *Captain Blood*, directed by Michael Curtiz, with Errol Flynn, Olivia de Havilland, Lionel Atwill, and Basil Rathbone, Warner Bros. Pictures, 1935. Other films, such as *Wuthering Heights*, based on Emily Bronte's novel, and *Goodbye, Mr. Chips*, appeared during the thirties based largely upon the Anglo-American cultural dialogue. See *Wuthering Heights*, directed by William Wyler, with Merle Oberon, Laurence Olivier, David Niven, Flora Robson, and Donald Crisp, Metro-Goldwyn-Mayer, 1939; *Goodbye, Mr. Chips*, directed by Sam Wood, with Robert Donat, Greer Garson, John Colley, Peter Colley, and Paul Von Hernried, Metro-Goldwyn-Mayer, 1939.

7 John M. MacKenzie, ed., *Imperialism and Popular Culture* (Manchester: Manchester University Press, 1986), 1-14.

8 Jeffrey Richards, "Boy's Own Empire: Feature Films and Imperialism in the 1930s," in *Imperialism and Popular Culture*, ed. MacKenzie, 140-60. Not all films of the decade embraced imperialism wholeheartedly. The British production *Rhodes*, for example, which appeared in America and detailed the life of empire-builder Cecil Rhodes, was actually critical of British imperialism in Africa. See Mark Van Doren, *The Private Reader: Selected Articles and Reviews* (1942; reprint, New York: Kraus, 1968), 321-4.

9 John M. MacKenzie, *Propaganda and Empire: The Manipulation of British Public Opinion, 1880-1960* (Manchester: Manchester University Press), 89.

10 *The Lives of a Bengal Lancer*, directed by Henry Hathaway, with Gary Cooper, Franchot Tone, Richard Cromwell, Sir Guy Standing, and C. Aubrey Smith, Paramount Productions, 1935.

11 Ferguson, *The Film Criticism of Otis Ferguson*, ed. Robert Wilson (Philadelphia: Temple University Press, 1971), 65-6.

12 Sennwald, "The Paramount Presents 'The Lives of a Bengal Lancer' and 'Enter Madame' at the Palace," *New York Times*, 12 January 1935, sec. I, p. 12; Sennwald, "Where Will They Be In December?," *New York Times*, 30 June 1935, sec. X, p. 3.

13 Joseph I. Breen to Paramount, 6 December 1937, *The Lives of a Bengal Lancer* File, Motion Picture Association of America-Production Code Administration Collection (hereafter cited as MPAA-PCA), Academy of Motion Picture Arts and Sciences, Beverly Hills, CA (hereafter cited as AMPAS).

14 Local censor boards in Algeria, Morocco, and Tunisia summarily rejected the film, while the Egyptian censors accepted it only after Paramount removed McGregor's quip. India's authorities took particular exception and demanded that the British launch a protest of the film to United States Secretary of State Cordell Hull. Although careful not to stir Indian discontent, British authorities, who throughout had advised Paramount to handle colonial relations with care, refused. James Wingate to Will H. Hays, 9 December 1932; Frederick L. Herron to Geoffrey Shurlock, 27 May 1935; Joseph I. Breen to Paramount, 19 November 1935; Breen to Paramount, 10 June 1940; "Films 'Vilification' of India," *The Statesman* (Calcutta), 19 September 1935, p. 1-3, all in *The Lives of a Bengal Lancer* File, MPAA-PCA Collection, AMPAS.

[15] Inter-Office Communication, Hal Wallis to Sam Bischoff, 8 January 1936, reprinted in Rudy Behlmer, ed., *Inside Warner Bros. (1935-1951)* (New York: Viking, 1985), 28-9. Perhaps the quintessential testament to the popularity of *The Lives of a Bengal Lancer*, and the attempts by other studios to capitalize upon this genre, was the production of *Bonnie Scotland*, a Laurel and Hardy parody of the former. *Bonnie Scotland*, directed by James W. Hogne, with Stan Laurel and Oliver Hardy, Metro-Goldwyn-Mayer, 1935. The adventure of the imperial film proved particularly popular during the Great Depression. Richard Hofstadter claims that depression-era psychology played a role in the physical imperialism of the 1890s. In the 1930s Americans similarly found escape from their sense of economic powerlessness in the popular imperialism of these films. For a discussion of psychology in physical imperialism see Hofstadter, *The Paranoid Style in American Politics and Other Essays* (New York: Alfred Knopf, 1965).

[16] Ben Shylen to Hal B. Wallis, 5 November 1941, *Sergeant York* Story File, Warner Bros. Archives (hereafter cited as WBA), School of Cinema-Television, University of Southern California, Los Angeles, CA (hereafter cited as USC); Robertson, *Casablanca Man*, 39; Roddick, *New Deal Entertainment*, 266.

[17] *The Charge of the Light Brigade*, directed by Michael Curtiz, with Errol Flynn, David Niven, Olivia de Havilland, Nigel Bruce, and G. Henry Gordon, Warner Bros. Pictures, 1936; Inter-Office Communication, Hal B. Wallis to Sam Bischoff, 8 January 1936, reprinted in Behlmer, *Inside Warner Bros.*, 28-9.

[18] Nugent, "Kiplings of the Pacific: Hollywood, In Its Imperialistic Sagas, Helps Bear the White Man's Burden," *New York Times*, 8 November 1936, sec. X, p. 5.

[19] *Gunga Din*, directed by George Stevens, with Cary Grant, Victor McLaglen, and Douglas Fairbanks, Jr., Radio-Keith-Orpheum, 1939.

[20] *Gunga Din*; Ben Hecht et al., "Gunga Din" (screenplay, *Gunga Din* Final Script File, George Stevens Collection, AMPAS, 1939), 1, 5-12, 113-21, 130-4, 165, and 174-5.

[21] The Kiplingesque views of race and imperialism permeated the film even though director George Stevens decided to add the superimposition of the poem "Gunga Din" over the final scene only at the last moment. Pandro Berman to Stevens, 5 August 1938, *Gunga Din* Production File, Stevens Collection, AMPAS.

[22] Nugent, "Kiplings of the Pacific," 5; Crisler, "Poets and the Cinema," *New York Times*, 29 January 1939, sec. IX, p. 5.

[23] Hecht et al., "Gunga Din," 120 and 158.

[24] Hecht et al., "Gunga Din," 38-9 and 56B.

[25] Ferguson, *Criticism*, 246-7.

[26] Dallek, *Roosevelt and American Policy*, 126-7, 131, and 135-6. For a discussion of Hollywood and the Spanish Civil War see Bernard F. Dick, *The Star-Spangled Screen: The American World War II Film* (Lexington: The University Press off Kentucky, 1985), 10-40.

[27] *Fire Over England*, directed by William K. Howard, with Laurence Olivier, Vivien Leigh, Raymond Massey, and Flora Robson, United Artists, 1937; James Wong Howe, "Fire Over England" (screenplay, *Fire Over England* File No. 48, James Wong Howe Collection, AMPAS, 7 June 1936), 9 and 56. The conflict between appeasement and a hard line policy towards Hitler had even greater resonance, of course, for British politics.

[28] *Fire Over England*; Howe, "Fire Over England," 70, 101, 103 and 111.

[29] Lorentz, *Lorentz On Film: Movies 1927 to 1941* (New York: Hopkinson and Blake, 1975), 140-41; *Fire Over England*; Howe, "Fire Over England," 112, 116, 118, 120 and 121.

[30] Dallek, *Roosevelt and American Policy*, 137, 140 and 147-52; Robert A. Divine, *The Illusion of Neutrality* (Chicago: University of Chicago Press, 1962), 211-4, 221, 228 and 334.

[31] Inter-Office Communication, Wallis to Warner, 30 April 1938, *The Dawn Patrol* Story File, WBA, USC; also reprinted in Behlmer, *Inside Warner Bros.*, 73.

[32] *The Dawn Patrol*, directed by Edmund Goulding, with Errol Flynn, David Niven, Basil Rathbone, and Donald Crisp, Warner Bros. Pictures, 1938; Seton I. Miller and Dan Totheroh, "Dwn Patrol" (screenplay, *The Dawn Patrol* Story File, WBA, USC, 1938), 6-9, 33-7, 44, 67-9 and 124-6.

[33] Fulton to Walter MacEwen, 31 December 1938, *The Dawn Patrol* Story File, WBA, USC; Nugent, "Chips Off the Yule Log," *New York Times*, 25 December 1938, sec. IX, p. 7; "War Again in Hollywood: 'Dawn Patrol' Remake Follows Chronicle of 'Sub Patrol,'" *Newsweek*, 12 December 1938, 25.

[34] *The Dawn Patrol*; John Alden, "'Dawn Patrol' Brings Thrills To Orpheum," *The Minneapolis Tribune*, 5 January 1939, p. 7, *The Dawn Patrol* Clipping File, WBA, USC.

[35] Breen to Warner Bros., 9 December 1940; 17 September 1940; 31 October 1939; 2 November 1939; 8 June 1939, all in *The Dawn Patrol* File, MPAA-PCA Collection, AMPAS.

[36] *The Dawn Patrol*; Miller and Totheroh, "Dawn Patrol," 48-55 and 58-64.

[37] Analysis Chart, by F. Stinnette, 6 October 1938, *The Dawn Patrol* File, MPAA-PCA Collection, AMPAS.

[38] "'Warner Bros.' Campaign Plan," 1938, *The Dawn Patrol* Publicity File, WBA, USC. Although Flynn held British citizenship, he was born in Ireland, grew up in Australia, and spent most of his adult life in the United States. See Flynn, *My Wicked, Wicked Ways* (New York: Buccaneer Books, 1959).

[39] LeJeune, "'The Dawn Patrol'-and A Tail-Piece," *The Observer* (London), 19 February 1939, p. 12, *The Dawn Patrol* Clipping File; Max Milder to S.E. Morris, 20 February 1939, *The Dawn Patrol* Publicity File; Telegram, Reg Whitley to Jack Warner, 16 February 1939, *The Dawn Patrol* Story File, WBA, USC. The film enjoyed a warm reception in London where it played to capacity crowds, even after ticket prices were raised, at the Warner Theatre for several weeks.

[40] Telegram, Eden to Lindsay, 10 March 1937, FO 371, vol. 20651, no. 91, cited in Thomas E. Hachey, ed., "Winning Friends and Influencing Policy: British Strategy to Woo America in 1937," *Wisconsin Magazine of History* 55, no. 2 (1971-72): 120.

[41] Dispatch, Lindsay to Eden, 22 March 1937, FO 371, vol. 20651, no. 247, cited in Hachey, "Winning Friends," 122-3, 126 and 129.

[42] Dispatch, Lindsay to Eden, 22 March 1937, cited in Hachey, "Winning Friends," 122-3, 126 and 129.

[43] Hachey, "Winning Friends," 122; Nicholas John Cull, *Selling War: The British Propaganda Campaign Against American "Neutrality" in World War II* (New York: Oxford University Press, 1995), 3-4 and 198-202.

[44] Lindsay specifically mentioned the positive impact that *Cavalcade* had on American opinion towards the United Kingdom. Dispatch, Lindsay to Eden, 22 March 1937, cited in Hachey, "Winning Friends," 122-3 and 126. Lindsay, however, was not the first Anglo bureaucrat to recognize the potential in film. In 1932 Sir Stephen Tallents, first secretary of the Empire Marketing Board who later moved on to the British Broadcasting Corporation, argued that it was essential "to throw a fitting presentation of England upon the world's screen." See MacKenzie, *Propaganda and Empire*, 83-4.

[45] Quote from Michael Korda, *Charmed Lives: A Family Romance* (New York: Random House, 1979), 138-9. Churchill to David B. Cunynghame, 22 October 1937, reprinted in Gilbert Martin, ed., *Winston S. Churchill* (Boston: Houghton Mifflin, 1983), 810-1; Lord Winterton to Churchill, 27 October 1937, in Martin, *Churchill*, 817-19; Churchill to Cunynghame, 3 November 1937, in Martin, *Churchill*, 823-6; MacKenzie, *Propaganda and Empire*, 89. For a full discussion of Churchill's relationship with Korda and cinema see D.J. Wenden and K.R.M. Short, "Winston S. Churchill: film fan," *Historical Journal of Film, Radio, and Television* 11, no. 3 (1991): 197-214. Korda's post-war efforts on behalf of British film are described by John Nichols elsewhere in the collection, ( ). 24

[46] Korda, *Charmed Lives*, 148.

[47] That *Hamilton Woman*, directed by Alexander Korda, with Laurence Olivier, Vivien Leigh, Alan Mowbrey, and Sara Allgood, United Artists/ Alexander Korda Films, 1941.

[48] Roscoe Williams, "That Hamilton Woman," *Motion Picture Daily*, 24 March 1941, *That Hamilton Woman* File, MPAA-PCA Collection, AMPAS.

[49] "That Hamilton Woman," *Variety*, 20 March 1941, p. 3; "'That Hamilton Woman'! Triumph for Vivien Leigh," *The Hollywood Reporter*, 20 March 1941, all in *That Hamilton Woman* File, MPAA-PCA Collection, AMPAS.

[50] Korda, *Charmed Lives*, 154-5; Gerald P. Nye, "War Propaganda," *Vital Speeches*, 15 September 1941, 720-3. A brief discussion of the Senate's investigation into suspected propaganda follows.

[51] Nye cited in Richard W. Steele, *Propaganda in an Open Society: The Roosevelt Administration and the Media, 1933-1941*, Contributions in American History, ed. Jon L. Wakelyn, no. 111 (Westport, Conn.: Greenwood Press, 1985), 165; Harold Lavine and James Wechsler, *War Propaganda and the United States* (New Haven: Yale University Press, 1940), 230-1.

[52] Lavine and Wechsler, *War Propaganda*, 230-1; John Selfridge, "Hollywood Crown Colony," *Scribner's*, January 1941, 45-9, Core Collection, British—Actors and Actresses File, AMPAS. These actors did not, of course, perform military service for the UK.

[53] Dick, *Star-Spangled Screen*, 41, 43-4, and 55-6; Clayton R. Koppes and Gregory D. Black, *Hollywood Goes To War: How Politics, Profits, and Propaganda Shaped World War II Movies* (New York: The Free Press, 1987), 4-5 and 8; Steele, *Propaganda in an Open Society*, 154. For a full discussion of the Warners' anti-Nazi activities see Christine Anne Colgan, "Warner Brothers' Crusade Against the Third Reich: A Study of Anti-Nazi Activism and Film Production, 1933 to 1941" (Ph.D. diss., University of Southern California, 1985).

[54] "22 Ambulances Donated," *New York Times*, 14 December 1940, sec. I, p. 4; "Movie To Buy Spitfires," *New York Times*, 11 February 1941, sec. I, p. 27.

[55] Dick, *Star-Spangled Screen*, 65-6; Koppes and Black, *Hollywood Goes to War*, 43-4; "Warner Bros.," *Fortune*, December 1937, 208 and 212.

[56] As the market changed so too did the PCA's prohibitions on depicting foreign nations or peoples unfavorably. By July of 1940, Hays helped organize the Motion Picture Committee Cooperating for National Defense, a liaison between the government and the film industry designed to fulfill the former's cinematic needs. Koppes and Black, *Hollywood Goes To War*, 20-2, 27-30 and 34; Steele, *Propaganda in an Open Society*, 152-5, 158 and 162; Black, *Hollywood Censored: Morality Codes, Catholics, and the Movies*, Cambridge Studies in the History of Mass Communications, ed. Kenneth Short and Garth Jowett (Cambridge: Cambridge University Press, 1994), 299-300. The growing flood of American pictures into England created some friction. As early as 1935 the English film industry lobbied Parliament to place an import quota on American productions. Representatives of the English film industry claimed that a quota was necessary to prevent American pictures from pushing British producers out of their own market. Parliament remained lukewarm on the issue throughout the thirties. See Bruce Allan, "British Producers and Critics Blame America for Low Profits," *Motion Picture Herald*, 30 January 1937, 59; Allan, "British Minister Discredits Talk of American Control of Industry," *Motion Picture Herald*, 6 March 1937, Core Collection, United Kingdom — Anglo-American Relations File, AMPAS.

[57] Film historians have noted the overt anti-Nazism of the era's films. See Colgan, "Warner Brothers' Crusade"; Dick, *Star-Spangled Screen*, 41-64.

[58] George H. Gallup, *1935-1948*, vol. 1 of *The Gallup Poll: Public Opinion 1935-1971* (New York: Random House, 1972), 184-88; Charles C. Alexander, *Nationalism in American Thought, 1930-1945* (Chicago: Rand McNally, 1969), 176-7.

37

[59] Roosevelt, *War and Neutrality*, vol. VIII of *The Public Papers and Addresses of Franklin D. Roosevelt*, ed. Samuel I. Rosenman (New York: Macmillan, 1941), 460-63, quoted in Robert A. Divine, *The Reluctant Belligerent: American Entry into World War II*, America in Crisis Series, ed. Divine (New York: John Wiley and Sons, 1965), 65-6; Allen, *Great Britain and United States*, 794; Dallek, *Roosevelt and American Policy*, 199.

[60] Quote from Divine, *Reluctant Belligerent*, 65.

[61] Gallup, *1935-1948*, 184-8.

[62] Nugent, "History, Histrionics and Humor," *New York Times*, 18 June 1939, sec. IX, p. 3.

[63] Analysis Chart, by Geoffrey Shurlock, 27 May 1939, *The Sun Never Sets* File, MPAA-PCA Collection, AMPAS.

[64] *The Sun Never Sets*, directed by Rowland V. Lee, with Douglas Fairbanks, Jr., Basil Rathbone, Barbara O'Neil, Lionel Atwill, and Virginia Field, Universal Pictures, 1939.

[65] The film implied, but never forthrightly stated, that Zurof was a Soviet spy encouraging socialist revolutions against western capitalist countries with his broadcasts. The implied anti-Soviet message was a tentative reaction to Josef Stalin's flirtations with Hitler that led to the signing of the Nazi-Soviet Non-Aggression Pact two months after the picture's release.

[66] *Sun Never Sets*; Nugent, "A Wild-Eyed Story of Empire Is 'The Sun Never Sets' at Music Hall," *New York Times*, 9 June 1939, sec. I, p. 26.

[67] Department of State, *Peace and War: United States Foreign Policy, 1931-1941* (Washington, D.C.: United States Government Printing Office, 1943), 547-8, quoted in Divine, *Reluctant Belligerent*, 84.

[68] Divine, *Reluctant Belligerent*, 86-8; Dallek, *Roosevelt and American Policy*, 221-32.

[69] *Foreign Correspondent*, directed by Alfred Hitchcock, with Joel McCrea, Laraine Day, Herbert Marshall, George Sanders, and Albert Basserman, United Artists/Walter Wanger Productions, 1940; Herb Sterne, "Foreign Correspondent," *Rob Wagner's Script*, 28 September 1940, 16, quoted in Slide, *Selected Film Criticism*, 77; Cull, *Selling War*, 111-2.

[70] Churchill, *1935-1942*, vol. VI of *Winston S. Churchill: His Complete Speeches, 1897-1963*, ed. Robert Rhodes James (New York: Chelsea House, 1974), 6231.

[71] "Errol Flynn Turns Sea Hawk," *Evening News* (London), 2 August 1940, *The Sea Hawk* Clipping File, WBA, USC.

[72] *The Sea Hawk*, directed by Michael Curtiz, with Errol Flynn, Flora Robson, Claude Rains, Alan Hale, and Brenda Marshall, Warner Bros. Pictures, 1940; J.G. Hawks, "The Sea Hawk" (screenplay, *The Sea Hawk* Story File, WBA, USC, 1924), not paginated; Seton I. Miller, "Sea Hawk" (screenplay, *The Sea Hawk* Story File, WBA, USC, 13 May 1939), 1-5; Miller and Howard Koch, "The Sea Hawk" (screenplay, *The Sea Hawk* Story File, WBA, USC, 30 January 1940), 1-2.

[73] *Sea Hawk*; Miller and Koch, "Sea Hawk," 2.

[74] *Sea Hawk*; Miller and Koch, "Sea Hawk," 5.

[75] *Sea Hawk*; Miller and Koch, "Sea Hawk," 6-7, 13 and 24; Philip M. Taylor, "Propaganda in International Politics, 1919-1939," in *Film & Radio Propaganda in World War II*, ed. K.R.M. Short (Knoxville: The University of Tennessee Press, 1983), 34-5.

[76] Miller to Walter MacEwen, 26 March 1940, *The Sea Hawk* Story File #1; Inter-Office Communication, Koch to MacEwen, 20 March 1940, *The Sea Hawk* Story File #2, all in WBA, USC.

[77] Advertisement, "The Sea Hawk," 1940, 4, *The Sea Hawk* Publicity File, WBA, USC.

[78] *The Sea Hawk*; Miller and Koch, "The Sea Hawk," 149-50.

[79] *The Sea Hawk*; Miller and Koch, "The Sea Hawk," 149-50.

[80] Koch, *As Time Goes By: The Memoirs of a Writer* (New York: Harcourt, Brace, Jovanovich, 1979), 45-6; Hawks, "Sea Hawk," not paginated; Miller, "Sea Hawk," 158; Outline, by Koch, n.d., 38, *The Sea Hawk* Story File, WBA, USC. Historian Rudy Behlmer claims that Elizabeth's final speech was cut from the American version of *The Sea Hawk* and was shown only to English audiences. (This is an important point for our purposes; however, the author has not yet uncovered primary evidence to confirm this assertion.) See Behlmer, ed., *The Sea Hawk*, Wisconsin/Warner Bros. Screenplay Series (Madison: The University of Wisconsin Press, 1982), 41-2. The Warner Bros. research department contemplated the relationship between the past and the present in creating the film. Warner's researchers compiled studies of sixteenth century navies, British and German fleets as they stood in 1940, and comparisons between the two. Inter-Office Communication, Herman Lissauer to Jack Kelly, 21 June 1940; Inter-Office Communication, Lissauer to Kelly, 22 June 1940, all in *The Sea Hawk* Research File, WBA, USC.

[81] "Swashbuckling on Warner Sea," *Newsweek*, 19 August 1940, 46.

[82] "The Sea Hawk," *The Daily Film Renter*, 31 July 1940, *The Sea Hawk* Clipping File, WBA, USC.

[83] Kenneth McCaleb, "Swashbucklers Fight It Out in 'Sea Hawk,'" *New York Mirror*, 10 August 1940, *The Sea Hawk* Clipping File, WBA, USC.

[84] Roddick, *New Deal Entertainment*, 268 and 281.

[85] Gallup, *1935-1948*, 233 and 243.

[86] Divine, *Reluctant Belligerent*, 91.

38

[85] Gallup, *1935-1948*, 233 and 243.

[86] Divine, *Reluctant Belligerent*, 91.

[87] Quote from Leo Gurko, *The Angry Decade* (New York: Harper and Row, 1968), 9-10; Dallek, *Roosevelt and American Policy*, 232; Gallup, *1935-1948*, 237-8; Divine, *Reluctant Belligerent*, 129-31.

[88] Divine, *Reluctant Belligerent*, 106.

[89] Nye, "War Propaganda," 721-2. FDR's son, James Roosevelt, provided another link between the industry and the administration. James Roosevelt, president of Globe production company, travelled to England in 1939 on behalf of Samuel Goldwyn to promote *Wuthering Heights*. See "James Roosevelt To Sail," *New York Times*, 28 March 1939, sec. I, p. 20; Koppes and Black, *Hollywood Goes To War*, 33-4.

[90] Philip Dunne, "Propaganda or History?," *The Nation*, 20 September 1941, 241; Dick, *Star-Spangled Screen*, 89; Steele, *Propaganda in an Open Society*, 155-7.

[91] Roosevelt, *The Call to Battle Stations*, vol. X of *The Public Papers and Addresses of Franklin D. Roosevelt*, ed. Samuel I. Rosenman (New York: Russell and Russell, 1969), 40-2; Koppes and Black, *Hollywood Goes To War*, 36; Memorandum, Mellett for Roosevelt, 17 March 1941, Folder, Mellett Papers, Franklin D. Roosevelt Library, quoted in Steele, *Propaganda in an Open Society*, 163-4.

[92] Nye, "War Propaganda," 720-3; Koppes and Black, *Hollywood Goes To War*, 40. For a discussion of the debate between interventionists and isolationists see Wayne S. Cole, *Roosevelt and the Isolationists, 1932-1945* (Lincoln: University of Nebraska Press, 1983).

[93] Gallup, *1935-1948*, 257; Divine, *Reluctant Belligerent*, 106-7.

[94] Inter-Office Communication, Buckner to Wallis, 4 June 1940, *Sergeant York* Story File, WBA, USC.

[95] *Sergeant York*, directed by Howard Hawks, with Gary Cooper, Walter Brennan, Joan Leslie, George Tobias, and Stanley Ridges, Warner Bros. Pictures, 1941; Abem Finkel et al., "Sergeant York" (screenplay, *Sergeant York* Story File, WBA, USC, 31 January 1941), 108-15.

[96] Crowther, "The Screen In Review," *New York Times*, 3 July 1941, sec. I, p. 15; Roddick, *New Deal Entertainment*, 209-12; Koppes and Black, *Hollywood Goes To War*, 37-9. For a detailed study of *Sergeant York*, see Michael Birdwell's essay in this collection ( ).

[97] *Sergeant York*; Finkel et al., "Sergeant York," 119; Analysis Chart, by F. Stinnette, 13 May 1941, *Sergeant York* Story File, MPAA-PCA Collection, AMPAS.

[98] "Sergt. York Visits with the President," *New York Times*, 31 July 1941, sec. I, p. 13; Roddick, *New Deal Entertainment*, 213-4.

[99] Roddick, *New Deal Entertainment*, 179, 210, 268-9 and 282.

[100] Peale to Warner, 2 July 1941, *Sergeant York* Story File, WBA, USC.

[101] Divine, *Reluctant Belligerent*, 131-5 and 143.

[102] O'Hara, "Blond Blitz on the R.A.F.," *Newsweek*, 6 October 1941, 59-60.

[103] *A Yank in the R.A.F.*, directed by Henry King, with Tyrone Power, Betty Grable, John Sutton, Reginald Gardner, and Donald Stuart, Twentieth Century-Fox, 1941.

[104] The best, and most contradictory, works on Roosevelt's diplomacy remain Dallek, *Roosevelt and American Policy* and Divine, *Reluctant Belligerent*. For a discussion of FDR's use of the media see Steele, *Propaganda in an Open Society*.

[105] Cultural differences, for example, played a role in creating the nineteenth century conflict between England and Germany, according to Raymond Sontag, *Germany and England: Background of Conflict, 1848-1894* (New York: Russell and Russell, 1964). Examples of the recent focus on unofficial, cultural relations, in diplomatic history include Michael L. Krenn, "Unfinished Business: Segregation and U.S. Diplomacy at the 1958 World's Fair," *Diplomatic History* 20, no. 4 (Fall 1996): 591-612; Reinhold Wagnleitner, *Coca-Colonization and the Cold War: The Cultural Mission of the United States in Austria after the Second World War*, trans. Diana M. Wolf (Chapel Hill: The University of North Carolina Press, 1994).

Michael Todd Bennett received both his B.A. and M.A. in history from Texas Tech University. Currently, he is working toward the Ph.D. with an emphasis on twentieth century American history at the University of Georgia. Bennett works as a teaching assistant and lives, with his wife Ginger, in Athens, Georgia

Frederic Krome

The True Glory and the Failure of Anglo-American Film Propaganda in the Second World War

The True Glory was the last great combat documentary made during the second world war. The film, which won an Oscar for the best documentary of 1945, was produced and released under the auspices of the Joint Anglo-American Film Planning Committee (JAAFPC). Introduced by Supreme Allied Commander in Europe, Dwight D. Eisenhower, the film tells the story of the last year of the war in Europe, beginning with the Normandy invasion and ending with the fall of Berlin. Animated maps along with scenes of combat help provide a visual dimension to the film's lyrical narration, which describes the inexorable march of the Allied Expeditionary Force towards the final destruction of Hitler's Third Reich. The film is a stirring tribute to the soldiers of the Anglo-American alliance who fought during that bloody time.[1]

Although an artistic and popular success, *The True Glory* is actually the story of a failure concealed behind the façade of an award-winning documentary, for the Joint Anglo-American Film Planning Committee was not formed to make an award-winning film. Indeed, the JAAFPC was created in March 1944 for the express purpose of producing a series of 'official films for world distribution showing Allied operations from a truly integrated viewpoint'.[2] Ironically, therefore, although it produced *The True Glory*, the actual mission of the JAAFPC was a failure. The story of its work, and ultimate end, also provides historians with an interesting case-study of inter-Allied tension during the last year of the war in Europe.

Prior to the formation of the JAAFPC, the only attempt at making a joint Anglo-American film occurred in 1943–4, when Frank Capra, then serving in the US Army Signal Corps, was sent to London. Capra's assignment was to co-produce a joint documentary on the North African campaign, incorporat-

---

1 Copies of *The True Glory* can be found in the Motion Picture Branch of the National Archives, Washington, DC. It can also be viewed at the Imperial War Museum's Department of Film.
2 Memorandum to Assistant Chief of Staff from General Frank A. Allen, Jr, 15 December 1944. Special Staff, Public Relations Division, SHAEF, Joint Anglo-American Film Planning Committee (hereafter JAAFPC) File, RG 331, Decimal 334, Box 11, National Archives, Washington, DC (hereafter NA).

ing footage from a British account of the campaign, entitled *Africa Freed*, with an American version of the film. What was supposed to be a co-operative effort, however, developed into a major crisis in inter-Allied propaganda between Capra and the British Army Film Unit. This crisis was caused by differences in personality and film-making techniques, as well as the cinematic presentation of the role of each nation in the campaign. The resultant tensions were in no way calmed by the completion and positive reception of the film *Tunisian Victory* in 1944.[3]

Although tension continued to exist between Allied propaganda agencies after the completion of *Tunisian Victory*, the US Joint Chiefs of Staff argued that the resumption of unilateral film projects would give 'the world an entirely false impression' about Allied unity. In early 1944, the Joint Chiefs felt that this appearance of Allied disunity was in 'urgent need of correction'. That perception was the major impetus behind the creation of the JAAFPC.[4]

It was hoped that the JAAFPC would eliminate, or at least reduce, the number of problems that plagued the making of *Tunisian Victory*. As with the previous attempt at a joint film project, however, the JAAFPC became bogged down in inter-service and inter-Allied rivalry that characterized much of Anglo-American relations during the last year and a half of the war.[5]

The JAAFPC was created in March 1944, when the War Department in Washington requested that George Stevens, the head of the Special Coverage Unit assigned to photograph combat operations for the Supreme Headquarters Allied Expeditionary Forces (SHAEF), prepare a plan for cinematic coverage of the coming invasion of France.[6] Stevens proposed that film coverage be divided into two parts. The first would be a series of short films, approximately two reels in length, covering specific sections of the coming invasion and subsequent campaign. Stevens divided the potential coverage into eight topics:

(a) Plan and Preparation
(b) D-Day
(c) 'The First Thousand Yards'
(d) Phase one
(e) Phase two

3   See Frederic Krome, 'Tunisian Victory and Anglo-American Film Propaganda in World War II', *The Historian*, 58, 3 (Spring 1996), 517–29; for another version see Tony Aldgate, 'Mr Capra Goes to War: Frank Capra, the British Army Film Unit, and Anglo-American travails in the production of Tunisian Victory', *Historical Journal of Film, Radio, and Television*, 11, 1 (1991).
4   Memorandum to Assistant Chief of Staff from General Frank A. Allen, Jr, 15 December 1944. JAAFPC, RG 331, Decimal 334, Box 11, NA.
5   Krome, 'Tunisian Victory', op. cit., passim.
6   Memorandum to General Davis on Film Production, 17 May 1944. SHAEF, JAAFPC File, RG 331, Decimal 334, Box 11, NA. George Stevens (1904–75) worked as a cameraman on the Laurel and Hardy comedies before directing *Gunga Din*. He joined the Signal Corps in 1942 and eventually was made head of SHAEF's Special Coverage Unit, which was responsible for producing combat documentaries of Allied operations in Europe.

(f) Phase three
(g) Phase four
(h) Capitulation[7]

Pursuant to War Department desires, the first of these short films, *Plan and Preparation*, was scheduled to be finished and available for release in the USA on D-Day. Stevens's draft script emphasized the importance of Anglo-American co-operation, the 'Single Instrument' as Eisenhower called it, with which the total destruction of the enemy would be achieved.[8]

In addition to the short films, Stevens also planned a larger project, tentatively entitled *Assault on the Continent*, compiled from the existing subjects 'and/or other topics as the campaign develops'. Since the invasion was a combined Allied operation, Stevens concluded his report by asking his superiors if he should proceed alone, or 'in any form of joint Anglo-American collaboration as may be directed by SHAEF'. Stevens's enquiry was not simply a desire to promote Allied unity, but came shortly after the Special Coverage Unit discovered that the British Army Film Unit was planning a similar series of films about the coming invasion and thus was made in the hopes of avoiding a potentially embarrassing diplomatic incident.[9]

Stevens's request for guidance came at a time when the lessons, and the production problems, of *Tunisian Victory* were still fresh in the propagandists' minds. The fiascos that resulted from Frank Capra's visit to London and the confusion and tension over the first Joint Anglo-American film project were lost on few. Robert Riskin, Chief of the Overseas Branch of the Office of War Information's (OWI) Motion Picture Bureau, argued that it was 'manifestly absurd, in view of the carefully-conceived plans for joint British–American execution of military campaigns, that the story of those campaigns should be told individually . . .'. Riskin contended that Allied propaganda efforts should mirror general military strategy and that propaganda films should be planned like any other joint campaign. Joint planning served two important purposes. The first was the appearance of Allied unity. Individually-produced films gave the impression that each nation was fighting the war alone. This was unsatisfactory because 'in neutral and allied countries, where we are striving to impress everyone with our complete unity, we fail miserably because the American and British newsreels tell individual stories'. The second and more immediate purpose involved soldier morale. Riskin believed that 'an American soldier in the United Kingdom, seeing a newsreel in which the British are winning the war singlehandedly, is ready to start a brawl with every English soldier he meets'.[10]

---

7 Major George C. Stevens to Lt-Col. J.B.L. Lawrence, 3 March 1944. SHAEF, JAAFPC File, RG 331, Decimal 334, Box 11, NA.
8 Ibid.
9 Ibid.
10 Robert Riskin to General Robert A. McClure (Chief of Publicity and Political Warfare, SHAEF), 31 March 1944. SHAEF, Special Coverage Unit File, RG 331, Decimal 062.2, Box 3, NA.

Riskin's implicit criticism of American volatility reveals several attitudes about Anglo-American relations. Even in early 1944, when it was obvious that the Allies were winning the war, concerns about Anglo-American tensions, which used to be an exclusively British occupation, had now become an issue for the Americans as well. Inherent in Riskin's remark, however, was not only a concern for the continuation of cordial Anglo-American relations, but also American jealousy that Britain might be getting more than its fair share of credit for winning the war. In order to avoid such problems and ensure fair and balanced coverage, Riskin, in conjunction with the Public Relations Office of SHAEF, ordered George Stevens to convene the first meeting of the Joint Anglo-American Film Planning Committee (JAAFPC) on 8 March 1944.[11]

Since the JAAFPC was supposed to represent Anglo-American interests, it contained an equal number of representatives from each nation and service organization concerned with publicity. The chairmanship was held jointly by Robert Patterson, head of the OWI's London Branch, and Jack Beddington, of the British Ministry of Information's Films Division. Representatives of the Public Relations Divisions of all Allied military organizations — army, navy, and air force — were also included, as were members of the film industry. Rounding off the membership were representatives from both the United States Army Signal Corps and British Army Film Unit. The actual number of the Committee's membership was never fully determined but was certainly well over two dozen.[12]

Not surprisingly, the JAAFPC recommended that the first joint Anglo-American film should be about the coming invasion. Pursuant to this, it named George Stevens and David MacDonald, of the British Army Film Unit, co-producers of the joint film project.[13] The two were ordered to meet and plan how best to combine the personnel from both film units 'into working teams . . . for practical production'. The JAAFPC decided to discard Stevens's existing plans and begin a new co-operative project. On an ominous note, Stevens and MacDonald were told neither how long the joint film was to be, nor 'what stage of events it should conclude' in its coverage. This lack of decisive guidance from the JAAFPC's leadership set the stage for a clash of ideas between the co-producers.[14]

Stevens argued that a short film on the preparations necessary for the invasion, similar to his initial plan for the War Department, should be the subject of the first joint project sponsored by the JAAFPC. Later, a longer film along

11   Memorandum on Organization of Joint Anglo-American Film Project as a Separate Unit, 15 December 1944. SHAEF, JAAFPC File, RG 331, Decimal 334, Box 11, NA.

12   Memorandum to Assistant Chief of Staff, SHAEF, Organization of the Joint Anglo-American Film Project as a Separate Unit, 15 December 1944. SHAEF, JAAFPC File, RG 331, Decimal 334, Box 11, NA.

13   David MacDonald (born 1904 in Helensburgh, Scotland), worked in Hollywood with Cecil B. De Mille from 1929 to 1936. He was a Major in the British Army Film Unit during the war and was the primary producer of Desert Victory.

14   Memorandum by George Stevens, March 1944. SHAEF, JAAFPC File, RG 331, Decimal 334, Box 11, NA.

the lines of a *Desert Victory* or *Tunisian Victory* could be made. MacDonald, however, favoured immediately moving to production of a feature-length film that would cover events to the conclusion of the 'first phase of operations', although he did not define exactly what chronological or topical events this would cover. MacDonald apparently saw less of a need for immediate propaganda and was concerned with maintaining the high quality of film propaganda set by previous British productions.[15] This initial conflict over the extent of coverage for the first of the joint film projects did not bode well for the future. As in almost all previous Anglo-American clashes, however, the Americans won, and a short film tentatively entitled *Preparation for Invasion* was again begun in late March 1944.

In addition to the Stevens–MacDonald controversy, inter-service rivalry, according to Ronald Tritton, the Committee's Secretary, also dominated the JAAFPC from the very beginning of its existence.[16] During the JAAFPC's first meeting, Tritton remarked that, as usual, the British Air Ministry 'was [being] unco-operative'. The Air Ministry argued that previous official films 'slighted' the role of the Royal Air Force in every other major campaign.[17]

The Air Ministry was also apparently jealous that army film personnel always seemed to dominate official productions. Indeed, upon learning the identities of the co-producers of the first joint films, both members of army film units, the Air Ministry demanded that a 'neutral producer' be named. It apparently believed that a 'neutral producer' would be less likely to ignore the role of the Air Force in the coming invasion. Although the JAAFPC held fast to its initial appointment, the infighting over such a trivial matter seemed to characterize the Committee's work.[18] In an even gloomier tone, Tritton also noticed that within a month of its formation the JAAFPC already had several sub-committees meeting to discuss problems, further confusing issues that needed to be addressed quickly.[19]

The situation in London was rapidly deteriorating into inter-service infighting. It became even more intense when, in May 1944, the JAAFPC found that it had problems with Washington as well. The War Department had somehow reached the conclusion that the creation of the JAAFPC had removed all editorial control of campaign films from the American military, a situation not

---

15   Memorandum by Stevens to Lawrence, March 1944. SHAEF, JAAFPC File, RG 331, Decimal 334, Box 11, NA.

16   Tritton, a civilian, was named Publicity Director by the War Office in 1940. In this capacity he was responsible for serving as liaison between the military and the newsreel companies. He was named Joint Secretary to the JAAFPC on 8 March 1944. The American Secretary was not named for several weeks. See Clive Coultass, *Images for Battle: British Films during the Second World War* (Delaware 1990), 60.

17   See Entry for 8 March 1944, Ronald Tritton Diary, Department of Documents, Imperial War Museum (hereafter referred to as Tritton Diary). His diary provides the only major British source on the JAAFPC.

18   Ibid. Upon hearing the Air Ministry request for a neutral producer, a committee member remarked, 'What do they mean, a Swiss?'. In all likelihood what they meant was someone not affiliated with the British or American army.

19   Entries for 8–10 May 1944, Tritton Diary, IWM.

at all to the liking of America's military leaders. In response to this perceived threat, the War Department refused to accept finished films emanating from London until it had a chance to approve of their cinematic content.

The War Department justified its stance by arguing that 'the Committee [JAAFPC], predominantly British, proposes to dictate the use of film material and personnel furnished by the United States and to dictate what combat pictures may be shown to the American public'. The War Department was obviously worried, as Riskin was earlier, that official films made under British domination would present a lopsided view of events and exaggerate the importance of the British military contribution. Washington continued to object, arguing that it was 'the function of the War Department to decide the best use of combat films and the function of SHAEF to see that proper films are taken'.[20] Somehow the War Department had reached the conclusion that the JAAFPC was under 'foreign' control and accordingly was a threat to the impartial coverage of the coming invasion.

Shortly after the initial War Department memorandum, the Chief of Staff of the United States Army, George Marshall, wrote directly to Eisenhower to voice his displeasure over the JAAFPC. Marshall accused Eisenhower of relinquishing editorial control of Allied film production to a committee dominated by the British. Marshall was also offended to discover that the British would apparently 'receive all combat footage, screen it, and select what they think should be released' to both Britain and the USA. Marshall informed Eisenhower that were this situation to become known it would 'have [the] most undesirable repercussions in this country'. In order to prevent this, Marshall insisted that 'no film covering the operation of American troops be released in London until your headquarters has been notified that it has been released in the United States'. He ended his harangue by noting that the first of the joint films, *Preparation for Invasion*, was apparently already far behind schedule, a sad commentary on the Committee's effectiveness.[21]

Eisenhower's response to Marshall incorporated a defence not only of the JAAFPC but of the very importance of Anglo-American film projects in general. His first objective was to disabuse the American Chief of Staff of the idea that the Committee was 'dominated' by the British. Indeed, Eisenhower provided Marshall with a breakdown of the membership of the JAAFPC, demonstrating to him that each Ally and service department was equally represented. The SHAEF Commander also argued that 'prior to the committee's formation, motion pictures had been produced showing only British or only American participation'. The primary reason for establishing the JAAFPC was to ensure that a properly balanced pictorial reflection 'of each Ally's contribution would be told in a fair and proper perspective to the whole'. Eisenhower continued:

20   Memorandum for the Chief of Staff by Major-General H.C. Ingles, Chief Signal Officer, 11 May 1944. Records of the Chief of Staff, RG 165, Decimal 062.2, Box 133, NA.
21   George Marshall to Eisenhower, 12 May 1944. Records of the Joint Chief of Staff, RG 165, Decimal 062.2, Box 133, NA.

> The harmony necessary for successful military operations would thus be brought home to the peoples of our respective nations through the medium of joint films. It has always been my policy to emphasize this teamwork, and I feel that great harm can come from independent pictures of exclusive British participation shown in Britain, or in America of exclusively American participation.[22]

As to Marshall's second point, Eisenhower noted that *Preparation for Invasion* was behind schedule not because of the vagaries of the JAAFPC, but because of structural problems inherent in combat film production. A full accounting of these difficulties was forwarded to Marshall in a separate memorandum.

The memorandum on the production problems of *Preparation for Invasion* cited four major factors delaying the film's completion. The first two were simply structural problems. Production on the film was stopped for four weeks by the Public Relations Office of the European Theatre of Operations while the advisability of establishing the JAAFPC was debated. Time was also lost in establishing a working liaison with the British to begin actual co-production. However, the major factor delaying production was the discussion between the co-producers and the JAAFPC to 'determine [the] length and subject matter that the committee desired to control'. In addition to the structural constraints, the problem was compounded by the War Department in Washington which withheld the necessary technicians and material needed to improve the speed of production.[23]

Eisenhower and his staff assured Marshall that most of these problems were solved and that the film would be ready by the end of May. He concluded with a plea for the continuation of the joint film project by arguing that 'any evidence of disunity at this point might go further than the subject of films'.[24]

Following the Marshall–Eisenhower exchange, members of the Signal Corps and Special Coverage Unit worked out a compromise with Washington on the major points of conflict. Colonel Curtis Mitchell, representing Eisenhower and the JAAFPC, negotiated an agreement with General Surles, head of the Signal Corps Photographic Section, by 'phone on 19 May. Mitchell promised Surles that the JAAFPC would serve as an 'advisory' body, making recommendations about film coverage, such as the pre-invasion film currently under production. When a film topic was agreed upon, the JAAFPC would first relay its decision to Washington and London for approval. Only after receiving the necessary approval would the Special Coverage Unit and British Army Film Unit appoint the necessary personnel to begin production. Mitchell claimed that this system was just the same as when 'Capra started. . .and when you worked out the arrangement with Brendan Bracken'. Unlike then, however, the Allies were not attempting to combine existing films but to start afresh on a joint project. This

---

22   Eisenhower to Marshall, May 1944?, SHAEF, JAAFPC File, RG 331, Decimal 334, Box 11, NA.
23   Memorandum to General Davis, 17 May 1944. SHAEF, JAAFPC File, RG 331, Decimal 334, Box 11, NA.
24   Eisenhower to Marshall, May 1944?, SHAEF, RG 331, Decimal 334, Box 11, NA.

arrangement did not prevent either the War Department or London from producing a similar picture unilaterally. Mitchell told Surles: 'We are completely free to act without them, but we can act with them, and thereby insure ourselves of all the film and all the co-operation that we could possibly expect out of the friendliest sort of relationship.'[25]

As for Washington's concern about loss of editorial control, Mitchell assured Surles that the Committee's decision to make a film did not automatically bind either side to accepting the finished product. The Signal Corps representative, who, after Mitchell left, would be J.B.L. Lawrence, would not commit the War Department to distribute any future joint project in the USA until after the Signal Corps High Command had been consulted. As for the nearly completed *Preparation for Invasion*, the JAAFPC promised to send the finished film to Washington on two separate reels, one containing the film and the other the soundtrack. The material forwarded to the War Department would be the already-approved British release print of the film. The War Department could then review the film in order to make the changes it felt necessary for American release.[26]

Although the compromise satisfied the War Department, it had, in one quick stroke, destroyed the major purpose behind the formation of the JAAFPC. The release of separate American and British prints of the film directly contravened the aim of the Committee to show Allied campaigns from a truly integrated perspective. After only two months of operation, the JAAFPC was stripped of its sovereignty, that is, its ability to act independently of interference from either Washington or London. Any future film projects would have to be approved not only by the JAAFPC, but by all the service organizations.

Despite the lack of co-operation from Washington, the JAAFPC was able to finish and release what it hoped would be the first of its series of short campaign films. *Eve of Battle*, the release title of *Preparation for Invasion*, was a 19-minute film detailing the preparations leading up to the actual landings in France. Although it was not available for release on D-Day itself, it was previewed in both America and Britain in late June 1944. The film contained some 'especially fine material of the air offensive', perhaps making the Air Ministry happy, as well as detailed scenes of troop training.[27] An ironic twist was the listing of David MacDonald as the primary producer, even though initially he had been against the making of this film.[28]

In the aftermath of D-Day, the JAAFPC was still committed to the continuation of joint film projects. Indeed, on the day before the Normandy

25 Colonel Curtis Mitchell to General A.D. Surles, Record of a Telephone Conversation on 19 May 1944 at 2304 hrs British Time. SHAEF, JAAFPC File, RG 331, Decimal 334, Box 11, NA, 1–3.
26 Ibid., 3–5. In order to allow easy re-editing, one reel did not have a soundtrack.
27 Coultass, *Images for Battle*, op. cit., 164. I am unable to discover why the working title of the film was changed for its release.
28 See the catalogue entry in Nicholas Pronay and Francis Thorpe, *British Official Films in the Second World War: A Descriptive Catalogue* (Los Angeles 1980), 155.

landings it had proposed, and received approval for, the making of '1 feature-length picture of the joint operation now in preparation'. This film would be along the lines of that proposed by MacDonald back in March 1944. In making its recommendations, the JAAFPC urged that 'speed is of vital importance, facilities and direction and production must be superlative to measure up to the historical importance of the assignment'.[29] The JAAFPC asked Washington to refrain from the production of any films that might overlap with the joint film project. The War Department, not surprisingly, refused to agree, citing the enormous number of short films and newsreels that would contain information about the invasion and the campaign.[30] In the matter of the proposed feature-length film, however, the JAAFPC did agree to abide by the existing agreement with Washington. The system of communication that was established was so complex that it almost certainly guaranteed that the one thing that could not be achieved was speed of production.[31]

By the time the JAAFPC had worked out its difficulties with Washington, the summer was well advanced and D-Day was fast becoming a memory. As British and American cameramen continued their work, the JAAFPC continued its deliberations on the nature of future joint Anglo-American film projects. R.E. Dupuy suggested that a joint Anglo-American film must show the steps leading to the creation of the Allied Expeditionary Force, the creation of an Allied command, as well as its planning, preparation, assault and ultimate victory over the enemy. Dupuy argued that the fact that the joint film was a historical document 'to be shown to the Allied and neutral peoples . . . makes it essential that it should stress, in broad and balanced outline, the joint efforts of the Allied nations'.[32] Obviously many officials in SHAEF still had high hopes and expectations of the JAAFPC.

Some time in the early autumn, the Committee concluded that a film exclusively about the invasion was no longer a valid subject for propaganda and, therefore, decided to expand the scope of its coverage. It seems that initially the JAAFPC hoped to extend the coverage to keep pace with campaign developments. This would, however, place the film-makers in an impossible situation. The increase in the scope of coverage meant that the joint film project constantly required further updates. As the battle for France developed

---

29 Eisenhower and the JAAFPC to Surles, 5 June 1944. SHAEF, JAAFPC File, RG 331, Decimal 334, Box 11, NA.
30 Surles to Mitchell, 8 June 1944. SHAEF, JAAFPC File, RG 331, Decimal 334, Box 11, NA. Specifically, Washington claimed that it was concerned that if they agreed to the JAAFPC request then the Army–Navy Screen Magazine, a bi-weekly newsreel, would not be able to show any of the events.
31 JAAFPC to Surles, 5 June 1944. On the complexity of the communication system, see 'Notification of War Department of US Aspects of Joint Anglo-American Film Committee and other Similar Activities', 15 May 1944. SHAEF, JAAFPC File, RG 331, Decimal 334, Box 11, NA.
32 Memorandum for Brigadier Turner by Colonel R. Ernest Dupuy, 26 July 1944. SHAEF, JAAFPC File, RG 331, Decimal 334, Box 11, NA. Dupuy was the Acting Chief of the Public Relations Division.

and Allied operations spread out, the film-makers found it virtually impossible to complete their work.

In late October 1944, therefore, the JAAFPC decided to change the course of joint film propaganda radically. The making of a series of short campaign films along the lines of *Eve of Battle* was abandoned. The Committee also discarded the idea of making several feature-length films on specific sections of the campaign against nazi Germany. Instead, in October 1944, the JAAFPC decided to concentrate on the making of a single joint film covering everything from D-Day to the eventual fall of Germany. Two representatives of the Committee, Lt-Col. Newman and Captain Fox, travelled to Washington to secure War Department approval of the decision. Once Washington and London had agreed to the new direction for joint film propaganda, all that was necessary was to name the co-producers.[33] In November, the British named Carol Reed, who had just finished his feature film *The Way Ahead*, to represent its interests, while the Americans appointed Garson Kanin.[34]

From the beginning of this final phase of the joint film project, which lasted from November 1944 to July 1945, American officials interfered continuously. Although General Surles of the Signal Corps concurred with the JAAFPC that the film should begin with D-Day and end with the fall of Germany, he expected that at least one third of the picture would describe the actual process of invasion, breakthrough and the subsequent campaign through Brittany. He demanded this format rather than the Committee's plan to devote the first third of the picture to the preparation and mobilization for D-Day. Washington also felt that it was more important that the film should 'tell the public how the Army operates, rather than merely showing its operations or explaining, for the hundredth time, why we are in the war'.[35]

Surles felt that these conditions were necessary because 'these things happened so rapidly that even the splendid coverage provided by the American press did not fully tell the story'. He apparently saw the joint picture more as a vehicle for bringing the American military achievement before the American public than as a means of showing Allied unity. In order to ensure what he considered 'proper' coverage, and incidentally to maintain War Department influence on the JAAFPC, Surles argued that a Signal Corps Official should be

33   Allen to Lord Burnham (Director of Public Relations, War Office), 24 October 1944. SHAEF, JAAFPC File, RG 331, Decimal 334, Box 11, NA.
34   Carol Reed (born 1906), had worked as an actor/screenwriter before moving to directing. During the war he was assigned to the British Army Film Unit. Garson Kanin (born 1912), worked as a producer in Hollywood in the 1930s. During the war he made several films for the Office of Emergency Management. See JAAFPC File, Correspondence of 14 December 1944, RG 331, Decimal 334, Box 11, NA. Although Nicholas Wapshott argues that Reed and Kanin were appointed joint producers before D-Day, JAAFPC records do not contain any reference to either man before November 1944. See Nicholas Wapshott, *The Man Between: A Biography of Carol Reed* (New York 1994).
35   Surles to General Frank Allen, 24 November 1944; and Memorandum to General Frank A. Allen, Jr (director, Public Relations Division), 7 December 1944. SHAEF, JAAFPC File, RG 331, Decimal 334, Box 11, NA.

dispatched to London. He felt that a SHAEF officer would be unsuitable to represent the War Department because SHAEF represented 'the entire Allied Expeditionary Forces' and not the War Department.[36]

Filming for the joint project continued even as the deliberations about its editorial content raged. The major technical problem continued to be the lack of permanent personnel. Throughout November–December 1944, key technical personnel were reassigned at critical moments of operation. The JAAFPC, lobbying for a continuance of the services of skilled technicians, promised to have a rough cut of the film finished by 1 February 1945 if only these technicians and film-makers would not be reassigned.[37] This promise was made when it was believed that the end of the war in Europe was only several weeks away. Naturally, this optimistic assessment, both of the time to completion of the film as well as of the war itself, was altered after the last great German counter-offensive of the war. In the early months of 1945, after the Battle of the Bulge had been won, the JAAFPC revised its tentative date of completion.

In February 1945, the JAAFPC promised to have a rough cut of the film completed by 19 March, in order to screen it for the 'representatives of the War Office, War Department and Supreme Headquarters'.[38] It fulfilled its promise. By the middle of March, the basic material of the joint picture, less the final stages of the campaign, was finished. The most difficult stage was therefore to follow, as the JAAFPC attempted to mould the final cut into a form that was suitable for the three masters — Washington, London and SHAEF — it served. The problem was even more acute because the JAAFPC was attempting to make a film 'from an entirely new angle'. Instead of producing 'a chronological, historical documentary', the JAAFPC planned to make a film about 'the soldiers themselves'.[39] Although no paper trail apparently exists to document the processes that led to this decision, it marks a fundamental change from joint films focusing on the strategic nature of the alliance to a film that concentrates on human interest.

After the rough cut of the joint film was previewed by service representatives in March, the actual revisions to the film began. The final months of production were filled with inter-service squabbles over the amount of coverage each branch, and each nation, would receive. For example, the Air Ministry continued to make an issue about the extent to which its activities were included in the joint picture.[40] In addition, the War Department expressed

36   Surles to General Frank Allen, 24 November 1944. SHAEF, JAAFPC, RG331, Decimal 334, Box 11, NA.

37   Memorandum from Public Relations Division by Edward M. Strode, SHAEF, JAAFPC File, RG 331, Decimal 334, Box 11, NA.

38   Memorandum by Edward M. Strode, 15 February 1945. SHAEF, JAAFPC File, RG 331, Decimal 334, Box 11, NA.

39   Colonel Newman to Colonel Curtis Mitchell, 15 February 1945. SHAEF, JAAFPC File, RG 331, Decimal 334, Box 11, NA.

40   Willoughby de Broke (Air Ministry) to Group Captain G.W. Houghton (SHAEF, Air Staff), 4 April 1945. RG 111, M1211 File, Motion Picture Branch, NA.

concern about the balance of coverage. Curtis Mitchell, speaking for that department, wondered 'just how far the Committee will go in balancing the National interests'. He noted, however, that at the present moment, the joint film showed American activities 'to such advantage that there may be considerable criticism from the British public'. This bias, however, did not seem to concern Mitchell greatly.[41]

The major problem facing the JAAFPC in the last months of production was, ironically, the War Department's relentless quest to correct small factual inaccuracies in the joint film. Although the position might seem a repetition of the Air Ministry's attitude towards *Eagle Squadron* three years earlier, in fact it was radically different. Mitchell argued that

> . . . in producing a motion picture to be shown to the citizens who supported and financed that effort, it is of the utmost importance that accuracy, complete and total, be the guiding star of the producers. It is not enough to be brilliant, or to be well-intentioned, or even partly right. One must be completely right, in fact and symbol. Only a film that is completely right can hope to contribute to Allied unity.[42]

Mitchell and the War Department actually used the issue of factual accuracy as a means of dominating the editorial content of the joint picture.

For example, Mitchell found that the section of the film describing the industrial build-up necessary for the invasion was 'almost exclusively British'. This was unacceptable, due to the 'great industrial achievement of the United States in manufacturing material for use by our armies in France and Germany'. Mitchell argued that since the USA had supplied most of the material, the greater part of this section of the film should be devoted to American industry.[43]

In a purely quantitative sense Mitchell was correct; American might did predominate. Yet if quantitative guidelines were the controlling factor, over 70 per cent of the film would have to be devoted to American arms, hardly qualifying it as a joint picture. Although Mitchell did cite several instances where the British military's role was greater than that of the Americans, they usually covered such activities as reconnaissance, an area not likely to be considered threatening to America's image as the dominant military partner.[44]

In these circumstances it was truly a credit to their combined talents that Kanin and Reed were able to produce such a coherent and brilliantly edited film as *The True Glory*. The final rough cut of the film was scheduled to be previewed by the JAAFPC on 18 May at the Ministry of Information headquarters in London. It included a hurried addition of scenes from Buchenwald and Bergen Belsen, as well as ruined Berlin. True to form, the JAAFPC

41   Mitchell to Surles, 30 March 1945. RG 111, M1211 File, Motion Picture Branch, NA.
42   Mitchell to the Joint Anglo-American Film Committee, 30 March 1945. RG 111, M1211 File, Motion Picture Branch, NA, 1.
43   Ibid., 1.
44   Ibid., 2. Another example was the assault on Holland, which was made by two American and one British Divisions. The film, according to Mitchell, seemed to show the British predominating.

squabbled over the title, settling on *The True Glory* only after prolonged and bitter debate.[45]

The True Glory follows the story of the Allied armies from the Normandy invasion to the fall of Berlin. General Eisenhower introduces the film, claiming it is a tribute to the men of the Grand Alliance who fought in the great battles during the last year of the war. Much of the footage is stirring, and frightening, in its intensity. Unlike previous campaign films that sanitized war, *The True Glory* contains scenes of Allied tragedy, such as a C-47 transport 'plane crashing as it disgorged paratroopers, to demonstrate to the viewer the human tragedy of war. Perhaps some of the most powerful scenes were the liberation of two of the death camps, Buchenwald and Bergen Belsen. The images of the emaciated survivors were sure to convince the audience of the justness of the Allied cause. As with *Tunisian Victory*, the narration was supposedly spoken by 'common soldiers'; however, prominent actors were used. The animated maps show the ever-widening extent of Allied conquest, each nation represented by a flag, as the final, inexorable defeat of Germany comes ever closer.

The film was pronounced completed in early June 1945. The finished copy was scheduled to arrive in Washington in early July, where Columbia Pictures was selected to distribute the film in the USA, Canada and South America.[46] Before the film arrived, however, a final problem, or perhaps commentary on Anglo-American affairs, developed. In July 1945, the War Department directed that the title cards of the film, which read 'The Governments of Great Britain and the United States Present', should be reversed before the film was cleared for release in America.[47] A compromise was apparently reached, as the next title sequence read 'Distributed by the US Office of War Information and the Ministry of Information'. That this last bit of pettiness was solved in this way was likely due more to exhaustion rather than any noble feelings of Allied unity.

The True Glory was finally released to audiences in Britain and the USA in August 1945. It went on to win an Oscar for the best documentary of the year and received critical acclaim on both sides of the Atlantic. Yet, ultimately, the joint film project must be regarded as a failure. Not only did it take the Joint

---

45   See the correspondence in the JAAFPC File for 23 April, 9 May, and 12 May 1945. RG 331, Decimal 334, Box 11, NA. For information on the fighting over the title, see Coultass, *Images for Battle*, op. cit., 183–4. *The True Glory* was part of a prayer Drake supposedly wrote before the defeat of the Spanish Armada in 1588.

> O Lord God, when Thou givest to thy servants to endeavour any great matter, grant us also to know that it is not the beginning, but continuing of the same, until it be thoroughly finished, which yieldeth the true glory.

46   Taylor Mills (Chief, Bureau of Motion Pictures, OWI) to Thomas Baird (British Library of Information), 18 June 1945. Entry 265, Box 1447, British Information Services File, RG 208, Office of War Information, Washington National Records Center, Suitland, Maryland.
47   Gordon Swarthout (Pictorial Branch) to Ralph Nelson, 18 July 1945. RG 111, Motion Picture Branch, File M1211, NA. Complaints were also voiced about the 'hells' and 'damns' in the film. See Memorandum to Chief Pictorial Branch, Bureau of Public Relations, 20 July 1945. RG 111, Motion Picture Branch, M 1211 File, NA.

Anglo-American Film Planning Committee more than 17 months to complete its masterpiece, but it must also be recognized that the path that eventually led to the making of *The True Glory* did not reflect any great vision on the part of the JAAFPC, or indeed, of any of the publicity organizations from which it drew its membership.

Instead of making policy and holding to it, as Eisenhower and SHAEF managed to do, the JAAFPC allowed itself to be bullied by the various Allied governments. If SHAEF represented the combined military interests of the Allies, then the JAAFPC should have served the same purpose in propaganda. Instead it became a political football, bounced and kicked around by Allied governments. That it still produced a brilliant film was a tribute to Kanin and Reed.

Washington's domination of the JAAFPC, primarily its ability to maintain editorial control, was indicative of the state of Anglo-American relations during the final year and a half of the war. The sheer extent of America's industrial might, combined with the total of American troops, made the final victory over nazi Germany possible. British interests rapidly became dependent upon American goodwill. Joint film propaganda, committed to making films about the Allied war effort from an integrated viewpoint, depended upon Allied selflessness. Unfortunately, by the beginning of 1944, once it was obvious that the Allies would win the war, American propagandists became intensely jealous of their British allies. The result was an ironic dénouement for the British who, as in the case of *Tunisian Victory*, feared that they would receive no credit for their accomplishments. As the final victory approached, American propagandists became less willing to share the glory and triumph with Britain, a sad commentary on Anglo-American relations at the end of the second world war.

Frederic Krome

is Lecturer in History at Northern Kentucky University and Adjunct Instructor in Judaic Studies at the University of Cincinnati. He is currently working on a study of Jewish soldiers during the first world war.

OWI GOES TO THE MOVIES: THE BUREAU OF INTELLIGENCE'S CRITICISM OF HOLLYWOOD, 1942-43

GREGORY D. BLACK AND CLAYTON R. KOPPES

The war had penetrated Tarzan's peaceful kingdom. Agents of Nazi Germany had parachuted into the jungle and occupied a fortress, hoping to exploit African oil and tin. But Tarzan rallied his jungle forces against the Axis. "Kill Nadzies!" Tarzan commanded the natives, all of whom were white. They nodded enthusiastically. The Germans were so despicable even the animals turned against them. Tarzan himself chased the head of the Nazi column deep into the jungle, and, just as the fear-crazed German officer frantically signaled Berlin on his shortwave radio, Tarzan killed him with his knife. In Berlin the radio operator recognized the distress signal and rushed out to summon the general in charge of the African operation. While Tarzan, Boy, and Jungle Priestess laughingly looked on, Cheetah the chimp chattered into the transmitter. Ignorant of the fatal struggle in the jungle depths, the general heard the chimp on the radio, jumped to his feet, saluted, and yelled to his subordinates that they were listening not to Africa but to Der Fuehrer.

These dramatic scenes are taken from a 1942 motion picture appropriately titled *Tarzan Triumphs* in which Johnny Weissmuller, a slightly flabby but still impressive noble savage, made the jungle safe for the Allies. To the Bureau of Intelligence (BOI) of the Office of War Information (OWI), however, Tarzan's triumph was a source of great concern. Despite the innocent absurdity of the plot and the triumphant denouement in a familiar movie serial, the bureau feared the film would harm the United States war effort. These government analysts decided *Tarzan Triumphs* did not take the war seriously.[1]

The intelligence bureau's criticism of the Tarzan saga was part of a series of analyses of the contributions of Hollywood movies to the United States propaganda effort in World War II. From October 1942 through

[1] Office of War Information, Bureau of Intelligence, Media Division, "Weekly Summary and Analysis of Feature Motion Pictures," no. 11, Feb. 26, 1943, pp. 19-20, Box 1945, Records of the Bureau of Intelligence, Records of the Office of Government Reports, Record Group 44, Washington National Records Center, Suitland, Md. (hereafter cited as RG___, WNRC). Despite the title, the summaries were issued irregularly, usually every two weeks.

56

TODAY
HIS BIGGEST!

Come subs or high-water, they get
the ships through! They're
heroes all in the Merchant
Marine — and its the most
heroic story of all for
Humphrey Bogart!

BOGART

Steams out of 'Casablanca' for

'ACTION IN THE NORTH ATLANTIC

WARNERS'
Thunderous story of the Men
of the Merchant Marine

RAYMOND MASSEY · ALAN HALE

JULIE BISHOP · DANE CLARK
Screen Play by John Howard Lawson
Based on a Story by Guy Gilpatric · Additional
Dialogue by A. I. Bezzerides and W. R. Burnett

★ THEATRE & DATE ★ BUY WAR BONDS ★
AT THIS THEATRE!

(Courtesy of the Wisconsin Center for Theatre Research)

March 1943 the bureau's media division, headed by Columbia University journalism professor Herbert Brucker, analyzed all of the approximately 250 feature pictures released in the United States. These analyses constitute an important, and hitherto untapped, source for the study of dominant themes in wartime movies, and for the analysis of the particular point of view of a government propaganda agency.[2] The bureau's analyses reveal a somewhat surprising mixture of liberal precepts with an extreme sensitivity to criticism of life in the United States. The bureau deplored racist portrayals of the American blacks and the Japanese enemy on the one hand, and severely criticized the portrayal of the police as corrupt or even incompetent. The analyses suggest, further, the dangers inherent in a government agency's examining multifaceted experiences through the lens of one concern—the war effort—and the desire to direct artistic expression into propagandistic channels.

In scrutinizing the movies, the BOI was carrying out part of its role of analyzing all media to assess "the war's impact in the terms in which it reaches the public." The purpose of BOI was essentially to gather and analyze data and then distribute the information gathered to the planning and policy agencies within the federal government "in ample time for

their decisions."[3] While these reports were concerned specifically with the images foreign audiences might receive from Hollywood films, also implicit was recognition that Americans too were drawing from Hollywood films concepts of the American war effort. As R. Keith Kane, chief of the BOI, wrote to Librarian of Congress Archibald MacLeish, an assistant director of OWI, "Any planning would be futile which failed to take into account the close interrelation between American opinion and the influences upon it and the opinion of foreign publics and the influences on them."[4] To the BOI Hollywood films represented a powerful influence on both the American and foreign public. BOI weekly reports on feature motion pictures were intended to provide Washington policy makers with an analysis of how popular films were presenting the image of the United States at war and how Hollywood explained the war, the issues, our allies, and our prospects of victory to foreign audiences.

The concern was not limited to Washington bureaucrats. Producer-director Walter Wanger, for example, wrote to OWI that Hollywood, because of its tremendous popularity overseas, should be considered by Washington as the heartland of world public opinion. Wanger recognized that if Hollywood was to serve effectively it would have to improve its ability to present the war issues more realistically. He therefore suggested that OWI might send to Hollywood a group of experts who would cooperate with the film-makers to insure that each film was "correctly researched and correctly emphasized."[5]

2 Useful secondary sources on OWI are sparse. The only full-scale study of domestic operations of the OWI is a journalism dissertation whose historical use is somewhat limited. See L. S. Mackay. "Domestic Operations of the Office of War Information in World War II" (Ph.D. diss., University of Wisconsin, 1966). Basic background materials include *Hearings Before a Subcommittee of the Committee on Government Operations, Report of Elmer Davis to the President on the Office of War Information*, 88 Cong., 1 sess., pp. 210-221; Bureau of the Budget, *The United States at War*. Historical Reports on War Administration no. 1 (Washington, D. C., 1946), pp. 220-233; Sydney Weinberg, "What to Tell America: The Writers Quarrel in OWI," *Journal of American History* 55 (1968): 73-89; Richard R. Lingeman, *Don't You Know There's a War On? The American Home Front, 1941-1945* (New York, 1970); and *Public Opinion Quarterly* 7 (1943).

3 BOI, "Outline of Operations," Nov. 18. 1942. Box 4, Philleo Nash Papers, Harry S. Truman Library; R. Keith Kane to Archibald MacLeish, Aug. 7, 1942, Records of the Chief of the Bureau of Intelligence, Box 1833, RG 44, WNRC. See also, Kane to Davis, "Distribution of Intelligence Reports," Oct. 13, 1942, ibid.

4 Kane to MacLeish, Chief of BOI Records, Box 1833, RG 44, WNRC.

5 Walter Wanger to Gardner Cowles, Jr.. July 30. 1942, Box 3, Records of the Office of the Director.

Propaganda, while always important in warfare, assumed new significance in the twentieth century when total war required the mobilization not merely of armies but of public opinion as well. The tremendous success of Nazi propaganda efforts was well known. Many persons attributed France's collapse in 1940 as much to the failure of national will as to the shredding of its armies. Although President Franklin D. Roosevelt and his advisers were reasonably confident that Americans would not buckle like the French, some trends were disturbing. Soon after Pearl Harbor public opinion analysts noted that many Americans exhibited excesses of pessimism or euphoria about the prospects of a United States victory in the war, often indicated willingness to negotiate a separate peace with Hitler, and betrayed little understanding of the reasons why America was fighting. The president's advisers believed that these weak timbers of public opinion needed immediate shoring up.[6]

The foreign situation was even more desperate. Just as surely as World War I, the Second World War was a battle of ideas. Whatever their long-run practicality, official pronouncements, such as the Atlantic Charter or Vice-President Henry A. Wallace's "century of the common man" speech, were designed to effect short-term propaganda victories. Major strategic decisions such as unconditional surrender were announced with one eye cocked toward their value as weapons of psychological warfare. The war was a clash of cultures, a global debate as to whether a totalitarian regime like Nazi Germany or a democratic system as practiced in the United States offered men the better life. Thus, the United States

and its allies were especially sensitive to portrayals of American life and ideals. If other nations, particularly those under Nazi domination, were to accept the American way of life, the United States had to be presented as prosperous, law abiding, moral, and free. If the Allies' propaganda efforts was to undermine enemy morale effectively, their cause had to be portrayed as more just than that of the Axis.[7]

In classic Rooseveltian fashion, four similar but autonomous public information agencies had been carrying on essentially the same activities since the late 1930s. With the advent of war consolidation was clearly in order, but Roosevelt, fearful of the suspicions that would be attached to any propaganda agency, was reluctant to consolidate until a prestigious figure could be appointed director. Wide support for Elmer Davis was indicated when *The New Yorker* editorially proposed the CBS news commentator. When the president appointed Davis head of OWI on June 13, 1942, the day he formed the office, *The New Yorker's* inimitable editor, Harold Ross, congratulated Davis, "Your amazing appointment is our first editorial accomplishment since getting the information booth at Pennsylvania Station moved into the middle of the floor fifteen years ago, and is unexpected and overwhelming." Despite Ross's conviction that Roosevelt was as open to influence as the Pennsylvania Railroad, the president more likely was persuaded by Attorney General Francis Biddle who had proposed in April that Roosevelt select Davis to head OWI.[8]

Davis had spent the years 1939 to 1941

Records of the Office of War Information, RG 208. WNRC.

[6] Richard Steele, "Preparing the Public for War: Efforts to Establish a National Propaganda Agency, 1940-41," *American Historical Review* 75 (1970): 1640-1653; Louis DeJong, *The German Fifth Column in the Second World War* (Chicago, 1956), pp. 39-143.

[7] James MacGregor Burns, *Roosevelt: The Soldier of Freedom, 1940-1945* (New York, 1970), pp. 381-389.

[8] BOB, *United States at War*, pp. 210-223; Mackay, "Domestic Operations of the Office of War Information in World War II," pp. 57-111; "The Talk of the Town," *The New Yorker*, Mar. 14, 1942, p. 13; Harold Ross to Davis, June 16, 1942, Box 1, Elmer Davis Papers, Library of Congress; Francis Biddle to Roosevelt, Apr. 22, 1942, Official File 5015, Franklin D. Roosevelt Library.

OWI AND MOVIES   47

covering the Nazi takeover of Europe for CBS radio, and his dramatic broadcasts of the invasion of Poland and the German bombardment of London had enhanced his reputation as a political commentator. When Davis went to Europe in 1939 he had questioned the wisdom of American involvement in any European war. Two years of firsthand observation changed this view, and on his return to New York he was quick to warn the American people that the war was very much an American war. London was the first line of American defense and were the United States to avoid a world dominated by totalitarianism, it would have to become involved. As Davis stated in reference to Britain's need for help: "They need bombers which can be flown over, but they need other things, tanks and guns and food, which must be shipped, and we may find that if we want Hitler to lose this war, we shall have to see that the stuff gets there. That means convoys, which may mean shooting, but if Hitler should win this war, there's likely to be some shooting afterwards which would no longer be on the other side of the Atlantic." [9] With Davis at OWI were men such as Archibald MacLeish, Leo Rosten, and Lowell Mellett, who shared his belief that totalitarianism formed a real threat to American security and democratic ideals.

The task of molding public opinion at home and abroad fell to the OWI. As the central coordinating agency between the government and mass media, Davis's organization was to inform the public of the "progress of the war effort and of war policies, activities, and aims of the Government." OWI promoted the war effort by such tactics as war bond drives, victory gardens, publication of the magazine *Victory*, assistance for writers, sponsorship of radio programs, and production of motion picture shorts. The office relied to a great extent on voluntary cooperation among the various media. Rent by internal schisms and frequent personnel changes, OWI ran afoul of Congress and of established information services in old-line departments like State and Agriculture dedicated to protection of their own domains. The agency was placed within the Executive Office of the President, but Roosevelt seldom intervened in behalf of OWI, and it lacked the clout produced by a politically potent constituency.[10]

A few days after Pearl Harbor, Roosevelt had declared that the motion picture, "one of our most effective media in informing and entertaining our citizens," could make "a very useful contribution" to the war effort. Rosten, novelist, Hollywood writer, and later a deputy director of OWI, explained why.

The movies can give public information. But they can do more than that; they can give the public understanding. They can clarify problems that are complex and confusing. They can focus attention upon key problems which the people must decide, the basic choices which the people must make. They can make clear and intelligible the enormous complexities of global geography, military tactics. economic dilemmas. political disputes, and psychological warfare. The singularly illuminating tools of the screen can be used to give the people a clear, continuous, and comprehensible picture of the total pattern of total war.[11]

Rosten's statement typified OWI's estimate of Hollywood's influence. In that pretelevision era movies were in their heyday. The motion picture industry in the United States produced five hundred pictures each year and controlled sixteen thousand theaters with a seating capacity of eleven million. Paid admissions during the war averaged eighty million viewers per week,

9 Alfred H. Jones. "The Making of an Interventionist on the Air: Elmer Davis and CBS News, 1939-1941," *Pacific Historical Review* 42 (1973) : 91.

10 Davis. *Report to the President on the Office of War Information*, 88 Cong.. 1 sess.. pp. 210-221.

11 Leo Rosten to Davis. Aug. 24. 1942, Box 13, Nash Papers.

equal to nearly two-thirds of the nation's population. Millions of servicemen trooped to no less than seven thousand on-base movie houses each week.[12]

Hollywood's influence was equally powerful abroad. Foreign exhibition, particularly in the British Empire and Latin America, spelled the difference between profit and loss for many pictures; the number of foreigners who saw an American film often exceeded its audience in the United States. Whether foreign viewers sought entertainment or enlightenment, the wide popularity of Hollywood films meant that millions of persons were receiving indelible impressions of American life. Because movies appealed to the full spectrum of classes and tastes, the cinema's influence was as potent as that of any medium. A basic tenet in the offices of OWI was that if foreigners were to be convinced America was fighting for a just cause, and if Americans themselves were to comprehend the war's issues, the movies must use their tremendous power responsibly.[13]

As Wanger wrote OWI domestic director Gardner Cowles, Jr., in the summer of 1942:

The American film is our most important weapon as no country has developed its film industry to compete with ours. The problem of enlightenment of the masses is a major problem and admittedly the film is the greatest visual educational factor accepted by the masses. The other great American means of communication, the radio and the press, are more limited. Very few people read American papers abroad and those you want to reach by short-wave radio cannot afford the sets. So you are back to the film again.

The producer went on to admit that the cinema had not yet contributed as much as

it should have to the war effort and suggested more government advice was needed for films to be "correctly researched and correctly emphasized."[14]

In mid-1942 OWI officials were alarmed at what Hollywood was doing—or rather, not doing—in response to the challenge. MacLeish, an assistant director of OWI, voiced a widespread concern: The movies were "escapist and delusive," MacLeish charged. Indeed, Hollywood bore "a primary and inescapable responsibility" for what he termed Americans' failure to understand either the events leading to the war or the war itself.[15] OWI officials realized that maintaining public morale would be especially crucial—and difficult—in the anxious first months of the war, when Allied forces reeled before the Axis and eventual victory seemed far from certain. At this ominous time the BOI movie analyses were deemed especially important.

The analyses paid particular attention to portrayals of the United States and treatment of war-related material. The bureau's aim was to "indicate material occurring in the picture which will enable judgments to be made about the desirability of its release abroad." An objectionable film would be disparaging to some aspect of life in the United States, and if shown to foreign audiences, would "put us in an unfavorable light." In analyzing war-related material, OWI's film critics again emphasized the importance of "picturing the conflict to foreign audiences in a way favorable to our side." A promotional film would contain "a convincing statement of the justice of

---

12 *Movies at War*, Reports of War Activities, Motion Picture Industry, 1942-45, vol. 1, no. 1, pp. 1-5. Today the industry produces less than 200 films a year.

13 "Weekly Summary," no. 1, Oct. 15, 1942, pp. 1-3, BOI Records, RG 44, WNRC; "United Artist," *Fortune* 23 (1941): 95.

14 Wanger to Cowles, July 30, 1942, Box 3, Director's Records, OWI Records, RG 208, WNRC. Interestingly Wanger also said in the same letter: "The film is of enormous value during the *war*, but its importance will multiply in the *post-war* period when our doctrine will have to be spread rapidly to counteract enemy propaganda. Beyond that in the rebuilding of the world, the film uses are too many to be listed."

15 MacLeish, address to annual meeting of American Booksellers Association, New York City, May 6, 1942, p. 5, Box 888, ibid.

our cause and the evil of the enemy's" and an objectionable movie would present material in a manner that might "throw discredit or an unfavorable light on our side of the conflict." [16]

The bureau's criticism of Hollywood focused on three complaints. Analysts objected, first, to the portrayal of the home front as unaffected by the war. *Andy Hardy's Double Life*, starring Mickey Rooney, Lewis Stone, and Fay Holden, drew the bureau's fire, for example, because the film depicted an upper-class family living in prewar comfort, enjoying ample food and luxuries, and sending their son to college instead of the army. The bureau voiced similar objections about two Henry Aldrich movies produced during this period; adolescence, not the war, was the main theme.[17] The bureau did not contend that all films should be built around the war. If movies about the home front, however, were to be exhibited abroad, where Allied peoples had undergone privations undreamed of in America, the bureau felt the pictures should make reference to civilian sacrifices and show that the average American understood the meaning of the war.

OWI was still more troubled about the large category of films that showed the United States infested with gangsters, corrupt judges, and incompetent police and undermined by sabotage. Films like *Boss of Big Town*, *Eyes of the Underworld*, and *Rubber Racketeers* emphasized aspects of American life that OWI thought unfit for foreign audiences at a time when America was fighting for freedom and democracy. Favorite plots showed crimes solved, spy rings broken, and criminals thwarted by average citizens while police stood by dumbfounded. In *Busses Roar* a bomb was timed to explode on a bus as the vehicle passed through an oil field, thus betraying the field's location to a Japanese submarine lurking offshore. The plot failed when an unidentified old man riding the bus suddenly discovered and defused the bomb. How the old man had enough knowledge to do this was never explained, but it was clear that he, not the police, had saved the day. The bureau objected to the popular Sherlock Holmes and Falcon films for similar reasons. Analysts criticized *The Falcon's Brother* because it contrasted the "dumb policeman" with the "clever amateur detective," and because the private detective broke up a Nazi plot to murder a Latin American diplomat while the United States government remained ignorant of the scheme. The bureau report termed the entire episode "incredible." [18]

Even the stock cowboy movie assumed ideological importance because a high proportion cast their villains as supposedly responsible heads of the community. This theme was prominent in *Dead Man's Gulch*, *Lost Canyon*, *Riders of the Northwest Mounted*, *Thundering Trails*, *The Lone Star Trail*, and *Pardon My Gun*, which prompted OWI to observe, "This plot is becoming a Hollywood habit, the men who should be the town leaders are bandit leaders instead, and some itinerant cowboy has to administer justice for the people." [19]

The bureau was concerned, secondly, that Hollywood's treatment of the issues usually lacked intellectual and ideological force. When an American film hero was faced with an opposing ideology, he generally responded with an "Oh, yeah?" followed by a smash to his adversary's jaw. Thus ended any discussion of the issues. The agency found no reference to the principles of the Atlantic Charter, for example, in any of the films reviewed. The movies emphasized too much of what the United Nations was

16 "Weekly Summary," no. 1, Oct. 15, 1942, p. 2. BOI Records, RG 44, WNRC.

17 "Weekly Summary," no. 12, Mar. 11, 1943, p. 3; "Weekly Summary," no. 2, Oct. 31, 1942, p. 4, ibid.

18 "Weekly Summary," no. 2, Oct. 31, 1942, pp. 4, 6; "Weekly Summary," no. 3, Nov. 12, 1942, pp. 3-6, ibid.

19 "Weekly Summary," no. 8, Jan. 14, 1943, p. , ibid.

Hollywood Canteen, one of the most famous musicals built around the war, had a slender plot and starred almost everybody including Joan Leslie and Robert Hutton, *center*. (Courtesy of the Wisconsin Center for Theatre Research)

fighting against, not enough what it was fighting for. It was not enough to point out that America was battling against an invasion of the homeland or against political and economic enslavement. Davis's office stressed that "we are fighting for the rights and dignity of the individual human being" and for the day "when the world will be governed by law and justice." Everyone, including minorities who OWI admitted had been mistreated, had a personal stake in victory. "Only under the democratic system is there any hope of achieving the goal of equal opportunity for all," the office asserted. Democracy was real and it worked, the agency continued, whether "in the community, in the factory, in our schools, or in the army." Finally, the dream of universal peace was not "wild" or "empty," but could be achieved as it had been in the Western Hemisphere where borders stood unfortified and "small and weak states" did not live "in constant fear of oppression by greater and more powerful nations." [20]

To the OWI it seemed that Hollywood simply was not taking this global conflict seriously. The industry exploited the war as a backdrop for frothy musicals such as *True to the Army*, starring Ann Miller,

[20] Office of War Information, Bureau of Intelligence, Media Division, Special Intelligence Report no. 77, "The Enemy in the Movies," Nov. 25, 1942, pp. 1-5, Box 4, Nash Papers; "Government Information Manual [for the Motion Picture Industry],"

Judy Canova, and Jerry Colonna, or *Star Spangled Rhythm,* or *The Yanks are Coming.* One typical musical comedy film, *Youth on Parade,* closed with the cast singing Sammy Cahn's "You've Got to Study, Buddy":

It's kids like us who'll win this fuss
and make the peace
No more Versailles treaties
cause it's proven they don't last.
Diplomats in their slick top hats,
Their day is gone and past. . . .
We've got a plan for every man
In which all hatreds are barred
So better study, Buddy, study hard.

Bureau analysts felt the kids would have been better off in the army.[21]

One of the most famous musicals built around the war was *Hollywood Canteen,* starring almost everyone. The cast included Bette Davis, the Jimmy Dorsey Band, Jane Wyman, Barbara Stanwyck, Jack Carson, John Garfield, Ida Lupino, Irene Dunne, Zachary Scott, and Jack Benny. *Hollywood Canteen*'s slender plot concerned a shy soldier on leave who wandered in and out of the canteen and managed to fall in love with Joan Leslie. After songs by Roy Rogers, Eddie Cantor, the Andrews Sisters, and the Golden Gate Quartet, Dennis Morgan and Joe E. Brown led the entire cast in "You Can Always Tell A Yank":

You can always tell a yank,
He's the kind of guy who's
Always ready to drive a tank to save
democracy
And save the world from tyranny.

Another quickie musical, *Johnny Doughboy,* featured a group of ex-child film stars who, hoping to regain stardom, put on a show for the local military base. In a film that had little to do with the war, the stars suddenly burst into a song glorifying the army private:

It takes a guy like I
to make the guns to boom, boom!
It takes a guy like I
to make the cannons roar.
You can tell F. R. we've crossed the sea
To get that so-and-so guy,
And it takes a guy like I.[22]

To BOI analysts these musicals provided no promotional material for the overseas audience nor did they even have the redeeming feature of introducing memorable patriotic songs. Typical war songs were "The Yanks are Coming," "I Must Have Priorities on Your Love," "There Will Be No Blackout of Democracy," and "The Flag Is Still There, Mr. Key." All were a far cry from "Over There" and "K-K-K-Katy."

The Devil With Hitler was just as bad, OWI thought. In this Hal Roach slapstick comedy hell's board of directors decided that Hitler should replace the devil. The tall, well-groomed Satan, who had spent a lifetime building his power in hell, did not want a "flash in the pan like Hitler" usurping his position. He became Hitler's valet, and, after a great deal of difficulty, forced Hitler to release two prisoners. Through Hitler's "good deed" the devil secured his position. The film also presented Mussolini as a pathetic tool of Hitler and a sneaky, simpering "Suki Yaki" as the stock Japanese.[23] OWI felt these films demeaned the war effort and were unacceptable for export to foreign audiences. OWI shuddered that the world might draw its opinion of the United States at war from these fantasies and worried that even the American audience might overlook the ideological issues at stake.

The bureau was disturbed, thirdly, by

Apr. 29, 1943, pp. 1-6, Box 1433F, Records of the Office of the Chief, Records of the Motion Picture Bureau, RG 208, WNRC.

21 Dorothy B. Jones, "The Hollywood War Film: 1942-44," *Hollywood Quarterly* 1 (1946-47): 11; "Weekly Summary," no. 3, Nov. 12, 1942, p. 15, BOI Records, RG 44, WNRC.

22 "Weekly Summary," no. 12, Mar. 11, 1943, p. 13, BOI Records, RG 44, WNRC.

23 "Weekly Summary," no. 3, Nov. 12, 1942, p. 6, ibid. For an interesting review of this film, see *Variety,* Oct. 21, 1942.

the portrayal of the enemy. In November 1942 OWI issued a detailed intelligence report analyzing the presentation of the enemy in Hollywood feature films. The bureau found that the enemy was not presented as an idea, philosophy, or way of life. Nor was the enemy treated as a threat to the American way of life. Not one film "represented the conflict as one, which if ending in defeat for us, would mean an end to our cherished and fundamental institutions." In short, the Hollywood view of the enemy was simply a "Man-with-a-gun" attacking the United States. Physical violence was the threat, and it was a challenge that could be defeated solely by superior force.[24]

Stand By for Action, starring Charles Laughton, Walter Brennan, Brian Donlevy, and Robert Taylor, was a typical Hollywood action film that told the story of the *Warren,* a reconditioned World War I destroyer. The only issue, unfortunately, OWI argued, was the defeat of the Japanese Navy. Laughton, playing Admiral Thomas, stated: "We've got to use everything we can float if we're going to survive. There is no discussion of ideology, it is a question of our armed strength against that of the enemy." Neither Laughton nor other heroes of action films were made to explain the reasons for the enemy's attack. The Japanese presumably fought from patriotism and loyalty to their emperor, and the Germans fought for their fuehrer. They were depicted as fanatically devoted to their country, a fact the bureau feared would arouse involuntary respect in movie audiences. The bureau also lamented that the enemy was never "persuaded to an opposite opinion or a realization of the baseness of that for which they fight."[25]

Hollywood had a distinct view of each of

the enemies. Germans were gentlemen with whom it was possible to deal as equals. As soldiers they were efficient, disciplined, and patriotic; the bureau was unable to find a scene in which the Germans were morally corrupt or delighted in cruelty. In *Eagle Squadron,* after shooting down a Royal Air Force plane, German fliers dropped a note on a British airfield that apologized for the death of an Allied pilot and questioned the brave British for their foolish resistance to Germany. Nazi officialdom, especially Gestapo agents, were pictured less charitably. While dedicated, they were typically cruel and incompetent, and were always distinguished from German soldiers and the German army. In *Miss V From Moscow* a German army officer ridiculed a Gestapo officer's fanaticism. In *Berlin Correspondent* a newspaper reporter had no trouble outwitting the Gestapo in Berlin. As a whole, the film showed the Gestapo as bunglers and fools, which the bureau felt understated the seriousness of the threat posed by the organization. The movies reviewed by the bureau rarely mentioned the German government. The impression lingered that a few leaders were responsible for the German plight, a point of view that alarmed OWI because it undermined the concept of unconditional surrender.[26]

The Italians were noteworthy for their absence. No Italian appeared as the leader of a spy or espionage group operating in the United States or Europe. The only film released during this period that dealt with the Italian role in the war was a British release, *Ships with Wings.* In this picture Italian soldiers ridiculed their officers as "overdressed dandies who are perfectly willing to have the Germans take over military leadership and the execution of plans." The Germans, of course, sneered at the Italians. Even the film industry with its vast imagination was unable to see Musso-

24 BOI, "The Enemy in the Movies," pp. 1-5, Nash Papers.

25 "Weekly Summary," no. 11, Feb. 26, 1943, p. 17, BOI Records, RG 44, WNRC; BOI, "The Enemy in the Movies," p. 1, Nash Papers.

26 BOI, "The Enemy in the Movies," pp. 19-23, Nash Papers.

OWI AND MOVIES 53

lini's military machine as a threat to Allied security.[27]

The Japanese received by far the worst treatment in Hollywood. Japanese soldiers were pictured as less military than their German counterparts and were almost universally cruel and ruthless. Japanese were short, thin, and wore spectacles. They were tough but devoid of scruples. In almost every film showing American-Japanese battles, the enemy broke the rules of civilized warfare. In *Manila Calling*, starring Lloyd Nolan—a film the bureau found objectionable because Filipinos were cast as a distinctly inferior race and suffered very messy extinction compared to the romantic deaths bestowed upon Americans—the Japanese sniped from trees, mutilated and tortured Filipinos, and obviously enjoyed their work. In *Wake Island* they shot wounded American soldiers and bayoneted defenseless men. *Submarine Raider* contained a scene in which a Japanese pilot flashed a toothy grin as he attacked the helpless crew of a torpedoed ship. By contrast Hollywood did not identify enemy European pilots and never had them revel in their deeds. A few films mentioned the Japanese government, which was usually pictured as cynical, corrupt, and deceitful. Frequent references were made to the treacherous attack on Pearl Harbor. *Wake Island* contrasted Japanese envoy Kurusu's peace trip to Washington during which he pledged peace and toasted Roosevelt with the violent attack on Hawaii.[28]

The racism implicit in the presentation of the Japanese as compared to the Germans was continually deplored by OWI. "This is not a racial war," OWI emphasized. Racist portrayals ran counter to the United Nations avowed goals of racial equality and civil rights. Moreover, OWI realized that millions of America's allies were non-white and pointed out that allies like the Filipinos would resent depictions of racial differences. OWI also was sensitive to American black opinion. In part because OWI officials were committed to racial justice but also because the office feared pockets of apathy or disloyalty could develop if blacks interpreted the conflict as a white man's war, OWI bureaus took pains to mute racial distinctions.[29]

Another complaint was that movies underestimated the enemy. While often shown as a formidable opponent, all too often any dumb American could easily defeat him. *The Daring Young Man* epitomized for OWI many of Hollywood's worst faults. Playing the role of Jonathan Peckinpaw, Joe E. Brown wanted to impress his girl friend by joining the armed forces. He was, of course, refused by all three branches because he was too small. To build himself up he started bowling. He became an overnight sensation because a local gambler used him as a stooge for a trick radio-controlled ball. Three Nazi agents discovered they could send messages to German submarines while standing near Peckinpaw when he bowled. FBI agents exposed the farce and Peckinpaw was disgraced. But he redeemed himself by capturing the Nazis singlehanded and being accepted into the army. The only salient point the bureau could find in the movie was the Nazi who had to say "Heil Hitler" three times as penance for accidentally using the word kosher. The bureau recognized that the film was simply a comedy,

29 "Government Information Manual," p. 2, Box 1433F, Bureau of Motion Picture Records, RG 208, WNRC. See OWI's continuing efforts in support of the black All-American Newsreel in BOI, "Newsreels and OWI Campaigns and Programs," Report no. 5, Dec. 15, 1942, p. 11, Report no. 6, Jan. 6, 1943, p. 11, Report no. 7, Feb. 3, 1943, p. 13, Report no. 8, Mar. 12, 1943, p. 10, Box 4, Nash Papers; Report no. 21, Records of the Division of Press Intelligence of the Bureau of Special Services, RG 208, WNRC; and for the concern over scenes of segregation see, Arthur L. Mayer to Lowell Mellett, June 23, 1943, and Mellett to Mayer, June 24, 1943, Box 1433G, Motion Picture Records, ibid.

27 Ibid., pp. 24-25, 29.

28 Ibid., pp. 23-24.

but it could see no reason to drag the war into a typical Joe E. Brown film. The bureau also condemned the film's presentation of blacks, who were "uncommonly stupid" and used only for comic relief. This element alone made the film unacceptable to the bureau.[30]

Not all Hollywood films were so lacking in sensitivity toward the issues of war. Some did deal with the war in positive terms. The bureau approved of *Night Plane from Chunking*, starring Robert Preston and Ellen Drew, because it offered a graphic illustration of Japanese aggression and portrayed the Chinese as stoical, dignified, and respected by Americans who were helping them defend democracy. The theme of Americans who were fighting as pilots in China was a favorite. The plot was usually complicated by one American among the fliers who flew only for money, until late in the film when the cynic was converted to the fight for freedom. *Flying Tigers*, starring John Wayne and John Carrol, was typical. As the film opened, Carrol dismissed China as just a name; if America had been under attack, he would have been ready to fight for a cause. He discovered, however, that China meant home to millions of people, and in the end he gave his life for them. *China Girl*, starring George Montgomery as an American photographer and Gene Tierney as the ever-present Chinese educated in America, followed a similar theme. The film opened with the following lines on the screen: "An American will fight for three things—for a woman, for himself, and for a better world. He was fighting for only two of these when the story begins, November, 1941." But the hero was soon converted to the third. The Japanese captured Montgomery in China and offered him $20,000 if he would photograph the Burma Road. Flying to Mandalay, he fell in love with a Chinese girl (Tierney) who, with her father, was fighting for China. When the girl was killed in a Japanese air-raid, the hero was converted to democracy. OWI felt this film showed realistically the difficulties the Chinese were facing and the heroic role some Americans had played in China. One scene in the film took place in a Chinese school where a teacher read a poem to her class as Japanese bombs fell:

No tyrants dream of earthly might
No cannon roar nor battle toll
Can quench this small but holy light
Of freedom rising from our soul.

Then, as the children responded "Our country is goodness . . . Our country is justice," a Japanese bomb hit the school, killing many of them. The film left no doubt that the Japanese would use any means to achieve victory over the long-suffering Chinese or that China was an important theater of the war.[31]

The bureau also liked *Chetniks*, a 1943 release featuring Philip Dorn. One of the few Hollywood movies to use Eastern Europe as a setting, the film boosted the concept of a United Nations, OWI felt, by portraying the Yugoslavian people heroically resisting the Nazis. *Chetniks* showed the resistance movement as unified under the firm leadership of Draja Mikhailovitch. Flanked by dignitaries of the church, he addressed the people: "I give you my solemn promise that I shall not lay down my sword until every inch of Yugoslavia is reclaimed from the invader. . . . Neither German might nor German frightfulness can deter us from the goal we have set—complete freedom for our people." Despite the historical inaccuracies, the bureau still termed the film "promotional." [32]

[30] "Weekly Summary," no. 3, Nov. 12, 1942, pp. 2-3, BOI Records, RG 44, WNRC.

[31] "Weekly Summary," no. 11, Feb. 26, 1943, pp. 13-14; "Weekly Summary," no. 1, Oct. 15, 1942, pp. 9-11; "Weekly Summary," no. 7, Jan. 7, 1943, pp. 3-5, ibid.

[32] "Weekly Summary," no. 11, Feb. 26, 1943, pp. 6-7, ibid.

The classic *Casablanca* received, with a few exceptions, a tepid review. Featuring a powerful cast including Humphrey Bogart, Ingrid Bergman, Claude Rains, Sidney Greenstreet, Peter Lorre, and Paul Henreid, the melodrama depicted several themes that the bureau applauded. Several scenes effectively portrayed the human tragedies resulting from the vast refugee problem created by Axis conquests. The bond of friendship and mutual respect between Rick (Bogart) and his black pianist, Sam (Dooley Wilson), while not without condescension, was for the time a positive statement of the race question. And one of the key issues of the war received brief attention when Rick, bandaging the Czech leader Victor Lazlo (Henreid), questioned the value of the resistance movement's suffering. Lazlo replied: "We might as well question why we breathe. If we stop breathing, we'll die. If we stop fighting our enemies, the world will die." But the analysts fretted over Rick's cynicism, and they disliked the dapper French prefect of police (Rains). "His main interest outside of gambling is pretty women," the bureau report lamented, "and his method of pursuing them is unscrupulous." Moreover, he played along with the Germans until the end of the film when he adroitly switched to the Free French.[33]

The analysts all but overlooked the essentially pro-Allied theme of *Casablanca*. One salient incident received no attention in the bureau's report. Lazlo, his wife, Ilsa (Bergman), and Rick descend the stairway from Rick's office to find the German officers singing "Die Vaterland" as the cafe patrons look on in stony silence. Lazlo has the band strike up the "Marseillaise," and the entire cafe quickly unites in a spirited rendition, drowning out the Germans who make a disgusted exit. Furthermore, the report paid only passing attention to the movie's

conclusion. Risking his life, Rick has helped the Lazlos escape to Lisbon; it is clear he has abandoned his cynicism and will continue to fight for the Allies. The prefect, too, is persuaded by the heroic example of the resistance fighters. Arm in arm, Rick and the prefect walk into the fog-shrouded night, the prefect uttering the deathless line: "This could be the beginning of a beautiful friendship." [34]

Even though Rick and the prefect have been converted to the cause, the intelligence analysts remained unsatisfied. The war issues had received little explicit discussion; the film ended without a ringing reaffirmation of the Atlantic Charter. The bureau was not content to let meaning emerge from the interaction of the characters or the overall story line. Instead of the "beginning of a beautiful friendship" it would have preferred a two-paragraph sermonette explaining Nazi aggression and the justice of the Allied cause. The effect on what was perhaps the most memorable film of the war period would have been incalculable.

The overt moralizing the bureau favored led it to endorse the forgotten *Immortal Sergeant* as the best Hollywood treatment of the war. Played by Henry Fonda, the sergeant was a young Canadian writer who had joined the British army in Libya. The picture compared the problems Fonda had encountered in civilian life—he had joined the army because he was unable to tell his girl, Valentine, he loved her—with the problems he was facing fighting for freedom. The bureau liked the movie because it gave the public a concept of the war in North Africa, but particularly because the film combined the concrete problems of an individual with those of a military campaign. *Immortal Sergeant*, like *Casablanca*, dealt in part with a man's increasing understanding of the war issues. But the last

---

[33] "Weekly Summary," no. 9, Jan. 28, 1943, pp. 6-9, ibid.

[34] Ibid.

Claude Rains, Conrad Viedt, Paul Henried, and Ingrid Bergman in *Casablanca*.

scene, in contrast to *Casablanca*'s, won the bureau's praise for its explication of the issues. Recovering from his wounds in an Allied hospital, Fonda began to understand the cruel necessity of war: "If I want Valenine or anything else worthwhile in life, I've got to fight for it. That's not a bad thing for a man to find out is it? Or for a nation either, for that matter, to fight." [35]

Immortal Sergeant was one of several movies released early in 1943 that encouraged OWI to believe that "some of the best films from the war information point of view" were at last coming out of Hollywood. An OWI analyst cited *The Moon Is Down* and *Hangmen Also Die* for powerful presentation of the issues. Movies produced later in the war that won praise from OWI included *Watch on the Rhine, Destination Tokyo, The Eve of St. Mark, A Guy Named Joe, Corregidor,* and *Sahara*. [36]

The delay in the production of feature films likely to please OWI was largely attributable to the inevitable time lag between a picture's conception and its release. Nine to twelve months was a typical gestation period for a major film; early 1943 was, therefore, about as early as improvement could have been expected. In the first months after Pearl Harbor, the "man-with-a-gun" interpretation of why America was at war was an understandable response. Some time was required for Hollywood—and the government itself—to marshal ap-

[35] "Weekly Summary," no. 10, Feb. 12, 1943, pp. 19-20, ibid.

[36] Bell to Mellett, Feb. 23, 1943, Box 890, Office of Government Reports Records, RG 44, WNRC; Jones, "The Hollywood War Film," pp. 1-13.

peals for the four freedoms and the United Nations.

Just as the upturn in the cinema was becoming noticeable, an angry Congress slashed OWI appropriations. Partisan congressmen charged that OWI had been working as much for Roosevelt's reelection as for Allied victory, and Southern legislators were incensed by OWI's solicitous treatment of blacks. Intelligence operations were among the first activities cut back, and analysis of motion pictures was suspended in the spring of 1943.[37]

During its brief life the BOI performed useful services through its movie analyses. First, the bureau proved helpful in flashing warning signals about films that would offend foreign sensibilities. The insensitivity of American film makers had provoked several unfortunate incidents in 1942. In *A Yank at Eton* the cocky American student (Mickey Rooney) who thumbed his nose at tradition upset the British. The portrayal of Iceland as a forbidding, frozen land populated by rather dimwitted citizens in the Sonja Henie vehicle *Iceland* had outraged that key island's population. And the proposed re-release of *The Real Glory*, which emphasized strife in the Philippines between Muslims and Christians and between Filipinos and Americans, had gravely offended Philippine President Manuel Quezon.[38] The greater understanding encouraged by the bureau's analyses helped reduce such incidents later in the war. Second, the bureau responded fully to its task of analyzing war themes in a vital medium. The need for pictures "correctly researched and correctly emphasized" was acute in the often depressing first year of war. By providing systematic, up-to-date intelligence reports, the bureau furnished the data needed for informed policy making.

Nevertheless, the bureau, by narrowing its focus to the treatment of war-related issues, lost a sense of perspective. Bob Blakely, an assistant to OWI domestic director Cowles, sensed this when he charged that the bureau reached "some rather ridiculous conclusions." He was astounded that analysts rated the comedy *George Washington Slept Here* as "possibly objectionable" because the Americans did not appear "as a normally intelligent group" and because there was "no feeling of cooperation in the community nor in the family." He also doubted that the corrupt judges and incompetent police who troubled the bureau put America in a bad light. American films were "good ambassadors," he argued, precisely because they did not make "any conscious attempt to create a certain impression of Americans." Foreign viewers did not conclude that all Americans were "crooks and fools and tyrants." They perceived instead that Americans "were all kinds of people just like themselves and that best of all the Government didn't beat the industry into conforming to a certain message." Composer Sam Barlow underscored the point after a trip to Latin America in 1943. Foreign audiences knew "perfectly well" the United States had "innumerable problems," he said; it solved nothing to show movies "of an utterly hypocritical sweetness and light." In fact, the United States gained respect by releasing films recognizing its problems. *The Grapes of Wrath*, produced in 1940, in particular, demonstrated to Latin Americans that the country "had ceased to be the Make-Believe Child, Goody Two-Shoes, and had really become adult."[39]

---

[37] Sydney Weinberg, "What to Tell America: The Writers' Quarrel in OWI," *Journal of American History* 55 (1968): 73-89.

[38] *New York Times*, Jan. 10, 1943; *Variety*, Oct. 21, 1942; Frederick N. Polangin to Mellett, Aug. 8, 1942, Quezon to Mellett, Aug. 17, 1942, Mellett to Goldwyn, Aug. 20, 1942, Goldwyn to Mellett, Aug. 24, 1942, Box 1433B, Motion Picture Records, RG 208, WNRC.

[39] Bob Blakely to Mike Cowles, Nov. 6, 1942, Records of the Office of the Historian, Director's Records, RG 208, WNRC; Sam Barlow, "Barlow Report," 1943, Box 28, Oscar L. Chapman Papers, HSTL.

The very diversity of American films was a more potent argument for the Allied cause than any OWI-inspired sermonette. When the movies poked fun at the police or spoofed the government, they demonstrated that freedom of expression was a reality. When Charlie Chaplin satirized a dictator or when a bumbling Joe E. Brown exposed Nazi spies, films did not minimize the totalitarian threat but pricked the pretensions of dictators.[40] At the same time, audiences could see the vivid contrast between democracy and totalitarianism, to which humor and satire were alien. When the clever amateur detective outwitted the police he reaffirmed the American belief in the resourceful individual who triumphed over the institution, and he reinforced a democratic theme—the worth and dignity of the common man.

With the myopia fostered by focusing on overt ideological content, the BOI overlooked the positive ideas conveyed in more subtle ways. Through its desire to press artistic expression into government-sanctioned molds, the bureau courted the danger of undermining the ideals for which it fought. The best argument for why Americans fought remained not the rhetoric, but the reality, of freedom. □

40 Gordon Allport, "Liabilities and Assets in Civilian Morale," *Annals of the American Academy of Political and Social Sciences* 216 (1941) : 93.

Ralph R. Donald
Southern Illinois University at Edwardsville

Awakening A Sleeping Giant:
The Pearl Harbor Attack on Film

The Film Archive

The Purple Heart (1944): Actor Richard Loo explains The Great Design.

Considering the success of the surprise Japanese attack on Pearl Harbor on December 7, 1941, Admiral Isoroku Yamamoto should have been happier. But the supreme commander of the Japanese Navy would not allow himself to become too elated: two vital aspects of this operation had failed. Although his battle plan was nearly flawlessly executed, Yamamoto had not achieved success in two important (and eventually critical) aspects. The admiral knew that the only way Japan could succeed in a war with the United States was if the conflict were a short one, won by a swift, decisive crippling of America's pacific fleet, followed by immediate American capitulation. Although the Pearl Harbor attack killed 2,403 people, destroyed or damaged 18 U.S. battleships, cruisers and destroyers and 188 airplanes, the Pacific Fleet's aircraft carriers were not in port at the time, and thus were spared. This Japanese "bad luck" caused not only the cancellation of the second phase of their attack, the invasion and occupation of Hawaii, but also led to their subsequent defeat in the battle of Midway, a turning point in the war in the Pacific.[1]

But of equal consequence was the fatefully bad timing of the Pearl Harbor attack. Although Japanese military history clearly demonstrates that they had always favored a swift, decisive blow that counted heavily on the element of surprise, the Pearl Harbor attack had to be handled a bit more delicately. This was because Yamamoto had lived and studied in the United States, and understood American culture well: he knew that the people of the U.S. despised deceit, and already thought of the Japanese as a sneaky and crafty lot. Thus, Yamamoto decided that thirty minutes prior to the attack, Japanese emissaries would inform American Secretary of State Cordell Hull that further negotiations between the two countries would be fruitless, and that thereafter a state of war would exist between the U.S. and the Empire of Japan. Then, the admiral reasoned, no matter how great an element of surprise achieved in the raid on Pearl Harbor, no one could call it a sneak attack conducted while peace negotiations were still underway in Washington. But the Japanese miscalulated the amount of time needed by their Washington embassy required to decode and type the ultimatum transmitted from Tokyo; as a result, the message was not ready in time for their meeting with the American secretary of state. Later, when the Japanese delegation finally presented itself and its ultimatum, the Pearl Harbor "sneak attack" had already begun. Disgusted and outraged, Hull quickly read the tardy transmission, and—with a hail of profane insults—dismissed the emissaries before they could explain or apologize. Most Americans responded the same as Hull: isolationist and unwilling to involve themselves in the war up to then, they were changed by the events on this "day of infamy."[2]

This background helps explain why, as Yamamoto received the warm congratulations of his staff, he appeared openly depressed. When asked why he was not more elated by such a one-sided victory, he replied, "I fear all we have done is to awaken a sleeping giant, and fill him with a terrible resolve."

American feature-length war films released from 1941 to 1945 such as *Across the Pacific (1942)*, *Air Force (1943)*, *Black Dragons (1942)*, *Blood On The Sun (1945)*, *Bombardier! (1941)*, *China (1943)*, *China Girl (1942)*, *Destination Tokyo (1944)*, *Eagle Squadron (1942)*, *The Fighting Seabees (1944)*, *Flying Tigers (1942)*, *God Is My Co-Pilot (1945)*, *Gung Ho! (1943)*, *Purple Heart (1944)*, *They Were Expendable (1945)*, and *Wake Island (1942)* were characteristic of the hundreds of American films that have dramatized events surrounding the attack on Pearl Harbor.

By the time the American public saw films such as these, the basic facts of the attack were well known. But through Hollywood's lens, the character and emotions of this angry, awakening American giant are portrayed and revisited. It is said that art imitates life: although most of these wartime epics were unrealistic, propagandistic, and certainly ethnocentric, they nonetheless provide a reasonably accurate mirror of the immense hate and disgust of the American people for the Japanese attack on Pearl Harbor.

In his analysis of World War I propaganda, Harold Lasswell noted that a key persuasive device is to direct the blame for the outbreak of war to the enemy. He categorized these scapegoating messages simply as "guilt." The guilt appeal stresses the fact that the propagandist's peace-loving nation would never covet its neighbor's holdings, or desire to rule its population. Thus, the deteriorated state of affairs leading to armed conflict is due, in one way or another, to the illegitimate desires and actions of the enemy. "They are the aggressor, not we." This particular propaganda device is often followed by yet another persuasive tool, which Lasswell dubbed "the illusion of victory" statement. In this instance, the illusion of victory state-

Across the Pacific (1942): Sequel to *The Maltese Falcon?*

73

ment stipulates that although the enemy may have initiated the conflict, our forces will put an end to it.

A typical combination of these devices is found in *Across The Pacific*. In this film the Japanese plan is to bomb the Panama Canal on the same day Pearl Harbor is attacked, delaying by weeks the arrival of naval reinforcements from the east coast. This is dialog from a scene between a man revealed to be a Japanese saboteur

Blood on the Sun (1945): Exposing the Tenaka Memorial Plan.

and an American counterintelligence agent, played by Humphrey Bogart.

> *American:* You guys been lookin' for a war, haven't ya?
>
> *Japanese Saboteur:* That's right, Rick. That's why we're starting it.
>
> *American:* You may start it, Joe, but we'll finish it.

As one can see, in the hands of 1940s Hollywood screenwriters, this propaganda appeal does not seem very mature. As a matter of fact, it greatly resembles the threats made by schoolboys on a playground.[3]

Such statements were not solely aimed at the Japanese. Their Axis allies, the Germans, received their share of revenge threats. In *Bombardier*, shortly before the protagonists find out about Pearl Harbor, the old sarge is reading a newspaper headline to the female lead, whose name is Burt. The report says, "Hitler Challenges American Navy: Fuehrer Warns U-Boats Ready To Return Fire on Ships."

> *Sarge* [fuming] That guy burns me up.
>
> *Burt:* [amused] Don't get excited. You'll start a war.
>
> *Sarge:* No, he'll start it, and the bombardiers will finish it.

In *Purple Heart*, Capt. Ross (Dana Andrews) gives an emotional speech to the Japanese kangaroo

court about to sentence him and his men to death for their part in the Jimmy Doolittle raid, America's act of revenge for Pearl Harbor. In this oration, he prophesies the fate in store for Japan for attacking the U.S., and in an eerie sort of way, seems to predict the future destruction of Hiroshima and Nagasaki:

> *Ross:* You wanted it, you asked for it, you started it! And now you're going to get it, and it won't be finished until your dirty little empire is wiped off the face of the earth!

A propaganda statement similar to "They are the aggressor, not we," maintains that Japanese imperialists had planned the Pearl Harbor attack long in advance. This helps explain to an audience that no single issue, nor any single recent incident, caused the enemy to go to war against us. Rather, this statement contends that their imperialistic goals required that the Japanese make war upon us, and that they spent many years carefully planning it. In both *Purple Heart* and *God Is My Co-Pilot*, two Japanese villains were portrayed by the same Chinese actor, Richard Loo (since by this time, nearly all Japanese on the West coast of the U.S. were incarcerated in internment camps). Loo's two hateful Japanese characters are shown to have been plotting the overthrow of America long before the attack at Pearl Harbor. In *Purple Heart*, Loo plays a Japanese general, chief of Army Intelligence. He tells captive American flyer Ross that he lived in Santa Barbara, California, in the 1930's, and worked on a fishing boat—all the time spying, "charting every inch of water from San Diego to Seattle." In *God Is My Co-Pilot*, Loo, who this time portrays Japanese fighter ace "Tokyo Joe," claims that he was sent by his government to Glendale, California, before the war to learn to fly "American-style." By inference this guilt statement implies that only this illicitly-obtained American know-how permits this Japanese flyer to defeat American planes in battle.[4]

The plot of the James Cagney spy film *Blood on The Sun* is to obtain and reveal to the American people the contents of the secret "Tanaka Memorial Plan," a document purported to be a step-by-step design for world conquest, written in the late 1920's by Japanese Prime Minister Guichi Tanaka. This scenario called for the conquest of China and Southeast Asia to acquire the raw materials and manpower for a sweep East to destroy Pearl Harbor, overrun the Hawaiian Islands, and then assault the U.S. mainland. As well, in *Purple Heart*, Loo's character also alluded to this same master plan. And during one meeting with Tanaka in *Blood on The Sun*, the famous and often-quoted boast of Admiral Yamamoto is repeated:

Yamamoto: I will be in the White House when Japan dictates her terms of peace.

Although the actual facts of the Pearl Harbor attack belie this statement, most American films produced during World War II steadfastly maintained that the attack was indeed premeditated deception, and not an unfortunate error in the timing of the delivery of the Japanese government's ultimatum. A crawl at the beginning of *Blood on The Sun*, states that Tanaka was "the Oriental Hitler. His plan of world conquest depended on secrecy for success." In the denouement of the film *China*, which takes place on the eve of the Pearl Harbor attack, a snickering Japanese general boasts to the American "Mr. Jones" (Alan Ladd) about what will be happening in Hawaii "in a few hours."

Likewise, in *China Girl*, with the month of November, 1941, prominently revealed on the calendar behind his head, a smarmy Japanese Army general tells an American journalist (George Montgomery):

> *General:* Japan is a friend of America:
> We are a peace-loving nation.

As most American audiences of the 1940's knew, Japan's peace envoys were in Washington for a new round of talks which both sides hoped would avert war between the two nations. In light of the timing of the Pearl Harbor attack, Hollywood often reminded audiences just how treacherous this ploy appeared to be. For example, *Black Dragons* begins with a shot of a headline that says, "Japs Bomb Honolulu During Peace Talks." In *Wake Island*, Marine and Navy officers actually wine and dine these same Japanese "peace envoys," whose plane stops overnight at Wake for re-fueling. Once again, the ubiquitous Richard Loo, this time made up to be a bespectacled, bucktoothed version of Japanese envoy Admiral Nomura, tells American officers he has "a message of peace" to President Roosevelt. The admiral solemnly swears that in the Japanese heart, FDR "will find no thought of war, but instead, wishes for a lasting peace." The film also shows a calendar to visually emphasize the date of this statement three days before Pearl Harbor.

In *Air Force*, the crew of the bomber "Mary Ann," en route to Hawaii Dec. 6, 1941, is listening on the radio to the evening news. The newscaster reads, "Mr. Kurusu (the other Japanese envoy) and Admiral Nomura have assured the President that Japan's intentions are wholly peaceful." Later, when the air crew finds out what happened at Pearl Harbor, Winocki (John Garfield) is livid in this conversation with the Chief (Harry Carey):

> *Winocki:* They send a couple of oily gents to Washington with an olive wreath while the boys back home clobber Uncle Sam with a crowbar!
> *Chief:* He's a tough old gent. You just wait 'til he gets annoyed.

To drive the point home more, *Air Force* director Howard Hawks depicts the "Mary Ann's" crew listening to a short wave broadcast of President Roosevelt's famous "Day of Infamy" speech.

> *FDR:* The attack yesterday on the Hawaiian Islands caused severe damage to American naval and military forces. I regret to tell you that many American lives were lost. But always will our nation remember the character of the onslaught against us . . . no matter how long it may take us to overcome this premeditated invasion, the American people, in their righteous might, will win through to absolute victory. We will not only defend ourselves to the uttermost, but will make it very certain that this form of treachery shall never again endanger us. Through our armed forces and in the unbounded determination of our people, we will win the inevitable triumph, so help us God.

This is perhaps the FDR recording most often used by Hollywood in its combat films, and it contains many propaganda appeals itself. Later, after the Mary Ann's aircrew lands at Wake Island, they listen to a wounded Major Bagley, the commander of the American-held island's defense forces:

> *Bagley:* I've studied all the wars of history, but I've never come across any dirtier treachery than [Pearl Harbor].

So emotional was this treachery theme that it came to be known by many negative colloquialisms. Hollywood, not to be left behind, borrowed from the standard terminology for a treacherous attack as found in the western, "shot in the back," and adapted it to the Japanese traditional affection for knives and swords. In the "Foreword" narration by Quentin Reynolds at the beginning of *Eagle Squadron*, he refers to the young flyers who joined the Royal Air Force before Pearl Harbor:

> *Reynolds:* This is a story of our countrymen who didn't wait to be stabbed in the back. (Later in this narration, Reynolds repeats this phrase.)

Destination Tokyo devotes a considerable

75

amount of time to this back-stabbing metaphor: Cary Grant, portraying a submarine captain, explains to the crew why a downed Japanese pilot stabbed a crewman (named Mike) in the back, although Mike was trying to rescue him from the water:

Captain: Mike bought his kid roller skates when the kid turned five. Well, that Jap got a present when he was five — only it was a dagger. His old man gave it to him so he would know right off what he was supposed to be in life. . ." [the Captain goes on to say how Japanese kids were indoctrinated in the ways of war] ". . . And by the time he's 13, he can put a machine gun together blindfolded. That Jap was started on the road 20 years ago to putting a knife in Mike's back. And a lot more Mikes are going to die until we wipe out a system that puts daggers in the hands of five-year-old children — That's what Mike died for — more roller skates in this world — and even some for the next generation of Japanese kids.

Although not every film scenario gave Hollywood the chance to tell the tale of the Pearl Harbor attack, this was one story that every American knew well. All it took to rekindle the emotions and hatred that the memory of this deed contained was a simple code, a shorthand: "Remember Pearl Harbor." This shorthand, or "cueing mechanism," has been used before. It was very successful in rallying U.S. support for the Mexican War and the Spanish-American War. "Remember the Alamo" and "Remember The Maine" made each war's call to action clear: Righteous anger, even revenge, was justified because of the heinous actions of an aggressor. So, after a time, recounting the entire litany of enemy sins was unnecessary. All that was required was a terse reminder, a cue to make audience recall the enemy's guilt. History itself testifies to the thunderous success of the slogan "Remember Pearl Harbor."

Typical of the subtle cueing is this scene from *Air Force*, in which the "Mary Ann's" captain, "Irish" Quincannon, (played by John Ridgely), flies over Pearl a few hours after the attack. As Ridgely banks the plane for a better look, he tells his crew on the intercom:

Quincannon: (solemnly) Pilot to crew. Take a good look: Maybe it's something you'll want to remember.

Tracking down the fuselage from a point-of-view outside the ship, Hawks' camera captures the faces of the crewmen, gazing out through port holes at the smoking remains of America's Pacific Fleet, their faces illuminated by the fires below. And in one of the wartime language dispensations from the Hays Office censors, Winocki (John Garfield) is allowed to exclaim:

Winocki: Damn 'em, Damn 'em!

There is a scene in both *Flying Tigers* and *Air Force*, in which the men sit around a radio, listening to Roosevelt's "Day of Infamy" speech. In both films, directors David Miller and Howard Hawks portray the nation's horror and disbelief by looking into the faces of the men as they react both to the news of the attack, and to the President's call to arms. Their faces and in their physical reactions reflect a determination to remember and to exact revenge.

In *Bombardier!*, the entire cast sits reverently in their chapel on Dec. 7, when a day room orderly (played by Robert Ryan), bursts in with the news, "the Japs have bombed Pearl Harbor!" Later in the bombing school office, with his officers gathered around him, Colonel Pat O'Brien points to the date on the calendar and says:

O'Brien: There's a date we'll always remember — and they will never forget!

Another cueing phrase for Pearl Harbor is found in *The Fighting Seabees*. This naval construction battalion's theme song, lustily sung at various times during the picture, features Sam Lewis' lyrics

. . . and we promise that we'll remember

the Seventh of December.

In *They Were Expendable*, the attack is announced during a party for U.S. Navy personnel at a Philippine night club. After receiving the word, they simply take a "stiff upper lip" and immediately depart for their duty stations. But later, director John Ford, a reserve Navy captain himself, takes some time recalling the greatest single tragedy of the Dec. 7 attack. The men of the P.T. boat squadron are shown surveying the wreckage of their quarters following a particularly devastating Japanese air raid. The squadron cook, who had formerly served on board the USS *Arizona*, says he wishes "the old Arizona" would soon come steaming up the harbor to help them. Since most of the men had not yet heard the details of the enormous losses the fleet sustained in the attack, "Cookie" had no way of knowing that the *Arizona* was sunk at Pearl Harbor with nearly all hands. Officers (played by John Wayne and Robert Montgomery) react to this by exchanging solemn looks, which were not lost on the Chief Boatswain's Mate, (Ward Bond.) The mate simply asks, "The *Arizona?*" Lt. Brickley (Montgomery) looks dejected, shakes and bows his head. Pearl Harbor is once again tacitly called to mind, and the defunct battleship is added to the list of effective Pearl Harbor cues.

Although in *Gung Ho!* Director Ray Enright uses the same approach, the references to Pearl Harbor range from not-too-subtle to heavy-handed. In one sequence the Marine Raiders' troop ship is shown passing by Pearl Harbor. As the director cuts away to stock footage of the aftermath of the Japanese attack, the Marines solemnly and silently gaze at the wreckage of the *Arizona* and other ships. But Enright felt for some reason that he needed to add to this moment a narrator's voice-over:

> *Narrator:* Pearl Harbor — Five months after the day of infamy —there are men in the Second Raider Battalion who lost brothers on those ships. Can we help even the score?

Earlier in the same picture, one Marine is asked why he volunteered for this especially hazardous duty. With malice in his voice and a look of hate in his eyes, he says:

> *Marine:* My brother died at Pearl Harbor (the music in the scene becomes suddenly somber). They didn't find enough of him to bury.

Yet another approach to remind audiences of the tragedy of Pearl Harbor is found in *Wake Island.* A pilot agrees to fly a suicide mission after hearing that his wife was one of the 68 civilians killed at Pearl Harbor. In *Air Force*, the airmen of the "Mary Ann" seek out the pilot's sister, who was wounded by a strafing Japanese plane. In the hospital, crammed with civilian casualties, a little girl with bandages on her eyes, reaches out her hands and asks, "Mommy, I can't see. Why can't I see?"

After Hiroshima, American war films changed, softening both in propagandistic tone and in their treatment of the Axis powers. Along with these changes came the eventual recognition that the incidents surrounding Pearl Harbor were more complex than these wartime propaganda films depicted. In films such as *Midway (1976)* and the U.S./Japanese co-production of *Tora! Tora! Tora! (1970)*, audiences discovered many new facts. Rather than portraying the Japanese attack as sneaky and villainous, these modern treatments dramatize a much more complex series of events in a more truthful retelling of the story. As Jeanine Basinger wrote describing the effect of viewing *Tora! Tora! Tora!*:

> [The Japanese] characters have dignity and pride, and telling the story of the bombing of Pearl Harbor from their point of view helps, finally, if not to compensate for, at least to offset the indignity of their presentation in so many American films of World War II. Watching *Tora! Tora! Tora!*, one can suddenly see the event of Pearl Harbor from another viewpoint—how daring a raid it was, what a military coup, and how bold the men who planned it and how brave the men who flew its mission. Our side appears remarkably inefficient, complacent, and disorganized by comparison, a fact which is doubtless historically correct. *Tora! Tora! Tora!* thus illustrates the power of film. By filming Pearl Harbor from inside the Japanese bombers, it can inspire the victims to cheer the attackers! This is not the point of the film . . . but it is the end result, particularly for an American who has never thought of Pearl Harbor as anything but a "dastardly deed."[5]

This, of course, is not surprising, since both history and the films that depict history are created to assuage the *current* beliefs of the writer and his/her public. But today, although many more Americans know these facts, "Japan-bashing," using the Japanese as scapegoats in the media and in the conversations and thoughts of the American people, continues.

Destination Tokyo (1943): A secret mission of revenge.

What might have happened if those Japanese envoys had delivered their ultimatum and declaration of war on time, before the attack. Would there have been so great an American outcry? Would it simply have been referred to in the history books and in the

While envoys talked on December 7, 1941.

films as "the battle of Pearl Harbor," the opening salvo of declared hostilities between America and the Empire of Japan? Would Americans still have rallied to the support of our government's war objectives and enlisted by the thousands on December 8?

What then would American filmmakers have used as a rallying cry? Would "Remember Bataan and Corregador" have replaced "Remember Pearl Harbor" as cueing phrases? And without the "treachery" of the Pearl Harbor attack to remember, would President Truman still have chosen to drop the A-bomb on Hiroshima? How might this have altered the Cuban Missile Crisis when President Kennedy rejected the advice to Bomb Cuba and invade because he did not want to be credited with "another Pearl Harbor." What if Kennedy had not been haunted by the specter of December 7?

But ambassadors Nomura and Kurusuu *were* late in delivering their ultimatum, providing American filmmaker/propagandists with an issue, a slogan, and a battle cry. The "sleeping giant" awoke, and Yamamoto's worst fear was realized.

Notes

[1]Toland, John. *Infamy: Pearl Harbor and Its Aftermath.*

(Garden City, N.Y.: Doubleday and Co., 1982): 13.

[2]Toland, 253, 12.

[3]Lasswell, Harold *Propaganda Technique in World War I* (Cambridge, MA: MIT Press, 1971): 47, 102.

[4]If there was any recurring character who seemed to typify American moviemakers' stereotype of an evil, sinister "Jap," is was Richard Loo. Although during the '40s the actor also played Hollywood's "good Asians," Chinese guerillas fighting alongside Americans against the Japanese in films such as *China*, the majority of his portrayals throughout the 1940s were of the archetypical "evil Japanese." The only significant difference between these portrayals of Japanese seemed to be Loo's makeup. Especially in the earlier 1940's war films, Loo was forced to enunciate his lines through false buck teeth and strain to see where he was walking through thick-lensed, black-rimmed glasses.

[5]Basinger, Jeannie. *The World War II Combat Film: Anatomy of a Genre* (New York: Columbia University Press, 1986), 193.

Ralph R. Donald is Professor and Chairperson of the Department of Mass Communication at Southern Illinois University at Edwardsville. He received the Ph.D. degree from the University of Massachusetts at Amherst and has taught broadcasting and film for twenty-three years. Editor of *Mid-Atlantic Almanack*, published by the Mid-Atlantic Popular/American Culture Association, he has also been a newspaper editor, radio/tv news producer, and a political campaign media consultant.

78

Pictures of the Enemy:
Fifty Years of Images of Japan in the American Press,
1941-1992

Susan D. Moeller

"Japan," noted author and columnist Pico Iyer, "is a product of our imagination, and the country that we see is only the one we have been trained to see" (Iyer 76). In the 50 years since the American entry into World War II, the American press has been the pre-eminent institution directing what the American public sees of Japan and the Japanese. The "reality" of Japan has been mediated through the press; the press has both documented events and been the prime instrument of assigning meaning to them. Images of Japan in American mass-market periodicals have created a fictional country. These images have been selective presentations of people, events, places and ideas. If not outright "inventions," they have been constructed ideological fabrications aimed at consolidating, perpetuating and extending the belief system of the United States. The print media has as much "interpreted" Japan and the Japanese, as "reported" on the international climate vis à vis Japan.

Images of Japan in the American press confirm that American images and representations of the "Other"—of "foreign" countries and "different" races, for example—are typically efforts by a dominant power group to impose clarity and order on an essentially complex and chaotic world. Photography, graphics (illustrations, cartoons and charts) and articles on Japan and the Japanese in fifty years of mass-market news and general-interest magazines and major market newspapers show that the American press has consistently constructed an image of Japan as the "Other," where the extent and type of "Otherness" has been determined by the American press's sense of comfort about the place of the United States in the global arena .[1]

"Relations of power inescapably color the ways in which we perceive ourselves in relation to others," Elizabeth Fox-Genovese has stated (25). The more strained the social, political and economic conditions under which "We," the United States, meet the "Other," Japan, the more the representations of the "Other" rely on stereotypes. American relations with

Japan have been strained since Commodore Matthew Perry's ships entered Tokyo harbor in 1853.[2] And certainly, as detailed in this paper, relations between the United States and Japan since Pearl Harbor have been colored by that cataclysmic social, political and economic event.

The communications revolution of the past 50 years has made surprisingly little difference in the amount of stereotyping. Said Joel Dreyfuss, the former Tokyo bureau chief of *Fortune* magazine, "Japan is the most important country in the world that Americans don't understand.... Maybe because Japan has become the first nonwhite country we are forced to deal with as an equal, we have explained away the challenges to our stereotypes by creating new ones: no longer considered an immature third world nation, Japan is now seen as a mystical blend of a 2,000-year-old culture and modern management" (Dreyfuss 8).

Many stereotypes about Japan have persisted through the years, and as *New York Times* critic Vincent Canby has written, "propaganda freezes interest in a culture that, just possibly, may have a great deal to teach us" (Canby H1). Japan, a country far away, across the broad Pacific, with a distinctive people and culture, has typically perplexed Americans and the American press; it has been the most mysterious nation in the mysterious Orient.[3] Near the end of the Second World War, *Newsweek* magazine argued, "Americans find it hard to understand such remote peoples as the Chinese, Indians, and Arabs." But in "dealing with" Japan, *Newsweek* believed, "Americans—and all other nationalities for that matter—are up against an absolutely unique nation. The mental and moral climate of Japan is...utterly different from any other in the world" (Pakenham "Mentality" 48). Fifty years after that comment remarkably little in that assessment has changed. The thoughtful *Atlantic Monthly* ran an article by journalist James Fallows entitled, "The Japanese Are Different from You and Me" (Fallows 35).[4] Harvard professor of strategic studies, Samuel P. Huntington,

79

wrote an op-ed piece in the *New York Times* stating that Japan "is a society and civilization unique to itself" (Huntington E19). And the review in the *New York Times* of Michael Crichton's best-selling thriller about Japanese business investments in the United States noted, "The Japanese are different, say Mr. Crichton. They think differently and act differently. They move through the world with assumptions about human society very different from ours" (Nathan 23).

Differences can, of course, be charming. Opposites do often attract. But at least as frequently, differences can be threatening, particularly if the differences between individuals, groups, or nations are so extreme as to threaten the core assumptions of each.⁵ "Only Japan," as Samuel Huntington has written, "is non-Western and modern" (Huntington E19). Japanese culture and character are perceived to be so different from those of the United States that Americans (as represented in the press) are concerned that they cannot succeed on Japan's terms (or vice versa). Therefore, a "win" for Japan implies a larger critique of American society. And, conversely, American success suggests that the basic tenets of Japanese culture and society are at fault. "I will confess," admitted Fallows, "that [the] distinction—between different and wrong—sometimes eludes me in Japan" (Fallows "Japanese Are Different" 36).

On occasion, the United States press has been intellectually fascinated by Japanese uniqueness; at other times, however, Japan has elicited the worst of the press's chauvinism. This essay will suggest that attitudes have been more cyclical than progressive, related distinctly to the political climate. When Americans feel insecure, they lash out. In periods of anxiety, when Americans doubt their own abilities to succeed in the global arena, anti-Japanese prejudice emerges in mass-market periodicals. When Americans are concerned about the health of their own institutions, when they worry that their pre-eminent position in the world is slipping, when, most importantly, they fear that Japan is surpassing them, the Japanese become a target of attack in the press. "In moments of international stress," wrote Harvard East Asian expert Peter Stanley, "the imagery of Japan almost invariably turns toward conspiracy, insidiousness, deceit, fanaticism, regimentation, and a kind of discipline and loyalty that is somehow less than fully human. This tendency in the imagery reminds us that we are dealing here with something very unusual, a big power relationship that is also an interracial relationship where distrust and caricature come easily" (Stanley 21).

The "Infamous" Enemy

On December 7, 1941, Americans were caught by surprise; the effrontery and success of the Japanese attack in Hawaii inspired a reaction of fear and racism: the Oriental menace, the Chinese "Yellow Peril" was back. Mass-market news publications seized on explanations for the phenomenon of triumphant Japanese aggression and concocted grounds for why that aggression would not be ultimately victorious. The two-faced, "topsy-turvy mind of the Jap" provided the rationale; the character of the Japanese was at fault. "The people of this world [Japan] are timid and childish, arrogant and guileful. They profess a code of absolute purity and integrity and will descend to any depth of depravity to uphold it. They say 'yes' when 'no' is intended and understood. They operate modern machinery and think in terms of a feudal system of five centuries ago. Their social code protects them in every dilemma, but this very formalism often proves their undoing" ("Explaining" 23). Japan appeared as an inscrutable enemy, unknowable, incomprehensible, and therefore, unarguably, indubitably, wrong.

With the "infamous" attack on Pearl Harbor, the terms of confrontation were set. In the press, Americans expressed horror not only at the massive devastation of Pearl Harbor, but even more so at the nature of that attack. The fact that the attack was a surprise was not seen, however grudgingly, as sound military tactics but as a barbarous display symptomatic of the Japanese national character. The Japanese were vilified in the media and entertainment industry's outlets.⁶ Articles, photographs, movies, posters and cartoons built up the case that all "Japs" were alike; they exploited the ethnocentricity of Americans who "could not tell them apart."⁷ An article in *Life* appeared two weeks after Pearl Harbor instructing the United States on "How to Tell Japs from the Chinese." With photographs of Japanese and Chinese marked for telltale physiognomic features, the copy pointed out psychological distinctions as well. "An often sounder clue" than facial appearance, one caption mentioned, "is facial expression, shaped by cultural, not anthropological, factors. Chinese wear rational calm of tolerant realists. Japs, like General Tojo, show humorless intensity of ruthless mystics" ("How to Tell" 81). John Ford's film, *December 7th*, produced while the mass internment of Japanese-Americans was taking place, insinuated that all resident Japanese in Hawaii were spies for their "Fatherland." While Japanese in the United States may seem loyal and while they may say they are loyal, the film stated, still "there are a *lot of them*." ("An American Portrait" 11).

Publications across the United States were quick to caricature the Japanese enemy. As *Life* magazine, the most popular weekly of the time, said that month, "The whole cartoon aspect of the Jap changed overnight. Before that sudden Sunday the Jap was an oily little man, amiable but untrustworthy, more funny than dangerous" ("How to Tell" 81). After December 7, the Japanese were depicted by stereotype. The Japanese, noted eminent columnist Ernie Pyle, "were looked upon as something subhuman and repulsive; the way some people felt about cockroaches or mice" (Pyle 5). The Japanese were routinely referred to and pictured as literal or figurative animals, something less than human—at best credited with "child minds" (Pakenham "Breaking Point" 35). The Japanese were compared to rats and ants, and, most consistently, considered ape-like, "almost simian."[8] Liberty Bond Drive posters depicted the Japanese as leering monkeys raping and pillaging Western women and civilization.

To illustrate articles on the enemy, editors chose photographs that emphasized and reinforced the notion that the Japanese were a subhuman race. Photographs depicted myopic, buck-toothed, weak-chinned, childish Japanese soldiers to underscore their inferiority to the firm-jawed, broad-chested Americans ("At last" 30). Images of the Japanese's barbarous treatment of Allied soldiers in the Pacific gave credence to the commentary and illustrations depicting the Japanese as animalistic. Photographs from the Bataan death march and a captured snapshot of a Japanese officer in the act of beheading an Australian flyer received universal attention. Other pictures, when they surfaced, were widely printed. Two photographs illustrated a March 1942 story in *Newsweek*. One showed a Japanese soldier straddling the beheaded body of a Chinese man; in one hand the Japanese held a sword, in the other he grasped the severed head. The second image pictured a half dozen Japanese in a ravine bayoneting bound but live human beings. Scores of other soldiers looked on. The captions reminded, "Acts in China such as beheadings...and bayonet drill with live targets forewarned of Japanese cruelty" ("Hong Kong" 15).

These images which documented the cruelty of the Japanese helped to justify the American press's publishing of graphic evidence of savage Allied and American treatment of the Japanese. One of the most notorious images of the war appeared in *Life* and pictured a burned Japanese head speared on top of a wrecked Japanese tank in Guadalcanal ("Guadalcanal" 26-27). The photograph elicited considerable mail; some readers were sickened by the image, charging that "the cruelty of war is no excuse for sadism. You had better leave that kind of stuff to Hitler and Tojo" ("Letters," Feb. 22, 1943, 8). Others, especially servicemen, felt "dead Japs make good pictures regardless of how they died" ("Letters," March 15, 1943, 4).

Perhaps the most egregious series of images to be published during the war appeared in several periodicals, *Newsweek* and *Life* among them. The page-long photoseries, concisely titled in *Life* "A Jap Burns," depicted six frames of an Allied soldier torching a Japanese soldier to death with a flame-thrower. The effect was of slow-motion photography; in each frame, viewers witnessed the excruciating death of a man. They saw the grimace on his face and his hand reaching to hold his belly, to protect his genitals. "One Jap's fate is a nation's if the Berlin ultimatum goes unheeded by Tokyo," read *Newsweek*'s caption ("Now the Jap" 20).[9]

Throughout the Second World War, the American press called upon all the slurs in its command to condemn Japan and to disparage its abilities. Qualities that would have been praised in Allied nationalities were maligned in the Japanese. The dogged refusal of the Japanese to accept defeat in the last months of the war, despite the bombings, starvation, and work details, was not evidence of patriotism or determination but of "unhealthy mental processes, an ingrained fixation by which a race has hypnotized itself" (Pakenham "Trick Mind"). The politeness, cleverness, diligence, strong group life and obedience to authority which had been admired elements of the Japanese character in the past were recast into pejorative traits. Politeness hid deceit, cleverness gave proof of a criminal mind, diligence concealed zealotry, a strong group life cloaked a society rife with regimentation and obedience to authority metamorphosed into fanaticism.

Periodicals cited behavior patterns of the Japanese as having been "warped" into belligerence. "In his native habitat the Jap is roughly kind, hospitable, considerate, and generous. His humor is animal, and he loves laughter, gambling, and drinking. There is little of the instinctive hero about him.... But introduce the simple formula of unquestioned loyalty to the emperor and you have a grim fanatic...whose mind stops working.... Put the simple villager in a uniform, send him abroad in his emperor's service, and he begins by slapping the faces of white women and ends up a devil incarnate, boasting of what he did at Nanking, Hong Kong and Manila" (Pakenham "Trick Mind" 33; "Mentality" 48).

"Uncle" Sam and "Nephew" Japan

Then Japan lost the war. With that loss, there was a perceptible, and almost immediate transformation of American media stereotypes about the Japanese. The United States had been vindicated; the press could afford to restrain—if not revoke—its diatribe. Certain articles, especially those centering on World War II figures, continued to emphasize the innate and perverted violent nature of the Japanese. Magazines and newspapers, for instance, made much of the botched suicide of military leader Tojo, showing gory shots of him in bloody agony. Accompanying captions and articles discussed the centuries-old custom of ritual disemboweling, and sneered that Tojo was so incompetent a military leader that he could not even properly execute himself—even though he had chosen to use a gun rather than the traditional sword.

Other articles continued to insist on the alienness of the Japanese, describing adult sumo wrestlers as "monsters," for example, and picturing obese children as freaks ("Tax" 44, "We Still Have Face" 36). Pejorative attitudes towards the Japanese also lingered in the rhetoric of discussion. The Japanese "aped" U.S. habits; they worked in an "ant-heap" of activity; and they still did everything "backward" (The Mysterious West" 23; "Trouble in Japan" 38, 36). But General Douglas MacArthur's encouragement of fraternization between the U.S. occupying troops and the Japanese civilians gave inspiration to a spate of positive, if patronizing, stories about Japanese who were eager to learn American ways. Articles appeared picturing GIs showing Japanese women American cultural fashions; GIs took them to the movies and the parks on "dates," and taught the women how to jitterbug and slow dance. Photographs showed smiling "geisha girls" enjoying the company of their soldier-tutors; the images suggested that the Japanese were "apt pupils" willing to cast off their own traditional habits for the more lively American customs ("Date" 64-65).

Newsweek reported in 1947 that Americans found themselves to be "popular conquerors" ("Trouble" 37). Beginning with the mass-market publications' surrender issues, the press depicted "Japan bowed in defeat," and paying its "respects" to the Americans (Cover caption, *Newsweek*, Sept. 10, 1945, 21). "The Japanese, with characteristic practicality," *Newsweek* wrote, "admitted the better nation had won and that starting the war had been their responsibility. Instead they talked with the utmost seriousness of becoming the 49th state" ("New Door" 33). Medieval fealty to the emperor, which had resulted in fearsome deeds, *Time* reported, was being replaced by obedience to the American flag, with its consequent advantages. "If democracy was the faith of the men who had beaten Japan," wrote *Time* in 1949, " it was probably a good thing; [the little man] would make obeisance to it, too" ("Japan: New Door to Asia" 33).

The press emphasized the imperativeness of teaching the Japanese the right democratic values. In the 1956 movie *Teahouse of the August Moon*, Colonel Purdy, commander of the U.S. occupation forces on the Japanese island of Okinawa, described his role: "My job is to teach these natives the meaning of democracy. And they're going to learn democracy if I have to shoot every one of them" (qtd. in McDermott A1).[10] The American press fell into a condescending, if paternalistic attitude towards the Japanese; "Uncle" Sam would adopt Japan as its nephew. The notion of the Japanese as nephews—as literal children—took hold in the pages of American magazines and newspapers; the limited "child-minds" ascribed to the Japanese people during the war gave way to articles which focused on the children and youth of the nation. "Disciplined and pliable," wrote one magazine in a cover story, children "are Japan's—and our—hope for the future. While the older generation finds it hard to undo ancient customs, real Japanese understanding of democracy will come from children educated in its precepts from earliest infancy" (Cover caption, *Newsweek*, Aug. 4, 1947, 13). Photographs of the older, repressed generation still paying homage to the past regime contrasted with pictures of the bright faces of children in uninhibited play ("Life in Tokyo" 106, Noble 9). General MacArthur's quixotic, idealistic effort of remaking Japan into a democracy in America's image was confirmed in its appropriateness by the press depicting Japan as a country of young students.

The "Alliance of Free Partners"

With the end of Occupation and the lifting of censorship in 1952, Japan began once more to reassert itself. A wave of anti-Americanism swept the nation. Articles in American periodicals wondered whether "Japan [Is] Hoping for World War III" to redress its losses (Bess "Is Japan Hoping" 26). Grim-faced Japanese once again appeared in photographs spouting comments insulting to the United States; for example, one Japanese businessman, publisher Otoku Obama, was quoted as saying that "Japan's affairs after the war were guided by 'inferior' Americans"

(Bess "The Japs Have Us" 24). Surprisingly, perhaps, the uncovered resentment of the Japanese for the Americans did not translate into a mutual reaction. There was no need; Americans continued to be secure in their pre-eminent world role. Indeed, Americans felt free to admire distinctly Japanese institutions; for instance, articles in various periodicals began to emphasize the aesthetic beauty of things Japanese. American magazines discovered the charm of traditional Japan; rather than criticizing the Japanese for adhering to "backward" ways as they had done during Occupation, stories in the press expressed appreciation for the grace of the Japan that was fast disappearing under the pressure of the Western-promoted modernization. Even businessmen and politicians were pictured against classic, pastoral—and benign—Japanese settings (Cover, *Time*, March 14, 1955).

Many of the images of the Japanese in the popular press continued to emphasize notions introduced during Occupation. Articles on and pictures of children underlined the concept that Japan's future was in the hands of the young.[11] Other articles continued to dwell on the differentness of Japan, but what were emphasized were quaint rather than disturbing differences—popular were illustrations of the extreme contrasts to be found in the postwar era: geisha girls on motorcycles and peasants with refrigerators.[12] Japan, so these images suggested, was at once alien and Westernizing.

The end of the censorship also made possible the publishing in U.S. periodicals of Japanese photographs taken in the hours after the dropping of the bombs in Hiroshima and Nagasaki.[13] Never before had Americans seen pictures of Japanese civilians caught in the backwash of the war. Never before had the American public seen so many, and such graphic photographs of Hiroshima victims and disabled war veterans.[14] Gritty, grainy images that depicted burned and bandaged children, dying families, mutilated soldiers, and devastated urban landscapes brought home to Americans the misery that they themselves had inflicted. In the Cold War years immediately following the Soviet detonation of an atomic bomb, Americans were fearful of a global atomic holocaust. In the 1950s, photographs from Hiroshima and Nagasaki acted as a warning to the world. Why did *Life* magazine publish photographs of "how an atomic bombing appears to people who experience it"? *Life* editors answered, "The motive for the first U.S. publication of the Hiroshima and Nagasaki collection is its terrible and vital pertinence to the age in which we live" ("Dead Men" 17). As related by the press,

Americans, overwhelmed by their own fear of the bomb, found new compassion for the Japanese.

Sympathetic portraits of the Japanese continued to appear in the press into the 1960s. Japan, which despite the fears of the 1950s had not turned communist—and indeed had become the bastion of anti-communism in Asia—was beginning to look very good to American commentators. Both countries found that they had a mutual interest in regional security. The "protective—and much resented—uncle-nephew relationship which had lingered from the U.S. occupation days" grew into an "alliance of free partners" ("How Different" 26). The gradual shift transforming Japan from being a U.S.-occupied country to being a U.S. "outpost" country—which had begun in the fifties with the end of Occupation and the Korean War—was complete. American troops in Japan could keep an eye on China and the Soviet Union, and their presence in Japan meant that the Japanese felt little pressure to funnel money towards their own defense.

Enter the "Colossus of the Orient"

Able to put all its capital into industry, by the 1960s Japan had become Asia's number one industrial power, its output two and a half times its prewar level—a well-noticed "miracle" of recovery. The United States had become Japan's biggest customer and Japan had become a significant consumer of American goods. Numerous business-related articles appeared in the American press applauding the Japanese transformation into the "Colossus of the Orient." Prominent business leaders as well as corporations such as Hitachi, Sony, and Mitsubishi became the focus of glowing stories lauding their achievements. Stories often emphasized Japanese companies' cradle-to-grave investment in and involvement with their employees. A feature on the manufacturer Hitachi, for example, mentioned that Hitachi employees "shaved with Hitachi razor blades, lived in Hitachi housing, read by Hitachi lamps, and when they died Hitachi buried them" (Smith 56A). The nineteenth-century paternalism of American capitalists such as Pullman, lamented by American conservatives, found outlet in sixties-era Japan. Explicit comparisons discovered the business talents of heroic Americans to be expressed by the Japanese; an article on Japanese entrepreneur Matsushita, for instance, titled him "Pioneer with a Touch of Ford and Alger" ("Pioneer" 10).

For all the admiration expressed in American periodicals for the successes of the Japanese economy, there remained a caveat to the Japanese-American "alliance of free partners." The American press understood that partnership to be an unequal one, made up of a senior and a junior member, not of two peers.[15] The United States, in the estimation of the press, remained on top. Such a senior-junior relationship suited Americans in two respects: first, the "partnership" meant that American post-war investment in Japan had been successful; and second, the teacher-student rapport which still existed served to stroke American egos about the continued superiority of the American way of life. Articles rarely failed to juxtapose images of Japanese Westernization with symbols of Japanese traditions: photographs of a kimono-clad Japanese girl car-hopping beer, of a geisha bowling, and of a Shinto priest exorcising a Tokyo gas station were typical ("Japan Today" 51; "Special Issue" cover; Steinberg 81). Such images suggested not only the quaintness of Japanese society, but implied an inherent inferiority; the successes of Japan were evident in these pictures, but the Japanese refusal to abandon their customs was interpreted in the American press as meaning that the Japanese would never progress to the point of challenging U.S. superiority.

Such complacency freed the press to admire rather than condemn the still striking cultural and social distinctiveness of the Japanese. The serenity of traditional Japan attracted the interest of the press; articles and advertisements geared towards men were especially drawn to the calmness and submissiveness of the geisha (Joseph 57, Brake 12) Feature stories and commercial advertisements claimed that busy executives could find relief from the stresses of their day with "beautifully coifed hostesses who hover around like handmaidens" ("Japan's Dazzle" 62-3, JAL advertisement 114-115). Less innocent "handmaidens" were also an attraction for the businessman on expense account; one article claimed that "the cabaret girls [are] much prettier than geishas...now strip shows stir more interest than geisha parties" (Penn 97). Other articles appeared, in news, travel, fashion, and architectural magazines, celebrating more restrained Japanese ideals of beauty and order. "Japan's aesthetics have produced depths of beauty of which we can be very jealous," wrote *House Beautiful* magazine. "Their understanding of great lasting beauty—in objects, in rooms, in color schemes—surpasses that of any other culture." For the first time it could be suggested that Americans could learn from the Japanese, although articles were careful to note that understanding "the attitudes and values that produced such sensitivity and awareness...can help us find our own American

way to the same rewarding ends" ("Why an Issue" 53,55).

Japan might well have been the first genuinely modernized nation in Asia, but it had become clear that it had managed to retain its unique core of traditional ideas, ethics, customs and institutions. Photographs of strange customs and rites, of exotic Kabuki actors and adult—and children—sumo wrestlers remained popular editorial gimmicks that never allowed Americans to forget the "Otherness" of Japan (Brake 21, 36-7; Joseph 57; "Traditional Look" 79). "In short," said *Life* magazine, "there are still question marks about the Japanese character, but they are not the old clichés about the mysterious East" ("How Different" 26). Still confident in the United States's dominance in the world, the American press continued to view the Japanese benevolently, as talented students who had applied their lessons on U.S. capitalism and democracy to their own singular situation. Japan still appeared in periodicals as a "baffling" and "topsy-turvy" land, but its "volatile moods" inspired "fascination," not fear or repugnance ("A Word with Our Readers" 53). The "delightfully mixed-up country—where many things seem to operate in reverse," *Reader's Digest* could jokingly observe, can cause Americans to wonder "which side is up after all?" (Nelson 203).[16]

The End of the Honeymoon

By the mid-to-late sixties that question had become a serious query. The quagmire of Vietnam and the unrest in the streets at home caused Americans and the press to reevaluate their attitudes towards Japan. The Japanese had become restive "in their nation's role of junior partner and 'Asian bastion' for the U.S." (Mydans and Mydans 101). Leaping into the status of the "free world's" number two producer, Japan had begun to talk back to the United States. By 1968 American exports to Japan totaled $3 billion. But Japanese exports to the United States totaled $4 billion. That billion-dollar gap drove the first substantial wedge into this "era of good feelings."

By Richard Nixon's presidency, the press could report that the Japanese had once again become a threat to Americans. "Made in Japan" had come to symbolize a mark of excellence, no longer a brand denoting inferior quality. Japan was challenging the United States not only in Asia, but in markets in the United States. With the creation of Japan as a new kind of world power—all the more remarkable for its being a power without any armed forces to speak of, without colonies or vast land resources or significant raw-material wealth—the happy enthusiasm for things

Japanese dissipated. The American press began to speak of the Japanese in terms reminiscent of thirty years previously. The Japanese were not the "apes" of World War II days, but they had become "economic animals [who] performed brilliantly" (Gibney 28).[17]

Interestingly, despite the constitutional prohibition against offensive rearming, American periodicals also started to refer once again to the Japanese as a warrior race. Reference to the Shoguns of the past became a new theme in writings about and illustrations of the Japanese. There had always been an undercurrent of articles in the sixties that spoke about "Troubled Japan" and claimed that "in the mass, [the Japanese] can be passionately excitable" (Ehrlich 21, 24-5). And in times of political disturbance, Americans had been reminded, for example, of the "pattern of assassination" in Japanese history—as had been the case in 1960 when the chair of Japan's Socialist Party, Inejiro Asanuma, was publicly stabbed to death ("Murder in Public" 24-5). But, beginning with the Nixon administration, such references became more common. Magazines gleefully listed aberrant violence within Japan as evidence not only of the hidden rage of the Japanese people, but of fatal flaws within Japanese society (Krisher 34-5).

At best, the American press was ambivalent about Japan's increasing power and prestige in the world. The Japanese had grown "up politically as well as economically, and [were now] ready to play a more independent role in the world" (Shaplen 105). But indicative of American reactions to Japan's greater autonomy were the so-called "Nixon shocks" to the Japanese: Richard Nixon's non-negotiated quota on Japanese textiles, his temporary surcharge on imports, his short-lived embargo on the export of soybeans (a mainstay of the Japanese diet), his sudden revaluation of the dollar in 1971, and his détente with China, initiated without a word to the Japanese allies. President Nixon's shocks were an attempt to publicly demonstrate to the world the political and economic superiority of the United States over Japan (and, concomitantly, the rest of the world). America's embarrassing loss of face by the military debacle in Southeast Asia in this view was compensated for by the effective exercise of diplomatic and economic muscle elsewhere.

An adversarial image of Japan reemerged in American periodicals that managed to be at once both hostile and patronizing. Means were found to suggest that Japan was not invincible. Japan's surrender to the United States in World War II received considerable attention in the press; 1970 was the twenty-fifth anniversary of the end of the war. Even articles that

castigated the United States for dropping the two atomic bombs, for example, still reminded that it was the United States which was the mightier nation ("25 Years Ago" 30). Publications also focused on internal traumas within Japan, making the point that Japan, as well, had its clashes between generations, its turmoil in the street and its pollution of the environment. Photographers and reporters documented, for example, the mercury poisoning of a Japanese fishing village by a Chisso factory. Stirring images of men, women and children ravaged by the pollution amply conveyed the message that the Japanese economic "miracle" had been a nightmare to some (Smith 80-1).

The long honeymoon was over. Mutual suspicion increased, although the special relationship, built on the twin pillars of trade and military security, continued, albeit shaken. American treatment of Japan improved briefly during the presidency of Gerald Ford, who was, remarkably, the first U.S. president to visit Japan. The worldwide recession eased friction for a time by reducing for a while the embarrassingly large trade surpluses that Japan was running up with the U.S. But as the seventies continued, the double oil shocks and Japan's successful surmounting of them caused the United States press to view Japan with an increasingly jaundiced eye. Japan had realized, in the words of Harvard professor and U.S. Ambassador to Japan Edwin O. Reischauer, "that they were a big, strong country that didn't have to be docile."

Some in the United States believed that Japan did not sufficiently acknowledge its heavy reliance on its Western ally. Treasury Secretary John Connally, an ardent nationalist, made numerous nasty comments: "Don't they remember who won the war?" As Japan surged to dominance in certain industries, the problem had become how "to integrate the new Japan into the world economy, in such a way that the 'fragile blossom,' as [National Security Advisor Zbigniew] Brzezinski called it, did not turn into Tokyo Rose" (qtd. in Cumings 181). By the end of the decade, as Japan's trade surplus rose while the dollar plummeted in value, Japan ranked with OPEC as the United States' most severe external economic threat (Stanley 18).

The "Economic Pearl Harbor"

By the beginning of the 1980s, prominent analysts in the press charged that the cultural and economic characters of the United States and Japan were "structured so differently that in important respects they no longer 'fit'" (18). Both countries had changed. Although reference continued to be made to the older brother-younger brother relationship between the two countries, such talk seemed strained. Even President Reagan, in his jocular fashion, acknowledged that a fundamental alteration in the relationship had occurred. After meeting with Prime Minster Zenko Suzuki early in his terms in office, Reagan observed that both he and Suzuki were 70 years old—with Suzuki being 26 days older. Noted Reagan, "We have decided that hereafter our relationship would be one in which *he* would be the older brother"—a comment taken as significant by observers in the press ("Pomp with Point" 28).

Few were as calm as Reagan about the change in status between the two nations. Rhetoric at the time made frequent, explicit and conscious reference to the previous world conflict; the *New Republic*, for instance, claimed that if the trade imbalance continued, "political pressure in the United States would lead to increased protectionism of a sort that could ignite a global trade war" (Stanley 18). A Japanese official was quoted as saying that "the sentiment in the U.S. is like that before the outbreak of war" ("Getting a Foot" 74). And U.S. experts quoted in *U.S. News & World Report* called Japan's industrial challenge "an economic Pearl Harbor" ("Samuri Spirit" 48). Conservative commentators argued that the Japanese regarded trade as a continuation of war by other means, and even liberals, such as Theodore White in the *New York Times Magazine*, warned that the Japanese were engaged in "dismantling American industry; their success at which will determine which country is the final winner of World War II" (White 18-23). By 1985 and the second Reagan administration, a top American official could snap, "The next time we send a trade negotiator to Tokyo, he may be sitting in the nose of a B-52" (Gergen 78).

Speeches emanating from Congress and the Reagan White House joined with cover stories in mass-market magazines and newspapers in "bashing" the Japanese. Articles and press releases talked about skirmishes and battles, dangerous confrontations, prize fights and war. Cartoons and illustrations showed a lean Uncle Sam squaring off against an immense Japanese sumo wrestler. Full-page photographs in a 1987 *Time* cover story pitted President Ronald Reagan and Japanese Prime Minister Yasuhiro Nakasone nose-to-nose: an angry, frustrated Reagan glared fiercely across the page at his antagonist; a calmer Nakasone gazed back ("Trade Face-Off" 28-29). Comparisons to Japanese wartime conquests were irresistible. One correspondent sourly noted that "the Japanese, without an army, have accomplished exactly what they set out to do during the Second World War—develop a Co-Prosperity

Sphere" (Fallows "Letter" 16). Another even more bitterly remarked that "in fact, [the new order] is much greater than the Greater East Asia Co-Prosperity Sphere that Japan strove so hard…to create during the Pacific War" (Hatcher 13).

Opinion polls in the eighties showed that the bulk of Americans held Japan responsible for their economic woes. Americans believed that a sizable proportion of Japan's prosperity was coming out of the United States' hide; they viewed Japan as greedy and unfair, conspiring against the United States (Gibney 7).[18] Periodicals described the U.S.'s major Pacific ally as "'Japan, Inc.' because of the belief that its industrial effort is a single piece of seamless fabric—companies interwoven with government" (Hatcher 14).[19] As measured by the sheer numbers of articles about Japan's industrial might, resentment of Japan's success mushroomed into an obsession in the press and in popular culture; even economists began to speak about the "post-American era." Conferences were called to discuss the historic shift of power (Fallows "Asian Journal" 20-21). And M.I.T. economist Lester Thurow warned that "we are all going to wind up working for the Japanese" (qtd. in "Hour of Power" 15).

A tinge of hysteria colored the press's reactions. American politicians smashed Japanese radios with sledgehammers; a photograph of congressmen pulverizing Toshibas made newspapers around the globe.[20] Publications called Japan "a bully—stomping into foreign markets" and advocated a "get tough" policy ("Trade War Ahead" 22). Florid language exacerbated the debate: a *Time* cover story began with the sentence, "Like a dazed and bleeding prizefighter trying to call time out in the middle of a round, America's automakers have been pleading for months for relief from the pummeling they have been taking from Japan" ("How Japan Does It" 54). Other magazines argued that the U.S. Congress should "kick the door in" ("Trade War Ahead" 22).

Japan's success bred enmity; the American press's characterization of Japan perpetuated a post-World War II order built on treating Japan as an enemy. "Our imagery," wrote Robert Samuelson in *Newsweek*, "is increasingly savage. The vision of refighting World War II is mindless jingoism." Instead of being pleased and flattered that Japan under the U.S.'s post-war tutelage had become such a brilliant success, Americans resented the idea of Japan's global achievements. As the columnist continued, "Americans cannot live with the idea that a nation we defeated in war now challenges us economically" (Samuelson 56). Daniel Burstein's economic study *Yen!*, for example, published in 1988, presented a worst-case scenario based on Japan's global economic power. It is possible, he wrote, that by 2004 Japan will be in a position to force the United States into financial receivership. He quoted a prominent Japanese securities broker as suggesting that when the time comes for Japan to bail out the United States, it should demand and be given the state of California, which would be turned into a joint U.S.-Japanese economic community. Daniel Burstein's study, together with such fiction-alized works as Michael Crichton's *Rising Sun*, encouraged simple-minded attitudes about the Japanese and reinforced the idea that the Japanese could be safely characterized as a "shifty, mendacious lot" (qtd. in Canby H1).

By 1992, with the trade gap at $49 billion, the American mood against Japan as expressed in the press was intolerant. "We will not be able to sustain our political partnership" if Japan's trade surplus continues to grow, cautioned Secretary of State James Baker (Woodruff B5). In a report entitled *American Public Opinion and U.S. Foreign Policy 1991*, the American public and American leaders were asked to evaluate threats to U.S. vital interests. Over 60% of both the public and American leaders targeted the "economic power of Japan" as the most critical threat to the United States. By substantial margins, more Americans said they feared Japanese economic power than they feared any other threat—including that of other nations' military power (Reilly 87).[21] The "Yellow Peril" was still perceived to be an active menace to the American way of life. As the *Washington Post* put it, "The Cold War and the Persian Gulf War may be over, but the Great Rice War is heating up" (Blustein A1).

"Japan-Bashing" Revisited

The American trans-Pacific namecalling would all be relegated to the pages of history books and to periodic curiosity on the occasions of military anniversaries, if it were not for the fact that much of the imagery and rhetoric of 1941 made a reappearance 40 and 50 years after that date. "Not since Pearl Harbor," wrote *New York Times* critic Vincent Canby in 1992, "has Japan-bashing been such big and popular business. It's easy to understand why. The Japanese are nouveau riche and we are their nouveau poor. They produce. We consume. We scrape together our last pennies to acquire a shiny new Acura we don't desperately need. We jog with Sony Walkmans that make our ears sweat. We watch Japanese-manufactured videocassettes on Japanese VCR's

through Japanese television sets. The purchase of Rockefeller Center was the last straw: who can take the Music Hall's all-American Easter pageant seriously, now that the Rockette-nuns are performing their sacred rites on what is, in effect, Japanese turf?" (H1)[22] Yet as Harvard economist (now Labor Secretary) Robert Reich mentioned in the *New York Times*, also in 1992, "Mitsubishi's purchase of a substantial interest in Rockefeller Center, Sony's purchase of Columbia Pictures and Nintendo's recent flirtation with the Seattle Mariners make the headlines, but in almost every controversial case, it has been the American owners who have initiated the deal. The British still own more of the United States than the Japanese do" (Reich 24).

As the last 50 years have shown, historically, when the American economy is in trouble, the realistic threat from Japan to American interests is exaggerated in stereotypes. "A considerable number of Americans still harbor latent or overt prejudice against the Japanese as a people," observed Asian expert and journalist Robert Christopher. "When the nations of Western Europe run a trade surplus with the United States, as they did last year, eminent Americans do not reflexively recall that it was Marshall Plan aid that put Europe on its feet and thereby tar all Europeans with ingratitude. And when Common Market countries use subsidies or other sly devices to help their farmers or manufacturers to outcompete ours, no one invokes memories of Nazi Germany, Fascist Italy or Vichy France" (Christopher 24).[23] Yet when Americans believe themselves to be in competition with the Japanese, the image of Pearl Harbor is evoked.[24] "Memories of the attack can be detected in the metaphors with which the Japanese challenge is described," noted Reich. He gave examples drawn from many of the late 1980s and early 1990s books on Japan. "Japan is 'targeting' our key industries (Holstein); it is 'raiding' our technologies (Dietrich); we are 'outgunned...in the battle for control of world financial resources' (Burstein); Japan is mounting a 'planned attack' on the United States through a 'new kind of invasion' (Crichton)" (Reich 24).

Over the last 50 years, Japan has served as a means for the American press to define the United States, its interests and its role in the world. Images of Japan have functioned in much the same way as those of the former Soviet Union: they have served to unify many disparate groups within the United States against a single foreign foe. They have served to distract public attention from domestic problems. Some critics of American society have observed that the real threat in the United States is an America that no longer coheres—an America wracked by class and racial divisions, by immigration, by bilingualism, by differences in religious and civic values, even by "multiculturalism." James Fallows urged Americans in his 1989 work about Japan, *More Like Us*, to "revive the idea that America is one coherent society, with bonds that are stronger than its internal differences. We understood this instinctively during World War II, but not often enough since then" (qtd. in Reich 25). The late 1980s-early 1990s Japan-bashing told more about the state of America than the country of Japan. It is no coincidence that the resurgence of images of Japan-as-enemy occurred at the close of the Cold War and the demise of the Soviet Union.

Since 1941, the quest for an American global culture and identity has been a critical concomitant of U.S. foreign policy. Taking its force from the collective expectations of Americans, the quest for global cultural dominance has been, at bottom, a search for confirmation of the original validity of American choices.[25] As depicted in the American press, relations with few other countries have illustrated so well the ups and downs of American interests and expectations. Reference to a chronology of events for the last half century tells much of the tale; when times were good, when Americans felt secure in their world, attitudes about the Japanese expressed in the press were magnanimous in their acceptance of Japanese social and cultural different-ness. When times were bad, the American press lashed out defensively. To investigate images of Japan in the American press is to chart the rise and fall not only of Japanese-American relations, but of America's sense of global well-being.

Notes

[1]For the purposes of this study, I looked at the printed media from 1941 to 1992. I used a broad base of magazines—those listed in *The Reader's Guide to Periodical Literature*. It should be noted, however, that because of the subject matter, more articles on Japan were found in the newsmagazines than in other varieties of mass-market, general-interest magazines. I also looked at major newspaper coverage of Japan, but my investigation of newspapers' treatment of Japan was less systematic than my analysis of magazines' coverage. Essentially, I looked at newspapers in major markets when I was cued by events that were likely to be articles in the press.

[2]For early perspectives on American attitudes towards the Japanese, see: Lafcadio Hearn, *Glimpses of Unfamiliar Japan* (1894) and Ruth Benedict, *The Chrysanthemum and the Sword* (1946).

[3]Compared to other nationalities, Americans as a people are not particularly xenophobic. Many American scholars, such as Ezra Vogel and Edwin O. Reischauer, and some notable American politicians, such as Mike Mansfield, have tried to be extraordinarily sensitive in their understanding and interpretation of Japan. Of course, even these observers have had personal reactions to Japan; they have employed their American value system as the model against which Japan has been judged. One of the typical judgments made by American scholars and journalists about Japan is that that society is more xenophobic than that of the United States. Many of the criticisms I make in this paper about American stereotyping of the Japanese can be—and have been—made about Japanese stereotyping. Masao Miyoshi, professor of Japanese, English and comparative literature at University of California, San Diego, in his book *Off Center: Power and Culture Relations Between Japan and the United States* (1991), uses literature, film and cultural criticism to examine the blindness both nations show towards each other. (John Dower, in his work on World War II, *War Without Mercy*, 1986, does the same.) Miyoshi argues that in Japan there is little appreciation of "the Other"; there is neither an openness to cultures outside its borders, nor an under-standing of its own strangeness to much of the rest of the world, especially the West.

T.R. Reid, the *Washington Post*'s bureau chief in Tokyo has noted the same tendency—albeit in stronger terms: "It must be said the Japanese are at least as likely to wallow in cliches about America. Judging from the Japanese TV stereotype, every American is either homeless, unemployed, a drug addict, an AIDS victim or recently acquitted on charges of decapitating his gun-wielding, 12-year-old homosexual lover" (Reid 68).

The rhetoric is not all one-sided, witness the brouhaha in the United States after a Japanese politician accused American workers of being lazy and stupid. Independent reporter Hedrick Smith, interviewed in 1991 on television's *Washington Week in Review*, quoted one Sony official saying to American industrialists: "You need an economic Pearl Harbor to wake you up," and another official as saying: "You're too complacent, lazy. We have to look hard for anything we want to import."

[4]Fallows, one of a group of "revisionist" thinkers on the U.S.-Japan relationship, including Pat Choate, Chalmers Johnson and Clyde Prestowitz, argues that fundamental differences in the way the U.S. and Japanese societies frame economic and historical issues make all the difference in the way each side views national

competitiveness. As he wrote in his new work, *Looking at the Sun: The Rise of the New East Asian Economic and Political System*, (1994), "Western societies, especially American, have been using the wrong mental tools to classify, shape and understand the information they receive about Asia" (qtd. in Cramer B19).

An earlier best-seller, *Japan as Number 1: Lessons for America* by Harvard professor Ezra Vogel, argued similarly that the United States' most critical challenge in the 1980s would be internal—the suppression of American hubris. Japan-bashing reflected, in his perspective, both Americans' refusal to confront the inadequacies of their own performance and their reluctance to retool their institutions to compete effectively in the world and Asian markets.

⁵Over the past 50 years, both in times of stress and in times of calm, American officials and the press have argued that the unique culture of Japan drives its economic and political system. To give several examples: the "peculiar Japanese mentality has shaped the Pacific war as much as any purely military or geographic factor," noted *Newsweek* during World War II (Pakenham "Mentality" 48). "Behind [the] power realities, what may matter most to the U.S.," said a *Life* editorial in 1960, "is the character of the Japanese people and nation" (How Different 26). "The Japanese are vastly different from all other peoples in Asia and...the things that make them unique are those that have enabled them to survive and prosper so spectacularly," wrote a commentator in the *New Yorker* in 1974 (Shaplen 105). And in 1994, James Fallows wrote that Japanese economic interests believe that the "way to be strong, to give orders, to have independence and control, is to keep in mind the difference between 'us' and 'them'" (qtd. in Cramer B19). Striking a similar note are those who have recently contended that Japanese economic policy is fundamentally distinct; a Republican congressman said in 1990: "Japanese style and customs [appear] to be 'out of sync' with the U.S./European system of thinking concerning trade policies" (Shumway 5). And *New York Times* staff writer David Sanger observed of U.S.-Japanese economic relations: "Indeed, for two countries as obsessed with each other as these, it is remarkable how out of sync they seem to be" (Sanger E5).

⁶For a comprehensive discussion of the racist nature of the war against the Japanese, see John Dower, *War Without Mercy: Race and Power in the Pacific War* (1986).

⁷American images and representations of the Japanese have typically been tied to those of Japanese-Americans—and at no time so much as during the war years. There have been occasions, however, notably recently, when rising U.S. hostility towards Japan has not translated into equivalent hostility toward Japanese-Americans. In the late 1980s and 1990s, for example, Japanese-Americans have

been prospering without serious impediments in Hawaii and on the mainland and intermarriage rates between Japanese-Americans and Anglo-Americans have soared. The media's treatment of this recent prospering of Japanese-Americans has been generally positive, while, as this paper shows, the media's recent view of Japan has been generally negative.

⁸See, for example: Pakenham, "Breaking Point" 35; "Creaking Economy" 38; "Japan: The Mysterious West" 23; and "Explaining Jones-san" 23.

⁹The article in *Life* appeared the following week: "A Jap Burns" 34.

¹⁰The Purdy quote makes one wonder if it was the original inspiration for the infamous quotation from the Vietnam War: "We had to destroy the village to save it."

¹¹See, for example, "Japan: Singer of Hymns at the Helm" 30; and "Japan: We Still Have Face" 36.

¹²See, for example, "Japan: The Happy Farmers" 31.

¹³Perhaps the best-known contemporary *written* media portrayal of the dropping of the bomb was the *New Yorker*'s giving over of an entire issue to John Hersey's work *Hiroshima*, later published as a book.

¹⁴See, for example, "Japan: Land of the Reluctant Sparrows" 36, and "When the Atom Bomb Struck" 19-25.

¹⁵See, for example, Mydans, "What Manner " 101.

¹⁶The notion of Japan as being a sort of Alice-in-Wonderland country where "many things seem to operate in reverse" or "backwards" has been a consistent theme and stereotype over the past 50 years, witness President Bill Clinton's leaked comment to Russia's President, Boris Yeltsin, in 1993, that "when the Japanese say yes to us, they often mean no" (Sanger E5).

¹⁷Gibney appropriated the phrase "economic animals" from a Japanese television program to which he referred in his article. On the program, the Japanese audience was asked: "Are we only greedy economic animals, who live only to consume?...Or can this country find some better, wider channels for its energies?"

¹⁸See also: Reilly 87.

¹⁹Scholar James Abegglen, a consultant and veteran Japan hand, was responsible for originally coining the phrase, "Japan Inc."

²⁰The photograph of Rep. Helen Delich Bentley (R-Md) and several other lawmakers taking sledgehammers to a Toshiba boom box on the Capitol steps in Washington became such a cause celebre that every new Toshiba Corp. recruit has to sit through a half-hour videotape featuring the footage. The company's 70,000 current Japanese employees have already seen the half-hour tape ("Corporate 'Boot Camps'" C2).

²¹Or as James Fallows noted, "What most Americans fear about Japan is precisely that it works so well" (Fallows, "The Japanese Are Different" 35, 36).

[22]It should be noted that the Japanese owners of Rockefeller Center put the center into bankruptcy.

[23]This sentiment has been expressed elsewhere. Jack R. Carreiro, a vice president of the Hawaii Vistors Bureau, noted shortly before the 50th anniversary of Pearl Harbor: "No one is talking about what Hitler or Mussolini did. We don't want to relive the war. We must look forward, not backward" (qtd. in Reinhold A22).

[24]There was a tide of books at the end of the 1980s and beginning of the 1990s demonizing Japan, suggesting a connection between the old military war and the new economic warfare. Several of the books even suggested that economic hostility between Japan and the United States would turn inevitably into a war of guns and bombs. Some of the most prominent of these works are: *Agents of Influence* (1990) by Pat Choate, *The Enigma of Japanese Power* (1989) by Karel van Wolferen, *In the Shadow of the Rising Sun* (1991) by William S. Dietrich, *Japanese Power Game* (1990) by William J. Holstein, *Trading Places* (1988) by Clyde V. Prestowitz, Jr., *Unequal Equities* (1991) by Robert Zielinski and Nigel Holloway, and *Yen! Japan's New Financial Empire and Its Threat to America* (1988) by Daniel Burstein.

[25]See, for example, Vlahos.

Works Cited

An American Portrait, "The Pearl Harbor Project." manuscript funding proposal for The National Endowment for the Humanities, 1988.

"At last Some Japs Are Giving Up, But Bloody War Still Lies Ahead." *Newsweek* 2 July 1945: 30.

Bess, Demaree. "Is Japan Hoping for World War III?" *Saturday Evening Post* 26 July 1952: 26.

___. "The Japs Have Us on the Griddle Now." *Saturday Evening Post* 4 April 1953: 24.

Blustein, Paul. "At Tokyo Fair, U.S. Booth Sparks Rift Over Rice." *Washington Post* 16 March 1991: A1.

Brake, Brian. "Restless Excitement and a Wealth of Paradoxes Set the Mood of Modern Japan." *Life* 11 Sept. 1964: 21, 36-37.

Canby, Vincent. "Japan Unfolds Through Many Images." *New York Times* 14 June 1992: H1.

Christopher, Robert. "Let's Give Pearl Harbor a Rest." *Newsweek* 14 Oct. 1985: 24.

"Corporate 'Boot Camps' Not What They Used to Be." *Seattle Times/Seattle Post-Intelligencer* 31 May 1992: C2.

Cover. *Time* 14 March 1955.

Cover caption. *Newsweek* 10 Sept. 1945: 21.

___. *Newsweek* 4 Aug. 1947: 13.

Cramer, Bernice. "The Business of Where, Why East Beats West." (review of *Looking at the Sun: The Rise of the New East Asian Economic and Political System* by James Fallows) *Boston Globe* 1 May 1994: B19.

"Creaking Economy." *Newsweek* 23 June 1947: 38.

Cumings, Bruce. "The Conjurings of Japan." *Nation* 13 Feb. 1982: 181.

"Date with a Geisha." *Newsweek* 22 Oct. 1945: 64-65.

"Dead Men Will Have Died in Vain If..." *Life* 29 Sept. 1952: 17.

Dower, John. *War Without Mercy: Race & Power in the Pacific War.* New York: Pantheon, 1986.

Dreyfuss, Joel. "They Owe It All to Themselves." (review of William Chapman's *Inventing Japan: The Making of a Postwar Civilization*) *New York Times Book Review* 12 Jan. 1992: 8.

Ehrlich, Henry. "Troubled Japan." *Life* 10 Aug. 1965: 21, 24-25.

"Explaining Jones-san." *Newsweek* 3 Sept. 1945: 23.

Fallows, James. "Asian Journal." *Atlantic Monthly* March 1988: 20-21.

___. "The Japanese Are Different from You and Me." *The Atlantic Monthly* Sept. 1986: 31.

___. "Letter from Tokyo." *Atlantic Monthly* Aug. 1986: 16.

Fox-Genovese, Elizabeth. "Between Individualism and Fragmentation: American Culture and the New Literary Studies of Race and Gender," *American Quarterly* 42.1 (1990): 25.

Gergen, David. "Japan: The New OPEC?" *US News & World Report* 1 April 1985: 78.

"Getting a Foot in Japan's Door." *Newsweek* 25 March 1985: 74.

Gibney, Frank. *Japan: The Fragile Superpower,* 2nd ed. New York: Norton, 1985.

___. "New Face of World Power." *Look* 21 Oct. 1969: 28.

"Guadalcanal: Grassy Knoll Battle." *Life* 1 Feb. 1943: 26-27.

Hatcher, Peter. "Confronting the Problem." *World Press Review* Aug. 1987: 13.

"Hong Kong Blood Bath." *Newsweek* 23 March 1942: 15.

"Hour of Power?" *Newsweek* 27 Feb. 1989: 15.

"How Different Is Japan?" *Life* 1 Feb. 1960: 26.

"How Japan Does It." *Time* 30 March 1981: 54.

"How to Tell Japs from the Chinese." *Life* 22 Dec. 1941: 81.

Huntington, Samuel P. "The Coming Clash of Civilizations—or, the West Against the Rest." *New York Times* 6 June 1993: E19.

"Interview with Ambassador Mike Mansfield: US-Japan: 'Most Important Relationship in the World,'" *US News and World Report* 27 Oct. 1980: 44.

Iyer, Pico. "What Oscar Wilde Knew About Japan." *Time* 25 May 1992: 76.

JAL advertisement, *Holiday* Oct. 1961: 114-15.

"A Jap Burns." *Life* 13 Aug. 1945: 34.

"Japan: The Happy Farmers." *Time* 6 Oct. 1949: 31.

"Japan: Land of the Reluctant Sparrows." *Time* 14 March 1955: 36.

"Japan: The Mysterious West." *Time* 4 Aug. 1947: 23.

"Japan: New Door to Asia." *Time* 9 May 1949: 33.

"Japan: Singer of Hymns at the Helm." *Newsweek* 20 Dec. 1954: 30.

"Japan: The Traditional Look." *Holiday* Oct. 1961: 79.

"Japan: We Still Have Face." *Newsweek* 18 Dec. 1950: 36.

"Japan Today—The Paradox." *Newsweek* 20 June 1960: 51.

"Japan's Dazzle After Dark." *Life* 23 Feb. 1962: 62-63.

Joseph, Richard. "Go Pacific and Rive the Rife of Liley." *Esquire.* Aug. 1962: 57.

Krisher, Bernard. "Who Are the Japanese?" *Newsweek* 17 July 1972: 34-35.

"Letters to the Editors." *Life* 22 Feb. 1943: 8.

___. *Life* 15 March 1943: 4.

"Life in Tokyo." *Life* 3 Dec. 1945: 106.

McDermott, Terry. "U.S. Went Back to Arm-Twisting with Japanese." *Seattle Times/Seattle Post Intelligencer* 12 Jan. 1992: A1.

"Murder in Public by a Berserk Boy." *Life* 24 Oct. 1960: 24-25.

Mydans, Carl and Shelly Mydans. "What Manner of Men Are These Japanese?" *Fortune* 1 Aug 1969: 101.

Nathan, Robert. "Is Japan Really Out to Get Us?" (review of Michael Crichton's novel, *Rising Sun*) *New York Times Book Review* 9 Feb. 1992: 23.

Nelson, George. "Upside Down in Japan." *Reader's Digest* April 1960: 203.

Noble, Harold. "We're Teaching the Children to Lead Japan." *Saturday Evening Post* 27 July 1946: 9.

"Now the Jap Knows How to Quit His War." *Newsweek* 6 Aug. 1945: 20.

Pakenham, Maj. Compton. "Does the Jap Soldier Have a Breaking Point?" *Newsweek* 30 July 1945: 35.

___. "The Japanese Mentality as a Factor in War." *Newsweek* 11 June 1945: 48.

___. "With His Trick Mind, the Japanese Fools Himself." *Newsweek* 2 July 1945: 48.

Penn, Irving. "Penn's Japan" *Vogue* 15 Aug. 1964: 97.

"Pioneer with a Touch of Ford and Alger." *Life* 11 Sept. 1964: 10.

"Pomp with Point." *Time* 18 May 1981: 28.

Pyle, Ernie. *Last Chapter.* New York: Popular Library, 1945.

Reilly, John. "Public Opinion: The Pulse of the 90s." *Foreign Policy* 83 (1991): 87.

Reich, Robert B. "Is Japan Really Out to Get Us?" *New York Times Book Review* 9 Feb. 1992: 24.

Reid, T.R. "'Japan Inc.': It's a Concept That's Bankrupt." *Boston Globe* 29 Aug. 1993: 68.

Reinhold, Robert. "As Pearl Harbor Day Looms, Sting of Old Wound Revives." *New York Times* 1 Sept. 1991: A22.

Samuelson, Robert J. "Our Japan Obsession." *Newsweek* 12 Aug. 1985: 56.

"Samurai Spirit Lives On in Japan's Economic Drive." *US News & World Report* 19 Nov. 1984: 48.

Sanger, David. "Head to Head with the Japanese." *New York Times* 18 April 1993: E5.

Shaplen, Robert. "Letter from Tokyo." *The New Yorker* 20 May 1974: 105.

Shumway, Norman. "Congressman: Stop Bashing, Start Reform. *Centerviews* [East-West Center, Honolulu] Sept.-Oct. 1990: 5.

Smith, W. Eugene. "Colossus of the Orient." *Life* 30 Aug. 1963: 56A.

___. "Death-Flow from a Pipe." *Life* 27 June 1972: 80-81.

"Special Issue: Japan." *Life* 11 Sept. 1964: cover.

Stanley, Peter. "Our Good China/Bad Japan Syndrome." *The New Republic* 17 Feb. 1979: 21.

Steinberg, Rafael. "A Proud New Jazzy Age." *Life* 17 Oct. 1964: 81.

"Tax on Monsters." *Newsweek* 7 March 1948: 44.

"Trade Face Off." *Time* 13 April 1987: cover, 28-29.

"Trade War Ahead?" *Newsweek* 15 April 1985: 22.

"Trouble in Japan:How the Struggle to Win the Peace...Now Threatens the Success of the American Occupation." *Newsweek* 23 June 1947: 36, 38.

"25 Years Ago: Two Cities, Two Bombs." *Life* 30 Jan. 1970: 30.

Vlahos, "Culture and Foreign Policy." *Foreign Policy* 83 (1991).

Vogel, Ezra. *Japan as Number 1.* New York: Harper Colophon, 1979.

Washington Week in Review (PBS television program) 15 Nov. 1991.

White, Theodore. "The Danger from Japan." *New York Times Magazine* 28 July 1985: 18-23.

"When the Atom Bomb Struck—Uncensored." Life 29 Sept. 1952: 19-25.

"Why an Issue on Japan?" *House Beautiful* Aug. 1960: 53, 55.

Woodruff, John. "U.S., Japan Are Poles Apart on Issues." *Seattle Times* 13 Nov. 1991: B5.

"A Word with Our Readers about Japan" *Holiday* Oct. 1961: 53.

Susan D. Moeller is an Assistant Professor of American Studies and the Director of the Journalism Program at Brandeis University, Waltham, MA 02254.

The Cultural Hero in the
World War II Fantasy Film

by Peter L. Valenti

In *The Hero with a Thousand Faces*, Joseph Campbell delin-
eates a pattern of cultural behavior common to virtually all
societies in which a previously unknown figure — for example
Aeneas, Huang Ti, Jesus — emerges from a society to lead his
tribe to some better state and embodies values crucial to the
survival of his culture. Often the hero must pass through an
underworld or other world which suggests eternity, in order
to provide some form of salvation for his mortal world; the
golden bough and the cross are the preeminent symbols of
this experience in western civilization. As Campbell states:

> Whether the hero be ridiculous or sublime, Greek or barbarian,
> gentile or Jew, his journey varies little in essential plan. Popular
> tales represent the heroic action as physical; the higher religions
> show the deed to be moral; nevertheless, there will be found aston-
> ishingly little variation in the morphology of the adventure, the
> character roles involved, the victories gained. If one or another of
> the basic elements of the archetypal pattern is omitted from a given
> fairy tale, legend, ritual, or myth, it is bound to be somehow or
> other implied. . . .[1]

The democratic nature of this hero who emerges from the ranks
of the people to demonstrate for all his fellowmen the potential
inherent in that society dovetails neatly with the wide audience
for film in the 1940s. If we remember that popular culture as
well as religion sets forth this heroic pattern, then we can
scrutinize more carefully filmic adumbration of general cultural
values. Leni Riefenstahl's *The Triumph of the Will* (1936)
abundantly testifies to the power of film to inspire a society in

time of war; even today its power is breathtaking. However, I wish to suggest that another less obviously and less consciously articulated category of film suggesting behavioral patterns for imitation might be found in the fantasy films made during World War II. Since the communal nature of American film production precludes formulation of exclusively individual concepts and produces mediated artifacts, one would expect a time of severe cultural stress — here World War II — to create more intense formulations of the pattern. Two examples in particular — *A Guy Named Joe* (MGM, 1943) and *The Enchanted Cottage* (RKO, 1945) — show how the individual tragedy of death or disfigurement can be turned to general social good through the example of a loving couple.

The tragic destruction and loss which accompanied World War II have been partially obscured by the passage of more than three decades. However, the horrors of that war — or of any genocidal conflict — can be borne by people only if they sense a reason, a higher purpose behind the catastrophe. Man hopes that by suffering severe trials now, his culture may pass to a higher or more nearly ideal state of existence in the future. "For this mythical drama reminded men that suffering is never final; that death is always followed by resurrection; that every defeat is annulled and transcended by the final victory."[2] Man finds solace in such sequential actions because mythical repetition allows ". . . an optimistic view of life in general; everything takes place cyclically, death is inevitably followed by resurrection, cataclysm by a new Creation."[3] Archetypal repetition, says Mircea Eliade, "alone confers a reality upon events; events repeat themselves because they imitate . . . the exemplary event."[4] To a world immersed in the difficult business of waging war and attempting to find some logical rationale for the wholesale destruction, the fantasy film offered a postulation of overarching mythic values in a contemporary setting.

Fantasy perhaps more than any other genre suggests those aspirations of a culture toward achieving a satisfactory relationship with the cosmic forces shaping the destiny of the mortal world. By ignoring those constraints which restrict not only daily life but also mortal possibility, fantasy posits a world where idealized patterns of existence prevail. Obviously, the films of the 1930s from the strikingly choreographed musicals to the deliriously happy comedies provide fantasy as a neces-

The ghost of Pete Sandige is displeased at the initial attraction as Al Yackey introduces Dorinda to Ted in *A Guy Named Joe.*

sary escape from the bitterly harsh world-wide depression. If such films as *Broadway Melody of 1938* and *A Day at the Races* (1937) promise a better day around the corner, then an even more universally positive projection can be found in those films of the World War II era which eschew reality in favor of supernatural events.

Fantasy was not a new genre after 1939, but its possibilities were tapped in an intriguing new way during the war.[5] Dramatic films such as *The Return of Peter Grimm* in 1935 and comic entires such as *Topper* in 1937 suggest the interesting possibilities of communication with the spirit world and the return of the dead to the world of the living in a manner far different from the standard shudder school of the horror film. The change in attitude during wartime can be seen in the 1944 film *Between Two Worlds,* which incorporates the basic plotline of the 1930 film *Outward Bound* with the notable addition of a World War II seaman who realizes that he has died for the good of his family and his country. That critics disparaged this film but audiences made it financially successful suggests that the message of death transcended by larger tribal values is a source of power in the fantasy film.[6] Another source of strength, particularly in *A Guy Named Joe* and *The Enchanted Cottage,* derives largely from literate and intelligent scripting. Dalton Trumbo wrote the former, while DeWitt Bodeen and Herman J. Mankiewicz did the latter. The language of both films stresses the shaping influences of cosmic spiritual powers over the mortal world.[7]

The title of the film *A Guy Named Joe* illustrates the pattern of transcendance because no notable character in the film is named Joe; the Joe of the title is the American Everyman in service. The account of one particular G. I. Joe is presented as the story of a flier's death unfolds. Pete Sandige, played by Spencer Tracy, is an Air Force squadron leader who has a bad habit of show-boating his considerable prowess in piloting his aircraft. Irene Dunne plays Dorinda Durston, the girl in the Ferry Command whom Pete meets and loves. We can quickly recall familiar romantic plots presenting John Wayne and Donna Reed or Tyrone Power and Anne Baxter in various branches of World War II service, but the twist in plot is notable here. Pete is killed in action on a daring raid, leaving Dorinda disconsolate. Their mutual friend Al Yackey (played by Ward Bond) attempts to cheer her up. However, a double-exposure Spencer Tracy remains in the film to aid the war effort in general and young pilots in particular. After an unusually dangerous battle we see Pete's plane go down. The film cuts to a medium shot tracking Pete as he walks through a foggy, shadowy plain that we soon learn is Heaven. Pete's dismay at finding himself in Heaven is mitigated by an invitation to join the celestial air force as a counselor and trainer. The General (Lionel Barrymore) of this heavenly force tells Pete about his new instructional duties and sends him back to earth. However, the General later recalls Pete and admonishes him to work harder and to emphasize the value of teamwork for the young pilots. Pete vows to build effective fighter teams as he goes back to fulfill his mission.

The most interesting angle of the film is the entrance of Ted Randall (played by a young Van Johnson), the pilot whom Pete must guide through the war. Though he is a young scion of wealthy and powerful family, he does not betray the democratic ideals embodied in Pete Sandige, a genuine populist hero. Rather, he evinces a genuinely compelling humanity as he inquires about the despondency of a young soldier, learns of the man's homesickness, and arranges a long-distance phone hookup with the G.I.'s family. Thus rough-and-tumble Pete and genteel Ted complement one another nicely. Things really become complicated when this young flier meets and falls in love with Dorinda. Pete's ghost is of course unhappy with the thought, but he realizes that Dorinda's happiness is more

Before their wedding, Oliver and Laura appear with their physical defects.

important than his ego, which is supposed to be dead now anyway. In the film's climax, Ted breaks away from his squadron to execute a number of dangerous but flashy aerial maneuvers as Dorinda and Al look on in amazement and horror. Colonel Nails Kilpatrick is the C.O. feared by all; he is played by James Gleason, who two years earlier had played the fight manager in Columbia's fantasy *Here Comes Mr. Jordan.* Everyone on the ground fears his reaction to the aerial stunting. Pete is behind Ted all the way as the young pilot demonstrates that he had learned the fine points of trick flying. "Show them what you

can do," urges Pete as the apprentice learns rolls and turns that
he never knew that he could perform. Almost miraculously,
after this demonstration Colonel Kilpatrick does not give the
young pilot the verbal abuse which the actors and the audience
expect; Dorinda and Al are left to wonder what has mellowed
the feisty Colonel. Dorinda and Ted become sure of their love
and provide the comic resolution that one expects from the
wartime romance.

What I would like to emphasize in the plot of *A Guy Named
Joe* is the apparent effect of the transformation upon the
Colonel. Kilpatrick had never been able to put up with Pete's
shenanigans in the air and was constantly calling him down for
his frivolous attitude toward his safety. That the Colonel could
countenance Ted Randall's gyrations suggests that the death of
Pete Sandige not only provided the guidance necessary to
change a sensitive rich boy into a determinedly efficient fighter
pilot, but also that the virtues of a departed member of a
fighter squadron unconsciously insinuate themselves into even
those persons who had previously been indifferent or even hostile to those characteristics. Thus Joe's death is the beginning
of the transformation of his maverick characteristics into the
general cultural good, an elevation of his virtues that would
not have been possible had he lived.

A cultural transformation of a different sort is evident in
The Enchanted Cottage. Again the danger facing World War
II fliers is demonstrated, and again a wealthy young man finds
romantic fulfillment after apprenticeship and trial, but this
film presents no travelers between heaven and earth. The
movement presented here is that of the serviceman returning
to civilian life, a critically important process for postwar America in 1945. Like Val Lewton's *The Curse of the Cat People*
released the year before, the narrative line of the film does not
depend on fantasy elements for its resolution; rather, all events
in the film may be considered psychologically realistic. The
young heroine of *The Curse of the Cat People* may only be
imagining Irena, the gorgeous Cat Woman. Her father, Mr.
Reed, would have us so believe. Likewise, in *The Enchanted
Cottage* the plot development hinges on the transformation of
Laura and Oliver from plain and deformed to vivacious and
handsome. However, the language of both films clearly indicates
the necessity of the audience's participation in what Coleridge
termed "the willing suspension of disbelief." The film opens

with a shot of a piano keyboard upon which John, the film's narrator, is playing. He proceeds to tell his guests a very strange story about the last two inhabitants of a magic little house, an enchanted cottage consecrated to the transforming power of love. Since John is blind, he is guided by his "taxi," a young boy named Danny. Danny takes John by a cottage where John feels even though he cannot see the power of imagination on this spot. Danny tells him that a "terrible ugly" witch lives there, but John cautions him that physical truth may not always be appropriate. The witch is Mrs. Minitt, the cottage's housekeeper, who lost her pilot husband in World War I. The Minitts were the last honeymooning couple there, where true lovers for centuries had etched their names on a window looking out of the cottage. She takes on as her helper a local girl who failed in her attempt to find a place in the world and has returned to her mother's house. Thus homely Laura Pennington (played by Dorothy McGuire) gets another chance at a fulfilled life. Laura shows a wealthy young couple the honeymoon cottage, explaining its idiosyncrasies and the difference between haunted (ugly) and enchanted (beautiful). Oliver Bradford (played by Robert Young) is a handsome pilot who is affianced to Beatrice, though he has to ship out on the day they were to have been married. The war prevents the marriage and disfigures Oliver's face so much that Beatrice recoils when she first views the returning warrior. Though she shares the name of Dante's famous heroine, she provides no spiritual leadership for her lover and he sinks into despondency. This mood is well counterpointed by the driving rainstorm which rages outside the cottage as the couple returns not for a honeymoon but for bitter parting.

Laura's fine sympathy ultimately brings Oliver out of his gloom and he proposes to the plain girl. Their wedding dinner is served at the cottage by an enthusiastic Mrs. Minitt. Gradually a miraculous change comes over the little room; as Laura plays the piano she feels the transforming power of love. The camera tracks around the room, emphasizing points of light which suggest the dazzle overcoming the newlyweds. The two become beautiful to one another, but the transformation is subtle on the screen: a slight change of Oliver's facial features, and a different hairdo for Laura. Perhaps the medium of film here suggests that the true power of love is not physical, nor can it be demonstrated with before-and-after shots. Rather, the camera must suggest a change — as *The Enchanted Cottage* does with the blurred spots of light in the dining scene — as a less empirically observed than emotionally felt development.

John shares the couple's bliss as he visits with them. The ultimate test of their marital happiness comes when Mr. and Mrs. Price, Oliver's snobbishly sophisticated mother and step-father (played by Spring Byington and Richard Gaines), come to visit. Oliver and Laura anxiously ask if the older couple can see the change, but the Prices' crestfallen faces give away their terror at seeing Oliver and Laura. The radiant beauty of the younger couple, with their by-now selfless love, contrasts markedly with the somber countenances of the elder Prices. The young lovers are badly shaken, but Mrs. Minitt tells them that a man and a woman in love have a special fire and that theirs, which flamed up the day of their wedding, must be kept burning. Even she, at her age (and bearing a strong resemblance to

After the transformation, John, Laura and Oliver meet in the garden of the cottage.

Margaret Hamilton), would be pretty to her husband if he were to return. As Oliver and Laura sit in shadows reminiscent of the day Oliver returned to the cottage, they reaffirm their vows and decide that the previous occupants of the cottage would want them to engrave their names on the window. As they begin this activity, the camera fades to the piano keys which opened the film and then outside the party to the front door as a couple approaches. Instead of knocking, they kiss; their radiance is obvious even though we see them only from behind.

The two films which I have roughly outlined present happy endings achieved through the intervention of powers above the mortal world. The celestial General of *A Guy Named Joe* and the power of love, represented as a miraculous transforming property capable of changing physical reality, allow the unions of soldier and loving wife. Both films show this power in dramatic fashion: we are anxious as we imagine what tragedy might befall Ted as he recklessly zooms around the sky and we are painfully aware that Mrs. Price's reactions might burst the balloon of the Bradfords' happiness. Ted returns safely to the ground to claim Dorinda, but the Bradfords sadly sit by the window of the enchanted cottage and etch their names. In both situations the final romantic union is preceded by a crisis which is resolved by a trip with a guide (the plane exhibition in *Joe*) or invocation of the enchanting power by a couple truly in love (the engraving of the names on the enchanted window at the threshold of the world of everyday reality).

These critically important events constitute the mythic fulfillments in the two films. The actions of both situations may constitute what Campbell terms the "unlocking and release again of the flow of life into the body of the world." He terms this physical location the world navel, from which the flow of life comes. "The torrent pours from an invisible source, the point of entry being the center of the symbolic circle of the universe, the Immovable Spot of the Buddha legend, around which the world may be said to revolve." "The tree of life, i.e., the universe itself, grows from this point." A dragon may guard this point, or the supreme hero himself may be fixed to the tree, as in the case of Jesus or Wotan; "for the hero as the incarnation of God is himself the navel of the world, the umbilical point through which the energies of enternity break into time. Thus the World Navel is the symbol of the continuous creation: the mystery of the maintenance of the world through that continuous miracle of vivification which wells within all things."[8]

If I may be allowed to elaborate upon Campbell's assertions, I would emphasize the democratic nature of the hero and the populistic nature of film produced during wartime which presents the lives of people in wartime conditions. The hero of myth learns that he has had within himself all the time the potential to lead or provide an example for his people after he has released the flow of energy into his society by leaving time to enter the threshold of eternity and ultimate power. Pete's advice to Ted and Ted's reactions to the instructions constitute the lesson learned from the spiritual leader much as Dante learned from Virgil; the fledgling pilot now shows to his closest associates on the ground below what he has learned and what skills he will be able to bring to his country in the war effort. Ted's phone call for the homesick soldier shows that Randall's character is already worthy. He has only to master the harsher realities of the world at war, the skill at maneuvering aircraft, to help the war effort. Likewise Oliver Bradford possesses those positive qualities even though they are dormant while he is thinking about his own misfortunes during wartime. He and Laura together look out the window and the enchantment strikes them, reaffirming the spiritual power of love to transform their lives and begin a new existence for them. The patriotic message of *A Guy Named Joe* is obvious at the midpoint of the war, and only slightly less obvious is the hopeful message of *The Enchanted Cottage* at the end of the war as a disfigured veteran returns home to pick up the pieces of his life and begin over again. The fantasy film provides a genuinely sustaining hope that common people — Pete, Dorinda, Mrs. Minitt, Laura — can help to ensure the good fortunes of their societies. Though Pete dies, as Christ also died, he has made a contribution that will be remembered and embodied in others.[9] Oliver's hideous wounds enabled him to find a love which transcends mortal limitations of the body and indicates the progression of the comic sustaining of life. The darkened theaters of America from 1940 to 1945 held more than escapist fare for people weary of their sustained efforts to win a war; films such as these two share with religion a common purpose and pattern of cultural sustenance as both present positive life situations sustained by omnipotent cosmic forces.[10]

NOTES

[1]Joseph Campbell. *The Hero with a Thousand Faces*. Bollingen Series XVII (Princeton: Princeton University Press. 1968 [1949]). p. 38.

[2]Mircea Eliade. *Cosmos and History: The Myth of the Eternal Return* tr. Willard R. Trask (New York: Harper Torchbooks. 1959 [1954]). p. 101.

[3]Eliade. p. 102.

[4]*Cosmos and History*, p. 90. Eliade distinguishes between history and myth: history is linear and thus does not return; myth is circular and thus cyclical. We do not learn from historical events in the same way that we do from mythical events because history shows that each event is unique while myth holds that every archetypal event recurs and that each repetition derives ultimate significance from the prototypical event. The fantasy film thus elevates World War II from the level of history to that of myth.

[5]For a suggestion of the varieties of fantasy during World War II. see my article "The 'Film *Blanc*': Suggestions for a Variety of Fantasy, 1940-45." *The Journal of Popular Film*, 6 (1978). 294-304.

[6]The reviews of fantasy films often suggest that these films promise much but deliver little. Scripts are interesting and well-paced. but the dramatic conclusions do not satisfy the viewers. See for example the New York *Times* reviews of December 24. 1943. and April 28. 1945. Perhaps mythic patterns must be considered if fantasy films are to be understood satisfactorily.

[7]*A Guy Named Joe, The Enchanted Cottage*, and *Between Two Worlds* evolve from earlier treatments of World War I. The two latter films are remakes, while *A Guy Named Joe* adapts a World War II setting for what is basically a World War I tale. Lt. Col. James N. Brink (USAF, ret.). a pilot and Operations Officer in the 382nd Fighter Squadron which suffered extensive casualties in World War II, states that such tales as the account in *Joe* of dead pilots' spirits returning to help other pilots as standard fliers' legends — which studio promotions suggested — were not accepted belief in World War II. In an interview conducted October 10, 1978, Col. Brink suggested that this fantasy is. rather. typical World War I pilot lore. Thus these films hearken back to earlier events and emphasize mythic qualities.

[8]Campbell, pp. 40-41.

[9]The films suggest transcendance of mortal limitations. "And when such a realization of the nonduality of heaven and earth — even of non-being and being — will have been attained and assimilated. life-joy will pour from all things, as from an inexhaustible cup. Ego sacrificed, it is given back, and the waters of deathlessness are released to be carried in all directions." — Joseph Campbell, *The Mythic Image*, Bollingen Series C (Princeton: Princeton University Press, 1974). p. 198.

[10]The experience of viewing a film in a darkened theater may be even closer to participation in a religious service: when my mother first went to a movie as a child in the 1920s, she genuflected in the aisle before taking her seat. She subconsciously transferred her experiences imbued from traditional Roman Catholic ritual to this new awe-inspiring setting.

Peter Valenti teaches courses in film and literature at Fayetteville State University in North Carolina. This article is part of a projected booklength study of fantasy films in America.

South Pacific and American Remembering; or, "Josh, We're Going to Buy This Son of a Bitch!"

PHILIP D. BEIDLER

For many post-1945 Americans, the title *South Pacific* does not describe a text so much as a process of remembering. For the cultural historian, it offers an account of production. It is the relationship of these that will be my subject. The pattern of the former will largely depend, of course, on the rememberer – something of a book perhaps, a play, a movie, a song, another song. The latter, albeit complicated, is traceable. It has a literary provenance in a 1947 collection of fictional narratives by James A. Michener entitled *Tales of the South Pacific*,[1] variously described as short stories or a novel, but always noted as winner of the Pulitzer Prize. In translation to Rodgers and Hammerstein's 1949 Broadway classic, it adds another Pulitzer and a paperback fortune for the original honoree[2] to one of the most celebrated runs in the golden era of the American musical. It parlays that success into one of the first widely popular $33\frac{1}{3}$ RPM long-playing records, memorialized in its dramatic connection by a cover photograph of Mary Martin and Ezio Pinza in the lead roles of U.S. Navy nurse Nellie Forbush and French planter Emile DeBecque. It then reappears as a 1958 movie musical spectacular, leading to another joyride of the Michener narrative on the best-seller lists,[3] and to yet another best-selling LP, now in stereo, with the cover photo of the lovers, here Mitzi Gaynor and Rozzano Brazzi, resituated against a Hollywood backdrop of

Philip D. Beidler is Professor of English at the University of Alabama, Tuscaloosa, AL 35487, U.S.A.

[1] James A. Michener, *South Pacific* (New York: Macmillan, 1947).
[2] Thomas Davis, *Two-Bit Culture* (Boston: Houghton Mifflin, 1984), 133. James A. Michener, *The World is My Home* (New York: Random House, 1992), 329.
[3] Davis, 213.

Journal of American Studies, 27 (1993), 2, 207 222 © 1993 Cambridge University Press

wide-screen tropical splendors. Along the way, it proliferates into endless road productions and revivals; television showings and VCR rentals; re-recordings and new recordings on LP, tape, and compact disk.

My purpose here is to inquire into the process of production so described – the movement from "history" through "literature" into various forms of "classic" entertainment. I wish to make such an inquiry a case study in the conjoined forms *and* economics of cultural mythmaking. My specific approach will be to ask what made possible, in a certain set of cultural contexts, such a series of artifacts with regard to this particular history. Accordingly, my inquiry will begin with some proximate responses, having to do with the history of this particular war, the American war of 1941–45 in the Pacific, against this particular enemy, the Empire of Japan. But it will shortly turn to the various "entertainment" commodifications of history described above as *themselves a form of history*. Finally, it will also attempt to locate such commodifications within a national poetics of history long achieving honored status – and often at the expense, I will propose, of the very idea of history as possessed of ideological content – as a kind of ultimate entertainment technology *itself* called American remembering.

The specific question that generates my inquiry, centered on the focal artifact, Rodgers and Hammerstein's *South Pacific*, is fairly simple: what kind of people, slightly more than seven years after Pearl Harbor and three years after Hiroshima and Nagasaki, could possibly make World War II against the Japanese into a Broadway musical?[4] The proximate idea I will advance involves a deeply American politics of constructing the racial other. Or, as regards the Japanese, that it was exactly Pearl Harbor first – the surprise attack on Paradise – and Hiroshima and Nagasaki last, the

---

[4] The oddity of this, when one thinks about it, may be suggested by the only corresponding instance, to my knowledge, of such a proposition's ever being ventured about the World War II Germans. It occurs in Mel Brooks' movie, *The Producers*, in which an ideas-man, at the end of his imaginative tether, comes up with a Nazi musical entitled "Springtime for Hitler." One may cite, of course, such disparate aberrations as *Hogan's Heroes*, or Rodgers and Hammerstein's own eventual *Sound of Music*. These concepts, however, would rely on the notion of the "good German," an idea for which, as noted by John Dower, "no Japanese counterpart" would ever exist "in the popular consciousness of the Western allies": John Dower, *War Without Mercy* (New York: Pantheon Books, 1986), 8. Such a bifurcation was required for the Germans, particularly in post-holocaust regard, probably because in their very *occidental* heinousness, they remained too much like us. Indeed, the only alternative recourse in humorous depiction would lie in the black comedy, say, of a Thomas Pynchon. The Japanese, being wholly other, allowed for the ease of erasure conventionally applied to the other. One could simply make them invisible. In contrast, the Germans remained both easily other and uneasily same.

grand visitation of avenging wrath – with a host of other death-orgies such as Bataan, Guadalcanal, Tarawa, Iwo Jima, and Okinawa sandwiched bloodily in between – that made such a grotesque transmission possible. But further, it also required precisely the ease of cultural erasure enabled by the figure of the Jap: the rat; the louse; the cockroach; the savage simian fanatic little yellow bastard; the garden keeper's nightmare; the exterminator's delight. This war musical, I would insist, could only have come, really, of what must to date remain the most American of all great American wars, the great Pacific War, compounded of its most virulent racisms, east and west; in John Dower's exact formulation, the "War without Mercy."[6]

At the same time, however, I will also suggest that a number of coexisting, high-investment media of popular entertainment – print, stage, sound recording, film – quickly operated to render that subtext of horror largely irrelevant within an autonomous genealogy of production *itself*, a conflation of tastes and technologies become self-reifying forms of cultural statement, entertainment visions of the world taken to be fundamental ways of experiencing the world. The result, I will suggest finally, would be a new version of the artifact known as the American popular classic. And to recreate the history of events whereby such a classic is produced, I believe, is thus to know something about a national habit of remembering that even today, and often in ways largely *un*-remembered, remains part of the fabric *and* the business of our daily lives.

To begin by looking at the 1947 text in which the enterprise originates is to undertake in itself a work of curious recovery. Here is a pre-industrial James Michener, an author in his debut having much in common with other up-and-coming "literary" chroniclers of the just-finished Pacific war – Thomas Heggen in *Mr. Roberts*, Herman Wouk in *The Caine Mutiny*, Norman Mailer in *The Naked and the Dead*, Leon Uris in *Battle Cry*. To be sure, one hardly finds a neglected classic, a latter-day *Red Badge of Courage* or a prophetic *Catch-22*. Yet as to the Pacific conflict, Michener's book speaks with a terse authority. There is the feel of the naval war, professionals and opportunistic martinets mixed with average men and women called to roles in which they must somehow become bigger than themselves. There is the enormous military-logistical sprawl, island after island, as the bases multiply, bringing the line navy, the PT daredevils, the aviators, the marines, the nurses, the supply, maintenance, and paperwork types, with war-exotics and fast operators abounding, American and

6 Ibid.

H 2

indigenous. There is the drama of interminable waiting, punctured by violence almost beyond belief. An ammunition ship, lying at harbor in a rear-area depot, is literally disintegrated with all aboard in an inexplicable accident. An entire unit, various members of which have become individualized to us, is annihilated by a single artillery hit on a landing craft.

Emerging in major roles, through complex narrative involvements, are six characters who will become the central figures of the Rodgers and Hammerstein play: Navy Ensign-nurse Nellie Forbush, from Arkansas, U.S.A.; her eventual husband, the handsome, mysterious French planter, Emile DeBecque; the bawdy, jovial, Tonkinese black-marketeer, Bloody Mary; the young Princeton lieutenant of marines, Joseph Cable; Liat, Bloody Mary's virginal daughter, soon to become the latter's tragic beloved; and, finally, the all purpose scavenger and rapscallion, Seabee Luther Billis. These are joined by others: a shadowy American intelligence operative, Tony Fry; the rakish pilot Bus Adams; the enigmatic narrator, a "paper-work sailor,"[6] as he calls himself, dispatched hither and yon through the combat theater; the exotic "Frenchman's Daughter," or, more properly, Madame Latouche DeBecque Barzan, daughter of the Gaullist renegade DeBecque, ex-wife of the Petainist traitor Achille Barzan, lover of Bus Adams, eventually wife of the doomed Tony Fry, exotic hostess at her island villa to the officers of all nations who come bearing the plunder of war; the Japanese lieutenant colonel, Hyaichi, Cal Tech engineer who, despite the blundering of his superiors, manages to turn the massively prepared-for expedition against Kuralei, the focal action of the book, into a near-disaster for the American forces making the attack.

Yet as one reads along toward the climatic battle through a seemingly endless proliferation of characters and texts – indeed, the extent is barely sketched out above – one has the distinct sense of having somehow been there before. Then the realization takes shape. If we are seeing all this in a war, we understand that we are also seeing it within rather a familiar kind of book. It is a South Seas travel-adventure book, as Melville's *Typee* and *Omoo*, or the Pacific sections of Twain's *Roughing It* and *Following the Equator* are travel books. Most especially, it is such a book as Nordhoff's and Hall's mid-1930s trilogy – *Mutiny on the Bounty*, *Pitcairn's Island*, and *Men Against the Sea* – are South Seas travel-adventure books. (Early chapters, in fact, under the pretext of building an airstrip, enable a long visit on Norfolk Island with the descendants of the old mutineers.)

---

[6] Michener, *South Pacific*, 3.

Similarly, its renegades, castaways, burnt-out cases, and sundry other isolatos seem often to owe less to contemporary historical action than they do to R. L. Stevenson, Joseph Conrad, or Somerset Maugham. In the matter of war reporting, even down to the paper, the print, the no-waste layout, the sections that begin and end in mid-page, the locus classicus is the journalist Ernie Pyle. In the depiction of non-western women, it is the painter Gauguin. And then, just there, the sensation of familiarity really hits. Often it is not really a book. Rather, it is a movie, a South Seas adventure movie. Or, to use a suitable figure, it is the accumulated flotsam of a 1930s tidal wave of them: "A" and "B," silent and sound, dramatic and musical, legendary and forgotten. In a recent memoir, amidst reflections on his return to the islands, Michener himself drops the names of a few – *Mutiny on the Bounty, The Hurricane, South of Pago Pago, Tabu*. To these might be added, by conservative count, at least 60 others, ranging from the *The Love Trader* (1930) through the Dorothy Lamour sarong classics *Jungle Princess* (1936) and *Jungle Love* (1938) to the immediately pre-war Hedy Lamarr-Robert Taylor vehicle, *Lady of the Tropics* (1939), set, of all places, in the harbor at Saigon. Thus we come to see why we feel so much of the time that the text at hand has seemed a familiar precinct to the degree that the war often falls somewhere between local adventure and romantic backdrop. The real terrain at hands turns out to be a mythic geography firmly in possession of its real owners, the American audience.[7]

Recent evidence would suggest also how thoroughly the author regarded the very project of the book as a basically literary "property." The ubiquity of the narrator, he reveals, turns out to have derived from a set of faked orders he managed to acquire allowing him unlimited travel to gather experience, a kind of passport to material. The experience of the war years spent in the Pacific, he freely admits, became mainly the experience of producing the text that was to comprise the account of these years.

Yet such attitudes of authorial commodification seem almost innocent compared with those shortly evinced by heavy production types such as Kenneth McKenna, Jo Mielzener, Joshua Logan, Leland Hayward, Richard Rodgers, and Oscar Hammerstein, to name just a few. Whatever the real story of Michener's version of the war without mercy, it now becomes wholly subsumed in the story of how it became the newest version of the Broadway-Tin Pan Alley-Hollywood Sure Thing.

How sure a thing is verified by accounts of the deal from the various principals. According to Michener, for instance, McKenna, head of a

---

[7] For a complete survey of the genre, see Roger Dooley, *From Scarface to Scarlett: American Films in the 1930s* (New York: Harcourt Brace Jovanovich, 1979), 205-16.

Hollywood "literary department" disappointed by the negative response of his superiors to the book's film possibilities, recommended it to Mielzener, his half-brother, and a New York stage designer. Mielzener says that he excitedly contacted Richard Rodgers, who in turn contacted Oscar Hammerstein, and that shortly he found them leagued, in his words, "with two outstanding talents, Josh Logan, the director, and Leland Hayward, the charismatic producer."[8] Rodgers, on his part, suggests that the "property" was suggested to him by Logan during what seemed a fruitless period of seeking "an idea for a musical that excited me."[9] Logan, in turn, remembers a dinner with Mielzener and McKenna at which the latter recommended the book as possibly helpful in providing "some color" for a current Logan project, *Mr. Roberts*. Logan took the book to Miami over a weekend with Hayward and their wives. Hayward borrowed it while Logan took a nap. Shortly, he exclaimed, "Josh, we're going to buy this son of a bitch!" "What are we going to do with the son of a bitch?", Logan replied. "We'll make some son-of-a-bitching movies, some musical shows, maybe a couple of straight plays," said Logan, "– how the hell do I know? We'll just buy it quick, before somebody else does, and then make up our minds."[10]

Whatever the handling of the property, all accounts agree on one thing: the focal item for the new project was a relatively incidental story among the nineteen fictions comprising the original, entitled "Fo'Dolla'," in which East meets West through a Tonkinese black-marketeer's sale to an upper-crust American lieutenant of her virginal daughter. Yet, as Rodgers recalls, there were obvious problems. First, they all wanted to avoid "just another variation of *Madama Butterfly*." More importantly, he goes on, "though we liked the story, we became convinced that it was not substantial or original enough to make a full evening's entertainment." It was thence, he says, that they turned to a second, parallel narrative found in "Our Heroine," a section containing the outlines of the love plot involving Emile DeBecque, a middle-aged planter possessed of two mysterious mixed-race children, and a young, ingenuous, provincial American nurse named Nellie Forbush. "This, we decided, had to be the main story." Yet here, too, were new problems. "All this was against the rules of musical-play construction," which insisted that "if the main love story is serious, the secondary romance is usually employed to provide

---

[8] Michener, *World is My Home*, 290.
[9] Richard Rodgers, *Musical Stages: an Autobiography* (New York: Random House, 1975), 258.
[10] Joshua Logan, *Josh: My Up and Down, In and Out Life* (New York: Delacorte, 1976), 209–10.

comic relief." The difficulty then was "two serious themes, with the second becoming a tragedy." However, in a good cause, he concludes, "breaking the rules didn't bother us, but we did think the show needed comic leavening, so we went to still a third story for an affable wheeler-dealer named Luther Billis and added him to the cast."[11]

Thus the transformation, or rather, as it is called in the business, the development. And it is against this backdrop of textual construction, rather than any one of putative history or ideology, that we must view perhaps the most cherished legend concerning the work's status as an American classic: and that is the legend of Rodgers and Hammerstein's attempt to use the Broadway theater to make a courageous statement against racial bigotry in general and institutional racism in the postwar United States in particular. After all, the story goes, central to both of the twinned romantic plots were complex issues of multi-cultural and inter-racial relationships. These, moreover, culminated memorably, the legend continues, in the "message" contained in the plea for racial understanding sung toward the end by Cable, shortly before his death, under the title "You've Got To Be Taught." And there is some happy, incidental truth to this. The touring play, we know for instance, as well as the 1958 movie, provoked anxiety among critics and certain active resistance in the American South. On the other hand, to arrive here, we have to work through a truly inspired layering of racial substitutions. To put it simply, although the "Jap" problem in the text has been dispensed with, we now face two others. Both stem from that old American favorite, miscegenation. The first is focused in the main, Forbush-DeBecque love plot, the "family" plot as it were. It is, to use Nellie's own phrasing, a "nigger" problem. Ingeniously, *it* gets resolved by her acceptance of DeBecque and with him the children he has fathered by a Polynesian. She may be from Arkansas, but she is also an ingenue, a nurse, and a nurturing adoptive parent "in love with a wonderful guy." (When we see her last, she is serving soup.) DeBecque has gone Asiatic but, because he is an

[11] Rodgers, 259. The two main plots were tied together by a behind-enemy-lines reconnaissance-mission subplot involving DeBecque (who survives) and Cable (who dies) drawn, as is not generally acknowledged, from the plot of another story introducing the shadowy American operative Tony Fry, a recurrent major character in the ensuing text, and his radio mission with the brave, tragic British coastwatcher called "The Remittance Man." Further to facilitate Billis's enlarged role, one other borrowing was also made for the accidental "diversion" created by having Billis stow away and then fall into the sea enroute to the DeBecque-Cable "mission" and thereby become the subject of a rescue struggle attracting most of the American and Japanese forces in the area. This, in the original, came from "The Milk Run," a story involving the pilot Bus Adams.

occidental, he can come back across the line. (Curiously, the fact that he has committed in his youth what would now be called second-degree murder is far more easily dealt with than the fact of the children.) The offending wife is dead. The cute mixed-race children, like puppies or kittens, are eminently adoptable.

The second problem, focused in the parallel relationship of Cable with Liat, engineered by her black-marketeer mother, Bloody Mary, proves not so easy to work out. To borrow a phrasing that other Americans would eventually find for it, it is a "gook" problem.[12] Accordingly, as if in expiation for the other, it must be allowed to find its eventuation in tragedy. Here, to be sure, in matters oriental, the Puccini kill-the-courtesan model – a lesson not lost on the makers of the recent Broadway blockbuster *Miss Saigon* – does not even have to be sold. All that is required additionally for moral punctuation is that the lieutenant, for his sins, undertake a secret mission and be killed. And thus the racial calculus is complete, with the "nigger" problem resolved in ways having, as usual, nothing to do with American realities past or present and the "gook" problem drawn in the long, prophetic shadow of future "Tonkinese" realities still to be reckoned.[13]

Yet none of this in either case makes the basic cultural legend untrue. It simply locates the truth elsewhere in cultural remembering, so to speak, as a truth not so much of history as of popular desire. That is, if love and war were the themes, and racial understanding the received moral, the business was entertainment; and particularly, for the moment at least, the business at hand was that classic entertainment called the Broadway Musical. For here, such bizarre hybridizations of "concept" had long seemed the norm rather than the oddity. In a single work, there could be grandeur of opera; the seriousness of "legitimate" theater; the comedic

[12] Here, as with "nigger' above, in its American usage the racist term has been culture-specific. As the former has been used to derogate Americans of African descent, the latter was, of course, one of the main racial epithets used by Americans in Vietnam. Its origins, however, go further back in American wars, perhaps including the one in question. One theory connects it with the Korean Conflict, as deriving from a word in the latter language for "foreigner." Others locate it in the pre-World War II American argot of the Pacific and even as far back as the Philippine Campaigns at the turn of the century.

[13] It is surely one of our supreme literary-historical ironies that Mary and her daughter Liat are identified as Tonkinese. That is, they are Indochinese, most likely brought to the islands where the play is set by migrating French colonials. To be exact, this also makes them North Vietnamese, from "Tonkin" China, the region of Hanoi and the Chinese border, as opposed to "Annam" or "Cochin" China, known to us once as South Vietnam.

possibilities of the variety show and vaudeville; the emotionality of melodrama.[14]

Here, then, seems to have been serious creative business and the business of popular entertainment, meeting in some common discourse of public interest and appreciation. Accordingly, critical response to *South Pacific* was lavish. One commentator praised the setting out of sensitive human drama – and remember, this is the play, not even the book – against "the callous misery, boredom, and slaughter of war."[15] Others noted the aesthetic uniqueness of something not really a musical so much as a structurally focused, thematically coherent interweaving of plots with musical score and libretto *creating* the drama at levels of extraordinarily high quality.[16] Many, not having had the benefits of a half century of shopping mall and elevator music, teased out the compositional excellences of solos such as "Some Enchanted Evening," "Bali Ha'i," "I'm Gonna Wash That Man Right Out of My Hair," "Love with a Wonderful Guy," "Younger Than Springtime," "This Nearly Was Mine;" showstopping chorus numbers such as "Bloody Mary" and "There is Nothing Like a Dame;" atmospheric framings such as the charming "Dites Moi." And in all these respects, it does seem to have been a tremendously innovative and well-integrated production, with an appealing theatricality (including, for instance, instead of extraneously gaudy production and dance numbers, a razzle-dazzle show-within-a-show surely invoking nostalgic remembrances of wartime special services productions); and uniting song and plot with unprecedented ease of

---

[14] As Paul Johnson has suggested, it may come as close to any American art form to being simply *sui generis*. *Modern Times* (New York: Harper & Row, 1983), 227. The underworld stories of Damon Runyon, for instance, could become *Guys and Dolls*. A musical play about a production of *The Taming of the Shrew* could produce *Kiss Me Kate*; *Faust*, by way of a baseball story by Douglas Wallop, became *Damn Yankees*. *Romeo and Juliet* could get street-ganged into *West Side Story*. For Rodgers and Hammerstein in particular, a run of such far-fetched transformations had already been effected: a minor play by Lynn Riggs called *Green Grow the Lilacs*, with a modern dance script by Agnes DeMille, had become *Oklahoma!*; a second-rate melodrama, *Liliom*, by an obscure central European, Ferenc Molnar, had become *Carousel*.
A prestigious recent consideration of the form, Gerald Bordman's, involves a highly elaborated aesthetic eventuating in one volume on American operetta and one on American musical comedy: *American Musical Comedy* (New York: Oxford University Press, 1982); *American Operetta* (New York: Oxford University Press, 1981). This would seem quite beside the point. The point, rather, would seem to be exactly the wildly syncretistic nature of the form itself, a form adapted in fact as a quite specific contextualized "vehicle" for American expression predicated on the multifarious demands of audience appeal it is prepared to meet.
[15] Rachel Coffin, ed. *New York Theatre Critics' Reviews*. Volume X. Number 11. Week of 11 April 1949, 312.   [16] Ibid., 312, 313.

staging and movement. Indeed, as one commentator accurately points out, here may have been the index of a real technical leap forward, the creation of as much a stage movie as a stage play for audiences increasingly accustomed to the fluidity of the newer medium.[17]

As noted above, equally in circulation, moreover, was generalized public discussion of a sort now largely lost to us, a kind of Talk of Broadway discourse that once seems truly to have been something of the talk of the country. There was, in a phrase, the serious matter of popular pride in the production itself as a major cultural artifact, whether one could go to it or not, either on Broadway or at one of the stops of a national touring company. Here was one last something of New York, of American theatrical excitement, of the hubbub and bustle of a place where the biggest variety show on television, in the innocence of a time before Elvis or the Beatles, billed itself quite unironically as The Toast of the Town.[18] One could catch, for instance, some of the energy by reading – in a city newspaper, perhaps, or in a big photographic layout in *Life* magazine, about the assemblage of an extraordinary cast. Mary Martin, the new heroine of Broadway, one would know as having been re-discovered, after being written off as the kitteness of "My Heart Belongs to Daddy," through her brassy replacement of Ethel Merman in the touring company of *Annie Get Your Gun*. Ezio Pinza, the most prominent bass in the Metropolitan Opera, would be described (amidst accounts of his heroine's trepidations about measuring up to his grandeur) as Don Giovanni himself translated in full glory to the Great White Way. One would hear of two exciting "finds": Juanita Hall as Bloody Mary and Myron McCormick as Luther Billis. During its run, one would read about the play's eventually breaking the record for the longest running Broadway show. (Today it still sits at a comfortable fifth.) In a novel media experiment, one could even look in through the fledgling medium of television at a live broadcast of a Sunday matinee. One could enjoy the fruits of an actual South Pacific production company offering various souvenir merchandise. Apace, one could partake in the media *and* in the marketplace of the fashion excitement generated by a novelty number, sung by Mary Martin in a makeshift shower stall, entitled "I'm Gonna Wash That Man Right Out of My Hair." Huge numbers of women,

[17] Abe Laufe, *Broadway's Greatest Musicals* (New York: Funk and Wagnalls, 1973), 130.
[18] How fully this was the end of an era for Broadway was marked by a notable conjunction of big time sports with the overnight ascendancy of television. An object case: in 1947, the World Series was telecast for the first time, and Broadway theaters underwent a 50 per cent decline in revenues. *This Fabulous Century, 1940–1950* (New York, Time-Life, 1969), 266.

apparently, wanted to know what happened to the hair. Did it get washed that often – that is, once every day and twice with matinees? If so, how could it be done? The result would be, of course, on the marketing end, the "concept" of once-a-day home care products, and on the purchasing, a highly manageable, easily dryable, cropped hairstyle that became instantly fashionable.[19]

It was, moreover, exactly this combination of serious cultural interest with popular appeal that facilitated the further, relatively novel, and instantly successful packaging of the property *in toto* into one quite attractive new form of commodity just appearing on the entertainment horizon, the $33\frac{1}{3}$ RPM long-playing record. Indeed here it seemed, almost by divine conjunction of technological accident with promotional opportunity, had appeared a new medium, in its own blend of popular appeal with minor cultural cachet, designed exactly to endow *South Pacific* with yet a new configuration of popular "classic" status. This latest had appeared amidst the cumbersome and expensive multi-disc 78 RPM collections required for opera and classical performances and the more common 78 middle of the road single. Soon, it would be joined by the mass-production 45, the vehicle of an insurgent rock and roll. Shortly would begin what one historian of the market has called the battle of the speeds, with the main results being that the 78 would disappear, the $33\frac{1}{3}$ would for the moment take over the "longhair" niche, and the 45 would begin a new evolution toward the pop single.[20] In the meantime, however, a major crossover market remained; and a good portion of its needs proved to be quite successfully filled by that new phenomenon, the $33\frac{1}{3}$ musical original cast album that would seem for one last moment to capitalize precisely on the marriage of its audience demographics with demographics of the soon-to-be-eclipsed Broadway form, elevated but not highbrow, popular but not plebeian. A groundbreaking experiment in the medium, actually, had been Rodgers and Hammerstein's own *Oklahoma*, which was the first original cast album to enjoy large sales. *South Pacific* exploited a newly proven market and repaid handsomely. Occupying the No. 1 sale position for 69 weeks in all, by 1958, when displaced by the soundtrack of the movie, the Broadway album had sold 1 million copies. Not surprisingly, the movie version began its own run.

[19] It would also be the Mary Martin hairstyle seen shortly in the enormously popular Broadway production, again among the first to be seen on national TV, *Peter Pan*, and again setting off sundry reverberations in popular fashion.
[20] Russell Sanjak. *From Print to Plastics: Publishing and Promoting America's Popular Music (1900–1980)* (Brooklyn, NY: I.S.A.M. Monographs, 1983), 39.

No. 1 for 54 weeks, including 2 years in the U.S. top ten, it became the biggest soundtrack of the decade, with sales of 5 million.[21]

So, to the ongoing sound of success, our account of ongoing production comes at last to the text of *South Pacific* probably now most remembered by Americans: *South Pacific*, the 1958 film. In terms of how it is remembered, moreover, it also seems historically the easiest to situate, especially as to how its issues of racial relationship were being contextualized by national events. 1954 brought the U.S. Supreme Court decision on Brown vs. The Board of Education, declaring unconstitutional legally mandated school segregation. 1955 was the Montgomery, Alabama, bus boycott. In 1956 pictures were blazoned across the world of police dogs attacking demonstrators in Birmingham, Alabama. By 1957, similar images of hate recorded the attempt to integrate Central High School in Little Rock, Arkansas. America had found its race problem. Since 1949, an Arkansas hick had been singing about the same race problem in America's favorite Broadway show. (In the show and movie, she got to be from Little Rock; in the book it had been Otolousa.) The Little Rock integration crisis was about children and education. The *South Pacific* song was entitled "You've Got to be Taught." New pieties were ventilated regarding the film's topicality and timeliness. In at least one state legislature, a resolution was authored in condemnation of such political meddling.

Yet here again, I would now propose, in any attempt to compound remembering out of such impressions of historicality, one must take care not to confuse the general productions of history with a particular history of production. For, if anything, the film production seems to have taken place when and how it did largely exclusive of anyone's notions of topical concern. The chronological movement from stage to film, for instance, as in all Rodgers and Hammerstein properties, depended on length of dramatic run. *South Pacific* was a monster, closing on Broadway in 1954. It lasted on the road well into the decade. It may make us feel virtuous to suggest that it was the film for the time. We would be more accurate if we just said that it was time for the film.

Equally important, as to film possibilities, was the fact that it was also technologically the right time. For, whatever the message, *South Pacific* the film proved a case of the medium triumphant. It made film history.

---

[21] Joseph Murrells, *Million Selling Records* (London: B. T. Botsford, 1984). In the age of Michael Jackson, it is hard to remember the significance that such figures once could claim. One might note, for instance, that the sheet music to the show at the time sold 2 million. Laufe, 128.

Cinematic splendors unimagined by the fondest South Seas devotee or musical fancier emerged through stunning advances in lens capability, color and sound reproduction, and projection technique. The film, for instance, remains notable today for being one of the first filmed both in Todd-AO *and* Cinemascope. Widely remarked on at the time were the color filters used to enhance (and in some cases render quite bizarre) the atmospherics of various musical numbers. Dubbing techniques were perfected allowing flights of song to be floated at will. Mitzi Gaynor and Ray Walston, experienced troupers, were allowed to go it on their own. The male lead, Rozzano Brazzi, on the other hand, preserving the Pinza tradition of operatic grandeur, was endowed with the voice-over talents of a singing compatriot, Georgio Tozzi.[22] On the receiving end of these effects, the film also benefited from settings and modes of presentation as close as the local theater. Rapidly vanishing were the days of "A" movies at theaters with names like the "Majestic" and "B" movies at picture halls with names like "The Strand." As television began to crowd the visual market, the theater industry re-concentrated its own infrastructure on what it could do best: the popular classic as wide-screen spectacular. The new emphasis would set in as quasi-Biblical – *The Robe*, *The Ten Commandments*, *Ben Hur*. Eventually it would lead to *Dances With Wolves*. But along the way, it would also provide the American musical with its own, last, spectacular flowering: *South Pacific*, *West Side Story*, *The Sound of Music*, *My Fair Lady*, and, perhaps writing the final nostalgia script of remembering for a country that somehow couldn't get over thinking of itself as a Broadway show with a noble message and a bittersweet ending, *Camelot*.

In addition, there were other new demographics of entertainment that *South Pacific* the movie also seemed uniquely to address. Chief among these was tourism. World War II had turned Americans into globetrotters scrawling "Kilroy Was Here" on everything from cathedral walls to coconuts. In the prosperous decades succeeding the event, they avidly pursued the habit. Given the political upheavals of post-World War II Europe, tourism turned them Pacific-ward in particular. (Besides, having been fought over so violently and exclusively by us, it certainly must have

[22] Oddly, someone found it necessary to dub Juanita Hall. One further prophetic "Tonkinese" connection is also worth mentioning: the casting of France Nuyen as Liat. Nguyen is the most common of all Vietnamese names. On the other hand, one can find such racial ghosts throughout. In the Broadway original, for instance, the "Polynesian" children were played by Hispanics. One of the DeBecque servants was also played by Richard Loo, *everyone's* movie caricature of the despicable Japanese officer.

seemed ours to enjoy.) In 1959, Hawaii became a state. Shortly, in the entertainment market, there ensued a spate of films: *Blue Hawaii, Hawaii, Gidget Goes Hawaiian*; then of course came the television series: *Hawaiian Eye, Hawaii 5-O, Magnum PI.*[23]

South Pacific made sure it got into the boom on the front end. Besides one song excised from the play, "My Girl Back Home," re-integrated for length and dramatic continuity, there was, the viewer would note, one decidedly major new addition to the film, the interminable, highly choreographed Boar-Tusk ceremony. It is, of course, the torchlight spectacle luau from the standard vacation package, itself largely come from the pagan fire dance in the big screen epic. (Not surprisingly, the one they used actually came from Michener, who already had it as part of the dramatic development in *his* South Seas spectacle.) Now it could also be fixed indelibly in the expectation or the memory of any vacationer in the Islands. Indeed, to this day, in any place with hotels it is almost impossible to take an evening walk without running into one. The *South Pacific* profit symbiosis, moreover, seems far from playing itself out. Also to this day, any tourist to Kauai sold on the spectacular helicopter tour will come home with a memory of having seen, just out to sea off the pristine West coast the *actual Bali Ha'i.*[24]

Meanwhile, a half century after Pearl Harbor, four decades after Hiroshima and Nagasaki, the Japanese own most of Kauai and a good part of the American entertainment business. Still, the musical comedy that is our subject trundles along, tailing the old subtexts and agendas. And one cannot leave the trail of evolving technologies and productions without at least mentioning a recent recording – a London-based studio

---

[23] As a measure of the skyrocketing attention paid to the 50th state, in contrast to the mild interest shown in the 49th, one can cite in the latter case but one movie: *North to Alaska.*

[24] Thus the relocation of *South Pacific*, Michener's South Seas movie of a book to every American tourist's possible movie dream of a South Seas isle. And thus, however, also one last other strange merging of entertainment with proximate Pacific history that cannot go unmentioned in the Hollywood connection. And that is the relation of all this to that utter anomaly of the period, the funny movie about World War II against the Japanese. To be sure, some of these, such as *Mr. Roberts*, themselves began as novels transferred to the stage. (In fact, as noted, the producer of *South Pacific*, Joshua Logan, was working on the stage version of Thomas Heggen's serio-comic book *Mr. Roberts* when he first heard about Michener's book, which, turned down by MGM as a stand-alone, had been suggested as a source of background color.) Others, such as *Don't Go Near the Water*, moved from book to movie. But most seemed mainly to spin off their own bizarre momentum. The list is staggering: *Francis, the Talking Mule; Operation Petticoat; Ensign Pulver; The Wackiest Ship in the Army; Father Goose.* If the "War Without Mercy" had been bought for a song, it often proved worth a laugh as well.

recording, in fact, designed for the cassette tape and compact disc market – that keeps the old story going and pretty much sums it up. It is a strange hybrid, not the movie, not the play, not the book, but an aural "staging," several features of which become newly instructive. Most telling, as to the latest conflation of the history business with the entertainment business, is surely the listing of the cast. The male leads: first, as DeBecque, in the operatic lineage of Pinza, the cinematic one of Brazzi, Italians who make good Frenchmen, a Spaniard, a renowned opera singer, Jose Carreras; second, as Cable, a mainstay star of the American musical stage, Mandy Patinkin, whose achieved persona, in the long tradition of Broadway, has been a celebration of his ethnicity. No Liat, of course, in this aural setting, is mentioned. Her part is silence. Her "Tonkinese" mother, on the other hand, here *does* achieve a kind of breathtaking final evolution, portrayed by the venerable American jazz singer, Sarah Vaughan. Finally, there is the gemstone role in the spectacle, that of Nellie Forbush; and now the whole business truly does come back to meet itself. It is sung by the operatic soprano, Dame Kiri Te Kanawa, a New Zealander herself of mixed-race Anglo-European and Maori descent. Out of this, of course, some may take heart in such a presentation of this American classic with such a multi-racial, multi-cultural cast, tease out some old lesson about the universality of music. That is certainly the "sell" implicit in the latest production described here, some misty moral that awaits every time the book is read, the show or movie seen, the sound track or recording heard.[25]

I, on the other hand, must reserve such judgments, especially having noted above the debut on Broadway of a latest American classic entitled *Miss Saigon.* Of this attempt, carrying an enormous weight of analogy to the one discussed here, and its relation to the packaging of American myth as self-congratulatory folk opera, Michael Feingold, waxing apocalyptic, if somewhat ungrammatical in *The Village Voice,* says, "every civilization gets the theater it deserves, and we get *Miss Saigon,* which means we can now say definitively that our civilization is over."[26] Robert Stone's comment in *The New York Times* is closer to the mark when he says that "with the New York opening of *Miss Saigon,* the Vietnam experience begins its final slide into the past, into history, make-believe, and

[25] It is all over the extensive liner notes with which the tape is accompanied. James Michener himself is even invoked suggesting "that although neither Cable nor Nellie is originally able to overcome personal prejudice to marry Liat and DeBecque respectively, it is Nellie, the Southerner, who is better able to deal with her conflicts than Cable, the Philadelphia-born, Princeton-educated Northerner."

[26] Michael Feingold, "Heat-Seeking Bomb," *Village Voice,* 23 Apr. 1991, 91.

melodrama. "[27] My point would be that we have been doing this for a long time, and pretty much in the terms Stone acutely triangulates. History, make-believe, melodrama. Many, indeed, will recognize here a common version of the official "literary" narrative of our historical culture: history *as* make-believe melodrama, the old serio-amusement, neither tragic not comic, not even tragi-comic, but rather, somehow, at once deadly earnest and deadly escapist; and for certain not ironic, for that would truly be to admit to the historicity of history. In the complex evolution of the American entertainment classic entitled *South Pacific*, the production of a history moves on apace with the history of a production, of a series of productions, in fact, comprising something called American remembering.

[27] Robert Stone, "'Miss Saigon' Flirts with Art and Reality," *New York Times*, 7 Apr. 1991, Sec. 2, 30.

Hollywood and the Holocaust:

Remembering *The Pawnbroker*

LEONARD J. LEFF

"Hollywood is just interested in making money .... No, to Hollywood, culture is just a dirty word. Callow, that's the word for American culture. They have so much to learn from the Europeans."[1]

Selig (the brother-in-law) in Edward Lewis Wallant's *The Pawnbroker*

In a 1961 novel by Edward Lewis Wallant, Sol Nazerman runs a pawnshop near the Harlem River in New York. A former inmate of the Nazi concentration camps, he has social contacts—a woman with whom he has sex, an assistant who helps him in the store, a sister and her family who share a comfortable suburban home in Mount Vernon with him. But he shuts out the world to grieve for himself and the wife and children he lost in the Holocaust. Grim and ethnic, peppered with phrases like *oy vay* and *gay shluphin*, the novel was unusual screen fare in the year that Elizabeth Taylor won an Oscar for *Butterfield 8*.

Gerald Mast notes in *A Short History of the Movies* that the American cinema of the 1960s "became more a directors' cinema."[2] As an account of *The Pawnbroker* shows, though, the roots of the so-called Hollywood Renaissance were not only exceptionally tender—especially for downbeat pictures—but nurtured as much by studios or producers as directors or auteurs. Adapted for the screen and released by Allied Artists, *The Pawnbroker* (1965) was a story of repression and survival. And so, behind the scenes, was the story of the independent producers who, in association with actors, artists, and technicians, created the first stubbornly "Jewish" film about the Holocaust.

Movie company story editors of the early 1960s read virtually everything, even fiction, that concerned the Holocaust. *The Pawnbroker*, though, was not only about the annihilation of the Jews and its consequences—that was rare enough in 1961—but had the rawness of a bleeding wound. The gloomy novel opens as the "subtly deformed" (31)

---

1. Edward Lewis Wallant, *The Pawnbroker* (New York, 1962), 28. Subsequent references to the novel will be from this edition, with page numbers indicated parenthetically within the text of the essay.
2. Gerald Mast, *A Short History of the Movies*, 4th ed. (New York, 1986), 430–31.

123

Sol Nazerman tramps to work. The snow he crunches could have produced a pleasant sound, but "the sight of the great, bulky figure, with its puffy face, its heedless dark eyes distorted behind the thick lenses of strangely old-fashioned glasses, dispelled any thought of pleasure" (5). For the anomic, the proper pronoun is indeed *its*, not *his*.

The story arc of *The Pawnbroker* rises, regressively, retrospectively, toward the death anniversary of Sol's wife and children. Instead of action, though, the novel works via memory and things, like glasses. Again and again the stolid pawnbroker dons or removes the "round, archaic" (197) glasses he had found during his internment. These "weird glasses" (168) lead his nephew to wonder whether Uncle Sol can "penetrate and understand" the "murkinesses" of the universe (75), and they so embarrass his niece that she wants to buy him "a decent pair . . . tortoise shell, those heavy, movie-producer kind" (29). The "unique spectacles" (71) "cut into the flesh of his nose" (191), but Sol goes on wiping (95) and cleaning (134) and rubbing them (85). They are his shield against past "spectacles" like the Holocaust and his weapon against present "spectacles" like Mount Vernon (and Harlem) culture, in one scene "picking up flashes of sunlight and flinging them at [another character] like tiny darts" (109).

Sol does not lack a sense of irony. When the Jewish cop on the beat tries to bully him into giving away a Hamilton Beach mixer, he merely shrugs. "Here he was in the classic role of the interrogated again, and Leventhal was playing the part of the oppressor. It was getting confusing; soon you wouldn't know the Jews from their oppressors, the black from the white" (44–45). He cannot be ironic about what haunts him, though, especially when it occurs with the force of a cinematic cut. "Suddenly [Nazerman] had the sensation of being clubbed. An image was stamped *behind* his eyes like a bolt of pain" (6). The horrendous scenes that follow, italicized in the text, do not conform to the usual survivor's dreams "of improbable paradises, of equally mythical and improbable enemies; cosmic enemies, perverse and subtle, who pervade everything like the air."[3] Instead, Sol's daydreams (or flashbacks) have the grit of documentary footage, as when he recalls the "*mountain of emaciated bodies, hands, and legs tossed in nightmare abandon, as though each victim had died in the midst of a frantic dance, the hollow eyes and gaping mouths expressing what could have been a demented and perverse ecstasy*" (146). Sol has seen too much. "*They could see the whole thing from where they stood in the camp square*" (76) on the night

---

3. Primo Levi, quoted in Lawrence L. Langer, *The Holocaust and the Literary Imagination* (New Haven, Conn., 1975), 51.

the dogs had hunted down Rubin. Now Sol makes love to Tessie, Rubin's widow, another aggrieved survivor, and struggles not to see the ghosts that surround them. "Yes," he tells her, "I have escaped. I am safe within myself. I have made an order for myself, and no one can disturb it" (91). On the final pages of the novel, though, when his assistant dies, Sol can no longer control his "glass-covered eyes" (6). The stoic weeps, and then, gradually, he "wiped his eyes clear again . . . . wetness dried on his cheeks and a great calm came over him" (205). He prays for the dead, his assistant and the others. More importantly, he forgives himself.

Like many in Hollywood, Paramount readers thought *The Pawnbroker* "tremendous" but found "no way to whip up any enthusiasm here, especially the moment 'small picture' was mentioned."[4] Metro-Goldwyn-Mayer had another idea. Bill Zimmerman (of the story department) and Red Silverstein (of foreign distribution) read the book and thought an adaptation at least possible, less as an MGM production than an MGM release. Though the novel was far darker and (apropos the Holocaust) more personal than *Exodus* (1960) or the forthcoming *Judgment at Nuremberg* (1961), it ended affirmatively and, if quickly produced, could perhaps ride the minor wave of box office interest in "Jewish" cinema. MGM's Joseph Vogel had once hoped to make "a succession of deals with Hollywood's independent producers to put M-G-M on a competitive par with its more alert rivals."[5] *The Pawnbroker* (likely to appeal to a maverick filmmaker) could test that plan.

Shortly after publication of *The Pawnbroker*, Zimmerman and Silverstein sent the novel to a confrere on the East Coast, the home of many of Hollywood's independent producers. Roger Lewis had worked in advertising at Warner Bros., 20th Century-Fox, and finally, throughout the 1950s, United Artists. He had served briefly as UA's director of promotion and exploitation, then resigned to write for television (he won an Emmy for an episode of "The Defenders") and look for "serious" work in motion pictures. *The Pawnbroker*, he later said, was so serious that it "scared hell out of me." He nonetheless took on the property when Zimmerman and Silverstein hinted that Rod Steiger, a "bankable" actor, was interested in the lead role. In fact, Zimmerman and Silverstein had never spoken to Steiger. Zimmerman knew that Steiger was in New York in a play and thought that Lewis could persuade him to shoot a picture during the day. Lewis was annoyed—and, worse, soon learned

4. Martin Rackin, Letter to Roger Lewis, 25 January 1962, Box 1, "Correspondence" Folder, Roger Lewis Collection, Western Heritage Center, Univ. of Wyoming, Laramie (henceforth RLC).
5. "Gun Fight at the M-G-M Corral," *Time*, 5 August 1957, 69.

that Joe Vogel, like Rod Steiger, had never heard of Wallant's novel. Silverstein hastened to explain that he and Zimmerman wanted Steiger engaged before they approached Vogel about the production: unless a star was attached, a movie about the Holocaust would languish in the front office.[6]

By early 1962 Steiger had read the novel and talked salary ($75,000 and ten percent of the net), but he wanted to see a screenplay before he committed.[7] MGM seemed more encouraging—only because it wanted to exploit the Eady Pool, a British law that afforded the American film industry a generous rebate of distribution costs for pictures shot in England. Since the smaller the budget the greater the protection against loss, MGM tentatively proposed a *Pawnbroker* shot in London for $400,000. Lewis was skeptical. The setting of the narrative thundered the new world, *New York*, and though $400,000 would buy more abroad than at home, it was still a paltry amount.[8]

As MGM tarried, Lewis formed a partnership with Philip Langner (whose father ran the Theatre Guild) for production of *The Pawnbroker* as "A Theatre Guild Film."[9] Langner put up $7,200 in exchange for one-third of the picture. "Without [Langner] the project would never have happened," Lewis told one interviewer, "so he's entitled to what he got. But I had to give away a hell of a lot for his $7,200."[10] Lewis and Langner optioned the novel for $1,000 and drafted a crude prospectus for private investors. *The Pawnbroker*, Lewis wrote, is "a vehicle that will garner attention and awards all out of proportion to the cost."[11] The announcement won notice. For instance, Groucho Marx (among others) wanted to play Sol—an odd but not inconceivable choice since Bert Lahr had starred in *Waiting for Godot* in 1956 and (as Bottom) in *A Midsummer Night's Dream* in 1960.[12] When no money appeared to be forthcoming, however, Lewis called on United Artists.

UA was the logical home for *The Pawnbroker*: the company not only had a long association with independents (Otto Preminger chief among

---

6. Roger Lewis, "Oral History," Audiotape, n.d., #3216, RLC.

7. Lewis, Letter to Daniel Petrie, 30 January 1962, Box 1, "Correspondence" Folder, RLC.

8. Lewis, "Oral History."

9. Ted Allan, "Foreword," Allan and Rod Steiger, *The Pawnbroker: A Screenplay*, Ts., n.d., Box 2, RLC.

10. Fred Baker and Ross Firestone, eds., *Movie People: At Work in the Business of Film* (New York, 1973), 17.

11. Allan, "Foreword."

12. Philip Langner, Letter to Lewis, 29 March 1962, Box 1, "Correspondence" Folder, RLC.

them) but experience with the Eady Pool, which was then financing the first of the James Bond pictures and Tony Richardson's adaptation of *Tom Jones*.[13] David Picker loved Wallant's novel yet referred Lewis to Arnold Picker, head of UA's executive committee and "a hard ass."[14] About "Jewish" pictures, Picker told Lewis, the figures spoke for themselves. UA had bought *Exodus* in manuscript for $250,000 plus five percent of the profits. As early as 1958, over one year before publication, UA told Preminger (the director) that the studio would promote *Exodus* not as "a book about ancient Israel, but rather one of events that took place in *contemporary* history" (emphasis added). The campaign, in other words, would "keep foremost the idea that this is not a book specifically for Jewish interest, but rather that its contents are exciting universally." *Exodus* stayed on the best seller list for 79 weeks and sold three million copies in paperback. The global box office was just under $20 million. *Judgment at Nuremberg*, on the other hand, produced one year later and encumbered in part by the salaries of its cast and the length of its narrative, had shown the concentration camps in documentary footage and was on its way to losing $1.5 million at the box office.[15]

Exodus and *Judgment at Nuremberg* (originally a television production) were pre-sold. Since *The Pawnbroker* was not, UA conditioned its support on Lewis' paring the budget to $350,000 and eliminating the Holocaust theme. "'People don't wanna see pictures about concentration camps,'" Picker told Lewis. Lewis argued. "'Well,'" Picker said, "'there're other injustices.'"[16] (In Hollywood each minority group had its season: when he adapted *The Brick Foxhole* for the screen, as *Crossfire* [1947], Dore Schary was forced to change the victim of Richard Brooks's novel from homosexual to Jew.) Lewis was disheartened. He was also $30,000 in debt.[17] Then Rod Steiger orally agreed to play Sol. MGM offered Lewis $2,000 to go to London to scout locations and a writer. At last *The Pawnbroker* was moving.

In London Canadian writer Ted Allan, who would later collaborate with Jan Kadar on *Lies My Father Told Me* (1975) and John Cassavetes on *Love Streams* (1984), agreed to adapt Wallant's novel for £6,000 (salary deferred) plus four percent of the net. To assure his fragile hold

---

13. Tino Balio, *United Artists: The Company That Changed the Film Industry* (Madison, Wisc., 1987), 237.
14. Lewis, "Oral History."
15. Balio, 213, 201, 133, 145.
16. Lewis, "Oral History."
17. Baker and Firestone, 22.

on MGM—and future access to UA—Lewis told Allan that the screen-play should deliver the "data" about the concentration camp "in [Nazerman's] words, rather than show it in literal scenes." He also wanted to alter the novel's presentation of two female characters. Tessie was another hostage of the Holocaust and too "depressive." Shimon Wincelberg (a Jewish friend) had told Langner that Tessie was "repulsive" and that "Wallant (though presumably a Jew) knows very little about lower-class Jews (or concentration camps, or nazis [sic]) and was able only to characterize them in crude stereotypes."[18] Wincelberg may well have been thinking of the appearance of Sol's lover at the beginning of chapter four:

> Tessie Rubin opened the door to Sol and gave him access to a different kind of smell from that of the hallway of the apartment house. The hallway, with its tile floors and broken windows, smelled of garbage and soot; Tessie's apartment gave forth the more personal odors of bad cooking and dust. . . . She had a large, curved nose, and her face was very thin; there were hollows in her temples, and her eyes, stranded in the leanness of all the features, were exceptionally large and dismal. She threw her arms outward, splayed her legs in exhaustion: their thinness was grotesque, because her torso was heavy and short, with huge breasts. (46–47)

The slovenly Tessie nurses both her father and her self-pity. Her dying father whines at her and bickers with Sol, whom she uses as willingly as do his sister Bertha, Bertha's husband, and their children. At dinner with the relatives he dislikes, Sol watches his brother-in-law and niece smile at each another "in a glow of intellectual rapport. You wouldn't even guess they were Jews, Bertha thought proudly" (27). No one reading the novel would guess otherwise. Wallant treats the needy customers of the pawnshop with a compassion he denies the other Jews of the story. From Tessie and Bertha to the venal cop Leventhal and the parasitical survivor Goberman (who collects for the Jewish Appeal), *The Pawnbroker* eerily echoes the Jews of the Nazi propaganda posters and the Cruikshank pen-and-inks for *Oliver Twist*. Roger Lewis was no doubt thinking of them when he asked the screenwriter to reconsider the "crude stereotypes."

The other female character of concern was the social worker, Marilyn Birchfield, who reaches out to the pawnbroker. Following a botched robbery of the shop, Sol's assistant takes a bullet intended for his boss. "For an instant [Sol] saw the immaculate face of Marilyn Birchfield and he said as in a dream, 'No, no, I am too dirty; you must go away from

18. Shimon Wincelberg, Letter to Langner, 26 July 1962, Box 1. "Correspondence" Folder, RLC.

me.' And then she was gone, banished by his voice, and for a moment he
thought he recognized the delicate shape of regret, until that, too,
disappeared" (201). Though Sol later calls on Morton (his nephew) for
support, Lewis thought that focusing on the social worker rather than
the young man would lend the movie audience "a sense of hope and
fulfillment that they, and the theme, deserve."[19]

Marilyn Birchfield "reads" gentile with her American smile and her
social philosophy of good deeds, and though Sol's returning to Morton
rather than her would loosen the thread of anti-Semitism that runs
through the novel, it would also help reassure Hollywood investors
accustomed to a fadeout on the heterosexual couple. Granted, Lewis
wanted a screenplay reasonably true to Wallant's novel. He also intended
to show MGM that the picture would be commercial, however, and to
that end he wanted to cast a Caucasian as the woman who played the
girlfriend of the Latino assistant. As he told Allan, "It's a chance, as in
the book, to give us a good sex bit."[20]

Ted Allan finished the first draft in spring 1962, when the studios were
retrenching and averse to Holocaust pictures, no matter how circum-
spect the "data." The screenplay was funereal and the ending dour;
unlike Sol in the novel, Sol in the script reaches out to no one—neither
his nephew nor Marilyn Birchfield. The screenplay was also chock-full of
Jewish characters and Jewish "bits." MGM's Bill Zimmerman read
Allan's work and found the "business of Sol's Jewishness" disagreeable.
"Granted that he is a Jew and one of millions persecuted or murdered by
the Nazis, our audience need not be reminded of it to the extent that this
script does it. For example, the Hebrew memorial candle on Page 34
(which, aside from this issue, is meaningless for the bulk of our
audience); the use of the word 'kike' on Page 25; the 'Jewish Holiday'
reference on Page 124." Also, the script "badly" needs comedy relief,
"easily available" fortunately in a scene featuring Jésus (the shop
assistant) and his "cronies and their easy girls in a jukebox bar, etc."
Finally, the picture needs an "obligatory" scene of Sol and Marilyn at the
close. The couple do not need "a sunset background, but at least they
should figuratively touch hands in some manner."[21]

Again The Pawnbroker stalled. MGM was "too financially destitute
at the moment," Philip Langner told one associate, too consumed by its

19. Lewis, Letter to Allan, 19 February 1962, Box 1, "Correspondence" Folder, RLC.
20. Lewis, "Notes on [Allan] Screenplay for 'Pawnbroker,'" Ts., n.d, Box 1, "Miscellaneous" folder, RLC.
21. WSZ [William S. Zimmerman], Comments on shooting script, Ts., 28 May 1962,
Box 1, "Correspondence" folder, RLC.

runaway production of *Mutiny on the Bounty* (1962) to bankroll *The Pawnbroker*. Confiding in *Variety* reporter Thomas Pryor in a personal letter whose typos and syntax mirror his indignation, Lewis said that he was "holding a nice fat bag which included a gaurantee [sic] to Steiger they [MGM] now found some legal techincaility [sic] for saying they were not bound by, and, of course, my own obligation for the the [sic] advance [on a screenplay]."[22] Though committed to the project, Ted Allan must also have been frustrated: he had not yet been paid and probably wondered whether he ever would be.

Steiger generally liked the screenplay, and by June 1962 Lewis was at work in London on a revised second draft that would hold Steiger yet lure backers (the producer hoped). Steiger was also in London, and nearby. "He would come in and he would have little notes and things about scenes that he had decided on or thought about the night before and he would act them out and he would weep, and I would weep almost," Lewis recalled. "And I would weep, not like Rod, who was moved by his own ideas and his own acting, but because it was so bad."[23] Looked at another way, the weeping marked the strong commitment of the actor. And, clearly, he was the production's linchpin.

The second draft of *The Pawnbroker* (according to the title page, "by Ted Allan and Rod Steiger") set the structure and retained the dark cast of Wallant's novel and Allan's first draft. Countering the opinion of the studios, Steiger thought that Nazerman's Jewishness and the accent on the camps were essential. Accordingly, the ending was bleak, with the pawnbroker slumped over the figure of Joseph, formerly Jésus. "Sol cries, his pain now finding full expression at the death of his 'son', at JOSEPH's sacrifice, and we know there is hope again for him—and for us." Though he had wanted a more explicit scene, with Marilyn, Lewis was not averse to shopping around the revised screenplay. In order to reproduce it, however, he had to ask his partner for money. "I don't have it," he told Langner, and "I will be digging into my slender resources before I leave here since the corp. account is practically nil." The screenplay was slender, not full length, the result of pruning Lewis had done "in anticipation of the director's involvement." At eighty-four pages it was too short. Rereading it months later, Allan himself conceded that "it needs a lot of work. It lacks passion and originality."[24]

---

22. Langner, Letter to Robin Fox, 7 June 1962, and Lewis, Letter to Thomas Pryor, 15 June 1964, both Box 1, "Correspondence" Folder, RLC.

23. Lewis, "Oral History."

24. Lewis, Letter to Langner; Lewis, Letter to Richard Gregson, 18 July 1962; Allan, Letter to Lewis, 2 August 1962; all Box 1, "Correspondence" Folder, RLC.

The screenplay alone hardly accounted for lack of interest in *The Pawnbroker*. One problem was budget. Lewis could pay no more than £10,000 for a director, and he had been cautioned against many who worked for less, as Hollis Alpert noted when he wrote Lewis "to warn you against John Cassevetes [*sic*]." Another factor was the London production base. "It was ridiculous," Sidney Lumet told one reporter, referring to Soho standing in for Spanish Harlem. "I had read the book before, loved Wallant's work, and was furious at the kind of treatment it had been given, so turned it down."[25]

Others responded negatively. Stanley Kubrick found Steiger not "all that exciting" and turned down the project. Karyl Reisz (whose parents had been interned and executed in Poland) told Lewis that for "deep, personal" reasons he "could not objectively associate himself with any subject which has a background of concentration camps." Mirroring the corporate culture of the studios, others saw *The Pawnbroker* as a professional cul-de-sac. Stage director Franco Zeffirelli was ardent for film credentials, but *The Pawnbroker* was "not the kind of subject [he] would wish to direct, certainly not as his first Anglo-American venture." More candid, producer Michael Balcon refused because of the "subject matter" and the fear (more than justified) that the major circuits would have "certain reservations" about the picture.[26] Lewis, who was speaking to agents rather than to directors or producers themselves, suspected that the go-betweens had not "made clear the fact that we are handling [the camps] symbolically, not realistically, in the script."[27] So unique—and so taboo—was the "realistic" content of *The Pawnbroker* in early 1962 that it discouraged both investors and artists.

In August 1962 Ely Landau stepped forward. An accomplished television producer, Landau was making his first picture, *Long Day's Journey into Night*, whose cast and theatrical origins would guarantee it wide press coverage and thus a fair chance at profit. He offered to pay off Lewis and Langner's past expenses on *The Pawnbroker* in return for eighty percent of the producers' share of the picture. Expecting far more than two-thirds of twenty percent of the picture (Langner would have taken one-third of that twenty percent), Lewis naturally made a counter-offer. Landau was "a mercurial guy who changes his mind ten times a

---

25. Hollis Alpert, Letter to Lewis, n.d., Box 1, "Correspondence" Folder, RLC; Sidney Lumet, "Keep them on the hook," *Films and Filming*, October 1964, 19.

26. John Boulting, Letter to Stanley Kubrick, 1 June 1962; Dan Cunningham, Letter to Lewis, 14 May 1962; Dennis van Thal, Letter to Lewis, 18 May 1962; Michael Balcon, Letter to Lewis, 26 July 1962, all Box 1, "Correspondence" Folder, RLC.

27. Lewis, Letter to Larry Backman, 22 May 1962, Box 1, "Correspondence" Folder, RLC.

day," Lewis told Ted Allan, "and, faced with our determination to draw the line and mean it, which [Landau] apprently [sic] didn't think was going to happen, he's already begun to back flip."[28] Lewis had no other prospects, though, and, faced with an able negotiator, sold Landau eighty percent of *The Pawnbroker*.

By early 1963, at his base camp in the Time-Life Building, Landau had read, without pleasure, yet another revision of Allan's screenplay, and by early spring he had asked Morton Fine and David Friedkin (who won sole screen credit) to rework it. Their 178-page first draft (dated 14 May 1963) was very descriptive, occasionally almost florid, and though they renamed the Jewish cop *Morrow*, their Sol was more Jewish than Allan's, especially in his morbid, dry humor.

Keenly attentive to point of view, as Resnais had been in *Hiroshima Mon Amour* (1960), Fine and Friedkin portrayed the scenes of Sol in the New York suburbs as though they were "all happening on this side of a swoon . . . no distortion, absolute realism . . . a constant flux of voices and figures which ebb in, then out of focus. And overlapping of dialogues [sic], so that oftentime a speech which starts to have moment becomes lost as something new starts. And during the INTERCUTTING, the rising emetic effect on Sol is patent." Lewis' desire for closure has Sol reach out, finally, for Morton. "I need you," he says into a pay phone after the shooting. "Come to me." Per Lewis' desire for a "good sex bit," the screenplay called for intercourse between Jésus and his girlfriend as well as Sol and Tessie—but no nudity, in those scenes or others.[29]

In their second draft dated 21 August 1963 and thirty-five pages shorter than their first, Fine and Friedkin revised, among others, the scene that would give *The Pawnbroker* its place in the annals of American film censorship. At the pawnshop Jésus' girlfriend unzips her dress a little.

As she does the CAMERA MOVES IN to hold [her and Sol] in a TIGHT TWO SHOT.

MABEL
Look . . .

Sol doesn't move. And now with a languid gesture, looking down at her own breasts, she reaches for Sol, her fingers in back of his neck: gentle gesture for him to look . . . to come closer . . . gently . . . soothingly urging him.

28. Lewis, Letter to Allan, 30 November 1962, Box 1, "Correspondence" Folder, RLC.

29. Morton Fine and David Friedkin. "First Draft Script." *The Pawnbroker*, 14 May 1963, Box 2, RLC.

MABEL
Just look, that's all.

As Sol looks, the voice of a concentration camp guard orders him to look at the Nazi soldier who sexually menaces Sol's wife, Ruth. The third draft, four pages shorter and finished seven days later, suggests that the producers were apprehensive about the nudity, for Fine and Friedkin designated "a TIGHT TWO SHOT *from over her shoulders*" (emphasis added). The decision on what to show would finally be answered on the set and, later, in the editing room. Already, though, before Landau had hired the director and editor who would win accolades for the film, *The Pawnbroker* was courting controversy, for, nudity aside, an honest presentation of the Holocaust would itself go well beyond the boundaries of "good taste" in American cinema of the early 1960s.[30]

"The successful adaptation," John Ellis writes in *Screen*, "is one that is able to replace the memory of the novel with the process of a filmic or televisual representation."[31] On those terms Fine and Friedkin's sixth draft (the shooting script) assured the film's success. Abandoning the pitch black tone of the novel, it nonetheless hews closely to the outlines of the story, especially the characterization of Sol, and yet is potentially strong enough to stand apart from the novel that had seeded it.

The shooting script is not conventionally faithful to the novel. It rearranges or omits scenes. It lightens the characterization of Tessie. It dampens hope at the end of the story. Subtly, it changes even Sol. During the Holocaust he had lost all that he loved, he confesses to Marilyn Birchfield late in the film. There was nothing he could do, and now, as the death anniversary approaches, he feels frightened. The emotion puzzles him. As he says, "It's been a long time since I felt . . . fear." Judith Doneson calls the pawnbroker "a weak, almost feminine, figure," and a link between "fear" and a humbled masculinity does not seem so remote, not according to the theory that the Holocaust "feminized [all] European Jewish men, who were castigated as incapable of protecting their families and were therefore led sheepishly to the slaughter."[32]

Seeing *The Pawnbroker* through the lens of gender rather than Jewish history could universalize the Holocaust, rendering it if not (as Doneson

---

30. Fine and Friedkin, "Revised Draft," *The Pawnbroker*, 21 August 1963, Box 2, RLC.

31. John Ellis, "The Literary Adaptation," *Screen*, May-June 1982, 3.

32. Fine and Friedkin, "Revised Draft," *The Pawnbroker*, 28 August 1963, Box 2, RLC; Judith Doneson, *The Holocaust in American Film* (Philadelphia, 1987), 112; Michael Kimmel, *Manhood in America: A Cultural History* (New York, 1996), 278.

says) a metaphor for all human suffering,[33] then a statement on masculinity and its discontents. More so than the novel, though, the screenplay and film treat the feminization without losing the specificity of the Holocaust. Sol is surrounded with weak men. His brother-in-law (not a Holocaust survivor) literally lies prostrate at the beginning of the film, content to be led by his wife and supported by Sol, the "man of the house." One pawnshop customer stutters (he's a pederast in the novel), another lisps. The gangster Rodriguez and the hood Robinson conde-scendingly call Sol *uncle*, grudgingly recognizing his masculinity, but to their consternation he does not flinch at gunpoint. They may also envy the pawnbroker: though neither "weak" nor "feminine," Rodriguez and Robinson are both gay and thus more "other" than Jews are.

Sol best shows his manhood through his paternal interest in Jésus, the one character in the film whose self-doubts change the direction of the story. In their kitchen, in an odd scene, Jésus' mother supervises her son's bath as he teaches her to say "I am a good boy" in English.[34] When he goes to a nightclub—where an artiste ends her dance act by tearing off her wig and showing she's a man—he tells Mabel that the pawnbroker's "been working my back off all afternoon." When he tells her they should "just go up and sit and talk awhile," she pins his lethargy on his weak sex drive and says heatedly, "I don't like you working too hard 'cuz I don't like you using all your energy." Later he will show her what he can do, he snaps back, but when they have sex, she mounts him. (In the crosscut scene, Sol mounts Tessie.) The barb about "using all your energy" burrows under Jésus's skin: as he knows, day in and day out, a man must *prove* his manhood. Accordingly, when the hoods taunt him about working in the pawnshop ("a chicken business") and about his on-again off-again plan to rob it, he finally cooperates with them not only to steal the money but to show that he's man enough to do so.

Sol may well feel anxious about his manhood: when forced to "look . . . look" (at Ruth and the German officer) he is unable to "act like a man." A minor but telling change from novel to screenplay lets us infer that his "fear" has cultural as well as gendered roots.

Wallant's Sol is Polish. As Dorothy Bilik says in her monograph on Holocaust fiction, the pawnbroker was one of the "secularly educated, assimilated European Jews." And as Annette Insdorf reports in her book on Holocaust film, "Polish-Jewish civilization was highly developed between the wars and included experimental education (a Montessori

---

33. Doneson, 11.
34. Unless otherwise indicated, dialogue from *The Pawnbroker* has been transcribed from the soundtrack of the film.

school in Vilna), progressive politics (the *Bund*, a Jewish Socialist party), and ripe artistic movements (Yiddish writers' groups like *Di Khalyastre*."[35]

The cinema's pawnbroker is German. As Rod Steiger's unaccented English (purged of "Jewish" syntax and Yiddish expressions) hints, the German Jews were not only the most assimilated of Europe but tended to consider themselves superior to others. They were free, they thought, of the Orthodoxy that characterized many Polish Jews and felt they were Germans before they were Jews. The death camps were in Poland, where the peasantry was notorious for its anti-Semitism, so when the German Jews were isolated from other German citizens they were puzzled, not least because they were so close to the social history that had produced the Nazis. If an awareness of the *shoah* dawned later—and more profoundly—on German Jews than on Poles, then the cinema's Nazerman may have found it harder than his counterpart in the novel to understand and accept what had happened to him as a man, a German, and a Jew. As such, the screen version of *The Pawnbroker* adds nuance to the character's fear.

The Pawnbroker was rehearsed and shot in New York in fall 1963, under the direction of Sidney Lumet and on a budget beyond the $350,000 once proposed. The principal set (only a few were constructed) was the pawnshop, created by Richard Sylbert and lit, coldly, carefully, by Boris Kaufman. It was (as Lumet wrote later) "a series of cages: wire mesh, bars, locks, alarms, anything that would reinforce a sense of entrapment,"[36] and Lumet used each barrier evocatively. Assistant director Dan Eriksen found many of the actual locations: the bleached landscape of Sol's Levittown home; the peculiar second-story church where Jésus's mother worships; the city park where Sol meets Marilyn for lunch (originally to have been the end of a dock, a movie cliche); Marilyn's Lincoln Towers apartment, whose balcony overlooks smoke-stacks near the center of the frame and a railroad yard of clattering and clanging trains; and the exterior of the pawnshop on 116th and Park Avenues, next door to the Radiante Bar that offers little light and less hope as Sol passes by at the end of the picture.

Along with the locales, the black-and-white cinematography hardens the grittiness of the production. In the 1950s even "small pictures" (like *Tea and Sympathy*) or serious dramas (like *Vertigo*) had been shot in

---

35. Dorothy Seidman Bilik, *Immigrant-Survivors: Post-Holocaust Consciousness in Recent Jewish American Fiction* (Middletown, Conn., 1981), 80; Annette Insdorf, *Indelible Shadows: Film and the Holocaust*, 2nd ed. (New York, 1989), xvi.
36. Sidney Lumet, *Making Movies* (New York, 1995), 102.

135

color to compete with television. Once color reached television in the 1960s, though, Hollywood returned to monochrome, and Boris Kaufman was one of its masters; he had worked on American documentaries before he turned to features, and pictures like *12 Angry Men* and *On the Waterfront* foreshadowed the "realism" of *The Pawnbroker*.

Lumet had good camera sense. He had collaborated with Kaufman on *12 Angry Men* and *Long Day's Journey into Night* and worked fast, usually with two or three takes per shot. He was generous with actors, and the performers responded well, especially Jaime Sanchez (Jésus Ortiz), Eusebia Cosme (Mrs. Ortiz), and Brock Peters, who plays the gay racketeer (Rodriguez) living in a white house with a live-in white lover. Thelma Oliver, portraying Mabel as vulnerable yet brash, had not known that she would bare her breasts; she cried when told, and since (as Eriksen recalls) no "protection footage" was shot, she knew that the nude scene would probably appear in the final cut.[37] Lumet shot the sequence on a cleared stage, and, characteristically, the production quickly moved on.

Rod Steiger was immersed in the role of Sol Nazerman. He had shaved his head (his own idea, he told reporter Arnold Abrams) and hidden "his strong upper lip" behind a gray mustache. "There may be more money to be made in a musical comedy," he told the press, "but at least I feel I've done something worthwhile when I complete a film like this."[38] Lumet and Steiger were especially attentive to Sol's glasses. He has two pairs, one modern with black rims (the "movie-producer kind") and the other round with wire rims, like those Wallant describes. He keeps the latter at the pawnshop and uses the others elsewhere, until the scene with Mabel. Then, during the last third of the picture, he wears only the older pair, the spectacles that augur the looming and long-suppressed confrontation with the memory of the Holocaust.

Steiger and Lumet worked well together, especially in the last scene. The old-fashioned glasses press against Sol's forehead as he kneels over the dead Jésus, as he shapes a cry that never comes. That mute scream anchors the picture in "Jewishness." According to Annette Insdorf it represents not only "the helpless reaction to continued anti-Semitism, as illustrated by the client who calls [Nazerman] a 'money-grubbing kike'" but also "the emblem of the Holocaust survivor, the witness of a horror so devastating that it cannot be told."[39]

---

37. Dan Eriksen, telephone interview with the author, 13 June 1996.
38. Steiger, quoted in Arnold Abrams, "Film Crew Gives Status to Back Yard on L.I.," 9 October 1963, 3, clipping, "Publicity" Folder, Box 2, RLC.
39. Insdorf, 33.

By Christmas 1963 *The Pawnbroker* was in the hands of the editor, Ralph Rosenblum, whose account of the picture in two chapters of *When the Shooting Stops* constitutes the only other production history of the film. Rosenblum and Lumet edited *The Pawnbroker* in January and February 1964. They cut out scenes of the cop and the parasite Goberman and, appeasing the brother-in-law in the Wallant novel (who says that Hollywood has "so much to learn from the Europeans"), added the Holocaust flashcuts which Rosenblum has discussed at length.

According to a February 1964 advertisement in *Variety*, the Landau Company was "dedicated to the production of quality motion pictures for that world-wide audience seeking meaningful and provocative screen entertainment."[40] The *meaningful* would not be the *provocative* shot of Mabel's breasts (assuming it passed the censors) but the integrity of *The Pawnbroker*'s representation of a cataclysmic moment in human history.

Throughout early spring 1964 Landau and Lewis looked on as Lumet and Rosenblum tuned *The Pawnbroker*, and by summer the filmmakers were ready to show the S930,000 production to potential distributors. The latter may have been wary of the content of the film, especially the nudity, which could attract audiences but also litigation. Hoping to establish the bona fides of the picture and soften the censors' anticipated resistance to it, Landau arranged to open *The Pawnbroker* abroad. Lewis later recalled that he had long wanted to screen *The Pawnbroker* at the Berlin Film Festival, and as the award-winning *Bicycle Thief* (1950) had shown, an international reputation could not only trump the Production Code Administration (PCA) office but help a "serious" film set box office records. In early summer 1964 a motion picture trade association panel sponsored by the United States Information Agency chose *The Pawnbroker* as the American entry for Berlin, where it could score an artistic—and political—coup. On 2 July, when the Festival screened the picture, Landau and Steiger were there (and lauded), apparently on the production's budget. Lewis and Langner were also present, on Langner's money, and feeling forgotten.[41]

Lewis was the one constant in *The Pawnbroker*, from the option on the novel through (and beyond) the international premiere of the picture, a point overlooked when Rosenblum says that Landau "found [Wallant's] book, optioned it, and hired two men to write the script before the director ever came on the scene. None of this can be fairly omitted from

40. Landau Company, Advertisement, *Variety*, 12 February 1964, 19.

41. Harold Myers, "'Pawnbroker' Scores in Berlin Fest; Ovation for Steiger," *Variety*, 3 July 1964, 1; Lewis, "Oral History."

the story of the film's success."[42] In fall 1964 Lewis could only watch as the months passed and the Berlin publicity evaporated. Lewis begged Landau for prints to show around Los Angeles, and Landau, through an intermediary, responded "that, at the moment, there are only two PAWNBROKER prints in the United States that have the final version. Both of these prints are being used for screenings here. At such time as we make others, I will notify you and will be happy to send one to you." Landau was probably showing *The Pawnbroker* to likely distributors, and probably garnering more compliments than offers. The nudity was one bottleneck, the Holocaust theme another. "I don't think that Hollywood should deal with anything but entertainment," Paramount head Adolph Zukor had told the press in 1939. "The newsreels take care of current events. To make films of political significance is a mistake."[43] As late as 1962 Paramount had turned down *The Pawnbroker* because it was a low-budget production; another factor was no doubt the "depressive" content.

Finally, one copy of *The Pawnbroker* reached Hollywood. Contravening the protocol for feature films, Landau had not sent the shooting script to the Production Code office for vetting,[44] so agency director Geoff Shurlock may have felt sandbagged. Shurlock quickly screened the picture, though, and on New Year's Eve 1964 told Landau that the bare breasts and one of the sex scenes of Jésus and Mabel were "unacceptably sex suggestive and lustful."[45] The phrase was boilerplate left over from the tenure of former PCA director Joe Breen and calculated to force the producers into concessions. Another month passed. On 29 January Landau pleaded the moral gravity of the picture but was told that the Production Code would continue to hold the line on nudity and that Landau's only recourse would be a formal appeal.

Another month passed. Landau had arranged for Allied Artists to release *The Pawnbroker*, which, technically, the company could not do without the Production Code seal. Bosley Crowther, whose *New York Times* censure of the PCA's treatment of *Bicycle Thief* helped gain wide release of the picture, reported on 9 March 1965 that the New York censors had licensed *The Pawnbroker* sans cuts and that the Motion

---

42. Ralph Rosenblum and Robert Karen, *When the Shooting Stops . . . the Cutting Begins: A Film Editor's Story* (New York, 1979), 165.
43. Alfred Markim, Letter to Lewis, 22 October 1964, Box 2, "Correspondence" Folder, RLC; Zukor, quoted in Neal Gabler, *An Empire of Their Own: How the Jews Invented Hollywood* (New York, 1988), 340.
44. Ely Landau, telephone interview with the author, 19 May 1980.
45. Geoffrey Shurlock, Letter to Markim, Landau Productions, 31 December 1964, Motion Picture Association of America, New York (henceforth MPAA).

Picture Association appeals board (the parent of the PCA) would soon hear the issue.[46]

On 29 March 1965 representatives of Allied Artists told the appeals board that *The Pawnbroker* "will play specialized theatres for the most part, catering to adult audiences."[47] Allied Artists could have released the picture via a subsidiary and thus saved the cost and suspense of a confrontation with the Motion Picture Association. Since 1958, however, Allied Artists (a publicly traded company) had been frequently in the red; the price of its stock was hovering in the low single digits, and its next earnings report would show a $1.5 million loss. Allied Artists needed more than an "art house" hit. A Production Code seal—and controversy—could only help sell an otherwise difficult picture.

Landau assured the appeals board that the nudity was necessary to *The Pawnbroker* and that, more important, he would not exploit it in the advertising. The debate that followed was vigorous. Joe Mankiewicz, the independent producer whose *Suddenly Last Summer* had been a Production Code cause célèbre, defended Landau and *The Pawnbroker* while Spyros Skouras, the former exhibitor whose *Cleopatra* had taken down Twentieth Century-Fox and his presidency of the studio, led the opposition. Another major player, not even present, was Ephraim London, whom Landau had talked with, probably openly, about his plans to sue the Association in the wake of an unfavorable decision. London, having argued the *Miracle* case before the Supreme Court and thus curbed the authority of state and municipal censors, would gladly have taken on the Motion Picture Association, and Landau wanted to do so—despite the thought that other independents producers would have been too soft to join in as plaintiffs.[48] Based on a 6–3 vote, though, the Association granted *The Pawnbroker* an "exception" conditional on "reduction in the length of the scenes which the Production Code Administration found unapprovable."[49] Paramount head Barney Balaban warned that "any self-serving statement that the picture is unique and the so-called 'exception' applies only to this particular film is meaningless. The decision is obviously a precedent for the next and the next and we will learn where it ends only after it is too late." Balaban (the son of

46. Bosley Crowther, "New Decision Due on Movie Nudity," *The New York Times*, 9 March 1965, 30.

47. "Code Seal For 'Pawnbroker' Is Indicated," *Motion Picture Daily*, 24 March 1965, clipping, *Pawnbroker* file, MPAA.

48. Landau, telephone interview.

49. Appeals Board, Motion Picture Association of America, MPAA, "Minutes," 23 March 1965.

Russian Jewish immigrants) was probably swayed by other factors. In 1948 he had told Harry Warner that the return of Loeb and Leopold in *Rope* would have an "adverse influence on [the] standing of our Jewish people in the nation." "Hollywood was itself a means of avoiding Judaism," Neal Gabler says, yet Balaban had toured the concentration camps; too shaken to tell even his family what he had seen, he may have been as averse to Jewish survivors as Jewish killers. Such points of view were not uncommon, as a prominent Los Angeles rabbi showed after release of *The Pawnbroker*. "All [the Jews] talk about is the Holocaust and all the sufferings," Edgar Magnin told Gabler. "The goddamn fools don't realize that the more you tell gentiles that nobody likes us, the more they say there must be reason for it."[50]

Whatever else, Balaban was right about precedents. The "reductions" of nudity were minimal, and the press cheered the producers' victory. "If the Motion Picture Code has been broken, it is time that it was re-written," James F. O'Neill wrote in the Washington *Daily News* in late spring 1965. "When you consider what the dirty-movie houses get away with, and what the legitimate stage is offering in the way of artistic achievement, and some of the trash which Hollywood uses to lure the morons, *The Pawnbroker* evolves as a most tasteful, dynamic and dramatic motion picture."[51] The unspoken achievement was of course the presentation of the Holocaust: *The Pawnbroker* was an acid test of Rabbi Magnin's point of view, and the fray over the nude scenes would be long forgotten before another "Jewish" film superseded the harshness of the concentration camp scenes in the Lewis and Landau production.

The Catholic Legion of Decency tabbed *The Pawnbroker* "C" (for "Condemned"), assured, as one official wrote, "that a condemnation is necessary in order to put a very definite halt to the effort by producers to introduce nudity into American films." Years before, when, according to one bishop, "Jewish control of the industry [was] alienating many of our people," the Catholics might also have been swayed by other factors. The times had changed, though, and *The Pawnbroker* would become the first "C" picture to play St. Paul, Minnesota, a strongly Catholic city; according to *Variety*, "this may mark a letting down of the bars here for such films."[52]

50. Barney Balaban, Letter to Ralph Hetzel, Acting President, Motion Picture Association of America, 29 March 1965, MPAA; Gabler, 300; Magnin, quoted in Gabler, 348–49.
51. James F. O'Neill, Washington *Daily News*, clipping, Pawnbroker file, MPAA.
52. "Draft," *The Pawnbroker* file, Legion of Decency Archive, Department of Communication, United States Catholic Conference, New York; Frank Walsh, *Sin and Censorship: The Catholic Church and the Motion Picture Industry* (New Haven, Conn., 1996), 85; *Variety Daily*, 1 June 1966, clipping, RLC.

Having cleared the censors, the producers now had the harder task of selling a Holocaust picture (the nudity notwithstanding) to an audience of Jew and gentile alike. Landau opened *The Pawnbroker* in Los Angeles at the Pantages Theater, "either suicide or prescient genius," noted the reviewer for the *Hollywood Reporter*. The theater generally screened standard American fare, such as the Sinatra "rat pack" farce *Ocean's Eleven*, which Lewis recalled (in an oral history) was playing in reissue the night *The Pawnbroker* previewed there. The Pantages was RKO's "'key West Coast theatre,'" and the fact that it played *The Pawnbroker* let other exhibitors know that Allied Artists and RKO saw the production as a "big" picture.[53]

Major bookings and critical acceptance of *The Pawnbroker* followed, and so did Academy Award nominations. Rod Steiger lost the Oscar to Lee Marvin (for *Cat Ballou*), and, worse for investors, Landau and *The Pawnbroker* lost to Fox and *The Sound of Music*. The outcome was no surprise to Quincy Jones, who scored the picture. "Hollywood has a funny sort of prejudice toward films that come out of the East and since *The Pawnbroker* was really an East coast production, the industry resisted everything about it."[54]

Playing only key cities, *The Pawnbroker* grossed almost $3 million. Then, for the smaller houses, American-International took over domestic distribution. A-I cut the nudity, won an innocuous "A3" from the Catholic rating board and thus, according to *Variety*, opened up the picture to five- to ten-thousand more bookings. A-I reported that *The Pawnbroker* was only two feet shorter: the shot of the bare breasts had been removed "by using a lab blowup that cuts the girl's body off at shoulder level."[55] (The video bears the A-I logo but is the original Allied Artists release.) Soon Landau rued his pledge about advertising, for *The Pawnbroker* took in $1.5 million in Italy alone, thanks to what the producer called the "sex pitch" that had "proved to be a mainstay" in Italian posters for the film.[56] Domestically, the Motion Picture Association suppressed one "prominently displayed" part of the movie poster "showing the negro prostitute on top of the man."[57]

---

53. Review of *The Pawnbroker*, *Hollywood Reporter*, 16 April 1965, clipping, RLC; Lewis, "Oral History."

54. Baker and Firestone, 189–90.

55. *Variety Daily*, 3 August 1966, clipping, RLC.

56. "'Pawnbroker' Tops Italo B. O. Chase," *Variety Daily*, 14 March 1967, clipping, *Pawnbroker* file, MPAA.

57. Michael Linden, Letter to Jack Goldstein, Allied Artists, 5 November 1965, MPAA.

A beachhead for nudity in motion pictures, *The Pawnbroker* has—unjustifiably—been seen less often as an important picture about Jews, Jewish survivors, and the Holocaust. In the late 1950s *Me and the Colonel* (1958) and *The Diary of Anne Frank* (1959) had touched on the war but tiptoed around the Holocaust. Business was business, even on Broadway. When he directed *Anne Frank* in New York, Garson Kanin had had the playwrights delete Anne's allusion to the constancy of Jewish persecution, "an embarrassing piece of special pleading," he said. "The fact that in this play the symbols of persecution and oppression are Jews is incidental, and Anne, in stating the argument so, reduces her magnificent stature."[58] Jews endorsed the strategy: when *Anne Frank* went to Hollywood, the Jewish Film Advisory Committee applauded the authors of the screenplay for expanding the "universal" meaning of the play.[59]

As Sidney Lumet understood and as Judith Doneson says, "Jewish particularism was not popular in the fifties." At the end of that decade Lumet had read Herman Wouk's *Marjorie Morningstar* and, eager to direct it, flown west to confer with Jack Warner, who had once said that had he known about the Jewish connection to *Rope* he "would not have made any deal to release the picture." Scanning early sketches for the major set of *Marjorie Morningstar*, Lumet was astonished that the resort looked more like Brentwood than the Catskills. Production designer Dick Sylbert was mute, so Warner explained. "'You see, Sidney,' he said, 'we don't want a picture with a narrow appeal. We want something more universal.' I said, 'That means we don't cast any Jews, right?' I was on the three o'clock plane home."[60]

Those associated with *The Pawnbroker* had had doubts about the "particularism" of the story. "In keeping with the screenplay and the original novel," noted Rosenblum, writing more than ten years after release of the picture, the flashbacks portray none of the gross Nazi atrocities. "There were no ovens or executions or horrid human experiments. The story revealed the destruction of an identity," a "human" rather than "Jewish" identity. *Pace* Rosenblum, the flashbacks are not about suffering but Jewish suffering, and they anchor the film in the memory and "particularism" of the Holocaust. *The Pawnbroker* is significant because Sol Nazerman, Jew, is the central character. Absent

---

58. Kanin, quoted in Lawrence Graver, *An Obsession with Anne Frank: Meyer Levin and the Diary* (Berkeley, 1995), 89.

59. Doneson, 72.

60. Doneson, 72; Jack L. Warner, Letter to Barney Balaban, 5 March 1948, *Rope* file, Warner Bros. Collection, Univ. of Southern California. Los Angeles: Lumet, *Making*, 54.

his Jewishness or his life in the Nazi camps there is (as Patricia Erens says) no story.[51]

What then accounted for the relatively brisk box office of *The Pawnbroker*? "Thelma Oliver reveals a forceful personality (and a lovely body, too) as the Negro prostie," *Variety* told industry readers. Though the controversy over the nudity of *The Pawnbroker* surely attracted audiences, current events also produced box office interest in the Holocaust and thus the picture. Raul Hilberg's *The Destruction of the European Jews* had been published in 1961, and Hannah Arendt's account of the Eichmann trial (which lasted from April to December 1961) had appeared in *The New Yorker* in 1962–63 and then, hardbound, in *Eichmann in Jerusalem* in 1963. Both books enjoyed chiefly an intellectual readership; as Irving Howe said, as maddening as were Arendt's views, they "enabled us to finally speak about the unspeakable."[62] The trial itself and the hanging in May 1962 had been one of the major stories of 1961 and 1962 in the American press. "We want the nations of the world to know," Israeli prime minister David Ben-Gurion had said of the accusations and the proceedings, and reporters had spread the word.[63]

McCarthyism was over and the flight to the suburbs and the attendant struggle for assimilation *fait accompli*. In Hollywood and beyond, though, as Stephen Whitfield notes, some Jews "began to realize that the Jewish legacy was perhaps worth nurturing, if the alterative was the blurring of the differences between Jews and their neighbors, if the social contract contained a clause envisioning the end of the Jewish people." More generally, as Lester Friedman notes, there was a burgeoning awareness of ethnicity. Jews and others were now proud to identify themselves as members of a minority group,[64] and *The Pawnbroker* may have garnered a Jewish audience interested in a taste of Jewish history, one that had been less whitewashed than *Gentleman's Agreement* and

61. Rosenblum, 149; Patricia Erens, *The Jew in American Cinema* (Bloomington, Ind., 1984), 285.

62. "Myro," review of *The Pawnbroker*, *Variety*, 6 July 1964, clipping, *Pawnbroker* file, MPAA; Howe, quoted in Howard Morley Sachar, *A History of the Jews in America* (New York, 1992), 841.

63. Ben-Gurion, quoted in Jack Wertheimer, *A People Divided: Judaism in Contemporary America* (New York, 1993), 29.

64. Stephen J. Whitfield, "Our American Jewish Heritage: The Hollywood Version," *American Jewish History* 75 (1986): 334; Lester D. Friedman, *Hollywood's Image of the Jew* (New York, 1982), 171.

Crossfire, one that addressed the screen taboo of the twentieth century, the Holocaust.

Both the "general American" and the "minority" audience of the 1960s were curious about others' heritage and history. And like a Western told by a Native American, a Jewish picture about the Holocaust was a novelty. On television in 1959, then on film in 1961, *Judgment at Nuremberg* had been the stalking horse for *The Pawnbroker*, less because, as Annette Insdorf notes, *Judgment* "fit the bristling new material of the Holocaust into an old narrative form, thus allowing the viewer to leave the theater feeling complacent instead of concerned or disturbed,"[65] than because it raised questions that *The Pawnbroker* could answer. Who were the (anonymous) Jews of *Judgment at Nuremberg*? Telling the story of six rather than six million and how they suffered, died, and were mourned, *The Pawnbroker* personalizes the past.

Finally, no less than Sidney Lumet, Boris Kaufman, Ralph Rosenblum, or others, Rod Steiger was crucial to the popular success of *The Pawnbroker*. Having won an Oscar for *On the Waterfront* (1954) and been nominated for *The Pawnbroker* before it entered general release, he had enough celebrity to sell tickets to the picture yet not so much celebrity that it absorbed the character he played. Justice prevails in *Judgment at Nuremberg* not only because the occasion demands it but because Spencer Tracy sits on the bench. More character actor than star, Steiger has no congenial screen persona that allows us to "excuse" or feel "complacent" about the pawnbroker. He brings Sol Nazerman (not Rod Steiger) dynamically to life, as a Jew, an abrasive, often unpleasant Jew, angry about the Holocaust; in short, he adds to the credibility and "particularity" of the character and assures the story the "small-picture" status that, paradoxically, makes it so powerful.

Ilan Avisar, author of *Screening the Holocaust: Cinema's Images of the Unimaginable*, finds *The Pawnbroker* offensive. Jésus' death, for instance, Christianizes Sol, who, when he presses his hand down on a receipt spike after the assistant dies, adopts the stigma of the cross. In a more persuasive reading, though, Annette Insdorf sees the spearing as the legacy of a Nazi rather than Christian concept. Sol "wounds himself, rendering flesh a mere object" and thus "makes concrete one of the film's central themes: survivor guilt."[66]

---

65. Insdorf, 7.
66. Ilan Avisar, *Screening the Holocaust: Cinema's Images of the Unimaginable* (Bloomington, Ind., 1988), 125; Insdorf, 33.

Avisar says that *The Pawnbroker* debases its Jewishness by drawing a "bogus analogy between the horrors of the Holocaust and living conditions in Spanish Harlem."[67] Lumet had drawn that analogy—but not without an awareness of its flaws, flaws that were, not coincidentally, present in the novel. The latter, for instance, opens on Sol at the pawnshop, where he has his first flashback. The film, on the other hand, opens on Germany before the war, then cuts to the suburbs, blunting rather than reinforcing a connection between the Holocaust and Harlem. And long before the Berlin screening of *The Pawnbroker*, Lumet had continually tinkered with shots of the three Nazis who arrest Sol's family—shortening the shots, then lengthening them, then shortening them again so that the comparison of the three Nazis and the three pawnshop robbers would be hinted at rather than hammered.[68]

Finally, Lumet and his collaborators erected a wall of more than italics (Wallant's device) to separate the concentration camp scenes from those in New York. Quincy Jones scored the present-day scenes with jazz and the backstory scenes with classical music. Boris Kaufman shot the latter to look hallucinatory—less dark, less "aural," less percussive, less densely composed than the New York scenes. And because the past unfolds in fractional seconds rather than whole seconds, it stands in keen and exceptionally filmic contrast to the present, a contrast sharpened by the fact that the concentration camp scenes (unlike those in the novel) are so elliptical that we cannot "read" them.

Roger Lewis once described himself as "often a little too concilliatory [sic]."[69] And so perhaps was *The Pawnbroker*, if not too conciliatory then (for some critics) too universal. The picture testifies nonetheless to the spirit of independent production and, more so, the horror of the event that the story both dramatizes and memorializes. As early as spring 1962, less than three weeks before Eichmann's execution, Lewis, a Jew and a former vice president for advertising, said that he wanted to do not *a* picture but *this* picture, *The Pawnbroker*, "because of the years I spent peddling millions of miles of horseshit on film and hating about 99% of it . . . and then having all the smart guys tell that this one wasn't commercial, would never go, etc."[70]

67. Avisar, 124.
68. Lewis, "Notes re Screening Revised Rough Cut 'The Pawnbroker,'" Ts., 14 February 1964, Box 1, "Miscellaneous" folder, 4, RLC.
69. Lewis, Letter to Allan, 19 February 1961, Box 1, "Correspondence" Folder, RLC.
70. Lewis, Letter to Allan, 9 April 1962, Box 1, "Correspondence" Folder, RLC.

This picture, *The Pawnbroker*, was the work of *collaborateurs* rather than *auteurs*, which may account for its strengths and no doubt its weaknesses. Whatever its inherent successes or miscalculations, it was the foundation for the widely seen American miniseries about the *shoah* and, later, for the most honored and widely seen of all such theatrical films, *Schindler's List*. As Jésus tells Sol, "You my teacher." For the Holocaust pictures that followed, *The Pawnbroker* served the same function.

Review Article

A Reel Witness: Steven Spielberg's Representation of the Holocaust in *Schindler's List**

Frank Manchel
University of Vermont

This essay explores why Steven Spielberg's *Schindler's List* is significant for American cinema, for movies about the Holocaust, and for the artist himself. Two primary concerns guide its search: (1) to review the relationship between film history's "prince of profit" and his account of the Holocaust and (2) to emphasize how moving pictures might offer us something not possible in academic historical studies. The thesis is that the movie and the filmmaker are inextricably intertwined and that an understanding of that bond is useful not only for appreciating the film but also for reducing misconceptions about depicting the Holocaust in a commercial medium.

My goal is to suggest to readers that movies do not function in a vacuum, that their ability to entertain and to educate is tied to uncertain market conditions, daily censorship battles, prevailing industry practices, and powerful financial considerations. The more one understands these aspects of the film's background, the more one appreciates Spielberg's challenges and accomplishments. Thus, a subtext of this exercise is that mainstream theatrical films are both a business and an art, that historical and biographical movies make use of the past to comment on the present, that the mass media mediate between us and the events they depict, and that audiences often mistake that mediation for reality.[1]

The reader should also know at the outset that the tone of this essay differs markedly from that of many film studies. Rather than denigrating pragmatic moviemakers for bowing to commercial realities, I want to explore how artists like Spielberg employ their box-office clout to express their personal visions to a mass audience. As William D. Romanowski aptly stated, "Film has long been realized as a powerful transmitter of culture because it transmits beliefs, values and knowledge; serves as a cultural memory; and offers social criticism. Consequently, the cinema remains a continual battleground in the cultural conflicts in America."[2]

* This work has benefited from the comments of the following colleagues at the University of Vermont: Virginia Clark and Littleton Long, English department; Jan Feldman and Alan Wertheimer, political science department; Dennis Mahoney, German and Russian department; and Denise Youngblood, history department. In addition, I owe a debt of gratitude to Martha Day for her generous help in securing research materials.

[1] For a more complete discussion of these assumptions, see Frank Manchel, *Film Study: An Analytical Bibliography*, 4 vols. (Rutherford, N.J., 1990).

[2] William D. Romanowski, "Oliver Stone's JFK: Commercial Filmmaking, Cultural History, and Conflict," *Journal of Popular Film and Television* 21, no. 2 (Summer 1993): 63.

[*The Journal of Modern History* 67 (March 1995): 83–100]
© 1995 by The University of Chicago. 0022-2801/95/6701-0004$01.00
All rights reserved.

Although released only in December 1993, *Schindler's List* has already become for the present generation the most important source of historical information affecting popular perceptions of the Holocaust. According to one trade publication, the film's global popularity, four months after release, had already netted its makers $170 million, an unheard-of sum for a movie about the Holocaust.[3] While some groups heap honors on those connected with the movie, other circles condemn its perspective and motives.

Such reactions make it clear that *Schindler's List* is not just a movie. It has become part of an ongoing worldwide cultural war that for decades has been debating both the nature and causes of the Holocaust and the advisability of having artists interpret the events surrounding the Nazi genocide. My observations on Spielberg and his work, therefore, are meant to provide a perspective on their place in this important cultural conflict.

A word on methodology. Rather than confining itself to a straightforward review of the movie, this essay examines Spielberg's treatment of the Holocaust in the light of his prior cinematic career.[4] The plan is to position the film in its historical and cultural context and then to speculate on why it took so long for the book to be adapted to the screen. I will focus on three major areas: the subject matter and its visual presentation; the challenges that filming the Holocaust presents; and Spielberg's interpretation of this uniquely monstrous event. Because I assume that artists stimulate our imagination and scholars discipline it, the essay is divided into two major sections reflecting these divisions.

STIMULATING THE IMAGINATION

At the end of World War II, Holocaust survivor Leopold Pfefferberg became obsessed with the idea of persuading some gifted individual to tell the inexplicable story of Oskar Schindler, an apparently amoral German-Austrian businessman who nonetheless saved the lives of 1,100 Jews. Finally, in 1980, a chance meeting with Australian writer Thomas Keneally resulted in the publication two years later of the novelist's critically acclaimed book, *Schindler's List* (in Europe, *Schindler's Ark*).

Based on more than fifty interviews with the *Schindlerjuden* (Jews saved by Schindler), it recounts the spellbinding story of the lustful Catholic industrialist and Nazi spy who came to occupied Poland in 1939 to exploit the persecution of the Jewish population. Using all the wiles of a master con artist, this enigmatic entrepreneur took over a confiscated enamelware factory and manufactured pots and pans for the Nazi war effort. Rather than pay wages to Polish workers, Schindler used Jewish slave labor. Eventually, he convinced the authorities that his

---

[3] James Ulmer, "In Transit: Schindler Dodges Unkindest of Cuts," *Hollywood Reporter* (April 8–10, 1994), p. 18.

[4] My focus on the director as an auteur, the primary author of the movie, is not meant to slight the collaborative process of filmmaking. Nothing could be more obvious than the fact that this film demonstrates Spielberg's dependence on the combined efforts of people like screenwriter Steven Zallian, cinematographer Janusz Kaminski, and editor Michael Kahn.

workers should be quartered on his factory grounds. Using his talent for scheming, bribing, and black marketeering, he not only amassed a sizable fortune but also endeared himself to the Nazi bureaucracy. Then, for reasons never explained, this most unlikely of heroes underwent a transformation and recklessly risked his life and literally gave away his wealth to protect his Jewish laborers. As the Nazi war effort began to fall apart in the waning months of 1944 and word came that all surviving Jews were being deported to Auschwitz, Schindler persuaded the authorities to transport his factory and its "essential workers" to his hometown of Brunnlitz in Czechoslovakia and there convert the plant into a munitions factory. A list of 1,100 Jewish names, "Schindler's List," was prepared. To get on the list was to escape extermination in the gas chambers. Shortly after the announcement of Germany's May 7, 1945, surrender reached Brunnlitz, Schindler, now a presumed Nazi war criminal, fled. In the years that followed, his marriage and business ventures failed. But his courageous actions during World War II earned him the gratitude of the Jewish survivors. In 1956, a carob tree was planted in his honor on the Avenue of the Righteous near the Yad Vashem Museum in Israel. When he died in Frankfurt in October 1974, virtually ignored by the German people, Schindler's body was transported to Israel and buried in the Catholic cemetery of Jerusalem.

Recognizing the stirring dramatic possibilities of the story and inspired by its heroic tale, Music Corporation of America (MCA) president Sidney Sheinberg immediately purchased the screen rights to Keneally's book. The powerful CEO believed that it was the perfect vehicle for his protégé, Steven Spielberg. More than ten years would elapse, however, before Hollywood's box-office king began shooting the film. Why? Clearly, it was not a matter of financing. Unlike other producers who wanted to put Schindler's story on the screen, Spielberg did not have to worry about either financing or distribution.[5] After all, as Richard Schickel observes, "Since no filmmaker has a track record like his, none had his power to encourage both a studio and the young mass audience to take a risk on a movie the subject of which is inherently repellent, not to say terrifying."[6]

Ironically, film is a medium where the more successful you are commercially, the less acceptable you are to the critical community. Not surprisingly, for years Sheinberg was one of the few people, including the director himself, who thought Spielberg capable of making a movie about the Holocaust. In 1982, the thirty-five-year-old phenomenon was markedly different from other Hollywood wunderkind types like George Lucas, Francis Ford Coppola, and Martin Scorsese, who had studied film in college. Spielberg basically learned what he knew from watching movies and making them. His more educated peers might frequent the art houses, appreciate the great subtitled masterpieces, and aspire to Andrew

---

[5] In 1983, Thames's Television produced a fine documentary on Schindler's life. Jon Blair was the writer, producer, director. *Variety* reports that producer Arthur Brauner, himself a Holocaust survivor, struggled ten years to get backing for *An Angel in Hell* (a film about Schindler) but was never able to raise the necessary funding (see Michael Williams, "Spielberg Adds DGA to 'List': Helmer Wins Friends on Euro Tour," *Variety* [March 7, 1994], p. 36).

[6] Richard Schickel, "Heart of Darkness: Ghosts in Their Millions Haunt Steven Spielberg's Powerful *Schindler's List,*" *Time* (December 13, 1993), p. 75.

Sarris's pantheon of cinematic masters, but he preferred the world of B movies: the serials, westerns, science-fiction films, action-thrillers, and war movies.[7]

A few years' work in television during the late sixties and early seventies had landed Spielberg his first theatrical feature, *The Sugarland Express* (1974). Although the public paid scant attention to the film, one critic, Pauline Kael, identified the strengths and weaknesses that would define Spielberg's work up to *Schindler's List.* Characterizing his first feature as "commercial and shallow and impersonal," the *New Yorker* critic also praised the director's ability to make the mundane entertaining. She then went on to write: "The director . . . is twenty-six; I can't tell if he has any mind, or even a strong personality, but then a lot of good moviemakers have got by without being profound. He isn't saying anything special . . . but he has a knack for bringing out young actors, and a sense of composition and movement that almost any director might envy."[8] Within six years, Kael would blame Spielberg, as well as his friend Lucas, for representing everything that was wrong with modern American cinema, especially the industry's emphasis on marketing rather than on creating a movie.[9]

By 1982, most critics echoed her influential judgments, with one major change: no one doubted that Spielberg's films were extremely distinctive. His brilliant cinematic technique had made him the most popular and commercially successful director in film history. Thanks to works like *Jaws* (1975), *Close Encounters of the Third Kind* (1977), *Raiders of the Lost Ark* (1981), and *E. T.: The Extra-Terrestrial* (1982), Spielberg had become the modern Walt Disney. Like his presumed model, he delighted in making movies aimed at entertaining the child in each of us. The phenomenal successes of *Indiana Jones and the Last Crusade* (1989) and *Jurassic Park* (1993) give him the current distinction of having made four of the ten top-grossing movies in film history.[10]

Judging *Schindler's List* from this perspective, one can easily recognize the work of a master film technician in love with the classical Hollywood tradition. Audiences are given not only what they know about the Holocaust from past films but also a format with which they are comfortable. We have a central figure, Oskar Schindler (played superbly by Liam Neeson), who faces a series of obstacles that occur in a specific way during a specific period and are resolved by the film's conclusion. Through a spectacular reconstruction of historical events—for example, the rounding up of the Polish Jews by the conquering Nazi forces in 1939, the establishment of the Podgorze Ghetto in March 1941, the construction the following year of the Plaszow Forced Labor Camp, the destruction of the ghetto in 1943, the dehumanization of helpless people terrorized by merciless guards, the exhuming and burning of ten thousand Jewish bodies in 1944, and the horrors of arriving at Auschwitz—Spielberg and his ingenious collaborators visually "document" Raul Hilberg's unforgettable explanation of how the Nazis adapted centuries of anti-Semitism to the three stages of their Final Solution to the Jewish problem:

[7] In fact, at one point Spielberg thought of turning *Schindler's List* over to Scorsese.
[8] Pauline Kael, "Sugarlands and Badlands," in her *Reeling* (Boston, 1976), p. 300.
[9] Pauline Kael, "Whipped," in her *Taking It All In* (New York, 1984), pp. 207–14.
[10] As of April 1994, *Jurassic Park* is in first place; *E. T.: The Extra-Terrestrial,* second; *Indiana Jones and the Last Crusade,* fifth; and *Jaws,* eighth.

"The missionaries of Christianity had said in effect: You have no right to live among us as Jews. The secular rulers that followed had proclaimed: You have no right to live among us. The German Nazis at last decreed: You have no right to live."[11]

For more than three hours the moving picture creatively reconstructs details of what only the survivors can remember. No films of the atrocities at Plaszow exist, and, as Janet Maslin reminds us, the only surviving photographic record is a set of stills produced by Raimund Titsch, an Austrian Catholic factory supervisor who ran a uniform plant inside the Plaszow Forced Labor Camp.[12] Thus, for countless viewers, Spielberg's staged recreation of the humiliation, torture, and murder of millions and millions of Jews becomes "proof" that the Holocaust occurred. Using actual locations in Poland to heighten the movie's claim to verisimilitude, the filmmaker parades thousands of extras before us to illustrate a mass exodus from the suburbs to the city, from the city to the ghetto, from the ghetto to the labor camp, from the labor camp to the extermination center.

In classical Hollywood style, the story of the millions is demonstrated by the fortunes of the few. We see how, in the early years, individuals plead hopelessly for help from the *Judenrat*—a council of twenty-four elected Jews given modest authority by the Nazis—who supervised and administered the conqueror's law. We watch in disbelief the displacement on March 20, 1941, of a rich Jewish family from its comfortable home and follow them as they join other refugees in the street on a forced march to a sixteen-square-block Krakow ghetto. The sound of Polish onlookers yelling "Goodbye Jews" is chillingly presented. Equally memorable are the images dramatizing the atrocities committed in the ghetto, the forced labor camp, and finally Auschwitz.

The narrative dictates the action, the pace, and the imagery. This is a story of a culture that disappeared in six horrifying years, and how the efforts of one man made a difference to the few survivors. Our emotions are powerfully evoked from the beginning as the opening shots, in color, focus on a Jewish family welcoming the Sabbath and then proceed to quick dissolves eliminating first the parents, then the one remaining child, to the single flickering candle and finally to a wisp of smoke that imaginatively transports us back to the black-and-white era of 1939, with the smoke rising from a locomotive carrying Jews to the Krakow railway station. We see a single clerk set up his typewriter, ink pad, pens, and table to register the dozens of Jews forced out of their neighboring communities and into the urban trap created by the Nazi warlords. In rapid order, a corps of clerks is registering the confused and bewildered Jews at the rate of ten thousand per week. In true Hollywood tradition, Spielberg synthesizes the process by which Hitler's minions meticulously constructed their death lists. Later in the film, Schindler and Itzhak Stern (magnificently portrayed by Ben Kingsley), his Jewish accountant, will repeat the process by compiling another list, but this time one of "essential workers," a list of life; theirs consisted of 1,100 names, constructed hurriedly over a few days in a poorly lit private room.

[11] Raul Hilberg, *The Destruction of the European Jews* (Chicago, 1967), pp. 3–4.
[12] Janet Maslin, "Imagining the Holocaust to Remember It," *New York Times* (December 15, 1993), p. C19.

Relying on the classic Hollywood technique of interpreting history through the actions of centrally motivated characters, Spielberg contrasts the fate of Poland's 3.3 million Jews with the fortunes of Schindler. The effect is fascinating. The camera introduces us to Schindler, the avaricious Nazi opportunist, by showing us not who he is but what he is: a man preoccupied with a decadent lifestyle. All we are allowed to see initially are his preparations for dining out. Still keeping his actual identity hidden from us, the film shifts to a raucous nightclub scene, where the playboy/opportunist systematically curries favor with the top Nazi brass. Slowly, Spielberg acquaints us with the film's major protagonist. First we see him physically: suave, stylishly dressed, amazingly confident, and incredibly presumptuous. Not until several people wonder aloud about the identity of this ebullient host are we told, "That is Oskar Schindler!"

Only in hindsight can we appreciate the reason for the detailed way in which the camera records Schindler's hypnotic style—bribing head waiters, ordering the best food and wine, spending money freely, ignoring anti-Semitic jokes, and having his picture taken with his honored guests. Throughout the movie, Spielberg repeatedly shows the successful results of Schindler's charming behavior; and each new time we witness the outcome of his charismatic ways, the rewards he receives take on greater significance. What is at first only an episode showing how a master manipulator gets valuable war contracts and weasels his way into owning an impounded enamelware plant eventually becomes a major motif in the film, educating us to the fact that it was these unique talents that saved over a thousand Jews from annihilation. As for Spielberg's reason for teasing us in the opening scenes with the secret of who this flamboyant man is, clearly the director is foreshadowing the fact that the reason for Schindler's heroic metamorphosis will forever be an enigma.

Besides its scenes of nudity, terrifying violence, outstanding performances by the film's three major actors, and spectacular cinematography—all ingredients that appeal to mass audiences—the film contains a macabre sense of humor. Initially, one is uncertain how to react. Then one is grateful for the momentary relief in tension. Consider the first exchange between Schindler and Stern. The former is trying to convince the accountant to become his bookkeeper. The latter points out that most people have more urgent problems at this time. Schindler replies incredulously, "Like what?" He then explains his scheme to acquire the enamelware factory. Stern listens in bewilderment and then says, "Let me get this straight. The Jews put up the money, and I do the work. What do you do?" Another scene shows the black market operating in the church during a mass. We see Leopold Pfefferberg (effectively portrayed by Jonathan Sagalle) complaining to his sources that recent merchandise he has bought from them and sold to the Germans was defective. They laugh at him and say that it is not their problem. He answers that he will give their names to the Nazis, and they quickly realize, "Now it's their problem."

As the fate of the Jews becomes more perilous, this humor is given greater scope and visual power. Consider the scene when Stern is put on the wrong list and placed on a deportation train. Schindler goes to the station and demands that a clerk remove Stern's name from the list and free him. The clerk refuses, and the unruffled Schindler tries an authoritarian bluff. He demands to know the clerk's name. The stakes escalate when a young German officer also insists that nothing can be done. At that point, Schindler assures both adversaries that they will be in the front lines within a week. Cut to the three men walking down the station, yelling "Stern! Stern!"

And once again in classical Hollywood style, we are given one of the screen's most unforgettable villains, Amon Goeth (memorably played by Ralph Fiennes), who epitomizes for the audience the horrors of the entire Nazi war machine. While the top brass routinely take bribes and individual soldiers only follow orders, Goeth is a psychopath who appears to murder indiscriminately. He is first seen killing an educated Jewish woman overseeing the construction of the Plaszow Forced Labor Camp, not because she is wrong in her opinion (he acknowledges that she is right) but because she criticizes Nazi incompetence. Later, we see him standing on the balcony of his home at the base of a hill overlooking the camp, watching the morning roll call and then casually, apparently randomly, shooting Jews for target practice. In the end, Spielberg shows an unrepentant Goeth executed by the Poles for crimes against humanity.

If one studies the general reception of *Schindler's List,* it is obvious not only that Spielberg's image has been transformed in the public's mind but also that the film's subject matter has affected our society. *New York Times* critic Janet Maslin echoed the sentiments of most of her peers when she declared, "Mr. Spielberg has made sure that neither he nor the Holocaust will ever be thought of the same way again."[13] Emilie Schindler, the eighty-six-year-old ex-wife of the film's hero, announced the official reaction of many Holocaust survivors from Buenos Aires, "That film is pure truth. It shows some ugly things, but when you realize it's the truth, it's more powerful. The truth was even worse than the film."[14]

Schindler's List also stimulated other interpretations. "Citing everything from the Hebron massacre, in which a Jewish extremist killed Muslim worshipers," explained reporter Bernard Weinraub, "to the assertion that the movie is 'propaganda with the purpose of asking sympathy' to the traditional Muslim abhorrence of nudity and sex in movies, various Islamic governments have given the film a cold, if not hostile, reception."[15] Art Spiegelman, the author of *Maus: A Survivor's Tale,* insists that the movie is not really about the Jews or the Holocaust: "It's a movie about Clinton. It's about the benign aspects of capitalism—capitalism with a human face.... Capitalism can give us a health care program, and it can give us a Schindler."[16] And to make matters even more curious, President Clinton—mired in the enormous dilemma of how to get the

---

[13] Ibid.

[14] "Schindler's Wife 'Lists' Stake," *Daily Variety* (February 10, 1994), p. 23. I write "official" because John Gross reported that Emilie Schindler gave a bitter interview about her ex-husband just before the film was released (see John Gross, "Hollywood and the Holocaust," *New York Review of Books* [February 3, 1994], p. 15). In "Schindler's Wife 'Lists' Stakes," we are told that she is currently negotiating for a percentage of the picture.

[15] Bernard Weinraub, "Islamic Nations Move to Keep Out *Schindler's List,*" *New York Times* (April 7, 1994), p. C15.

[16] Reported in *"Schindler's List:* Myth, Movie, and Memory," *Village Voice* (March 29, 1994), p. 30.

American public to support military action in Bosnia to stop two years of "ethnic cleansing"—urged everyone to view Spielberg's film.

Whatever interpretation one gives to *Schindler's List,* it is undeniable that the public has reacted strongly to Spielberg's supposed documentation of the Holocaust. Worldwide audiences applaud its seeming authenticity, they marvel at his visual virtuosity, they honor his storytelling genius, and they are inspired by his humanity. But these were all strengths that he displayed in 1982. For more than a decade, serious students of the cinema have known about Spielberg's artistry in creating worlds others cannot imagine and making them visually unforgettable. His emphasis has always been on the emotional rather than on the intellectual. He enjoys making the epic event personal. Why should anyone be upset with such a virtuous production?

DISCIPLINING THE IMAGINATION

To understand why there has been a significant backlash to *Schindler's List,* we need to return again to the years between 1982 and 1993. If box-office clout and cinematic talent were not the problems in delaying the screen adaptation, what were the difficulties? Clues to what worried Spielberg surface in his recent statements to the press. For example, after receiving the Directors Guild Award on March 15, 1994, he commented that, "when I first read this book, I said, 'There are a lot of directors in this world who are much better than me to make this picture.' I did not *see* it when I committed to direct it in 1982. I didn't see it because I wasn't ready to see it . . . I didn't want to see it." On another occasion, he said, "I've never given up the ghost of my childhood. . . . I've been hanging on to that. I really feel I stopped developing emotionally when I was 19."[17] To one reporter, the genre director talked about how making the film made him feel "liberated for the first time in my career."[18] To another reporter, Spielberg explained that the film's length and black-and-white monochrome photography are the result of his commitment to remaining "true to the spirit of documentaries and stills from the period."[19] Other interviews reinforce his litany of self-doubts about his need to grow up, to reject his strictly Hollywood orientation, and to deal, on the screen, more truthfully with life. They also dwell on his "born-again Jewishness," how "I was so ashamed of being a Jew and now I'm filled with pride."[20] In talking about his Arizona childhood, he frequently admits that "I was always attempting to assimilate into popular culture."[21]

In reporting these quotations, my intention is not to suggest that they necessarily represent Spielberg's true feelings. Who knows what agendas he had in mind to

[17] *The Economist* in Spielberg List [online], December 25, 1993; available from NEXIS Library, NEWS File: CURNWS.

[18] Schickel (n. 5 above), p. 76.

[19] Andrew Nagorski, "Spielberg's Risk: The Director Takes a Chance with a Holocaust Drama Shot in Black and White," *Newsweek* (May 24, 1993), p. 60.

[20] John N. Richardson, "Steven's Choice," *Premiere* 7, no. 5 (January 1994): 72.

[21] *Atlanta Journal and Constitution* in Spielberg's Crusade [online], December 12, 1993, sec. N, p. 1; available from NEXIS Library, NEWS File: CURNWS.

promote his picture, to change his image, or to curry favor with different award-granting organizations? Spielberg's comments, therefore, can be seen as a shrewd businessman's public relations strategy. He knew that to make his Holocaust film attractive to hesitant mass audiences it had to be a hit at the box office, and that required a special type of marketing approach guaranteed to produce major awards and public approval. One can see such an approach in the filmmaker's concluding remarks in his interview with the German news magazine *Der Spiegel*, where he stated, "If the German reaction to my film should be shame, then it is important to me that the viewers understand, that shame also motivated me to this film. Namely, the shame of having been ashamed to be a Jew."[22]

More to the point, Spielberg's comments suggest that in 1982 the Hollywood-oriented director realized the immense problem of making a Holocaust film, as well as his professional and intellectual limitations. He also may have suspected that the time needed to do justice to the subject matter might best be handled on television rather than in the movie theater. He would not have been alone in that opinion. After all, the Holocaust had become an effective moral catharsis for American viewers after the Vietnam war. Between 1978 and 1989, no less than six major network miniseries dramatized the monstrous events: *Holocaust* (1978), *Playing for Time* (1980), *The Wall* (1982), *Wallenberg: A Hero's Story* (1985), *Escape from Sobibor* (1987), and *War and Remembrance* (1988–89). The reception of those uneven but often gripping projects would make almost anyone realize that professional artistry is no substitute for comprehending the subject matter. Nevertheless, Spielberg understood that film's rare ability to delude viewers into believing that they are experiencing reality carried with it tremendous responsibilities.

To be fair, problems related to treatment and reception were not unique to Spielberg. They are part of the cultural wars. They are part of the tools that scholars use to discipline our imaginations. For example, the issue of whether the Holocaust is an appropriate subject for the arts started when Auschwitz was liberated. Those who have studied the work of such Holocaust scholars as Primo Levi, Elie Wiesel, Theodor W. Adorno, and George Steiner know far better than I their arguments that silence is preferable to almost any fictional reconstruction. For such people, it is incomprehensible that there is an art in reconstructing atrocities, beauty in authenticating horrors, and a profit in dramatizing human misery. These are not, of course, idle or irrelevant arguments. Those who raise them are drawing an aesthetic line not just for Spielberg but for anyone who makes a film about the Holocaust, and most especially for American movies and television features where entertainment is the primary goal.

That having been said, it is also important to appreciate that artists seek to create a world of illusions to provide experiences that enable us to better understand ourselves and the human situation. They force us to examine the unexamined, to imagine the unimaginable. Even mawkish and melodramatic works like the groundbreaking *Holocaust* force the public to rethink its attitudes toward the role

---

[22] "Die Ganze Wahrheit Schwarz auf Weiss" (The whole truth in black and white), *Der Spiegel* (February 21, 1994), p. 186. Translated for me by Dennis Mahoney.

of the media, the meaning of the event, and the responsibility of individuals in our society.

Imagine the questions that Spielberg probably considered. His entire career had been devoted to making sentimental movies with optimistic endings, always reassuring his audiences that they can triumph over their fears if they have the courage and the will to do so. Is that an appropriate approach for interpreting the death of six million Jews? His box-office appeal rested, in large part, on his ability to manipulate people's emotions through the recycling and revitalization of film clichés and stereotypes. Does one bear witness to the past by using trite and trivial imagery? If the film industry demands stars more than statistics, fun more than fact, is film a suitable vehicle for examining the essence of evil? Does it make sense to mix entertainment and education? And what about ratings and box-office grosses? As the history of show business demonstrates conclusively, those who work regularly are those who have the attention of the public. Does one's drive for popularity require misrepresentation? If so, is the danger of factual distortion more disturbing in film because the work is accessible and acceptable to more people? And are factual distortions about the Holocaust insignificant? If the argument is that film will become the visual witness of the past for future generations, what can we do to insure that audiences observe the difference between perception and reality? How can we ensure that they understand that the representation is not the event itself? And what if exposure to a representation misleads the spectator into believing that, having experienced the event itself, there is no need to examine it any further?

I suggest that Spielberg's approach to these types of questions in *Schindler's List* is related to his shame about being Jewish, his orientation to filmmaking, and his exposure to films that he had seen about the Holocaust. I further contend that the film's reception is also related to legacies associated with class, age, race, education, and status. Moreover, the cultural and historical context in which film is received assures us that one cannot control the public's reaction or the use it will find for the movie. If it is true, as Walter Lippmann argued decades ago, that first we define and then we see, it is important to understand that it is only in the last fifteen years that public education has begun to elevate the story of the destruction of the European Jews from the status of a footnote in twentieth-century history to a serious place in the curriculum. No one should be surprised, therefore, that different groups not only see *Schindler's List* differently but also battle each other over its relevance to the past, the present, and the future.

For Spielberg's generation and those who came earlier, television and the movies were their primary classrooms on racism and the Holocaust. This is not the place to review the complex and controversial combination of world events, domestic crises, the nature of acculturation, and the difficulties in attaining basic human rights that affected the policies and practices of the Jewish film moguls who ruled Hollywood. Suffice it to say that American films for the first half of this century struggled to make Jews acceptable to the Gentile world and therefore changed from decade to decade to keep pace with the minority's desire for economic, social, and political freedoms. During Spielberg's personal and professional formative years, the screen image of Jews underwent radical changes. Freedom from studio domination and from a conservative Motion Picture

Production Code allowed filmmakers to reexamine their conservative attitudes toward ethnicity and to stress diversity rather than conformity. The new emphasis on cultural pluralism produced a range of Jewish characterizations with multifaceted personalities. Not all of the images were positive, and many people began to talk openly about screen anti-Semitism and vulgarity. In considering how he was going to present the image of Jews, Spielberg no doubt was influenced by the debates over whether negative ethnic characterizations contribute to or undermine racial bigotry.[23]

Another legacy of American film and television history that influenced Spielberg's sense of Jewishness was the Holocaust productions themselves. Most informed viewers realize that the majority of popular productions stress how catastrophic World War II was for people other than the Jews, that victimization was not limited to one race, and that performances are prized more highly than are honest scripts. Scholars would find it difficult to locate a single American film or television miniseries on this monstrous subject that was not accused by at least one noted commentator of being too melodramatic, simplistic, and trivial. But we need to put such glib positions in perspective. European films also have shortcomings, which rarely get mentioned. Raul Hilberg, for example, is one of the few intellectuals who has dared to criticize *Night and Fog* "as an erroneous and dangerous presentation of the facts. . . . [Because] in it the gas chambers appeared to be destined for Belgian, French or Dutch prisoners, without . . . the Jews . . . being mentioned once."[24]

This essay is not the place to debate the biases of critics. Let me just say in vastly oversimplified terms that conventional wisdom castigates America's film approach to the Jewish catastrophe on four specific grounds: (1) we place too much emphasis on emotional rather than informational issues; (2) we dishonor history by emphasizing the sensational rather than the factual; (3) we underestimate the intelligence of our audiences by oversimplifying complex material; and, worst of all, (4) we sin against the victims of the Holocaust by universalizing the Jewish experience.[25] Only the European filmmakers seem acceptable to a certain class of scholars, mainly because their theatrical works and documentaries are perceived to take great intellectual risks, stress original interpretations, explore complex moral positions, and deal sensitively with the pain associated with the memories of the past.

Sensitive to these issues and haunted by *Schindler's List*, Spielberg began a new cinematic journey after 1982. As Kathleen Kennedy, the former production head of Spielberg's company, stated in 1994, "I have known him for fifteen years . . . and he has spent twelve years talking about it."[26] During that period, he tried to

---

[23] For a discussion on books, films, and articles dealing with the history of Jews in film, see Manchel, *Film Study* (n. 1 above), 1:818–51.

[24] Sylvaine Pasquier, "Raul Hilberg: Un Acte Majeur" (Raul Hilberg: A major act), *L'Express* (February 24, 1994), p. 92. Translated for me by Dennis Mahoney and Eileen Riley.

[25] For useful material on these issues, see Ilan Avisar, *Screening the Holocaust: Cinema's Image of the Unimaginable* (Bloomington, Ind., 1988); and Annette Insdorf, *Indelible Shadows: Film and the Holocaust*, 2d ed. (New York, 1989).

[26] Jacques Buob, "L'honneur de Herr Schindler" (The honor of Mister Schindler), *L'Express* (February 24, 1994), p. 90. Translated for me by Stephanie Giry.

break out of his "Peter Pan" mode by making serious films like *The Color Purple* (1985) and *Empire of the Sun* (1987), although with very mixed results. Particularly significant were his comments in 1983, when he told the *New York Times* that he was troubled about "doing a movie [*The Color Purple*] about people for the first time in my career" and that he feared he'd be "accused of not having the sensibility to do character studies."[27] His forays into World War II had started earlier with *1941* (1979) and *Raiders of the Lost Ark* (1981), and they continued not only with the remainder of the Indiana Jones trilogy (1984, 1989) but also with *Empire of the Sun*. One need only study his treatment of the Germans and the Japanese to see how Spielberg's maturity was tied to his choice of scriptwriter and cinematographer. For that matter, you could gauge how far his sensitivity to Jewish pride had come from his productions of *An American Tail* (1986) and *An American Tail: Fievel Goes West* (1991), two animated cartoons starring Jewish immigrant mice. His intellectual shortcomings in these efforts contrast enormously with the substantive progress he demonstrates in *Schindler's List*.

The question of what approach to take to Keneally's novel, however, was paramount. To help decide, Spielberg (and later his collaborators) studied movies about the Holocaust. Surely he examined films like *The Shop on Main Street* (1965), *Wallenberg: A Hero's Story*, and *Shoah* (1986), all of which include Christians who risked their lives for the benefit of Jewish victims. Clearly he benefitted from the 1955 documentary *Night and Fog*, where Alain Resnais contrasted the past, using black-and-white photography, with the present, using color film, and made a point of showing how the Nazis made use of everything that the Jews owned or wore or had. Obviously, Spielberg must have studied *The Sorrow and the Pity* (1970) and *Shoah* to grasp the importance of displaying hatred and anti-Semitism rather than merely describing it. And certainly he was aware that impolitic casting (Vanessa Redgrave in *Playing for Time*) and inappropriate analogies (comparing the Vietnam war to the Holocaust in *The Memory of Justice*) had created storms of controversy in the past.[28] He may even have discussed the problems of interpreting social issues with William Styron, the author of *The Confessions of Nat Turner* and *Sophie's Choice*.

And how could Spielberg have ignored the fact that the Europeans were the only ones ever to win Oscars for films about the Holocaust? Up to 1990, for example, only four American movies treating the horror had ever been nominated: *The Diary of Anne Frank* (1959), *Judgment at Nuremberg* (1961), *Ship of Fools* (1965), and *Cabaret* (1972). None of them won. In contrast, ever since the foreign film category was introduced in the late 1950s, seven European features about the Holocaust had been entered—*The Shop on Main Street, The Garden of the Finzi-Continis* (1971), *The Tin Drum* (1979), *The Boat is Full* (1981), *The Assault* (1986), *Au Revoir les Enfants* (1987), and *The Nasty Girl* (1990)—and only three times (1981, 1987, and 1990) did one of them fail to receive an Oscar. The Motion Picture Academy of Arts and Sciences has even given an Oscar to the French

---

[27] Cited in Pauline Kael, *Hooked* (New York. 1989), p. 81.
[28] See Frank Manchel, "A War over Justice: An Interview with Marcel Ophuls," *Literature/Film Quarterly* 6. no. 1 (Winter 1978): 26–47.

documentary *Hotel Terminus: Klaus Barbie* (1988). For a man who by 1983 had been nominated three times for best director yet had failed to receive the honor, the European successes must have meant something to Spielberg. What was just as evident was that the American films did well at the box office, while their award-winning counterparts were rarely seen outside intellectual circles.

My contention is that this ingenious filmmaker designed a self-study program to discover what distinguished filmmakers like Alain Resnais (*Night and Fog*), Marcel Ophuls (*The Sorrow and the Pity, The Memory of Justice,* and *Hotel Terminus: Klaus Barbie*), Claude Lanzmann (*Shoah*), George Stevens (*The Diary of Anne Frank*), Stanley Kramer (*Judgment at Nuremberg*), Sidney Lumet (*The Pawnbroker*), and Alan Pakula (*Sophie's Choice*) had accomplished.[29] His purpose presumably was to find a way to merge the documentary approach of Europe with the box-office appeal of Hollywood.

In essence, then, Spielberg the businessman and Spielberg the artist knew that getting his movie across to the public and having that film's message have a significant impact on society depended on approaching the project in a specific way. The film had to account for the attitudes of Holocaust survivors toward the subject matter. The screenplay must incorporate Hollywood's tradition of making an epic story personal. Spielberg would have to distance himself from his commercial interests and convince the public that the film was made out of commitment beyond personal gain. Moreover, the sheer number of Holocaust films on television and on the big screen required his approaching the by-now "familiar" material with a "new look." The manner in which he depicted the events would also provide the opportunity to improve his stature in film history. Finally, Spielberg had to find the right time to release the movie—not just the season of the year but also the moment when society could appreciate its relevance to the present.

His conclusions can be seen in *Schindler's List.* For our purposes, let me indicate five specific areas: (1) the re-creation of sensitive historical incidents, (2) the black-and-white cinematography, (3) the issue of how one survived the Holocaust, (4) the characterizations of Schindler and Goeth, and (5) the ending of the film.

Nowhere is there a greater danger of misunderstanding or misusing *Schindler's List* than in the area of re-created historical incidents. With all due respect to the film's imaginative depictions of the destruction of the ghetto, the selection scenes in the labor camp, and the shower incident at Auschwitz, they are dramatizations, even though a large portion of the public assumes that what they see are the actual events. It is not, as some critics have suggested, just a question of fidelity to detail, or even of the filmmaker's humility in the face of such adversity. Even as far back as Plato's *Republic,* responsible critics realized that art was imitation and several steps removed from reality. If we understand the power of the medium to shape cultural and historical values, then we must curb our enthusiasm for an

---

[29] Other possible filmmakers who may have influenced *Schindler's List,* mentioned by reviewers, include Andrzej Munk, Aleksander Ford, Andrzej Wajda, D. W. Griffith, Orson Welles, and David Lean.

extraordinary piece of filmmaking and discipline our imaginations to the difference between fact and fiction. While I might put it less harshly than commentators like Frank Rich, Leon Wieseltier, or Philip Gourevitch, *Schindler's List* is not an antidote to the 1993 Roper Organization poll, which indicated that nearly 25 percent of all Americans doubt that the Nazis murdered six million Jews;[30] nor can brilliantly re-created scenes of misery and cruelty be used to disprove Holocaust revisionism. But because such scenes have the ability to affect people's values and attitudes, we assume that the most such attempts at authenticity can do is connect us to the event and stimulate our intellectual curiosity about the reality of the past and the possibilities for the future. In such instances, it is not, as Wieseltier suggests, Hollywood's honor that is at stake but education's. It is we, not filmmakers, who are responsible for teaching visual literacy to the public, so that they can recognize the distinctions between perception and reality.

Turning to the issue of the black-and-white cinematography, one clearly sees the lessons that Spielberg learned from European film culture. The quasi-documentary style, making masterly use of German Expressionist lighting, offers striking allusions to the perils of living in Nazi-occupied Poland from 1939 to 1945. Working with his great Polish cinematographer, the director uses his hand-held cameras to show not tell us how human beings could be degraded, humiliated, and dehumanized. The cinematic world that we are given offers unforgettable images of Nazi soldiers who enjoy killing helpless people, horrifying reminders of the lengths to which the Germans went to get gold from their victims, and the painful choices that the hunted had to make in their struggle to survive. Rarely in film history have we witnessed details of a road being built with the gravestones from a Jewish cemetery, or of children innocently singing as they are driven off to their deaths.

But black-and-white cinematography and the avoidance of Hollywood crane and dolly shots do not translate into documentary footage. No pictures, "documentary" or otherwise, can capture the misery, fear, illness, and suffering that occurred, and it is foolish to assert, as some viewers do, that *Schindler's List* can replace the true witnesses of the Holocaust. When Spielberg defends himself by arguing that he did not make a movie about the Holocaust but only "one story from the Holocaust," he misses the point.[31] One major lesson that Spielberg did not learn from artists like Resnais, Ophuls, and Lanzmann is humility in the presence of complexity. The fast-paced shooting and the audacious voyeurism of the Hollywood production place far more emphasis on the emotions than on the intellect, on the art rather than on the event. That is not to say, however, that one style is better than the other. Stirring emotions is one powerful way to get millions of uninvolved and uninterested audiences into examining a complex issue. Spielberg's way is not the Europeans' way, and the two should not be confused.

[30] Frank Rich, "Extras in the Shadow," *New York Times* [online], January 2, 1994, sec. 4, p. 9; available from NEXIS Library, NEWS File: CURNWS. Leon Wieseltier, "Washington Diarist: Close Encounters of the Nazi Kind," *New Republic* (January 24, 1994), p. 42. Philip Gourevitch, "A Dissent on *Schindler's List*," *Commentary* (February 1994), pp. 49–52.

[31] Martin A. Grove, "Hollywood Report: *Schindler* Global Hit; *Maverick* Sneaks Well," *Hollywood Reporter* (April 6, 1994), p. 8.

Much thornier than these aesthetic concerns are the intellectual issues raised by *Schindler's List.* Consider the question of how the film presents the question of survival. Spielberg demonstrates the conventional wisdom that survival depended on chance, that there was nothing anyone could do to outlast the Nazis' barbarism. One sees scenes of hiding places being discovered, of accidental encounters with murdering soldiers on snow-covered streets, of random shootings among prisoners when one of their peers escapes from a work detail. But the film also shows that there were things people could do to improve their own and others' chances. The rabbi who at first survives because Goeth's gun refuses to work is immediately transferred to Schindler's factory by Stern. The daughter who dresses up to gain entrance to Schindler's office does save her parents from death. The quick-thinking child who identifies the dead man as the thief who stole the chicken is rewarded by Schindler, who gets him transferred to the factory. And most important, Goeth does not kill prisoners randomly from his balcony. He shoots only those who are resting. Once the other prisoners begin running, the shooting stops. Even the shooting of the boy whom he twice "pardoned" is the result of an individual not performing his job according to Goeth's twisted standards.

Again, let me make it plain that I am not endorsing Spielberg's interpretation of why people survived the Holocaust. How could I? What do any of us know about the totality of that monstrous experience? J. Hoberman is quite right in arguing, "In the Holocaust, Jews were not saved. Were not snatched from the jaws of Auschwitz. The showers didn't sprout water."[32] That is true. But it is also true that some people did survive. With hundreds of movies being made about the absence of choices, what is wrong with skillfully created films examining another perspective? What I am arguing is that the director, the screenwriter, and the cinematographer offer convincing arguments that many of the 1,100 *Schindler-juden* survived because of individual initiative. Considering that many Holocaust historians take the opposite point of view about how one survived the Holocaust, it is a bold and courageous interpretation to make in a Hollywood movie.

But that daring stance is overshadowed by the brilliance of the film's approach to Oskar Schindler and Amon Goeth. In many ways the film's treatment of these two men appears to be modeled on Plato's discussion of the differences between the virtuous man and the tyrant; and the comparison seems designed to demonstrate Plato's concept that when the state goes bad, salvation can be found in those individuals who put morality above self-interest.[33] Or, as Plato would argue, virtue is its own reward whatever the consequences. We are also told in the *Republic* that the difference between the good man and the tyrant is razor thin. Thus, what distinguishes the virtuous man from the tyrant is often very difficult to discern—as the comparison of Schindler and Goeth demonstrates.

---

[32] J. Hoberman, "Parting Glances," *Village Voice* (January 11, 1994), p. 49.

[33] I can't help noting in Spielberg's marketing strategy for *Schindler's List* the extent to which he portrays himself as the virtuous man, stating that profits from the film will be turned over to Holocaust charities and that his intention is to benefit those who do not know, not those who do. Remember, Plato argued that disassociating oneself from the benefits of one's art, understanding its nature, and understanding one's audience were signs of virtue.

How one becomes virtuous is developed in the film through the use of editing and irony. Consider first a handful of parallels between Schindler and Goeth. Neither one acts virtuously when we first meet them. Schindler goes to the *Judenrat* to get Stern's help in running his business; Goeth arrives at the construction site of the forced labor camp to establish his authority. Both Schindler and Goeth use Jewish slave labor to operate their "businesses." Just as Schindler interviews ten Jewish women for a secretary's job, focusing on their physical beauty rather than on their professional skills, so Goeth "interviews" a line of Jewish prisoners for a maid's position, selecting the one least qualified for domestic work. Following the massacre in the ghetto, Schindler reflects on the tragedy by looking down from his upstairs office on the empty factory floor below, while Goeth looks down from his balcony on the morning roll call. When Schindler first meets Goeth, their initial conversations are about clothes, money, and business pressures. In short, both are consumed with material pleasures, and both eventually are perceived to be "mad" by those closest to them.

Their differences are not as obvious as one might suspect. In fact, there is a crucial scene where Schindler defends Goeth to Stern, arguing that you have to understand the commandant's position: "He has a lot to worry about." It's the war that's making Goeth behave as he does. (Earlier, the industrialist had explained to his wife that the war is the reason for his success.) Schindler argues that Goeth is really not such a bad fellow and that the two of them have a lot in common: womanizing, drinking, a love of the "good life." It is at that point that Stern reminds Schindler and us that the chief difference between the two men is that Goeth is a killer. Spielberg then intercuts Goeth's random shooting of twenty-five laborers in a returning work group. The point is again brought home in a drunken balcony scene, where Schindler lectures Goeth about the importance of temperance, power, and justice. He tells him the parable about the emperor who had the ability to execute but preferred to pardon. Goeth tries to apply this principle but is unable to do so. Schindler can. And near the end of the film, after we have been shown countless examples of Schindler's ability to bribe officials successfully, we see Goeth trying to imitate his friend to get him out of jail and failing miserably. Lest anyone forget the comparison, Spielberg lets Schindler bribe the commandant of Auschwitz to free the three hundred imprisoned Jewish women. Of particular importance is the fact that the film omits the novel's references to how much Schindler hated the Nazis. That omission intensifies the parallels between the industrialist and the commandant.

The difference between the virtuous man and the tyrant becomes clear when one realizes the loyalty that Schindler feels for "his family" (the *Schindlerjuden*) and that Goeth feels for money. In a telling scene, the two men bargain for the fate of 1,100 "essential workers" while visually a window post divides the pair. Schindler gives away all that he owns in order to save his workers; Goeth takes all he can get but complains that he just does not understand the scam Schindler is playing on him. And lest anyone miss the message, there is the ring-giving scene outside the factory, where Stern explains that the caption on the ring is taken from the *Talmud:* "Whoever saves one life saves the world entire." The final touch is to show that both men died with all their material goods taken from them. Nothing mattered in the end except virtue.

Throughout the film, Spielberg and his technical crew reinforce this Platonic idea by the use of chiaroscuro lighting, reminding us of the *Republic*'s explanation that light allows one to see knowledge and wisdom but that these forces can be eclipsed by darkness, filth, and duplicity. Thus, Schindler's triumph lies not only in seeing the error of his ways but also in doing something about it.

Crediting Spielberg with such a quantum leap in intellectual content is a double-edged sword. On the one hand, it acknowledges the substantive merits of the luminous script and rejects the idea that either Spielberg or Hollywood is limited to merely manipulative, emotional exercises. On the other hand, it illustrates once again how the uniqueness of the Holocaust is universalized. Clearly, one can see why the filmmaker is so intent on showing his movie to children, and why state governors are eager to use it as a means of combatting racial intolerance. At the same time, it obscures the fact that the Holocaust is a specific event in history, not a generalized horror.

My last concern is with the final scenes of the film. Schindler gathers his factory workers, persuades the Nazi soldiers to disperse, explains why as a "war criminal" he has to flee, and then breaks down over the realization that he could have saved more Jews if he had sold his Nazi pin (worn prominently throughout the film) and expensive car. Most reviewers comment negatively about the melodramatic nature of the scene and its overly sentimental presentation. Others attack it for its downright dishonesty, pointing out that Schindler was too scared about his fate to say anything, that the car was lined with money for a safe getaway, and that he fled not only with his wife but also with his mistress. Equally important, Steven Zallian admitted that including the ring-giving ceremony—an incident not described in Keneally's novel—was done precisely to remind the audience "that although Schindler saved some 1,200 people, 6 million more died during the Holocaust."[34] Here one must decide how much dramatic license we are willing to give the artist, whether one wants the work to be faithful to the world of illusions or to the world of reality, and whether factual truth is an aesthetic requirement for art.

A similar point can be made about the final scene, where the players and their true-life counterparts file past Schindler's grave on Mount Zion. Many people believe that this is a striking reminder of what the Holocaust was about, as a printed screen statement tells us that only four thousand of the 3.3 million Polish Jews survived but that there are six thousand survivors and descendants of the *Schindlerjuden*. I believe that statement is necessary at the end of the film because emotionally audiences are mourning Schindler, not the Jewish victims. At the same time, I am certain that there are those viewers who see the statistics as yet another reminder about Schindler, not the Jews. Thus, no matter whether one is uplifted by Schindler's heroism or saddened by his death, once again a film about the Holocaust has used the Holocaust as a backdrop to a powerful historical drama.

Schindler's List illustrates many important ideas not only about Spielberg but also about the problems associated with depicting the Holocaust in the mass media. First, its images remind us of previous movies about the Jewish

---

[34] "Backstage at the Oscars," *Variety* (March 22, 1994), p. 35.

catastrophe. A careful study of this film reveals the artist's debt to other works, as well as his many new contributions to the subject matter. Second, the questions raised about the movie's authenticity and historical relevance serve as meaningful reminders about the cultural debate surrounding aesthetic works about the Holocaust. The discussion reminds us anew that there is a difference between history *on* film and history *in* film. The former refers to historical dramas like *Schindler's List* that try to re-create the past. As historical records of the subject matter, they fail to measure up to the criteria used in judging historical evidence. History in film, however, refers to the medium's relation to society: how it reflects and affects people in a particular place, time, and period in history. Here, Spielberg's work provides invaluable documentation on the attitudes and values of society in 1994. Third, an analysis of why the movie is so popular worldwide reveals that many of the cinematic techniques used in *Schindler's List* can be traced back to the director's skill in his earlier works. It is a mistake to assume that this movie is not based on decades of training and expertise. Fourth, the accolades bestowed on Spielberg and his film, while richly deserved, also tell us about the critics and *their* maturity in finally recognizing a very talented filmmaker. Fifth, the critical reception of the film reinforces the notion that there is no way that artists can control how an audience interprets and uses their motion pictures.

Once we understand that movies do not appear in a vacuum and that their ability to entertain and to educate is tied to industry practices and to audience expectations, we recognize that movies can be, and often are, misunderstood and misused by the public. *Schindler's List* demonstrates that art is not about factual truth but about experience and that experiences are provided by artists who use the legacies of the past to interpret the present. Recognizing that each experience is different, we should realize that one film need not compete with or replace other works on the Holocaust. In this case, *Schindler's List* takes its place as one of the great achievements in the history of motion pictures, for it teaches us that momentous experiences must always be critically examined as both history and art.

What Combat Does to Man
Private Ryan and its Critics

__Eliot Cohen

Among the groups of scared, tired riflemen along the beach were a few intrepid leaders—officers, non-coms, and privates on whose individual backs the big responsibility at the moment lay. They began by example and exhortation to prod the men to get up, leave such poor shelter as they had found, and walk or crawl across the beach flat and up the hills where the enemy was dug in with rifles, mortars, and machine guns.

—U.S. Army history of the Normandy invasion[1]

T HE FIRST MOVIE audiences to see *Saving Private Ryan* went in to watch it with the usual accompaniments of that form of entertainment—boxes of popcorn and noisy banter. Two hours and forty minutes later they streamed out in stunned, wet-eyed silence. Veterans of World War II (even those, such as Paul Fussell, who are most caustic about the gulf between those who live war and those who write about it) testified to its fidelity to reality. A chat room devoted to the movie on America Online attracted ten thousand postings in a week, many from veterans or their children, paying tribute to the film. The American Legion created a "Spirit of Normandy" award for Steven Spielberg, and the U.S. Army, in the presence of its chief of staff, General Dennis Reimer, gave him its highest civilian decoration. The

Marine veteran who edits the semi-official *Proceedings of the U.S. Naval Institute* saw it, came back to his office, shut it down for the day, and took his entire staff to see it.

Oddly enough, however, highbrow critics across the political spectrum had little good to say about *Saving Private Ryan*. Perhaps understanding the movie better than their colleagues on the Right, some on the Left thought that although the movie portrayed war as horrific, it said too many nice things about military virtue. Vincent Canby in the *New York Times* sneered that "with *Saving Private Ryan* war is good again", expressing surprise that the movie suggests, "without irony, if obliquely—that Mom and apple pie were what Americans were fighting and dying for."[2] Writing in the *New York Review of Books*, Louis Menand complained that movie viewers would not be as horrified by German deaths as by American ones. He urged upon the reader the notion that "what makes war appalling isn't the possibility that someone will maim or kill you; it is the possibility that you will maim or kill someone else."[3] One doubts that many infantrymen would share

---

Eliot Cohen is professor of strategic studies at the Paul H. Nitze School of Advanced International Studies, Johns Hopkins University.

[1]Gordon A. Harrison, *Cross-Channel Attack* (Washington, DC: Department of the Army, 1951), p. 320.

[2]Vincent Canby, "War Movies: The Horror and Honor of a Good War", *New York Times*, August 10, 1998.

[3]Louis Menand, "Jerry Don't Surf", *New York Review of Books*, September 24, 1998.

such philosophic detachment, or, frankly, that responsible citizens (let alone parents and wives) would wish them to. In a protracted polemic directed against not only Spielberg but historian Stephen Ambrose, whose work inspired the film-maker, John Gregory Dunne in *The New Yorker* disdained as "butch and bluster" the views of op-ed writers who found something profound or moving in the movie.[4]

Conservatives have given Spielberg much rougher handling.[5] Some of this reflected personal animus against a well-known liberal, and descended into *ad hominem* accusations. Thus, even one of the more thoughtful critics, Christopher Caldwell, began his essay with an extended discussion of Spielberg's politics, and concluded with grudging praise, but also with a swipe at Spielberg as a representative of his generation. The movie, he wrote, may suggest that the Baby Boomers "understand the stakes of World War II, and the rightness of World War II. But it leads one to suspect that, all the same, they would never have fought it themselves."[6] Setting aside those hundreds of thousands of Baby Boomers who dutifully trooped off to the Vietnam War, how does Spielberg's movie reveal that, one wonders? Other conservatives were harsher yet. John Podhoretz in *The Weekly Standard* decided that the movie showed Spielberg's "limitations not only as an artist but as an adult." And Richard Grenier concluded, egregiously, that, "In Mr. Spielberg's view, the Stars and Stripes, worn on the shoulder, are almost the equivalent of the Swastika."

Many of the conservative critics deplored the movie's failure to rub its audiences' noses in the view that World War II was a Noble Cause, to which Charles Krauthammer aptly replied, "World War II speaks for itself. It needs no spin. Only a moral idiot can doubt its justice."[7] In fact, soldiers at the time (witness Bill Mauldin's Willie and Joe cartoons in *Stars and Stripes*) would have squirmed at patriotic declamations. As Mauldin noted in *Up Front*, the GIs referred to the Germans as "krauts", not "Nazis", and had little use for overt attempts to inspire them to do their

job.[8] Still, unlike such movies as *Paths of Glory* or *Platoon*, there can be no question but that *Saving Private Ryan* is suffused with patriotism. It begins and ends with a waving flag; features a dignified George C. Marshall quoting a heartrending letter by Abraham Lincoln to the bereaved mother of five sons; and portrays heroic acts by men of all ranks.

One scene, overlooked in the gore and noise of the battle pieces, makes this point particularly vividly. It depicts the administrative office in Washington where a clerk notices that three boys named Ryan have died within a week, leading to the discovery that all came from the same family. The clerks and their superiors (including a one-armed colonel commanding the unit) are serious and alert; the narrator reading excerpts of letters

---

[4]John Gregory Dunne, "Virtual Patriotism: Feeling Good About War", *The New Yorker*, November 16, 1998.

[5]John Podhoretz in *The Weekly Standard* ("All Guts No Glory: Steven Spielberg's World War II", August 3, 1998), Richard Grenier in the *Washington Times* ("Gandhi Spielberg", August 11, 1998), and John Simon in *National Review* ("The Best, or the Biggest?", August 17, 1998) all panned the movie; while the centrist *The Economist* and *The New Republic* were no better than tepid in their treatment of it. Stephen Hunter of the *Washington Post* wrote the most perceptive review ("*Private Ryan*: Steven Spielberg's Unflinching Tribute to the Men Who Conquered Hell", July 24, 1998) and a cutting critique of the critics ("Strafing *Private Ryan*: Conservatives Say Spielberg's Film is Too Far Left. They're Wrong. It's Conservative, and Right", August 9, 1998).

[6]Christopher Caldwell, "Spielberg at War", *Commentary* (October 1998).

[7]Charles Krauthammer, "Debating *Pvt. Ryan*", *Washington Post*, August 14, 1998.

[8]Bill Mauldin, *Up Front*, reprinted in *Reporting World War II* (New York: Library of America, 1995), vol. II, p. 315. This, the second in a two-volume collection of reportage, depicts well the kinds of characters and situations covered in the movie.

---

of commanders to bereaved families describes only good soldiers and fine men. A satirist or a skeptic would not depict that kind of military bureaucracy as efficient or humane. Spielberg, however, allows not a whiff of irony to drift into this scene.

THE MOVIE'S apparent theme is whether it is worth risking the lives of eight men to save one. Captain John Miller, played by Tom Hanks, begins by describing the effort to locate the last Ryan boy as a "public relations mission." During the interval between the movie's two great battle scenes he and his men wrestle with the problematic nature of their task. "We got mothers too", one private remarks sarcastically, and then, pausing, "except maybe the captain." But a tall paratroop captain through whose unit Miller passes surprises him by affirming the worth of the mission. By the time he and his squad have found Ryan, the tough, simple, and unsentimental Sergeant Horvath concedes that this may be the "only worthwhile thing we've done in this whole awful shitty mess." Even the most bitter and skeptical member of the squad, Private Reiben, who is prepared to despise the man whom they have come to rescue, has reconciled himself to the mission. Reiben, who feels particularly keenly the losses suffered to this point, finds himself in a foxhole with Ryan just before the climactic battle with the advancing Germans. In one of several brilliant moments of wordless acting, he gives Ryan a hard look and a slight nod, indicating that he too has accepted not only Ryan, but the value of their task.

The movie's conclusion makes it clear that the most important soldier of them all, Miller, has come to believe that the mission has indeed been worth it, with one haunting proviso: the survivor must attempt, somehow, to redeem the sacrifices made by those who fell. The basic problem here—pulling back a sole surviving son from combat—was a real one in World War II.[9] The broader question of risking many men to save one occurs fre-

quently in war, as Americans have seen even in the last few years when pilots have had to bail out over hostile territory in Bosnia and Iraq. In fact, however, the movie's importance does not lie in its treatment of this question. Rather, it resides in its depiction of men in battle, and of the nature of military leadership.

Even Spielberg's sharpest critics concede his artistic skill in depicting combat. Still, several of the more desperate commentators attempt to demonstrate their bona fides as military historians by resorting to quibbles—heaping scorn, for example, on the rank insignia painted in white on Miller's helmet, which, they insist, would merely have made him a target for German snipers. Richard Grenier remarks, "I know—unlike the captain in *Private Ryan*—that officers never wear insignia of rank in combat." Untrue, as it happens, since policy on this matter has varied widely from war to war and unit to unit, and more than one officer has chosen to disregard higher authority on this issue. More to the point, the army official history of the Normandy invasion has in it pictures of two battle-stained captains with white bars prominently displayed on the front of their helmets.[10]

A fair-minded and better read military historian would point to more substantial and serious divergences from D-Day reality, such as the absence of naval gunfire, often delivered at pointblank range by destroyers operating perilously close to the shore, which helped suppress the German positions dominating the beach. More serious yet is the implausible nature of the tactical problem inherent in the final shootout between an understrength pla-

---

[9]See Donald F. Crosby, S.J., *Battlefield Chaplains: Catholic Priests in World War II* (Lawrence: University Press of Kansas, 1994), p. 136, for one such episode.

[10]Harrison, pp. 316, 439. In truth, to this day American soldiers will often wear "subdued" (i.e., black or darkened) rank insignia on battle uniforms, although at various times and in various units even these will disappear.

toon of American soldiers and what looks to be a company-strength German mechanized task force, an episode that despite all of its drama has too much Hollywood in it. This scene escapes reality in certain technical and tactical aspects that undermine its plausibility, as when Corporal Upham waits until the shooting starts to begin delivering ammunition to a machine gun in a tower.

At a deeper level yet, one might note that no one can hope to portray combat per se: battle produces unique hells in air, on land, and at sea, in different theaters of war, and at different times and places. Movies, moreover, invariably create distortions of time, atmosphere, and emotional experience that prevent them from duplicating reality.[11] But these reservations, though better founded, also miss the point. Spielberg has captured battle with as much fidelity as one can outside of pure documentary, and in some ways rather better.

Paul Fussell has suggested that the first twenty-five minutes of the movie be made into a documentary entitled, "Omaha Beach: Aren't You Glad You Weren't There?" Indeed, the heart-stopping realism of the D-Day scene alone would make the movie worthwhile. That realism, however, goes far beyond a naturalistic rendition of maimed bodies and screaming men. The movie's uniqueness lies less in its graphic depiction of what combat does to man—the exposed viscera, spouting blood, and headless bodies—than in its portrayal of how man fares in combat. One lesson concerns the harsh penalties often exacted by sentiment or folly in war: a soldier trying to rescue a French girl dies an agonizing death from a sniper's bullet, and a glider reinforced to protect one man's life—a general's—becomes unmanageable and crashes as a result, killing almost all on board. Other movies show blood and guts aplenty, but few show death catching men so randomly, before they have had a chance to fight, or (in this case) even to disembark to prepare to fight. Randomness pervades the movie, to include the basic premise: the death of the three other Ryan brothers, necessitating the rescue of the fourth.

Not merely randomness, but a realistic weirdness characterizes Spielberg's portrayal of war. The eery dialogue in the death grapple between a knife-wielding German soldier and one of Miller's men at the very end of the film, the murderous cool of the squad sniper as he mutters Old Testament prayers while marking the range to his victims, the darkly comic confrontation of two soldiers with jammed weapons who throw their helmets at each other before reaching for pistols—all of these scenes have occurred, we know, in real war, and all reveal something of human nature.[12] "Why can't you bastards give us a chance?", screams the medic after a burst of fire kills the man whose wounds he has just staunched. Small wonder that another soldier shouts, "Let them burn!" after a flamethrower turns the German occupants of a machine gun nest into human torches. Veterans have long known (although rarely reported to the folks back home) that sometimes they take prisoners and sometimes not, and sometimes they may shoot a few before battle fury subsides and then let the rest survive. These scenes too have a terribly convincing quality. Horrible as some of these deeds are, American soldiers appear not so much to be committing atrocities as yielding to a kind of combat insanity. Their callous joking while sorting through the dog tags of dead soldiers contrasts with the tenderness with which they care for a dying comrade, which contrasts yet again with their hard desire to shoot in cold blood the hapless German soldier who also was only doing his duty in gunning down their buddy.

Spielberg captures the strange mind tricks played by combat. Several times during

---

[11]A competent military historian, Peter Maslowski, has explored these issues thoughtfully in "Reel War vs. Real War", *Military History Quarterly* (Summer 1998).

[12]For example, during the second Battle of Bull Run during the Civil War, Union and Confederate soldiers suddenly meeting one another in the woods threw stones at each other before using their weapons.

the movie Captain Miller, stunned by noise and what he has seen, becomes weirdly detached from a reality that seems to have become suspended, silent, and remote. Within a few seconds he returns to the here and now, in a phenomenon reported by veterans of infantry combat. He suffers, moreover, from the physical manifestations (in particular, an unstoppable tremor) of the combat fatigue that was only beginning to be fully understood during the Second World War as something altogether different from lack of resolve or mere cowardice. This too is subtly portrayed: at several points Miller tells Sergeant Horvath that he doubts his ability ever to explain to anyone what they have seen and done. When he says that he has journeyed so far from home that he doubts he can ever return, he refers not only to the physical distance and mortal perils that lie between Normandy and small-town Pennsylvania.

The truthfulness of the movie thus extends to the non-combat scenes as well. The mock homosexual banter of the soldiers, the assortment of human types found in any military unit, the pathetic wish of the outsider (Corporal Upham, the morally problematic translator dragged along on the mission) to be accepted and the reluctance of the veterans to have him—these ring true. So too does Ryan's adamant refusal to abandon his exposed comrades when Miller finally finds him. He expresses a sentiment shared by countless soldiers when he tells rescuers that these are the only brothers he has left. There are other poignant moments, as when Miller and Horvath remember, with mirth ever so slightly tinged with hysteria, some of the characters who have served with them—and suddenly realize that all of these men are gone, and that they are mocking their idiosyncrasies. There are grimly comic moments too, as Miller begins to despair of ever finding Ryan after several false starts.

When Miller reports back to the beach a few days after the landing in order to receive his new mission, he glances at a couple of GIs eating fresh salami sandwiches and shaving

with hot water. In an instant one sees on his face (again, without a word) the resentment and then the resignation that front-line soldiers feel when they see rear-area troops enjoying what civilians think of as the most trivial luxuries. In the same instant the thought occurs to the viewer that we, so far removed from this world, would normally have thought of the lounging men as combat troops (they are, after all, no more than a couple of miles from the front); but, in fact, they are almost as distant from what Miller and his men have gone through as we are. A similar sense of distance begins and ends the movie, when, in a contemporary Normandy cemetery, an aged veteran comes to terms with the aching losses the movie depicts. On the faces of his pleasant and attractive blonde grandchildren one reads a vague concern about the old man, but a complete lack of understanding of what he has experienced, and how it consumes him still.

SAVING PRIVATE RYAN's essential psychological truth supports its second great theme: leadership. Reviewers who, in a curiously confessional mood, declared with Roger Ebert that, "I identified with Upham, and I suspect many honest viewers will agree with me", missed this point.[13] To be sure, part of the movie's power lies in the anxiety it engenders in its viewers that, in similar circumstances, they might have acted like Upham rather than, let us say, Reiben. Still, Upham is, in fact, a minor and certainly unattractive figure: his last act is a cowardly murder, committed in a hopeless attempt to recover some self-respect following his failure to come to the aid of a comrade in combat. Rather, the men to watch are those in the original squad led by Hanks' character. In this regard, the D-Day sequence bears watching (if one has a strong stomach) more than once. The first time the viewer sees chaos and horror simply: death hammering on the ramps of tossing landing

---

[13]Roger Ebert, *"Saving Private Ryan"*, *Chicago Sun-Times*, July 24, 1998.

craft before men can get out, and the scourge of shot and shell on that open beach. The second time, however, one notes other things, in particular the improvisation and determination that, in the end, made the landings there a success. A thread of tactical skill, only intermittently visible to those watching, underlies the wiping out of a German bunker, and Miller's company's passage to the exit paths that were, in fact, the tactical objectives of the improvised teams of men at Omaha. In that breakthrough Miller does not indulge in heroics; he makes decisions, gives orders, and sends his men first into the fire when that makes sense. It is Sergeant Horvath who yells, "We're in business!", and leads the breakthrough.

Tom Hanks clearly has some leadership ability himself. When the other actors mutinied against the retired Marine veteran who put them through ten days of misery to prepare for the combat scenes, Hanks shamed them into staying the course. His portrait of Miller as a leader is flawless. If civilians should see the movie to remind themselves of, in Siegfried Sassoon's words, "the hell where youth and laughter go", second lieutenants should see it to reflect on what it means to lead men in battle. Miller manages a delicate balance between intimacy with his men and a carefully maintained distance from them. He treats the fumbling and panicky Upham with amused authority, but subtly pulls him into the unit. He gently helps Ryan to remember his fallen brothers, and then, equally gently but firmly nonetheless, declines to let the private peer into his new commander's soul. His personal background is a mystery to his men, and he keeps it that way, playing on their curiosity to serve the ends of discipline. He encourages them to gripe, but reminds them that gripes "only travel up, never down": he will never complain to them. He participates in their banter, but there is no doubt that he is the boss. That, as he says to Private Ryan at the end, "is non-negotiable." Even so, Miller cannot always bark orders; he must at times persuade, cajole, and even manipulate his men in order to get them to do what he wants. A

military historian once observed that in all armies there is a silent vote that occurs before men move forward, and this too we see in *Saving Private Ryan*.

Miller's men have noticed his hand shake as he tries to hold a compass, and although he attempts to joke them out of their anxiety, they eye him with a mixture of solicitude for a beloved leader and raw fear of losing the man they need to keep them alive. In yet another wordless moment, when overcome with grief at the death of one of his men, he manages— but just barely—to find a shell hole to yield to the emotional storm, so that his men will not see him crack. The frantic look he casts over his shoulder to make sure that he is hidden from view reflects the instincts of the leader dominating and controlling, with a supreme effort of will, the anguish of the man. It is not just that he has seen too much horror, or that he grieves over a single man. A young officer learns that he must place in strict order of priority "my mission, my men, myself." Miller keeps his own fears and longings very much to himself, but he broods about the price his men have paid to achieve their missions ever since his war began. He attempts to convince himself that the men he has killed—and by this he means his *own* men, who have died carrying out *his* orders—have, through their sacrifices, saved the lives of many more. He recognizes the tenuousness of this rationalization, but he clings to it to stay sane.

Real-life combat leaders exude the kind of quiet self-confidence and purpose that Miller displays on film. They also suffer the kind of pressures that bring him close to the breaking point on numerous occasions—as when he begins shouting at a passing column of paratroopers, or when his men nearly dissolve in mutiny before he intervenes to get them in hand. In the end, their men follow the Millers of this world not simply because of The Cause or even formal discipline and mere habit, but because of a moral authority rooted in competence and character. Miller's men, on the other hand, prove themselves, with one exception, to be average heroes: guys who hate their duty but do it, and do it to a high standard and despite their fears. Miller himself appears to us as an altogether believable leader of a type always in scarce supply, but frequently enough encountered to be familiar to those who know soldiers.

IF *SAVING PRIVATE RYAN* offers real insight into the nature of battle and leadership, why so little attention to these aspects of it on the part of critics? There is a personal reaction to Spielberg here, puzzling if only because no evidence suggests that he is anything other than a considerably nicer type of human being than many other spectacularly successful Hollywood producers. As for his politics, they have nothing to do with whether he has created great art. Perhaps distortion has arisen from many critics' temptation to discuss a movie genre—"the war flick"—rather than to discuss war, particularly if they have not experienced it themselves. A desire to fight cultural battles rather than meditate upon real ones has similarly distorted much of the reaction to the movie.

There is, however, a deeper explanation for critical disquiet with *Saving Private Ryan*. The movie offers no easy way out for its characters or its audience, and hence for critics. D-Day was, we all know, a smashing strategic success—but now we have an inkling of the horrors that accompany even lopsided victories. Miller's mission is a morally just one, we come to believe—but not so unambiguously right that survivors of it can brace themselves up and say, "Yes, the casualties were worth it." Miller is a great leader—but he has killed his men when he could have kept them alive, and teeters on the edge of psychic collapse. Courage and skill bring success—but never seem able to guarantee physical survival or psychological peace: the lone surviving veteran in the cemetery at Normandy can never know that he has "earned this." Most troubling of all, the men who fought this great war did their duty and achieved one of the most monumental victories of all time—but their children and grandchildren, the beneficiaries of their sacrifices, can only stare in sympathetic puzzlement at them. The movie raises troubling questions, and too many critics insist on having them answered. *Saving Private Ryan* challenges our moral seriousness, and that is a daunting thing for a summer film to have done. But it is also what distinguishes a great piece of art from a merely good one. □

Only Yesterday–II

Above all—what Keegan calls 'the ultimate mystery'—why did men continue to fight for so long under such appalling conditions? . . . For a generation that has never known war and is encouraged to seek counselling and compensation if they fall down and graze their knees, it may well be the most difficult to answer. Was it indoctrination of patriotism in youth? Press propaganda? Intimidation? The actual pleasure in fighting and killing? Or what the Germans termed *Grabenkameradschaft*, the comradeship of the trenches, the determination not to let one's mates down? Anyone with actual military experience is likely to discount all these except the last, and all the literature shows its enormous importance.

—Sir Michael Howard, *The Times Literary Supplement*, November 13, 1998

THE NEGRO SOLDIER (1944): FILM PROPANGANDA IN BLACK AND WHITE

THOMAS CRIPPS
Morgan State University

AND

DAVID CULBERT
Louisiana State University

AFTER YEARS DURING WHICH BLACKS AND POLICE ENGAGED IN PITCHED battles in small Southern towns and large Northern cities, Nicholas Katzenbach, Attorney General under Lyndon B. Johnson, termed television "the central means of making a private moral conviction public, of impelling people all over to see and confront ideas they otherwise would turn away from." Black activists considered television, in the words of a network producer, "the chosen instrument of the black revolution."[1] But television was not the first electronic medium used to further social change. The United States Army's orientation film, *The Negro Soldier*, released in January 1944, is one of those rare instances which allows the historian of mass media to speak confidently about conception, execution, and—to a degre.—results both intended and unintended, of a specific controversial film. The uses eventually made of the Army's motion picture illustrate the difficulty of gauging in advance the impact of mass communication on social change.

During World War II the Army was officially committed to maintaining existing patterns of segregation. But the liberal rhetoric of official war aims proved fatal to thoughts of maintaining the *status quo* at home. By inducting 875,000 Negroes into a fighting force of some twelve million, the Army discovered that it was operating a social relations laboratory.[2]

---

[1] Quoted in Thomas Cripps, "The Noble Black Savage: A Problem in the Politics of Television Art," *Journal of Popular Culture*, 8 (Spring 1975), 687–95.

[2] See Ulysses Lee, *The Employment of Negro Troops: Special Studies* (Washington, D. C.: Office of Chief of Military History, U.S. Army, G.P.O., 1966), a volume in the official series, *The United States Army in World War II;* see also Richard M. Dalfiume, *Desegregation of the United States Armed Forces: Fighting on Two Fronts, 1939–1953* (Columbia, Mo.: Univ. of Missouri Press, 1969); and Alan M. Osur, *Blacks in the Army Air Forces During World War II: The Problem of Race Relations* (Washington, D. C.: Office of Air Force History, G.P.O., 1977).

In spite of the wishes of many whites, the Army became a half-way house for those who believed that wartime should bring substantial racial progress.

The relationship between racial tensions and film can best be explained by a metaphor. The biologist defines symbiosis as an association of two different organisms which live attached to each other and contribute to each other's support. This article will describe the making and distribution of *The Negro Soldier* as an example of social symbiosis, for the idea did not come from one person, but emerged from a coalition of four wary interest groups which came together in antagonistic cooperation. The film offered important lessons to those who made post-war Hollywood "message" films, while black pressure groups discovered a new way to further social change through the distribution of motion pictures.

In retrospect, the four groups and their aims are easy to identify. First is the Army itself. By the time of Pearl Harbor both civilian and military leaders in America recognized motion pictures as a significant propaganda medium; they believed film could instill in citizens a spirit of patriotism and a will to fight.[3] Chief of Staff George C. Marshall believed that film should play a major military role in wartime.[4] Convinced that lectures about patriotism and recent history generally made no impact on draftees, he concluded that film could present serious material in a lively and interesting fashion. Thanks to Marshall, the Army chose Hollywood's Frank Capra to head an elite film unit assigned to make feature-length morale films intended to build enthusiasm for official war aims. To Marshall the key to morale for the educated soldier was to give a reason for fighting.[5] Capra's *Why We Fight* series, mandatory viewing for every

[3] Roger Manvell, *Films and the Second World War* (South Brunswick, N. J.: A. S. Barnes, 1974); David Culbert, "Walt Disney's Private Snafu: The Use of Humor in World War II Army Film," in Jack Salzman, ed., *Prospects: An Annual Journal of American Cultural Studies*, 1 (Dec. 1975), 80–96, and Richard Dyer MacCann, *The People's Films: A Political History of U.S. Government Motion Pictures* (New York: Hastings House, 1973).
[4] For an introduction see Richard Griffith, "The Use of Films by the U.S. Armed Forces," in Paul Rotha, *Documentary Film* (3d ed.; London: Faber and Faber, 1952), 344–58; on Marshall see Forrest C. Pogue, *George C. Marshall: Organizer of Victory 1943–1945* (New York: Viking, 1975), 91–92; Frank Capra, *The Name Above the Title: An Autobiography* (New York: Macmillan, 1971), 325–70; and three official histories from *The United States in World War II*: Dulany Terrett, *The Signal Corps: The Emergency (To December 1941)* (Washington, D. C.: Office of the Chief of Military History, U.S. Army, G.P.O., 1956), 78–82, 223–30; George Raynor Thompson et al., *The Signal Corps: The Test (December 1941 to July 1943)* (Washington, D. C., 1957), 387–426; and George Raynor Thompson and Dixie R. Harris, *The Signal Corps: The Outcome (Mid-1943 Through 1945)* (Washington, D. C., 1966), 540–79.
[5] There is a vast literature about morale and its importance. See Wesley Frank Craven and James Lea Cate, eds., *Services Around the World*, vol. VII of *The Army Air Forces in World War II* (Chicago: Univ. of Chicago Press, 1958), 431–76, for a good introduction to the

soldier, defined official war aims in a way no other medium could match. Marshall hoped that a Capra-unit film about the Negro would provide a reason why racial tolerance was necessary to a unified military effort.

Capra's credentials for his assignment were considerable. A Sicilian immigrant, he began his Hollywood career by working on comic short subjects. Every film he made in the 1930s showed the "little guy" as eventually triumphant, a message bound to find a sympathetic reception in hard times. Above all, Capra's name became synonymous with the box office: no other Hollywood director could match his unbroken string of hits: *It Happened One Night* (1934), *Mr. Deeds Goes to Town* (1936), *Lost Horizon* (1937), *You Can't Take It With You* (1938), *Mr. Smith Goes to Washington* (1939), and *Meet John Doe* (1941). Capra was living proof that the American Dream did come true; to him patriotism was a high calling, though he masked his ardor with a deft comic touch. Capra's War Department film unit quickly attracted many of Hollywood's most talented cutters, scriptwriters, and directors. When the unit's first *Why We Fight* film, *Prelude to War*, appeared in November 1942, Capra's preeminent position in military filmmaking was assured.[6]

The second group is the blacks themselves, who saw World War II as a time to bring an end to longstanding discrimination. To black America, Franklin D. Roosevelt's Four Freedoms—freedom of speech, freedom of religion, freedom from fear, and freedom from want—were totally incompatible with segregation. The desires of black America must not be measured by the standard of today's activist rhetoric. In World War II most Negroes sought "racial tolerance" as a first step. Though there was violence, particularly race riots in Detroit and Harlem, the National Association for the Advancement of Colored People (NAACP), headed by Walter White, looked to the courts, and to white liberals, to bring about gradual change.

Earlier government films relating to blacks suggested progress more glacial than gradual. In World War I official Signal Corps footage used

---

problem. The scientific study of morale was an outgrowth of World War I. See Edward L. Munson, *The Management of Men: A Handbook on the Systematic Development of Morale and the Control of Human Behavior* (New York: H. Holland Co. 1921); Munson's son became Capra's superior in I&E; he too wrote a widely used guide to morale: Colonel Edward Lyman Munson, Jr., *Leadership for American Army Leaders*, in The Fighting Forces Series (rev. ed.; Washington, D. C.: The Infantry Journal, 1944).

[6] Production files for "Prelude to War" are located in 062.2 ocsigo, Box 1, Records of the Chief Signal Officer, RG 111, Film Section, National Archives, where a viewing print may also be found [hereafter FS-NA]. See also 062.2 ocsigo, Box 12, A52-248, Washington National Records Center, Suitland, Maryland, for additional production material [hereafter WNRC-Suitland]. Concerning the optimism of Capra's films see Robert Sklar, *Movie-Made America: A Cultural History of American Movies* (New York: Vintage Books, 1976), 205–14.

Negroes for comic relief. During the 1930s, Pare Lorentz's conservationist films, *The Plow That Broke the Plains* and *The River*, contained only a few black faces. The first two years of the war saw little change. Blacks were patronized in the few films with specific Negro themes released by federal agencies, either by overpraising Jim Crow schools (*Negro Colleges in Wartime*), or by celebrating "safe" heroes such as George Washington Carver.

Henry Browne, Farmer, a Department of Agriculture film, failed to convince anyone that racial tolerance was desirable. Browne was the perfect obedient Negro: possessor of forty acres, some chickens, a son in the black 99th Pursuit Squadron, and a willingness to grow peanuts because his country needed their oil. To make matters worse, a low budget made the entire enterprise look second-rate. The Negro journalist who originally suggested the idea termed the finished product "an insipid little story far from our original purpose."[7]

Something more substantial was needed because the 1940 Selective Service Act prohibited racial discrimination. The Army looked to Negro manpower. At the same time, military compliance with segregation somehow did not, as the approved Army manual phrased it, "endorse any theory of racial superiority or inferiority."[8] The resulting situation was made worse by a pervasive hostility toward Negro soldiers, who tended to score lowest on the Army General Classification Tests. Deputy Chief of Staff Joseph T. McNarney voiced a prevalent Army attitude: "there is no use having colored troops standing by and eating their heads off if their lack of aptitude is such that they can never be used overseas."[9]

---

[7] Claude A. Barnett, head of the Associated Negro Press, to Victor Roudin, copy, March 26, 1953, in Barnett MSS, Chicago Historical Society, Chicago, Ill. As one black critic suggested, "Is there only one Negro family in the war and is the only thing they are doing farming?" William Ashby, Springfield [Ill.] Urban League, to Elmer Davis, Box 1431, entry 264, RG 208. Prints of both films are located in FS-NA. An official OWI analysis of *Negro Colleges in Wartime* is located in Box 1490, entry 271, RG 208; the script is in Box 1569, entry 302, RG 208; Box 1571, entry 302, RG 208, has nearly fifty photographs "taken for Negro Colleges but scenes not included in film"; stills from *Henry Browne, Farmer* are in Box 1569, entry 302, RG 208; the lack of appeal of *Negro Colleges in Wartime* is discussed in "Distribution of and Use of OWI Non-theatrical Films in April 1943," Box 1483, entry 268, RG 208, where only one film of all in OWI distribution had fewer bookings per print. All in WNRC-Suitland.

[8] [Donald Young], *Leadership and the Negro Soldier*, Manual M5 (Oct. 1944), 4. In keeping with wartime practice the author's name is not given. Culbert interview with Donald Young, Macungie, Pa., February 13, 1977. A copy of Manual M5 is located in Box 1011, Records of the Assistant Secretary of Defense, Manpower Personnel & Reserve, Record Group 330, Modern Military Records, National Archives, Washington, D. C. [hereafter MMR-NA].

[9] Secret Minutes, Meeting of General Council, May 31, 1943, 3-4, 334 cos, Box 30, Records of the Office of Chief of Staff, RG 165, MMR-NA.

Bitter racial prejudice did not distinguish among aptitude scores. Lacking an effective means of mass persuasion, the Army could only place "excessive faith in the effectiveness of hortatives" as a means of encouraging black and white soldiers to fight together for democracy. This approach was not enough. Secretary of War Henry L. Stimson's Civilian Aide for Negro Affairs, William Hastie, collected a file of outrageous racial incidents in which black soldiers, trained for the most part in the South, had been beaten by local rednecks. Such incidents, reported in the black press, offered a compelling reason for Negroes to reject official pleas for wartime unity.[10]

A group of leading social scientists employed by the Army's Information and Education Division (I&E) felt that scientific research could identify precisely what kind of film might bring white and black America closer together; these civilians made up the third group, and they wanted a documentary film about the Negro.[11] The idea for using motion pictures for persuasion was greatly aided by the fact that Capra's unit and the Research Branch worked side-by-side in I&E.

Brigadier General Frederick H. Osborn headed the Division. A wealthy New Yorker without prior military service, Osborn had family connections and a flair for administration. His father was one of Stimson's close friends, and an uncle, Henry Fairfield Osborn, had been largely responsible for bringing New York's Museum of Natural History to international prominence. Osborn, a board member of the Social Science Research Council (SSRC), had a scholarly study of eugenics to his credit. He came to the Army persuaded that morale could be determined by scientific means, and that traditional morale boosters—sports, camp songfests, "decks of cards and dice and tonettes"—belonged to a bygone era.[12] Osborn's advocacy, together with the support of both Marshall and Stimson, proved crucial to the military's adoption of both film and social science research.

Osborn was in an ambivalent position. Personally interested in statistical research, he headed a division concerned more with practical education and morale services within the Army than matters of sampling technique. I&E represented an unstable alliance between Capra's faith in film as entertainment, and faith in film as pedagogical tool, the latter the

[10] Lee, *Employment of Negro Troops*, 330.
[11] For a fine discussion of I&E see Neil Minihan, "A History of the Information and Education Division," manuscript loaned to Culbert. Also helpful is "Study of I&E Activities in World War II," typewritten, copy in Box 1, Francis Spaulding MSS, Archives of Harvard University, Cambridge, Mass.
[12] Interview with Donald Young, February 13, 1977; telephone interview with Frederick Osborn, November 5, 1976; telephone interview with Paul Horgan, November 10, 1976; Osborn, *Preface to Eugenics* (New York: Harper, 1940).

attitude of Samuel Stouffer, the University of Chicago sociologist who headed the professional staff of the Research Branch.[13]

At the same time, everyone in I&E shared an ardent belief in salesmanship. Wartime was no time for recondite speculation. Ideas were measured by their practical value. Capra needed no instruction in sales techniques: since the days of *Mr. Smith Goes to Washington* (1939) he had been selling democracy in his feature films. Less familiar, however, is the hucksterism of the social scientists. The Research Branch published its findings in *What the Soldier Thinks*, where numerous graphs and charts promoted the technique of "scientific" sampling along with practical results assured by asking questions incapable of complex answers.[14]

The social scientists realized that a morale film about race relations was a perfect place to test ideas about social engineering.[15] This outgrowth of behaviorial psychology argued that human behavior could be manipulated towards socially desirable goals. Critics of industrial societies had long complained that as technology spread its benefits, it also eroded traditional values. Stouffer and Donald Young, the War Department's official expert on race relations, believed that a "humane" or "liberal" use of film could reaffirm the values of a democratic society.[16] They also accepted a doctrine employed by most American propagandists in World War II—the "strategy of truth" or "propaganda of fact."[17] One was scrupulous about that which supported one's side while passing over the

[13] Culbert interview with Donald Young, February 13, 1977; letter of Young to Culbert, December 27, 1976.

[14] Stouffer publicized his attitude surveys in *What the Soldier Thinks*, complete copies of which are found in RG 330, MMR-NA, along with supporting unpublished data. In summary form they appear in Samuel A. Stouffer, et al., *Studies in Social Psychology in World War II: Vol. I, The American Soldier: Adjustment During Army Life; Vol. II, Combat and Its Aftermath; Vol. III, Experiments on Mass Communication; Vol. IV, Measurement and Prediction* (Princeton, N. J.: Princeton Univ. Press, 1949-50). The methodology of these surveys is brilliantly attacked in Jacques Ellul, *Propaganda: The Formation of Men's Attitudes* (New York: Vintage, 1973), in particular 259-302.

[15] A good discussion of social engineering is found in Robert K. Merton, *Social Theory and Social Structure* (rev. ed; Glencoe, Ill.: Free Press, 1957), in particular chapter 16, "Science and Democratic Social Structure." See also Alvin M. Weinberg, "Can Technology Replace Social Engineering," in Albert H. Teich, ed., *Technology and Man's Future* (New York: St. Martins, 1972), 27-35. For the origin of the term see H. S. Person, "Engineering," in Edwin R. A. Seligman, et al., eds., *Encyclopedia of the Social Sciences*, volume V-VI (New York, 1931), 542.

[16] For Young's pre-war work see his *Motion Pictures: A Study in Social Legislation* (Philadelphia: Westbrook, 1922); he also edited two special issues of the *Annals of the American Academy of Political and Social Science: The American Negro*, 90 (1928) and *Minority Peoples in a Nation at War*, 223 (1942).

[17] For a good discussion of the problem see Paul F. Lazarsfeld and Robert K. Merton, "The Psychological Analysis of Propaganda," in *Writers' Congress. The Proceedings of the Conference Held in October 1943 under the Sponsorship of the Hollywood Writers' Mobilization and the University of California* (Berkeley, Cal., 1944), 362-80.

rest in silence. The result often sounded like a lawyer's brief pretending to objectivity.

The fourth group was the Hollywood film community. The fact that Capra's unit was staffed with regulars from the major studios, and that the films were actually made in Hollywood, meant that military filmmaking was followed on a daily basis. *The Negro Soldier* played a significant part in furthering a dramatic shift in the kinds of roles blacks received in feature films; after 1945 the era of the "message" film was at hand. Only *The Negro Soldier,* of all wartime films depicting blacks, actually tried to weave the Negro into the fabric of American life; this characteristic made the Army's film a model for filmmakers wishing to break through ingrained industry stereotypes.

Before 1939, virtually every black role was intended as comic relief.[18] The War Department's officer's training manual, *Leadership and the Negro Soldier*, described this stock figure vividly: "When the Negro is portrayed in the movies, or elsewhere, as a lazy, shiftless, no-good, slew-footed, happy-go-lucky, razor-toting, tap-dancing vagrant, a step has been taken in the direction of fixing this mental picture of the Negro in the minds of whites."[19] The NAACP's Walter White went to Hollywood twice in 1942 to urge a better future for blacks in feature films.[20] White, according to producer Darryl F. Zanuck of Twentieth Century-Fox, wanted Negroes "used as often as possible in the more heroic roles—in the positions which they occupy in real life."[21] In *Sahara* (1943), a black even acted as spokesman for democratic values. But such roles, however well-intentioned, were but more sophisticated versions of earlier attempts which overpraised Negro colleges.

To understand *The Negro Soldier* as a product of Hollywood technique and social science prescriptions, it is necessary to follow the evolution of the script. In March 1942 Frank Capra asked the Research Branch to draw up a list of "do's and don'ts" regarding the cinematic depiction of blacks. Sociologist Donald Young, who had devoted his pre-war career to the study of racial minorities and the impact of motion pictures, prepared a memorandum filled with well-meaning cautions, the ideas of a liberal who above all sought racial tolerance: avoid stereotypes such as the Negroes' alleged affinity for watermelon or pork; also avoid strong images of racial identity ("play down colored soldiers most Negroid in appearance" and

---

[18] Thomas Cripps, *Slow Fade to Black: The Negro in American Film, 1900–1942* (New York: Oxford Univ. Press, 1977).

[19] *Leadership and the Negro Soldier,* 4.

[20] Cripps, *Slow Fade to Black,* 375–76.

[21] Zanuck to screenwriter Eric Knight, July 22, 1942, Eric Knight MSS, Quakertown, Penna.

ɔmit "Lincoln, emancipation, or any race leaders or friends of the Negro"). Young also favored intraracial politesse: "Show colored officers in command of troops, but don't play them up too much. The Negro masses have learned that colored men who get commissions tend to look down on the masses."[22]

The first script for *The Negro Soldier* was prepared by Marc Connelly. As writer for *Green Pastures* (1930) he had a reputation for sympathetic treatment of Negro themes.[23] Connelly began working in Washington in May 1942 and followed Capra to Hollywood when the unit moved there in June. The script, which has disappeared, was deemed "too dramatic" for the Army's tastes. A second draft, prepared by Ben Hecht and Jo Swerling, was also rejected because I & E continued to insist that the Negro film be "documentary"—i.e., an example of the "propaganda of fact."[24]

During script revisions, Capra gave little attention to the project; in fact, he planned to assign the film to his friend William Wyler, but the latter "got a better offer from the Air Force." In the fall of 1942 Capra chose Stuart Heisler, a comparatively young director (see Figure 1).[25] Heisler already had extensive experience as a studio technician and seemed knowledgeable about racial matters after having made *The Biscuit Eater*, a 1940 film shot on location in Georgia with an interracial cast. Heisler immediately accepted the offer, asking only that Capra provide him with "somebody that *really* knows the background of the Negro."[26]

As a result, Carlton Moss, a black writer, was pressed into service. Moss had attended Columbia University and had worked for the Federal Theater Project under John Houseman, who in turn recommended him to Capra. According to both Heisler and Moss the two "hit it off like magic." Moss remembers working on his version of the script in Washington at the Library of Congress, but not because it put him near the books he needed. It was hard to write about racial harmony while eating in Jim Crow restaurants; the Library's cafeteria was an unsegregated "oasis."[27]

[22] "Suggested Motion Picture of the Negro in the U.S. Army," n.d. [Mar. 1942], copy in Young to Culbert, December 27, 1976; the final memorandum is discussed in Lee, *Employment of Negro Troops*, 387; Culbert interview with Donald Young, February 13, 1977.

[23] Capra, *Name Above the Title*, 337.

[24] Carlton Moss to Donald Young, August 26, 1942; Box 224, Records of the Civilian Aide to the Secretary of War (Hastie File), RG 107, MMR-NA.

[25] Cripps interview with Frank Capra, La Quinta, Cal., December 31, 1976; Axel Madsen, *William Wyler: The Authorized Biography* (New York: Crowell. 1973), 224–25.

[26] Cripps telephone interview with Stuart Heisler, February 17, 1977.

[27] Cripps interviews with Carlton Moss, Hollywood, Cal., June 1970; Boston, Mass., April 1973; Iowa City, Iowa, July, 1974. Moss attended Morgan State College and wrote radio scripts for Dr. Channing Tobias, head of the black YMCA.

Figure 1. *The Negro Soldier* was directed by Stuart Heisler, shown here at left. Copy in Stuart Heisler MSS. Theater Arts Library, UCLA. (Courtesy of UCLA.)

Shooting began in January 1943. Heisler, Moss, Research Branch representative Charles Dollard, and a camera crew travelled the United States, visiting nineteen Army posts, virtually every location where black troops trained in large numbers. In Philadelphia, Donald Young arranged for added scenes to be shot at the homes of prominent Negroes. Heisler prepared a number of sequences in which black officers directed the training of soldiers. Most of this footage never appeared because the final version relied more on a docudrama than a documentary style.

The finished film, 43 minutes long, received official approval in January 1944.[28] *The Negro Soldier* (OF 51) unfolded in classic studio style, with a narrative spinning out a flashback device, flawless lighting, and technically perfect optical effects punctuating the sequences. To black audiences, in particular, this technical quality was especially significant. Never before had a film purporting to document black American achievement been made with such professional competence. At the same time, the movie served the Army as propaganda for both black and white troops and as a teacher of comradely regard across racial lines without explicitly violating Army policy toward racial segregation.

A summary of the film's visual content shows how this was accomplished. Neat, clean, orderly, responsible, patriotic: these are the middle-class values which the film presents in image after image. Following the opening credits, a wide establishing shot places us in a splendid stone Gothic church. From the point of view of the congregation we see a black soldier, in uniform, singing a solo; we hear a chorus of extraordinary ability. As the last notes fade away a handsome young preacher (played by Carlton Moss) turns from his prepared text to introduce representative soldiers in the pews.[29] The camera cuts to a sailor, a soldier, even a beautiful light-skinned WAC, ''Private Parks, First Class.'' ''First class, indeed,'' says the preacher with undisguised pride.

The well-dressed, attentive congregation, full of servicemen in uniform, inspires Moss to reflect on the achievements of black Americans: newsreel clips show Joe Louis with his ''American fist'' recovering the heavyweight championship from Max Schmeling; black athletes defeat Nazi Germany's best at the 1936 Berlin Olympic games. It seems that black America is showing the world what democratic competition can do, and what happens when a Negro gets a fair chance to compete on equal terms. Moss reminds his congregation that the war is being fought to

[28] A copy of the original version of OF 51 is found in FS-NA.

[29] A complete copy of the final photographic scenario, May 31, 1943, plus an earlier version dated September 17, 1942, may be found in proj. 6022, 062.2 ocsigo, Box 12, A52-248, WNRC-Suitland. Moss ended up playing the preacher himself only after rejecting a succession of Hollywood Negroes who seemed tied to traditional black acting styles.

defend the American way of life. A Nazi training film shows Schmeling learning to be a parachutist; more newsreel footage shows Joe Louis, in uniform, going through Army basic training. Moss produces a copy of *Mein Kampf* and reads a passage in which Hitler describes the futility of teaching a "half-ape" to be a doctor or lawyer. The congregation looks appropriately shocked to learn what the Nazis really think about Negroes (see Figure 2).

Moss then reflects upon the heroism of blacks in earlier American wars. To recreate historic battles, Heisler used neither complete reenactment nor mere reproduction of old paintings and engravings. The shooting script called for transparencies or "glass shots" made from contemporary illustrative materials, while black and white actors dressed as soldiers passed in the foreground carrying powder and shot to their cannons.[30] The "glass shots," intercut with interracial closeups for emphasis, illuminated the black role in earlier wars, along with the settlement of the West. To Negroes the very idea of any black past other than slavery was for the most part a complete surprise. Here was visual proof that America owed its freedom to its entire population. This lesson in race pride made an indelible impression on those whose education included virtually no mention of black history.

For events after 1898, it was possible to use newsreel footage. Flickering images drawn from archival film allowed audiences to see documentary evidence of Negroes in Cuba and laborers digging the Panama Canal. A wonderful character ("Hi, I'm Jim"—who looks old enough to have fought in 1898) is superimposed over the documentary footage. He tells us about "cleaning up" in Cuba and digging the canal. He sounds so matter-of-fact that we are swept along into accepting the unspoken message: patriotic, dependable blacks have been working to keep America safe all along. For World War I there is footage of the 369th National Guard in the uniform of the French Army. The historical account ends with a staged sequence featuring a black sailor, sure to be taken for Dorie Miller, a steward in the segregated Navy who had taken up a fallen gunner's weapon at Pearl Harbor and became the first black in World War II

---

[30] The script's shooting instructions for achieving this result are instructive: "(NOTE: This scene will be used as a transparency to work in two or three Negro soldiers with white soldiers passing in the foreground carrying shot and powder for cannons.)"; "(NOTE: Beginning with the Revolutionary period, down through all the wars, including World War I IMPRESSIONISTIC CLOSEUPS—white and Negro—mostly recognizable Negro faces—will be shot for dressing up and emphasizing that there were Negro soldiers in all of these wars.)" Script, May 31, 1943, p. 12, A52-248, WNRC-Suitland. The official production budget under the heading "Bits and Extras" called for "Battle of New Orleans. 5 Negroes 1 day at $10.50 a day." Copy in 333.9, ig, Box 1160, Records of the Inspector General, RG 159, WNRC-Suitland.

Figure 2. Carlton Moss, holding a copy of *Mein Kampf*. Moss not only wrote the script but also starred as the minister.

to fire at the enemy. The Japanese attack provides Moss with an opportunity to make another point: "And there are those who will still tell you that Japan is the saviour of the colored races," thereby suggesting the opposite—neither Hitler nor Hirohito have anything but contempt for Negroes.

The film now makes an abrupt transition from past performance to present opportunities. Mrs. Bronson, a handsome middle-aged woman wearing a suit and small fur stole (a scrupulous middle-class image in keeping with Donald Young's prescription), stands up in church to read a letter from her son who has just become an Army officer. As she reads the letter, the film cuts to scenes of basic training. Young Bronson is the very picture of light skinned, muscular leadership. He drills in the snow, goes to a segregated dance, meets a nice young girl, and back at camp, is introduced to the poetry of Langston Hughes. After soldiering all week Bronson heads for church on Sunday. The camp chaplain offers a pep talk describing improbably broad opportunities for blacks to get into Officer Candidates School and even West Point; Army units are shown as eager to

accept black recruits (see Figure 3). The film ends back in Mrs. Bronson's
church as the congregation rises to sing "Onward Christian Soldiers"
which segues into "Joshua Fit' de Battle ob Jericho," over which we see a
montage of marching men and women. The songs and images combine in
a final emotional appeal for wartime unity.

At first, *The Negro Soldier* was intended solely for black troops.
Donald Young wrote an official manual, *Leadership of Negro Troops*, to
be used by the white officers who commanded black units in World War
II.[31] But even before the film was released, two of the four groups, the
social scientists and the blacks, began to agitate for wider military and
civilian distribution.

Such talk resulted in an extraordinary amount of official debate. The
film's director, Stuart Heisler, remembers representatives of more than
fifty federal offices screening the rough cut and reading revisions of the
script.[32] Nobody seemed sure what the impact of the film might be on
black soldiers. To learn if the film would encourage rioting by Negro
troops, Heisler, Moss, and Charles Dollard, the Research Branch representative, took their product to a "Negro camp outside of San Diego."
The commander, who "knew" his men, insisted that the film would pro-
voke violence. He brought in a special unit of nearly one hundred military
police to prevent trouble. The result was hardly what the commander
expected. Enthusiastic black recruits threatened to riot unless *all* Negro
troops on the post saw the film.[33]

White soldiers offered a different problem. Here another group, the
Army leadership, took a direct hand to ensure that the final product would
be safe enough to appeal to the widest possible audience. Anatole Litvak,
Heisler's superior in the Capra unit, hand-carried the completed "answer
print" of *The Negro Soldier* to the Pentagon in October 1943. Marshall,
Stimson, Osborn, the head of the Army's Bureau of Public Relations,
General A. D. Surles, and Assistant Secretary of War John J. McCloy

[31] Osur, *Blacks in the Army Air Forces*, 80–81, notes opposition within the Army to
issuing Manual M5. The foreword to *Leadership and the Negro Soldier*, p. iv, specifically
suggests that *The Negro Soldier* be shown as part of the course of instruction, "preferably
the second meeting," and also suggests, p. 64, that one of the Capra *Why We Fight* films,
Divide and Conquer, be shown to combat racial "hate" rumors within the United States.
Gunnar Myrdal's *An American Dilemma: The Negro Problem and Modern Democracy*
(New York: Harper, 1944), is given particular emphasis in the manual's list of suggested
readings, p. 101.
[32] Cripps telephone interview with Heisler, February 17, 1977; *The National Film Board
News Letter*, February 4, 1944, 2, reported that "in Washington there are about sixty
different bureaus or sub-bureaus of the U.S. Government concerned with either the production, distribution, or utilization of films." Copy in Box 1486, entry 269, RG 208, WNRC-
Suitland.
[33] Cripps interview with Heisler, February 17, 1977.

Figure 3. Location footage of black troops revealed a wide range of military special-
ties and roles of blacks along with continuing segregation. (Courtesy of Film Stills Archive,
Museum of Modern Art.)

personally viewed the film. On November 1, after much discussion, Litvak received a detailed memorandum outlining specific changes intended
to make the film more factually accurate and to mollify racial sensibilities
of audiences.[34] Heisler had already been ordered to cut the footage showing men "under the command of Negro officers."[35] War Department
officials insisted that a section of the film dealing with World War I include "a small amount of footage which would show that Negroes did
something other than engage in combat in the front line." Emphasis on
black combat experience in the current war also had to be "toned down"
since it "would give an erroneous conception of the overall job of the
Army." Finally, every nicety of customary racial etiquette was to be
preserved. For example: "The sequence showing a [white] nurse or
physiotherapy attendant massaging the [black] soldier's back will be
eliminated."[36] This momentary visual breach of racial and sexual taboos

[34] Munson to Litvak, November 1, 1943, 062.2 cos, Box 304, Records of the Chief of Staff,
Troop Information & Education, RG 319, MMR-NA.
[35] Cripps telephone interview with Heisler, Feb. 17, 1977.
[36] Munson to Litvak, Nov. 1, 1943, Box 304, RG 319, MMR-NA.

could not be shown though the Army did use white staff to treat injured black soldiers.

In January 1944 the Army agreed to use the film in basic orientation for Negro troops, while continuing to debate further distribution.[37] The Research Branch conducted a "scientific" survey to see what statistics might say about wider reception. This was the wartime pattern: what individual commander's prejudice could compete with the scientifically measured opinion of the entire Army? The survey reported that almost ninety percent of black soldiers questioned wanted the film shown to white soldiers as well as black. Almost eighty percent thought civilians should see it. The surprise came in the white response, for almost eighty percent of those questioned favored showing the film to both black and white troops; nearly eighty percent wanted the film shown to white civilians.[38] Still, some military leaders insisted that the film be accompanied by printed material designed to blunt the message of racial tolerance. The Research Branch, particularly through the efforts of Donald Young, successfully insisted that the film stand alone.[39] In spite of itself, and in opposition to the wishes of some military leaders, the United States Army had a film based on social engineering precepts to teach racial brotherhood.

In the end, OF 51 became "mandatory" viewing for all troops at replacement centers within the United States.[40] Between February 1944 and August 1945, when the order was rescinded, almost every black in the Army and Air Corps saw this film; millions of white soldiers also viewed it as part of I&E's standard orientation program.[41] Though overseas combat zones could not enforce mandatory viewing for all soldiers, the Army still used the film late in 1946. Harry Truman's 1948 desegregation order marked the end of OF 51's official usefulness.[42]

The film had been made for military audiences. What would happen if it joined the ranks of a few other Army orientation films (including *Prelude to War* and *The Battle of Russia* from the *Why We Fight* series) and found

[37] Karl Marks to John Hubbell, Jan. 12, 1944, copy in OF 51 production files, 062.2 ocsigo, Box 14, RG 111, FS-NA.

[38] Report B-102, "Reactions of Negro and White Soldiers to the film *The Negro Soldier*, April 17, 1944. 439 blacks and 510 whites at Camp Pickett, Virginia, previewed the film. In addition almost 91 percent of the whites described it as "very good." Copy in Box 992, RG 330, MMR-NA.

[39] Memorandum, Maj. Gen. Ray Porter, Assistant Chief of Staff G-3, to Osborn, May 4, 1944, 413.53 ag, Box 3241, Records of the Adjutant General, RG 407, MMR-NA; Karl Marks to ocsigo, Apr. 15, 1944, 062.2 ocsigo, Box 44, A45-196, WNRC-Suitland.

[40] War Department Circular 208, May 25, 1944, 413.56 ag, Box 3241, RG 407, MMR-NA.

[41] War Department Circular 283, September 19, 1945, 413.53 ag, Box 3237, RG 407, MMR-NA.

[42] Brig. Gen. C. T. Lanham, Director, I&E Div., to Karl Korter, June 6, 1946, 062.2 cos, Box 374, RG 319, MMR-NA.

commercial distribution to movie theaters all over the United States? Would white patrons pay regular admission to see a film about racial tolerance? Distributors felt sure the answer was no. Blacks thought otherwise; they recognized that the official nature of the film would make it an effective weapon in the struggle for civil rights if it were widely seen by civilians.

The first step was official approval from Elmer Davis, head of the Office of War Information (OWI).[43] He and several members of his staff screened *The Negro Soldier* and demanded yet a few further changes. Davis concluded that the film "probably would be perfectly passable in any theatres whatever in the North; and that the only risks . . . would be attendant upon showing it in, say, Atlanta, or some such Southern center." One member of his staff introduced a new area of possible opposition—whether or not "the Negro press" might consider the film "just icing."[44]

OWI fears led in January 1944 to a private showing at the Pentagon for nearly two hundred black journalists. Frank Capra, though he had little to do with the film, arrived in Washington to show "his" production. Most of the audience wrote favorable—even glowing—reviews, passing over the omission of slavery and the realities of discrimination. Activist groups such as the NAACP and the National Negro Congress praised the film as "the best ever done" and called for its widespread distribution.[45] In April 1944 the Army officially released the film to civilian audiences.

It was one thing to make the film available to civilians, another to have it seen. From April 1944, the fate of *The Negro Soldier* increasingly turned on the activities of blacks, in particular Carlton Moss and Truman K. Gibson, now Stimson's Civilian Aide for Negro Affairs. Both proved adept at rallying Hollywood opinion in the film's favor, and overcoming a mixed critical response. Bosley Crowther of the *New York Times* thought the film "questionable" because it "sugar coats" and "discreetly avoids the more realistic race problems." James Agee, the Southerner who covered cinema for the liberal *Nation*, termed the film "pitifully, painfully mild" although he recognized that blandness made it more saleable. Few white critics shared Agee's insight into black attitudes toward the film. "Straight and decent as far as it goes," he wrote, it "means a good deal, I

[43] A good introduction to the OWI is Allan M. Winkler, *The Politics of Propaganda: The Office of War Information, 1942–1945* (New Haven: Yale Univ. Press, 1978); for Davis' pre-war radio experience see David Holbrook Culbert, *News for Everyman: Radio and Foreign Affairs in Thirties America* (Westport, Ct.: Greenwood, 1976), 125–52.

[44] Paul Horgan to Lyman Munson, Nov. 6, 1943, 062.2 cos, Box 304, RG 319, MMR-NA.

[45] Capra, *Name Above the Title*, 358-62. Mabel R. Staupers, NAACP, to Maj. Gen. A. D. Surles, February 25, 1944; and telegram, National Negro Congress to Surles, February 19, 1944, RG 107, MMR-NA.

gather to most of the Negro soldiers who have seen it." Moss agreed, telling a *Time* reporter that the movie would "mean more to Negroes than most white men could imagine."[46]

Civilian distribution depended on resolving a longstanding debate between the Army and the War Activities Committee (WAC), the group representing commercial distributors in negotiations for circulation of government films.[47] *The Negro Soldier*, at 43 minutes, or roughly half of normal feature length, would remain unpopular with bookers because no matter what its merits, the film required a change in the standard length of programs.[48] To combine an educational film of "excessive" length with OF 51's subject seemingly restricted viewing to black theaters.[49] But Army enthusiasm prevailed over WAC opposition. *The Negro Soldier* was released to those theaters which requested it from a national total of 16,203 "pledged" commercial houses. Accurate attendance records, kept in part to stave off possible government regulation, revealed that in calendar year 1944 the film was a commercial bust. It played in only 1,819 theaters in contrast to most OWI shorts which played in more than 13,000 theaters, or the Air Corps combat film *Memphis Belle* (in Technicolor), seen in over 12,000 theaters the same year.[50] Because of its awkward length, fears of resentment of its special pleading, and the normally low grosses generated by slack summer attendance, OF 51 in its first run seems to have done more poorly than any other film released by the government for commercial distribution.

Leading Hollywood producers, urged on by Moss and Gibson, tried another way of beefing up attendance. Litvak and Heisler re-cut the film to a 20-minute two-reeler, enabling the Army to offer two lengths of

[46] *The New York Times*, Apr. 22, 1944; *Nation*, March 11, 1944, 316; *Time*, March 27, 1944, 94, 96.
[47] For an excellent discussion of how the WAC functioned see mimeographed analysis of theater booking practices prepared for War Manpower Commission, n.d. [July 1944] in Taylor Mills to Francis Harmon, July 22, 1944, Box 1488, entry 269, RG 208; see also Mills to Truman Gibson, May 1, 1944, Box 1484, entry 268, RG 208, both in WNRC-Suitland.
[48] War Activities Committee, *Movies at War 1945* (New York: War Activity Committee, 1945), 42, copy enclosed in Francis Harmon to Culbert, January 26, 1977; information about exact bookings of OF 51 in each of thirty-one exchanges is found in Box 1485, entry 269, RG 208, WNRC-Suitland.
[49] Peter Noble. *The Negro in Films* (New York: Arno Press, 1970), 99–100 lists numbers of black theaters by state.
[50] Telegram, Lehman Katz to Lyman Munson, n.d. [June 19, 1944]; unsigned memorandum, n.d. [June 28, 1944], both in proj. 6024, 062.2 ocsigo, Box 12, A52-248, WNRC-Suitland. The short and long versions were both made available to commercial distributors in July 1944. Publicity release WAC, July 21, 1944, copy in Box 1, Albert Deane MSS, Museum of Modern Art Film Library, New York, N. Y. A print of Of 24 is available from the Army Training Support Center, Tobyhanna, Pa.

the same film to civilians, beginning in July 1944.[51] As OF 24, but with the same title, the film is virtually identical to OF 51, though omitting entirely Mrs. Bronson and her son's experience at Officer Candidates School. At the end a few added shots of black pilots and black construction workers in India helped give a wider visual sense of Negro involvement in the war. Only *The Negro Soldier*, of all films produced by the military during the war, was available in two versions at the same time. Moss estimated that possibly 5,000 theaters eventually showed the shorter version.

Civilian distribution still faced one last hurdle, a lawsuit from a white Jewish filmmaker who had also made a movie about race pride. Jack Goldberg, president of The Negro Marches On, Inc., for years had produced "race movies," a genre of cheaply mounted productions for distribution in Negro neighborhood houses. He sued in federal court to restrain the WAC from booking *The Negro Soldier*, claiming that it competed unfairly with his own film, *We've Come a Long, Long Way*, which dealt with roughly the same subject (see Figure 4). Goldberg's film possessed a certain credibility in black circles owing to its sponsorship by Elder Solomon Lightfoot Michaux, a radio evangelist well-known to Negro listeners.[52]

At this point the NAACP entered the controversy. Roy Wilkins helped Truman Gibson assemble a "confidential" list of white liberals to "assist distribution," including Nelson Rockfeller, Fiorello La Guardia, Cardinal Spellman, and the *New Yorker's* Harold Ross. NAACP special counsel Thurgood Marshall joined Gibson in filing an *amicus curiae* brief, insisting that the WAC provided "the only available medium" for circulating a film that "proceeded on the premise that racial prejudices which divide our population will have their effect minimized by the dissemination of facts." Marshall and Walter White then prodded the liberal Hollywood Writers' Mobilization into endorsing the film as a "real contribution to national unity" and a repudiation of "racist lies."[53] Gibson and Moss arranged for

[51] "Weekly Report on Film Production Activities," Lehman Katz to Paul Horgan, May 3, 1944, 319.1 cos, Box 370, RG 319, MMR-NA. Specific suggestions from the producers are quoted in Gibson to Anatole Litvak, Apr. 14, 1944, proj. 6024, 062.2 ocsigo, Box 12, A52-248, WNRC-Suitland.
[52] The Goldberg film was based on the OWI pamphlet *Negroes and the War*. Jack Goldberg to Francis Harmon, February 28, 1944, Box 1488, entry 269, RG 208.
[53] Wilkins to Gibson, January 3, 14, 15; February 1, 3, 1944; Wilkins to Maj. Homer B. Roberts, February 9, 1944; United States District Court, Southern District of New York, *Negro Marches On*, Plaintiff, v. War Activities Committee, Defendants, copy, n.d.; Gibson, *amicus curiae* brief, 2 pages, n.d.; Thurgood Marshall to Pauline Lauber, executive secretary, Hollywood Writers' Mobilization, May 2, 1944; Robert Rossen to Frank Capra, March 30, 1944, all in Box 277, Records of the National Association for the Advancement of Colored People, Manuscript Division, Library of Congress, Washington, D. C. [hereafter NAACP Records].

Figure 4. *The Negro Soldier* diverted attention away from Jack Goldberg and Elder Lightfoot Soloman Michaux's *We've Come a Long, Long Way,* one of the last "race movies" that seriously challenged Hollywood's version of the Negro. (Advertisement in NAACP Records, Library of Congress.)

gala Hollywood receptions in May and June 1944 to drum up support for both versions of "their" film. Black actress Lena Horne praised the film and major Hollywood producers provided blurbs, most more convincing than that offered by Columbia's Harry Cohn: "the greatest War Department Picture ever made."[54]

The NAACP, which had nothing to do with the making of OF 51, now promoted the film as if it were its own. "NAACP Deplores Legal Action Against Film *The Negro Soldier*," declared a press release which claimed that Goldberg's film was "insulting to Negroes," in contrast to *The Negro Soldier's* "enormous potentialities for good in stimulating the morale of American Negroes and in educating white Americans." White also persuaded liberal Jewish groups to repudiate Goldberg, thereby avoid-

[54] Quoted in Gibson to Anatole Litvak, April 14, 1944, proj. 6024, 062.2 ocsigo, Box 12, A52-248, WNRC-Suitland.

ing the appearance of a "Jewish vs. Negro situation." Goldberg was termed a longtime exploiter of black audiences. In the end Goldberg lost in court and settled for a few days' "clearance" to allow his film a brief run and give him a chance to get back part of his investment.[55]

The Negro press continued its campaign to gain wider distribution. It urged the National Council of Negro Women "to rally the public and force the special film, *The Negro Soldier*, to be released in full to audiences of both races." In Los Angeles press support led to a preview under the auspices of the mayor's Civic Unity Committee at a leading hotel.[56] Educators invoked the arguments of the scientific sample to promote the film. They tested OF 51 as a tool for teaching "inter-cultural education" and "living together," and ranked it third in effectiveness out of seventeen films studied.[57]

The campaign soon included plans for distributing the film to civilian audiences outside the commercial circuit. The coming of age of 16 millimeter film (at the time still called "substandard" film) proved a major means for spreading government information throughout the country. Indeed World War II marked the apogee of non-commercial distribution of films in the United States.[58] The OWI and the Army's Public Relations Bureau waged a tedious administrative battle over distribution. In April 1944 the OWI won the right to distribute the long version (OF 51) non-theatrically to a network of film departments in public libraries, schools, and colleges in every state.[59] The Film Library of the Museum of Modern Art in New York, which developed educational distribution of "classic" films in the late 1930s, helped promote *The Negro Soldier* by including it

[55] Goldberg to Congressman Andrew J., May, April 1, 1944; Goldberg to White, May 25, 1944; Ralph Cooper to White, June 8, 1944; Julia E. Baxter to Wilkins, November 4, 1943; press release dated April 27, 1944; White to Marshall, May 4, 1944; all in Box 277, NAACP Records.

[56] Clippings from black press; and invitations to Moss from the Civic Unity Committee and Charles U. Shellenberg, Los Angeles YMCA, April 24, 1944, in personal files of Moss, copies sent to Cripps; trade paper clippings in Stuart Heisler MSS, Theater Arts Library, UCLA.

[57] Discussed in Leonard Bloom, *California Eagle*, March 16, 1944; and Esther L. Berg, "Films to Better Human Relations," reprinted from *High Points* (New York: Brooklyn Jewish Community Council, n.d. [1945]), copies from personal files of Moss sent to Cripps.

[58] RG 208 has the extensive records of OWI's Non-theatrical Division of the Motion Picture Branch. See also Film Council of America, *Sixty Years of 16mm Film 1923–1983: A Symposium* (Evanston, Ill., 1954), 148–59.

[59] Curtiss Mitchell to Stanton Griffis, April 12, 1944, Box 1484, entry 268; Taylor Mills to Edgar Baker, June 8, 1944, Box 1486, entry 269; methods of distribution are discussed in C. R. Reagan to Congressman Louis Ludlow, June 10, 1944, Box 1581, entry 305; all in RG 208, WNRC-Suitland.

in a special series of Capra-unit films shown in New York to capacity audiences in July 1944.[60]

Black groups throughout the country were soon enthusiastic over "their" film and eagerly booked it for church and civic functions.[61] *The Educational Film Guide for 1945*, a standard guidebook for users of documentary film, praised OF 51's technical quality: "good photographs, a nice variety of scene, some flashes of humor and excellent musical background."[62] The film's superb technical quality made it the hit of the season in nontheatrical distribution. The film bureau of the Cleveland Public Library, for example, indicated frequent requests for the film in its monthly reports to the OWI, listing such groups as the "Woodbridge School & PTA" and the "Zion Methodist Church."[63] Not every report indicates attendance figures—nor are such figures capable of verification—but yearly estimated attendance at OWI films distributed nontheatrically numbered over 7.5 million, and that represents only domestic distribution.[64] The film was also used extensively in Latin America, particularly in Haiti, with its predominantly black population.[65]

With the release of OF 51, Moss lobbied for a second film, eventually called *Teamwork* (OF 14), a more self-conscious advocate for racial integration. The motion picture shows blacks in combat against the Nazis. A sequence shot on a Hollywood back lot has Nazi cannoneers shell black troops with a flurry of leaflets reminding them of the "lousiest" jobs and housing awaiting them at the war's end. The blacks toss aside the flyers, as they advance under fire. The narrator grants that "nobody thinks the United States is perfect."[66] Joe Louis is quoted as saying "there's

---

[60] Iris Barry, Curator, Museum of Modern Art Film Library, to Rudolph Montgelas, Bureau of Public Relations, n.d. [Aug. 1944], War Dept. folder, Central Files, Museum of Modern Art Film Library, New York, N. Y. 3,250 persons saw OF 51 (from July 24-30, 1944).

[61] Not every group had a choice: "Mr. E. J. Welch, D. C. Reformatory, Lorton, Va., is anxious to obtain the film, THE NEGRO SOLDIER, for a showing at the reformatory." Catherine Preston, to Joseph Brechsteen, September 13, 1944, Box 1483, entry 268, RG 208, WNRC-Suitland.

[62] Dorothy E. Cook and Eva Rahbek-Smith, compilers, *Educational Film Guide* (New York, W. W. Wilson, Co., 1945), 152. This annual compilation first appeared in 1936.

[63] "OWI Monthly Report of Government Film Showings for October 1944," Cleveland Public Library, Box 1640, entry 362, RG 208, WNRC-Suitland. Boxes 1624–1647 cover every state with varying degrees of completeness on a monthly basis.

[64] C. R. Reagan stated that he distributed 138 of his 150 16mm prints for 15,600 showings with an estimated total audience of 3,220,000 between June 15, 1944 and January 1, 1945. Reagan to Gibson, January 4, 1945, Box 224, RG 107 (Hastie File), MMR-NA.

[65] In June 1945 OF51 had been shown 69 times to 43,025 persons in Haiti. See monthly "16mm Films-Latin American Program-Summary by Title," Copy in Box 218, central files 3, Records of the Coordinator for Inter-American Affairs, RG 229, WNRC-Suitland.

[66] There is a print in FS-NA. The Script and production records are found in proj. 11,015, 062.2 ocsigo, Box 19, A52-248, WNRC-Suitland.

nothing wrong with America that Hitler could fix!" A timid, much less elaborate production than OF 51, *Teamwork's* modest "message" about integration nevertheless alarmed some in the Army. The film received belated military release only in January 1946, thanks in part to the efforts of the NAACP. Roy Wilkins attended a sneak preview of the film at the Signal Corps Photographic Center on Long Island. Wilkins lobbied for release and the NAACP felt the film could "do much to promote racial unity *now and for the future.*" By the summer of 1946, *Teamwork* also went into civilian distribution.[67]

What in retrospect can be concluded about the direct and indirect impact of *The Negro Soldier* on postwar American race relations? We believe this film represented a watershed in the use of film to promote racial tolerance. *The Negro Soldier's* influence can be seen in three areas: promotion, production, and the demise of "race films."

1) Promotion. Black pressure groups learned that film was a tool for social change. The Army did not recognize how much the technical quality of the film suggested to viewers a military commitment to equality of opportunity. The existence of such a film indicated change within the Army— why not also in the civilian world? Carlton Moss, handsome and eloquent, was the educated preacher who moved his listeners with facts and force of logic. Mrs. Bronson, in her suit and fur, seemed to prove that a black mother was the same as other middle-class women, save for a slightly darker skin color. Moreover, the Army considered Mrs. Bronson's son a valuable asset and trained him thoroughly. His hard work paid off in an officer's commission. Was not this visual evidence of equality of opportunity? How about Private Parks, First Class—wasn't she attractive and competent no matter what her racial background? And that fine church and all those well-dressed people who took their civic responsibilities seriously—all America could see these were valuable citizens. Such images provided visual proof of why racial equality was not just morally but logically justified. Why not everywhere? As Moss put it, he set out to "ignore what's wrong with the army and tell what's right with my

[67] Wilkins to Surles, August 22, 1945; White to Marshall, Harrington and Wilkins, April 17, 1946; White to Arthur Mayer, May 21, 1946; White to Robert Patterson, May 9, 1946; Jeannette E. Samuelson, public relations director, Arthur Mayer and Joseph Burstyn Theatres, to "Friend," mimeographed, July 11, 1946; Ida Long, 20th-Century Fox to Fred S. Hall, December 27, 1944; Hall to White, December 29, 1944; Wilkins to Maj. Homer B. Roberts, January 2, 1945, all in Box 277; White to Wilkins, Marshall and Harrington, April 24, 1946; Wilkins to Julia E. Baxter and Harrington, October 21, 1946; White to Patterson, April 24, May 9, 1946, all in Box 274; all in NAACP Records. Samuelson to W. W. Lindsay, Army Pictorial Service, June 12, 1946, proj. 11, 015, ocsigo, Box 19, A52-248, WNRC-Suitland.

Figure 5.   Goaded by NAACP pressure in support of wartime calls for "unity," "toler-ance," and "brotherhood," Hollywood movies sometimes included blacks in the ranks of the peoples fighting against fascism, as here in the case of Alfred Hitchcock's *Lifeboat* (1944), featuring Canada Lee. (Copyright, Twentieth Century-Fox Film Corporation.)

people," which, he hoped, would cause whites to ask "what right have we to hold back a people of that calibre?"[68]

The NAACP now understood how potent indirect messages in films could be. It produced a brochure promoting "audio-visual aids" for "teaching democracy." It formed a new national committee to deal with matters of film propaganda and encouraged film distributors to circulate inventories of films urging "tolerance" and "brotherhood" such as *Teamwork* and *Americans All*, produced by *The March of Time*. The National Conference of Christians and Jews joined what promised to be a new movement, discussed in journals with titles like the *16mm Reporter*.[69] Getting films off of shelves and before commercial and non-commercial audiences was a specific goal capable of fulfillment by any number of black pressure groups. The NAACP could echo the sentiment of an earlier enthusiast for social experimentation: "I have seen the future and it works."

[68] Moss clipping file, March 1944, in personal files of Moss, copies sent to Cripps.
[69] Press clippings in Box 274, NAACP Records.

Figure 6. The trend of wartime liberalism exemplified by *The Negro Soldier* persisted into the era of the so-called "message movie" such as Elia Kazan's *Pinky* (1949), a story of "passing" from black to white, starring Ethel Waters and Jeanne Crain. (Copyright, Twentieth Century-Fox Film Corporation.)

2) Production of "message films." A black journal's headline at the time of OF 51's release makes the point: "Army Shows Hollywood the Way."[70] The postwar era of feature films with "messages" about racial liberalism can be traced directly to the humane, natural realism of *The Negro Soldier*, though it would be simplistic to insist that a single film was the sole cause of every "message" motion picture produced after 1945. A number of examples demonstrate the connection.[71] Jester Hairston arranged the choral parts for *The Negro Soldier*. After 1945, Dimitri Tiomkin, who wrote OF 51's score, used Hairston for entire films, a startling change from "before the war [when] the studios only called us when they had 'Negro music' to be sung."[72] Stuart Heisler, director of *The Negro Soldier*, went on to make *Storm Warning* (1950), a harsh indictment of the Ku Klux Klan. Ben Maddow came from a background in wartime documen-

[70] *Negro*, II (Sept., 1944), 94, Johnson MSS.
[71] The tendency is described in Samuel Goldwyn, "How I Became Interested in Social Justice," *Opportunity*, 26 (Summer 1948), 100–01.
[72] "Movie Choir," *Ebony*, 4 (Oct. 1949), 25–27.

tary film to write the screenplay for Faulkner's *Intruder in the Dust* (1949), an urgent plea for mutual respect across racial lines in the South. Carl Foreman, who began the war by writing the Dead End Kids' *Spooks Run Wild*, worked for Frank Capra's film unit. Afterwards he wrote *Home of the Brave* (1949), in which the black hero was named "Mossy" as a tribute to a wartime friendship with Carleton Moss. Stanley Kramer, the producer of *Home of the Brave,* had worked at the Signal Corps Photographic Unit on Long Island during the war. His entire postwar career was devoted to "message" films, including *The Defiant Ones* (1958) and *Guess Who's Coming to Dinner?* (1967), both vehicles for Sidney Poitier and racial liberalism (see Figure 6).[73]

3) The demise of "race movies." The failure of Jack Goldberg's suit signalled an end for the "race movie." When feature films began to depict blacks as human beings, there was no longer a need for third-rate films designed especially for Negro audiences. After 1945 it was soon hard for anyone, black or white, to remember when as a matter of course separate-but-unequal "race movies" were a staple of the American scene. The humanity of *The Negro Soldier* had done its work well.

The historian is always interested in cause and effect, but perhaps a sense of irony is essential in understanding the impact of *The Negro Soldier.* Who would have thought that the Army, officially committed to segregation, would end up with a film which symbolically promoted the logic of integration? Who would have predicted that a documentary-style film about black history and opportunities for military advancement would spawn a generation of feature films calling for racial tolerance? Who would have thought that a military orientation film would make black civilians glow with pride? Minority pressure groups cannot help appreciating such ironies. Merely to show a film is no guarantee of anything, but screening a "message" film for a variety of audiences clearly can achieve results not originally conceived of. This is arguably the symbiotic potential of all mass media, a potential realized in the midst of total war, when the Army used film to show not just Hollywood but all America that civil rights was not only a moral but also a logical necessity. Such conclusions led Walter Fisher, one of a handful of black officers assigned to I&E, to remember this pioneering film a third of a century later. Although "we knew . . . the day of jubilee had not arrived," he considers *The Negro Soldier* "one of the finest things that ever happened to America."[74]*

[73] Cripps telephone interview with Carlton Moss, July 8, 1977; Cripps telephone interview with Stanley Kramer, July 11, 1977; Cripps telephone interview with Carl Foreman, July 12, 1977.

[74] Culbert and Cripps interview with Walter Fisher, Washington, D. C., July 12, 1977.

* We would like to thank the Woodrow Wilson International Center for Scholars, Smithsonian Institution, Washington, D. C., for support in preparing this essay.

IT'S EVERYBODY'S WAR

Racism and the World War Two Documentary

By GREG GARRETT

World War Two has been described by Studs Terkel and others as the last "good war," the last war in which Americans felt a sense of solidarity and the awareness that this was a fight all needed to support if we were to win. That sense of camaraderie and cooperation did not come about overnight, of course; before (and even after) Pearl Harbor, there were people who thought that, for whatever reason, this wasn't their war. For that reason, American wartime propaganda of all kinds tried to redefine the democratic principles we fought for and to emphasize that it was a battle every American had to support, regardless of race or color.

A position paper released by the Committee for National Morale early in 1941, for example, argued that American wartime propaganda should be "loyally and consistently democratic, seeking to preserve, extend, and realize the full implications of the democratic ideal. It must defend the essential freedoms and seek for a dynamic interpretation of the ideal of democracy" (Culbert 8). After Pearl Harbor, documentary scriptwriter Eric Knight agreed that the theoretical emphasis on democracy and inclusiveness was vital—that "Democracy, being built on individual free will, must have intellectual and moral unity"—and he concluded that documentary film was the medium best qualified to spread this message of inclusiveness and unity to Americans because of film's broad audience, expressiveness, and apparent truth (Culbert 108, 109–11). But did American documentary films of the wartime era achieve that democratic ideal any better than our society as a whole? With few exceptions, many of them scarcely known today, they did not. Although the war industries were just recently

Frank Capra's documentaries showed geographic or religious diversity before racial diversity.

(and uneasily) integrated by executive order, the armed forces remained segregated and most documentary films of the period also divide wartime America into whites and all others, with white America extolled almost without exception as the only America.

Of the many documentaries designed to encourage American unity, one of the best-known efforts was *It's Everybody's War* (1942), narrated by Henry Fonda and produced by Twentieth Century Fox under the auspices of the Office of War Information. *It's Everybody's War* tells the story of Jefferson, a representative American town, and its growing involvement in the war after its boys in the local National Guard unit go off to fight. After basic training, the soldiers are sent off to the Philippines, and the film shows the reactions of the locals to

Most documentary films of the period divide wartime America into whites and all others, with white America extolled almost exclusively as the only America.

news of the Japanese overrunning the islands, to the first KIA telegram being delivered, to the fall of Corregidor and the capture of all the American forces there. The people of Jefferson, left behind on the home front, resolve to work harder, sacrifice more, and buy more war bonds so that American soldiers will never again have to surrender because they don't have the materials they need to fight. "All America would learn what we learned the hard way," Fonda says, that this conflict was "war for every foot of

American soil, for every home and field."

The film is a stirring call to arms for the entire nation, except for one nagging detail, readily apparent to modern audiences: all of the inhabitants of Jefferson—the men in uniform, the citizens along the parade route, the farmers, the bond salesmen, the churchgoers—are white. Because of their lack of racial inclusion, in a sense the message of this film, others with the same purpose (Joseph von Sternberg's *The Town* is another prominent example), and virtually every other World War Two documentary—whether intentional or not—becomes "It's a white war."[1] While the government occasionally made films to explain that minorities were also involved in the war effort, the far greater number of lily-white documentary films suggests that it wasn't really everybody's war after all. Those propaganda, combat, and training films produced by or for the government during the war allow us to assess the society that produced them, for as David Denby had pointed out, they may be regarded as "a capsule of political attitudes and hopes," as well as "a repository of American myths, dreams, fears" (33). By studying the treatment—or lack thereof—accorded people of color in wartime documentaries, we may establish the true states of democracy, racism, and tolerance at home during this great struggle against foreign tyranny.

We must grant at the outset that the majority of Americans at this time were white, as were the majority of American fighting men and women; no one objects to those contributions being depicted and memorialized on film. What is objectionable about the majority of wartime documentaries, however, is that collectively they attach little importance to the efforts of people of color, and few demonstrate an awareness of America's diversity. Certainly history is aware: large numbers of Native Americans joined up to defend the nation that had offered them citizenship less than twenty years earlier; a Japanese American battalion liberated the Dachau concentration camp while many of their own families were interned behind barbed wire, and the unit to which they belonged, the 442 Regimental Combat Team, was both the most decorated regiment in American military history and the one sustaining the highest casualties; black soldiers, sailors, nurses, and pilots played important roles both in and out of combat although they were generally segregated into all-black units ("Reunion" 32). One would be hard pressed to discern this record from the majority of documentary films, however. Instead, non-white Americans were generally ignored or vilified in documentaries, with the result that even today few people realize how America's minorities helped win this last good war.

Many of the best-known films do seem to be making an effort to suggest America's diversity coming together to fight, as the morale theorists had suggested. Frank Capra's *Why We Fight* films, *Prelude to War* and *War Comes to America,* for example, contrast diversity and democracy in the "free world" versus the regimentation and mob mentality of the "slave nations" by generally balancing recognizable individuals in America against crowds or soldiers marching in lockstep in Japan, Germany, or Italy, but "diversity" in these and other films is generally defined only in terms of religion, vocation, or geographical region, not by racial identity. The religious iconography used in the Capra films and elsewhere is drawn from Catholicism, Protestantism, and Judaism, and *Prelude to War* proclaims that the tenets by which the free world—"our world, the democratic world"—exists are drawn from these religions as well as the Koran and Confucius. *Wings Up!* (1943), a documentary about officer candidate school for airmen, goes out of its way to show that the candidates may choose from Protes-

tant, Catholic, and Jewish clergy. Capra's *War Comes to America* emphasizes that "We have every denomination on earth . . . and no one tells us which one to go to," and the idea of religious tolerance even

man who prefers to spend his Sunday morning fishing bidding farewell to his son, who is headed for church. These and many other films effectively celebrate America's religious diversity.

Pvt. Joe Louis says_

"We're going to do our part ... and we'll win because we're on God's side"

extends to those who are not religious, as the narrator of von Sternberg's *The Town* notes: "All faiths have found a place here. No one interferes with the other's journey to heaven or to hell"; the montage of spires and worship services is followed by a scene showing an old

World heavyweight champion Joe Louis figured prominently in wartime messages aimed at African Americans.

Other documentaries record how people from different livelihoods, social classes, and geographic regions of America have cast aside their differences for the common cause. *Wings Up!*, a training film about air force boot camp, is narrated by Clark Gable, who describes himself as just another airman; some of the other representative airmen depicted range from Hollywood personalities to athletes, executives, college students, farmers, and blue-collar workers. And geographic diversity is also noted, as in the make-up of the crew of the *Memphis Belle* and the opening narration of *Welcome Home*, which points out that the war pulled men from everywhere: "The farms, the shanty on the tracks, the lavish apartments, the uptown flats, the shrubbed estates, the modest houses of the suburban streets."[2] But again, only rarely are minorities represented as part of that diversity in films not explicitly intended to deal with racial questions.

Of the best-known documentary films made during wartime, only three actually include racial diversity: Frank Capra's *War Comes to America*, John Ford and Gregg Toland's *December 7*, and John Huston's masterpiece, *Let There Be Light*.[3] *War Comes to America* is the culmination of the *Why We Fight* series and is intended to summarize the American experience and show why that experience separates us from the Axis nations. Its rendering of American history recognizes that many different peoples came together in this country: "The sweat of the men of all nations made America—and the blood." While it ignores indignities to Native Americans and Japanese Americans and never even mentions slavery as it recaps our history, its casual inclusiveness is nonetheless encouraging. Capra's rapid-fire editing makes an exact count difficult, but blacks are depicted in at least half a dozen scenes, including one showing a black gun crew in combat, while Japanese Americans are shown picketing in support of America's embargo of Japan.

In *December 7*, Ford and Toland

show us a black gunner (perhaps intended to represent Doris Miller, one of America's first heroes of the war) in action alongside white soldiers and sailors, and Asian American civilians, including a worried child, who are terrified by the ferocity of the Japanese attack. Most importantly, the honor roll of the Pearl Harbor dead, given substance by showing us pictures of those who lost their lives and taking us back to

Let There Be Light is startling in that it depicts blacks and whites not only in integrated units, but being given equal treatment.

the states to meet their families, attains true diversity. This roll call goes farther than just including whites from widely scattered locales or different religions; it acknowledges black, white, and Hispanic casualties. The narration, melodramatically, perhaps, emphasizes this true democracy by lingering on a new grave and inquiring of the last of those pictured casualties, a Lt. William R. Schick, "How does it happen that all of you sound and talk alike?" "We *are* all alike," is Schick's reply. "We are all Americans."

Let There Be Light is even more impressive in its inclusiveness, for, without drawing attention to it, it makes no racial differentiation in its story of psychically scarred combat veterans: all are equally visible in the process of healing covered by the film, from the lengthy intake interviews through group therapy sessions to rest and relaxation. Given Hollywood films of the era—which

either delete blacks or derogate them by lumping them into one or another offensive stereotype—and the lily-white content of other documentaries, *Let There Be Light* is startling in that blacks and whites not only are depicted in integrated units, but are shown being given equal treatment, and it is possible that this early vision of equality may have been a factor in the military's controversial decision not to release the film for general viewing.[4] But these three films are definite exceptions. Huston's documentary was not given wide release until decades after the war ended, and for the most part, Native Americans, Japanese Americans, and African Americans disappear from the official cinematic record.

The tale of Native American representation in the World War Two documentary is quickly told: there is, apparently, none. While segments of newsreels occasionally cover Indian ceremonies for visiting dignitaries or scenes of reservation life, including several Paramount newsreels from 1942 and 1943 that show Navajo or Pueblo Indians collecting scrap metal or making clothing for the war effort, none of the American wartime documentaries sampled for this article devotes time to American Indians, nor has the author turned up evidence of other documentaries that might tell, even in small part, the role of American Indian soldiers.[5] This oversight seems startling for several reasons. First, Indians were widely represented in World War Two. According to Alison R. Bernstein, around 25,000 Native Americans served in the military, a small number, perhaps, until you consider that the figure represents over a third of all able-bodied Indian males between the ages of eighteen and fifty; some tribes sent as much as seventy percent of their male population (40). Second, American Indians distinguished themselves in combat. Ira Hayes, one of the flagraisers on Iwo Jima's Mt. Suribachi, may be the best known of these men, but in general, Native soldiers won a disproportionate amount of attention for their military prowess, including General Douglas MacArthur's characterization of the Indian soldier as "particularly able" (Bernstein 46). While these opinions may in part represent the stereotype of the fierce Indian warrior, there seems little question that these service men and women performed admirably. Finally, many Hollywood films were populated by Indians with a singular skill; they could send an encoded call for help in their unique languages back to a counterpart at headquarters. In fact, Vine Deloria has observed that apparently

Each platoon of red-blooded white American boys was equipped with its own set of Indians. When the platoon got into trouble and was surrounded, its communications cut off except for one slender line to regimental headquarters, and that line tapped by myriads of Germans, Japanese, or Italians, the stage was set. . . . Anyone watching war movies during the '40s would have been convinced that without Indian telephone operators the war would have been lost irretrievably. (589)

In fictional films, ironically, the Indians saved John Wayne, Tyrone Power, or Randolph Scott on a regular basis by calling in the cavalry, but their real-life exploits have not been recorded for posterity. For that reason it is fortunate indeed that two of the best-known novels by Native Americans, N. Scott Momaday's Pulitzer Prize-winning *House Made of Dawn* and Leslie Marmon Silko's *Ceremony*, each relates the difficulties of returning Indian veterans, since otherwise the Native American experience in World War Two might be lost to the rest of America.

Japanese Americans suffered a worse fate than simply being ignored; they were actively vilified, with great numbers of them rounded up and placed in concentration camps because the government feared disloyalty. Perception of the

Japanese as a "yellow menace" was not a new development—a 1922 Supreme Court ruling banned Japanese immigrants from attaining citizenship, while national immigration quotas, a few years later, set

Japanese immigration at zero—but anger over the attack on Pearl Harbor led *Time* to report the national mood: "What would the people . . . say in the face of the mightiest event of their time? What they said—tens of thousands of them—was: 'Why, the yellow bastards!' " (Friedrich 33). Hollywood films of the day continued the trend. Frederick C. Othman noted how the war had created plenty of nasty villains and their hierarchy: "The Nazis make

heavy heavies, the Italians light heavies, the Japs the cruelest of all" (446). The perfidious assault on Pearl Harbor explains much, as do other Japanese atrocities, but "the coarseness and pervasiveness of

Wartime documentaries typically featured the Japanese as monolithic—"The Jap."

plain anti-'yellow' race hate throughout the war"—and, consequently, the hatred directed at Americans of Japanese descent—remains disturbing (Dower 10).[7] We seemed to enjoy hating the Japanese, a phenomenon that may even be observed today in the revival of Japan bashing.

Documentaries followed the lead of fiction films in consistently presenting the Japanese as "other," depicting them in the stereotypical fashion as bandy-legged, buck-toothed, big-spectacled, and barely human; physical characteristics subsume human identity. In *Camouflage* (1943), for example, an animated training film, Japanese pilots are depicted as buck-toothed, ape-like—Dower notes simian imagery as being the most pervasive view of Japanese animalism in wartime popular culture—and speaking gibberish, as are Japanese characters in Private Snafu cartoons in the *Army Navy Screen Magazine* (81–87). In *Prelude to War* the narrator argues that Hitler and his "buck-

descent were also vilified; while *Our Job in Japan* runs a preliminary title about the Nisei (second generation Japanese Americans) who, "however much they resemble our enemies in physical appearance," distinguished themselves in combat in Europe, many Americans, submerged in a flood of hate from newspapers, cartoons, public figures, and the powerful images of photographs and films, could not look beyond appearances.

One documentary film which we today might expect to portray Japanese Americans sympathetically, *Japanese Relocation*, does not do so, at least not consciously. In fact, its conscious aim is to defend the 1942 internment of 110,000 persons of

loss of money, jobs, property, and most important, self-respect; the film describes the Japanese Americans as "cheerfully" helping with the paperwork involved in the "migration." Although the narration remains consistently optimistic, the images often undercut this message. Shots of the homes and businesses left behind (some with "x"'s chalked on their doors) and notices posted to "all people of Japanese descent" are reminiscent of similar scenes in Germany; one would not be surprised to read "Achtung, Juden" on these posted handbills.

Other films produced by the War Relocation Authority, the agency in charge of the internment, reflect similar tensions between a national urge for security and a wholesale breach of civil rights. *A Challenge to Democracy*, intended for a general audience, as was *Japanese Relocation*, vacillates between the two tensions, as its title suggests. The narration explains that these Japanese Americans are "not under suspicion, they are not prisoners, they are not internees. They are merely dislocated people, the unwounded casualties of war." The most common term used in the narration for these "unwounded casualties" is "evacuees." On one hand, the film emphasizes the many hardships of the camps, suggesting some sympathy for the internees, while in almost the next breath, the narrator scurries to assure the American general public that these camps were built on lands that had "never been occupied or farmed," that wages in the camps, "by outside standards, are low," that "very little government money has been spent for strictly recreational purposes." The film ends with footage showing the many Nisei and Issei (first-generation emigrants) who have been relocated outside the camps (far away from their former homes and businesses on the West Coast) and are contributing to the war effort, especially those Nisei soldiers, whose bravery is also celebrated in the War Relocation film *Go For Broke*. Both these

toothed pals" won't stop until the whole world is under their control. The many derogatory references to the physical differences of the Japanese have the effect of making everyone of Japanese ancestry an enemy; unlike the racially similar Germans, who could be divided into "Nazis" or "good Germans," all Japanese became simply "Japs." This officially sanctioned attitude toward racial differences explains why those Americans of Japanese

Capra's *Prelude to War* portrayed Germany as regimented and a "slave nation."

Japanese ancestry living in California, Oregon, and Washington, to create a "historical record" of the act that the American Civil Liberties Union has called "the worst wholesale violation of civil rights of American citizens in our history."[8] The documentary minimizes the effect of the relocation, the resulting

films insist, without apparent awareness of the irony, that these soldiers fight for the American ideals of democracy, freedom, and equality, "regardless of race, creed, or ancestry." In fact, racism is never even mentioned in these documentaries, nor does it appear in a WRA film intended strictly for Japanese Americans within the camps, *The Way Ahead,* which urges them to relocate outside the camps so that their abilities can be put to use for the war effort. The film admits, "Of course, it isn't all easy out there," but the only difficulties presented to these Nisei being enticed to leave the camps are those encountered by everyone on the home front: housing shortages and rationing. In the film, a Nisei woman is depicted striking up a conversation with a white woman in a grocery store, while the narrator asserts, "It isn't hard to make friends." These Japanese Americans who had been forced from their homes, schools, and businesses almost solely because of the way they looked would surely have been justified in retaining skepticism about this sugar-coated version of the world outside the guard towers.

The documentary film that best represents the internees' experiences was not produced by the WRA, but by the Presbyterian National Board of Missions, using footage recognizable from the WRA films. That documentary, *Barriers and Passes,* is silent, relying on title cards and the visuals themselves to create meaning, rather than on the typical documentary narrator who tells the audience how to interpret the footage. These images of the wastelands where the camps were built speak loudly enough, with their blowing dust or muddy streets, but the title cards also allow the internees to speak for themselves. One says that worse than the crude conditions was "our discovery that we were actually prisoners behind barbed wire, guarded by armed men," while another says, "We've been wronged . . . but we will be serious about

being good useful loyal American citizens." Many of the internees feared that they would never ever leave the camps because of the "rising tide of race prejudice." The film shows the Japanese Americans build-

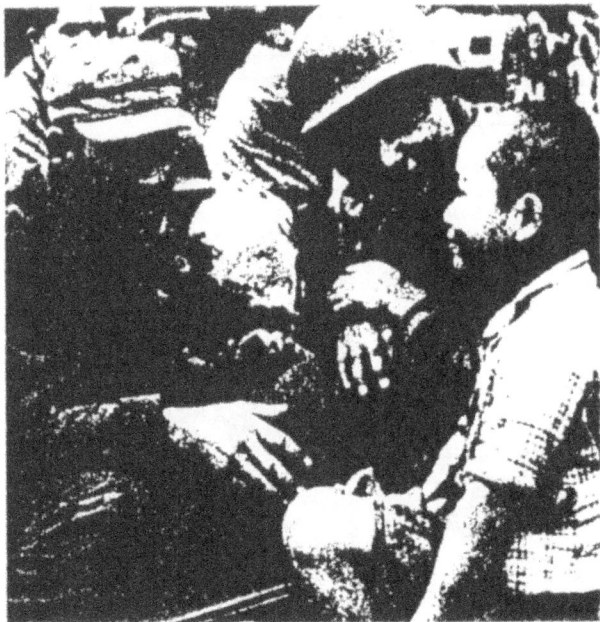

As this still from *Our Job in Japan* shows, films released after Japan's surrender were more conciliatory toward the Japanese.

ing permanent school buildings and beautiful gardens, and a title explains that there is "a strong feeling among the old Japanese that they will be permanently segregated and become wards of the United States like the American Indian." For any who have missed the sympathetic thrust of the film, the final title cards ask its audience, "Do we believe in democracy? Are we truly Christian?" and suggests that the "overwhelming majority" of the internees have given every evidence of their loyalty. Perhaps it is difficult for us to recapture the terrible spirit

of panic and paranoia in which, without real evidence against them, 110,000 Japanese Americans could be shipped off to remote concentration camps, forfeiting their land, businesses, and possessions; but still

it remains startling that the only film clearly and evenhandedly representing the Japanese American internship had to be pieced together from footage already in the hands of the government.

In comparison with the nonexistent Native Americans and the reviled Japanese Americans, on those rare occasions when black Americans do appear in World War Two documentaries (as we've noted, they too are almost always ignored in favor of whites), they seize center stage, and in contrast to their typical depictions in popular culture, the blacks in these films are intelligent, competent, and brave.[9] One film, *The Negro Soldier,* received wide public exposure, and others, *Teamwork, Wings for this Man, I've*

Been Working on an Airfield, and *The Negro Sailor* have the same basic purpose of fighting German race-baiting propaganda and pointing out how blacks were vital to the defense of America.[10]

The Negro Soldier, yet another product of the Capra unit, was, according to production files in the National Archives, one of the first projects Capra envisioned when he came to work for the military.[11] Framed around a sermon delivered in a black church, the film contrasts *Mein Kampf,* "the gospel according to Hitler," which calls blacks "half-ape," and the history of black soldiers, scientists, and athletes like Joe Louis in America. There is no mention of the native-grown variety of racism or the segregation of the black units in the armed forces, but the film still manages to stirringly show how American blacks are putting the lie to Hitler's words.

The other films received less widespread exposure, but utilized a similar rhetorical strategy. *I've Been Working on an Airfield* shows black engineers working on an airfield and talks about the unit's "long and hard pilgrimage." *Wings for this Man* relates the story of the Tuskegee Airmen. Other films on the black contribution to the war tiptoe around the question of racism, but *Wings for this Man* chooses to address it directly. While the film represents the bootcamp experience of "a group of average Americans," the narration also notes that before their training camp could be built, there was "misunderstanding, and distrust, and prejudice to be cleared away," and asserts that

> You can't judge a man here by the color of his eyes or the shape of his nose. On the flight strip, you judge a man by the way he flies. Here's the answer to Adolph and Hirohito. Here's the answer to the propaganda of the Japs and Nazis. Wings for this man. Wings for these Americans.

By contrast, *The Negro Sailor* makes no references to German propaganda. Instead, the film begins in a black newspaper office, and proceeds to follow a recently drafted employee through his Navy training. The sports editor who narrates the film naturally thinks of the war as a team effort, and while not everyone can be quarterback, "every sailor plays a vital position." Bill Johnson, our representative sailor, eventually serves on a destroyer's escort "manned by a predominantly Negro crew," although they serve under white officers.[12] During his training, Bill learns about the different positions blacks fill in the Navy, from steward's mate to chaplain, and about black heroes of the war like Doris Miller and Leonard Roy Harmon.

Teamwork shows how blacks and whites worked side by side throughout the war; skillful editing disguises the fact that its depicted units were segregated.

Teamwork also uses the team metaphor, but seems most interested in responding to the question of German propaganda discussed in earlier films.[13] Released in 1946, it serves in effect as a retrospective of race relations during the war. Originally titled *Negro Soldiers in Supply and Maintenance, ETO,* the scope of the film was expanded to include combat in January 1945, while the side-by-side depiction of blacks and whites in similar jobs also dates from a January memo, in which Lt. Col. Charles Dollard reasoned that this would do two things: It would prevent assigning "entire credit" for the miracle of battlefield supply to blacks, while it would also avoid the implication that blacks were only given jobs fetching and carrying.

The film begins with images of the Nazi "arsenal of words" that sought to divide and conquer and follows it with a scene staged at Twentieth Century Fox that depicts Nazi brass who plan to split American blacks away from the whites by playing on "frictions that already exist." The film goes on to show how blacks and whites worked side by side throughout the war, despite the flood of Nazi propaganda, skillful editing disguising the fact that all of the units depicted are segregated, and closeups are generally interpolated with stock footage of ships being unloaded or convoys rolling down the road. The film gains much of its effect by contrasting images with the stereotypical traits used by the Nazis: while the narrator remarks, "They said this man was shiftless. Lazy. Stupid. Irresponsible," the footage shows black communication workers or mine detectors hard at work. The film effectively demonstrates black intelligence, persistence, and courage, despite its self-serving motive of debunking German propaganda.

Of these films discussing black contributions to the war effort, only *The Negro Soldier* was widely released, and although it drew enthusiastic audiences, especially in the black community (W. C. Handy, who also appears in the film, wrote the filmmakers that he had seen it twice in one day "and in all probability will see it again"), it is, as we have seen, one of only a handful of documentaries produced for the war effort to center on non-whites. White chauvinism extends even to cases where it is patently ridiculous, such as *The Winged Scourge,* made by the Disney studio to explain conditions contributing to malaria in Latin America. The film was shown to over four million people in virtually every nation south of the border, yet the malaria victim depicted in the cartoon is a white farmer whose farm seems to step straight from the paintings of Grant Wood.[14]

This Latin farmer from the American midwest is a fitting final example of the casual chauvinism with which people of color were excluded from most American cinematic representations of the war.[15]

NOTES

1. And of course, the message was generally "it's a white man's war," although even films focusing on women and the war effort, such as *Glamour Girls of 1943* and *It's Your War, Too* are all white, despite *Glamour Girls'* narration: "every woman who can possibly help is wanted."

2. The 1991 feature film remaking *Memphis Belle* continued this long tradition of "All-American" fighting units, whites of various ethnic groups, educational and economic levels, and so on, coming together to fight.

3. The longer original version of *December 7*, directed by Toland, has been recently made available to the public, but the film credited to Ford and Toland was the one circulated during the war years and afterward.

4. I have written elsewhere about the thirty-five-year repression of *Let There Be Light*, which may never be adequately explained. See *"Let There Be Light* and Huston's *film noir," Proteus* 7.2 (1990): 30-33, and "Muffling the Bell of Liberty: Censorship and the World War II Documentary," *Journal of the American Studies Association of Texas* 22 (1991): 63-73.

5. I have consulted over forty wartime documentaries in preparing this article, including all of the best-known films (those affiliated with Frank Capra's unit, John Ford, John Huston, William Wyler, Joseph von Sternberg, and Pare Lorentz) and a number of other training and informational films issued by the government, many of which may be viewed only at the National Archives in Washington, D.C. It remains possible, of course, that other newsreels may discuss Native Americans in combat; the point is that these government-sponsored documentaries do not.

6. Alison Bernstein does discuss programs that put Indians, particularly Navajos, to work encoding or decoding messages. Some 400 worked as "Code Talkers" by the end of the war, hardly one for every platoon (49).

7. John W. Dower's *War Without Mercy* provides a logical and detailed analysis of the impact of race on the war in the Pacific. I highly recommend it.

8. Although it seems too apt to be true, the same individual, Dillon S. Myer, served as commandant of the Japanese relocation and later as head of the Bureau of Indian Affairs. What these two jobs may have had in common I will leave to the reader's judgment and to Richard Drinnon's *Keeper of Concentration Camps: Dillon S. Myer and American Racism.*

9. The award-winning 1987 documentary *Ethnic Notions* shows a 1941 cartoon of the various offensive black stereotypes whose images had "permeated American culture," but perhaps the depictions of blacks in wartime documentaries, as well as black participation in the war effort, were steps toward the more realistic and human images of blacks in films made following the war.

10. "Roll of Honor," a short segment of *Film Communique 4*, a 1944 film program shown to American workers, depicts an all-black unit rebuilding an airfield in the Southern Pacific. It also has the same general purposes as the longer films mentioned above.

11. This and subsequent unattributed citations are drawn from production files in Record Group 111, National Archives.

12. The film depicts Bill training alongside a multi-ethnic group of comrades—Bob, Pedro, Ole, and Lee—although, as Reese Erlich reports, the Navy did not abolish racial segregation until 1946, after a series of strikes by black seamen and pressure by groups such as the NAACP forced their hand (12).

13. Although it does not mention blacks specifically, *Army/Navy Screen Magazine #37* also confronts Nazi propaganda in the animated segment "Weapon of War," which features a huckster (given voice by Mel Blanc) pitching "Dr. Hitler's Blood Tonic" to unreceptive Americans.

14. Attendance figures through April 1945, according to *16mm films—Latin American Program—Summary by Title*, a file from the Records of the Coordinator of Inter-American Affairs reproduced in Culbert's *Film and Propaganda in America*, 471-73.

15. I gratefully acknowledge the Baylor University Research Committee for its generous financial support of this and other research, and Dean William Cooper and the Baylor College of Arts and Sciences for the 1992 summer sabbatical during which I researched and wrote this article.

WORKS CITED

Bernstein, Alison R. *American Indians and World War II: Toward a New Era in Indian Affairs.* Norman: University of Oklahoma Press, 1991.

Culbert, David, ed. *Film and Propaganda in America: A Documentary History.* Vol 3, Pt. 2. New York: Greenwood Press, 1990.

DeLoria, Vine, Jr. "We Talk, You Listen." *The Portable North American Indian Reader.* Frederick W. Turner, III, ed. New York: Penguin, 1974. 587-96.

Denby, David. "It's a Wonderful War." *Premiere* January 1990: 33.

Dower, John W. *War Without Mercy: Race and Power in the Pacific War.* New York: Pantheon, 1986.

Drinnon, Richard. *Keeper of Concentration Camps: Dillon S. Myer and American Racism.* Berkeley: U of California P. 1987.

Erlich, Reese. "Navy Reopens WWII Black Mutiny Case." *Christian Science Monitor* 10 April 1992: 12.

Friedrich, Otto. "Day of Infamy." *Time* 2 December 1991: 30-45.

Othman, Frederick C. "War in the World of Make Believe." *The Movies in Our Midst: Documents in the Cultural History of Film in America.* Chicago: U of Chicago P, 1982. 445-53.

"Reunion." *The New Yorker* 11 Nov. 1991: 32-33.

Riggs, Marlon, producer/director. *Ethnic Notions.* 1987.

Journal of American Studies, **31** (1997), 3, 385–405. Printed in the United Kingdom
© 1997 Cambridge University Press

What in the World interests Women? Hollywood, Postwar America, and *Johnny Belinda*

LEONARD J. LEFF

During World War II, when the Office of War Information urged the American film companies to help the nation win the war, the OWI's Bureau of Motion Pictures delivered both moral support and guidance. The BMP "Manual" (1942), for instance, encouraged producers to show women dropping off their children at day-care centers, then cheerfully heading off to jobs where they enjoyed equal opportunity and equal pay. Scenes like those may have been fantasy, and for some women wryly amusing, and yet, in the late 1940s and beyond, as one historian says, World War II came to be thought of as "the best war ever," the war, according to myth, where there were no tensions over class, or race, or gender.[1]

"The broad consensus after the war was that women with children should not work unless circumstances were severe," D'Ann Campbell reports in *Women at War*.[2] According to Hollywood, though, the consensus (like the myth) was dotted with rupture and resistance. In *Sitting Pretty*, a top-grossing release of 1948, Maureen O'Hara spends hours in her apron, in her kitchen, sweating. Moreover, she lets her husband (Robert Young, later the sage of television's "Father Knows Best") see and know how hard she toils. She was the ordinary housewife, *in extremis*. The "message" of the story turns more complex once the

Leonard J. Leff, Professor of English, teaches literature and film at Oklahoma State University, 205 Morrill Hall, Stillwater, OK 74078-0135, USA. (email: leff@osuunx.ucc.okstate,edu)

[1] Garth Jowett, *Film: The Democratic Art* (Boston: Little, Brown, 1976), 312; Michael C. C. Adams, *The Best War Ever: America and World War II* (Baltimore: Johns Hopkins University Press, 1994). The author wishes to thank Professor Linda Austin of Oklahoma State University for her constructive comments on an earlier version of this essay.

[2] D'Ann Campbell, *Women at War with America: Private Lives in a Patriotic Era* (Cambridge: Harvard University Press, 1984), 232.

family hires a nanny. O'Hara pursues her interest in sculpture; however, she works in her living room, where she is constantly reminded of her accountability as wife and mother. And, while the nanny denotes the postwar prosperity that rewarded the woman who stayed home, the sexual identity of the nanny (played by Clifton Webb) accents postwar bewilderment about gender roles. Finally, then, if the debate over feminism and World War II narrows to two points of view – the war as watershed, and the war as witness to the endurance of custom and tradition – one can hardly look to motion pictures as conclusive proof of one or the other.

Hollywood in the 1940s (as Mary Ann Doane, Andrea Walsh, and others have written) was pulled in two directions. The stress was inherent not only in the period, but also in the medium and in the genre of the so-called woman's picture: American movies were both a conservative art form that reinforced the status quo *and* a popular art that catered to its audience, in the case of the woman's picture its female audience*s*. Motion pictures strove to portray women as they were in the 1940s, as (per Walsh) "strong, maternal, and sisterly; desiring yet distrusting and angry toward men; excited about as well as ambivalent toward and frightened of independence and autonomy."[3] Walsh treats almost two dozen films at length and another several dozen more (as Doane does) in brief. Neither Walsh nor Doane nor others, though, offers more than an aside on one of the top-grossing releases of 1948, one that helped crystallize the debate over womanhood in postwar America.

Johnny Belinda, a woman's picture, bends the often rigid features of its genre. The representative woman's picture, usually set indoors, features "indoor" concerns, like romance or sexuality, and focuses on (as Walsh says) "the conflict between femininity and achievement."[4] *Johnny Belinda* places the heroine out of doors, in the field and the mill, where she plows and she lifts, and where, in short, she does "man's work." And it introduces sex not as love, or seduction, or even adultery, but as rape – a plot point rare in *any* film of the Hays Office era and one that, here, occurs virtually outdoors, in a dark corner of an apparently doorless mill. Finally, Belinda McDonald's "achievement" exceeds that of even Mildred Pierce, for, while the latter (in the 1945 film *Mildred Pierce*) advances from pie cook to restauranteur *par excellence*, the former grows from a girl who

---

[3] Mary Ann Doane, *The Desire to Desire: The Woman's Film of the 1940s* (Bloomington: Indiana University Press, 1987); Andrea S. Walsh, *Women's Film and Female Experience, 1940–1950* (New York: Praeger, 1984), 4 and passim.   [4] Ibid., 161.

most people thought was retarded into a confident young single mother and nascent matriarch.

As (again) Doane, Walsh, and others have argued, woman's pictures of the 1940s generally contained contradictions: the pictures hallowed, devalued, championed, and underrated women. *Johnny Belinda* contains contradictions, and yet in another sense cannot "contain" them. Supervised by Jerry Wald, released by Warner Bros., *Johnny Belinda* lays bare a masculinist motion picture industry and American culture richly ambivalent about woman and womanhood. As such, because it swings so widely and obviously between sympathy and suspicion, because it cannot decide, finally, just how it feels about woman and womanhood, *Johnny Belinda* speaks eloquently of the anxiety about gender conventions in the postwar 1940s.

Johnny Belinda opens on a map of Nova Scotia and the island of Cape Breton. A dissolve leads to a shot of waters lapping the island, and a montage follows. According to a March 1948 Warner Bros. press release about the opening series of moving shots, Paul Ivano "manned the camera" from a helicopter that flew over the northern California towns (Ft. Bragg and Mendecino) that stood in for the cliff-lined lip of the island. An offscreen male voice narrates. The Scotch burr and dropped consonants sound native.

The island of Cape Breton, the northeastern end of Nova Scotia, is just a small chunk of land stickin' out into the Atlantic. Roads haven't been built through everywhere yet; you mostly have to come in from the sea. It needs an old hand to navigate through the shoals offshore, especially during the storms that come up suddenly in the summertime. And the little lighthouse has saved many a life. The village isn't much to shout about. Just a quiet, peaceful place where the people are proud o' their church, built with their own hands and what little money they could scrape up. Their farms don't bring in much. But for a few months each year when the cod are runnin' there's a lot of excitement. You should see the harbor then, alive with boats. They leave the women to take care o' the potatoes and livestock and put out to sea. Not many of them are lucky enough to have their own boat, but they all get a share when the catch is paid for at the cannery. A fair sized haul means everything. It means food for the long winter, new blades for tools, grain bought for cattle. That's why we watch each vessel as she comes in, to see how low she sets in the water.[5]

---

[5] Warner Bros. Press Release (untitled), 3 Mar. 1948, *Johnny Belinda*, United Artists Collection, Wisconsin Center for Film and Theatre Research, State Historical Society of Wisconsin, Madison, P68–1989, Microfilm. Unless otherwise indicated, dialogue cited in the text has been transcribed (as was "The island of Cape Breton ...") from the soundtrack of *Johnny Belinda* (Warner Bros., 1948).

211

While a woman usually narrates the woman's picture, as she does in *Rebecca* (1940), *Since You Went Away* (1944), *Mildred Pierce*, *I Remember Mama* (1948), *A Letter to Three Wives* (1949), and others, a man narrates (or at least introduces) *Johnny Belinda*: he is an early sign of the danger the heroine and her story pose. The male narrator here has dominance and authority. He comes in (via helicopter) over the sea, "you" come in *from* it. He uses relentlessly penetrative images, too, from the land "stickin' out" and the roads "built through" to the hands that navigate dark shoals, and the phallic shapes of church steeples and lighthouses that, as super-man, he calls "little." He admires "the people" and the church *they* have constructed with the money *they* have earned on the land *they* have farmed. Who are "the people"? "*They* leave the women," the narrator says toward the end of his speech, and thus renders "the people" "the [male] people." Once again in the final sentence, the narrator works pronouns as clay. As the "documentary" shows men lined up on the wharf, watching Locky McCormick's boat enter the harbor, the narrator's *they* becomes *we*. The Author God has passed His agency to His heir. The story proper may now be told; that it will turn on rape – an enforcement of sexual division that has the clarity of a Punch and Judy show – should not surprise us.

On hardscrabble land in Cape Breton, Black McDonald farms with two other workhorses, his sister Aggie and his adolescent daughter, the deaf mute Belinda. The dummy (as the locals call her) runs the McDonalds' mill, and, though she can neither hear nor speak, she has acquired language. "She's learned to identify every man by his mark," her father says of the account book where he records each order and Belinda, as she processes each, crosshatches through the line he has made. Another man, Robert Richardson, the new local doctor, teaches Belinda yet another language. Her first lesson concentrates on the signs for *rooster* and *hen*, then *tree* and *water*, on "marks" of gender, in other words, and notions of fertility.

One evening, a band of revelers stops at the mill. Belinda has washed her face and hair and, apparently for the occasion, put on a plain but pretty dress. As she watches the dancers, Doctor Richardson lays her hand on a fiddle, and soon she steps in place to the cadence she feels. "She looks cute, don't she?" says Locky McCormick, the burly fisherman. Stella (Locky's girlfriend) bristles. And so does Black, since, on the site of goods processed and exchanged, where she stands next to the bachelor local doctor, Black now sees Belinda as both chattel and daughter.

Everyone leaves, Locky and others for a party, Black and Aggie for the train that will speed her to another of her kin. Black worries about Belinda alone in the mill. "Nobody'd bother stealin' her," Aggie snaps. Playing at dark comedy, Aggie uses *stealin'* rather than *kidnappin'* to annoy her brother and derogate Belinda. Unintentionally, though, she concedes that "things" have value, and Black can infer what, thanks to Hollywood censorship, Aggie cannot say: "Nobody'd bother stealin' her... virginity." For Black McDonald, *her* virginity and *her* fertility represent *his* property.

Locky returns alone to the mill. "Look what I brought you," he says to Belinda. She draws near and places her hand near the *f* holes of the stolen fiddle he bows so roughly. The rasping chords constitute a *danse macabre* as Locky, in a cruel and grotesque parody of seduction, approaches Belinda, then seizes her. Here *Johnny Belinda* turns into a notably frank motion picture: it will portray the rape that follows *as* rape – and boldly so, and harshly so.

Until the advent of the Production Code Administration in 1934, rape had been at once screen perennial and screen puzzle. Though rapists had usually been degenerates and morons, like Popeye in *The Story of Temple Drake* (1933), even the corncob scene of Paramount's adaptation of *Sanctuary* had baffled Miriam Hopkins. "Jean, are my legs opened at the right angle?" she asked Jean Negulesco, her "technical advisor" on the rape. "Shouldn't my dress be up higher? Do I scream? And are my eyes opened in terror of what I see? Or do I close my eyes and let things happen? Jean, do I enjoy it?" With that, Negulesco later recalled, "the laughter exploded all around."[6]

Like Hopkins, the Motion Picture Production Code also confounded seduction and rape.

II. 3. *Seduction or Rape*

A. They should never be more than suggested, and only when essential for the plot, and even then never shown by explicit method.
B. They are never the proper subject for comedy.

Seduction or *Rape*, persuasion or force, pleasure or pain. The "undecidability" of *Seduction* or *Rape*, on screen and off, endured well into the 1940s, when Warner Bros. assigned Irmgard von Cube and Allen Vincent to adapt *Johnny Belinda* for the screen. "Every time I see one of the numerous pictures in popular movies or magazines showing an anthropomorphous ape or a powerful, bearlike masculine creature with a completely helpless female in his arms," Helene Deutsch wrote in 1946,

---

[6] Jean Negulesco, *Things I Did and Things I Think I Did* (New York: Simon and Schuster, 1984), 92.

"I am reminded of my old favorite speculation: thus it was that primitive man took possession of woman and subjected her to sexual desire." Locky indeed appears ursine as he crooks his arms and spreads his fingers and reaches out for the defenseless Belinda, saying, "I caught a seagull once... It had – the same scared look." And, according to the 29 March 1947 screenplay, he seizes Belinda and "kisses her savagely." But *Johnny Belinda* was no *King Kong*. The long low-angle shadows and the struggle of Belinda before the fade out suggest that the rape will have no silver lining, and that what Deutsch called "the powerful embrace of the prehensile arms" and "the defensive counterpressure" will not induce "strong pleasure sensations in the woman's entire body."[7]

Three transitional shots follow the fade out on Locky and Belinda. An aerial shot of the Cape Breton shore uses water as the "mark" of sexual discharge. Standard Hollywood iconography. The next two shots are raw and novel, one a distant shot, the other a closeup. Belinda pushes a wheelbarrow along a bleak landscape ruled by desiccated fence posts and stumps, and in both long shot and closeup the phallic shapes that bisect the frame convey not only her awareness of male dominance, but also her

[7] 1930 Production Code, quoted in Leonard J. Leff and Jerold Simmons, *The Dame in the Kimono: Hollywood, Censorship, and the Production Code from the 1920s to the 1960s* (New York: Grove Weidenfeld, 1990), 285; Helene Deutsch, *The Psychology of Women: A Psychoanalytic Interpretation* (New York: Grune & Stratton, 1994), 222–23; Irmgard von Cube and Allen Vincent, *Johnny Belinda*, Screenplay, 29 Mar. 1947, United Artists Collection, Wisconsin Center for Film and Theatre Research, State Historical Society of Wisconsin, Madison, MSS 99AN Series 1.2, Box 208, page 45; subsequent references to this and the 22 Mar. 1947, 1 Aug. 1947, and 22 Aug. 1947 screenplays will be cited parenthetically within the text. As mediators between film and audience, posters and ads for *Johnny Belinda* spoke (in code) of rape – the fear, the pain, the sad consequences. "A story that has sensation written all over it! Never a picture like it! So daring it must be seen – this story of shame that came out of the shadows." In the strong slanted lines of the key art, Locky McCormick towers over Belinda with his arm crooked and his fingers spread; she cowers, but with arm crooked and fingers spread, as though, at least graphically, per Helene Deutsch, what follows were "natural," as though once Warner executives had seen what Warner producers had done, they were nonplussed about whether the shame that comes out of the shadows was his, hers, ours, theirs, or no one's (Warner Bros. Pressbook [undated, unpaged], *Johnny Belinda*, United Artists Collection, Wisconsin Center for Film and Theatre Research, State Historical Society of Wisconsin, Madison, P68–1989, Microfilm). *Johnny Belinda* nonetheless foreshadowed – and authorized – the candor of Warners' *A Streetcar Named Desire* (1951), which the Production Code office approved with the understanding that the ads would forgo the sensational. "I think Joe [Breen] felt he was letting us down very easy as far as the seal requirements went," Elia Kazan told Jack Warner, "and didn't want to be put further on the spot by the Ads which might, as the 'BELINDA' Ads did, be selling the rape scene" (Kazan, Letter to Jack L. Warner, 7 Dec. 1950, *A Streetcar Named Desire* file, Motion Picture Association of America Collection, Margaret Herrick Library, Academy of Motion Picture Arts and Sciences, Beverly Hills).

separation from the audience and – more important – from herself. The three transitional shots were apparently added during production as replacements for a more conventional scene between father and daughter. "It was the only time in my experience that an actor (Charles Bickford) argued against his scene," Jean Negulesco, the director of *Johnny Belinda*, wrote. "'Unnecessary to the story – a silent mood shot of Belinda's day's work on the farm will be more significant.'"[8]

The three transitional shots nullify the prospect of "pleasure sensations" and, because of Belinda's manifest innocence, make *Johnny Belinda* a "woman's picture" in more ways than one. Rather than another word for intercourse, or seduction, or masked pleasure, rape in *Johnny Belinda* constitutes an "act of cutting, of dividing the flesh, destroying its wholeness, hence the subject," an act that "alienates the victim from herself *and is meant to do so*."[9] Thus *Johnny Belinda* draws a line infrequently seen in the period, even in the social sciences of the period. Moreover, as the final reels of the picture show, the heroine suffers acute emotional suffering because of the "cultural conditioning" that silences her version of the assault. In *Johnny Belinda*, rape becomes the negation of female desire and female voice, *rape* and not *seduction*, force and not persuasion.

The rape creates enormous compassion for Belinda McDonald. As the introductory monologue hints, though, rape belongs to a larger and more disturbing pattern in the film. Belinda's education, however elementary, functions as her initiation into the adult world and thus, potentially, her acquisition of the independence and "looks" of the postwar woman. As an abusive correction to the limits of female autonomy, the rape shows us the price that man may put on that new freedom. It also offers proof of how woman and womanhood threaten man and, potentially, manhood. The "broad consensus" of postwar America notwithstanding, one scene after another reveals an anxiety over gender and gender roles.

In reel one, for instance, Locky McCormick passes by a young woman (Dolly) who guts fish. (She has a "repetition job" typical of the ones that

[8] Negulesco, 127. In *Things I Did and Things I Think I Did* Negulesco does not identify the scene. *Johnny Belinda* has only one unforgettable "silent mood shot," though, and it occurs immediately after the fade out on the rape.

[9] Mieke Bal, "The Rape of Narrative and the Narrative of Rape: Speech Acts and Body Language in Judges," *Literature and the Body: Essays on Populations and Persons*, ed. Elaine Scarry (Baltimore: Johns Hopkins University Press, 1988), 20. On rape and negation, see Coppélia Kahn, "Rape, Repression, and Narrative Form in *Le Devoir de Violence* and *La Vie et Demie*," in *Rape and Representation*, eds. Lynn A. Higgins and Brenda R. Silver (New York: Columbia University Press, 1991), 150; see also "Mourning and Melancholia" in Sigmund Freud, *Therapy and Technique*, trans. Joan Riviere (New York: Macmillan, 1963).

women had before and after – but less so during – World War II; despite her presence in the work force, she also has a name that reinscribes her in the austere sexual economy of the introductory monologue.) Once Locky fiddles with her scarf, and her feelings, he runs into Pacquet. Locky's catch has been too small, says the local entrepreneur, fanning two fingers three inches apart; he also pokes Locky's chest to italicize the point. Locky slaps Pacquet's stomach, and then, leveling the long stem of a pipe at him, he threatens to gut him. Like the appearance of the Author God, this scene on the dock, alluding to size and evisceration, overdetermines and lays open the brittleness of masculinity.

As Roger Horrocks (among others) has noted, masculinity must ever convey the message, "I am not a woman,"[10] and indeed both the tender Doctor Richardson and the violent Locky McCormick have an investment in sexual difference, an investment that uses Belinda as collatoral. For instance, Belinda does not recognize her "nature" until the doctor and (in another sense) Locky school her. Only days after the rape, the doctor confesses to her that the war "and all that came after" caused him to "lose faith in everything, myself, too." Belinda does not respond, and he goes on. The longer he goes on, the more he reminds us that it was his attention, early on, that gave Belinda an awareness of her social and sexual role as a woman, and thus fit her to hear his confession and thus assure that his weakness does not jeopardize his manhood. "I need you," he says, another endangered male who crooks his arms and spreads his fingers and reaches out for her. "Oh, Belinda, don't let me think I've failed again." The plea calls on Belinda to make her mark, the crosshatch that shows she has done as she was ordered.

Later, Doctor Richardson asks to have Belinda, sad and distant, "looked at" by a specialist. Her father accedes, and the prospect of visiting nearby Charlottetown perks her up.[11] On arrival in the town – whose late model automobiles on the fringe of one shot fix the time as contemporaneous with the production of the picture – she and Richardson come on a Nova Scotian marching band with players dressed in kilts. Belinda looks puzzled. Having learned to identify the man by his mark, she signs, "Women?" "Oh, no," Richardson responds, "men." Belinda smiles, tentatively. Once the marching band passes, Belinda and the doctor peer into a store window at "an array of frilly lingerie of all descriptions, wispy stockings, girdles. A little on one side, a legless

[10] Roger Horrocks, *Masculinity in Crisis: Myths, Fantasies, and Realities* (New York: St. Martin's, 1994), 33.
[11] The screenplays rather than the film identify the place as Charlottetown.

manikin posing seductively, smiling blankly, clad in nothing but a girdle and brassiere of black lace." Though the film tones down the 22 August 1947 screenplay, the "array" restores the gender boundary that the musicians have transgressed: it associates women with adornment and fetishism and (in so far as the "array" connotes "plenitude") fertility. Belinda answers the question, what do women want? She asks for the scarf she sees in the window, and when the doctor buys it, she smiles full force.

In his Charlottetown office, Doctor Gray (part physician, part scientist, or *Naturforscher*, literally "nature-poker") examines Belinda's throat and ears, then searches lower and discovers the pregnancy that, seemingly, valorizes the rape. As Kaja Silverman says in *The Acoustic Mirror*, the pregnancy

gives Belinda what psychoanalysis is always quick to propose as the final solution to the problem of female desire, the one thing able both to make good woman's lack and to give her an ideologically recognizable and coherent "content" – a baby. That "supplement" also provides her with a surrogate voice, capable of emitting that most exemplary of female sounds (at least within classic cinema): the cry.[12]

That voice proves astonishingly dogmatic. When she learns of her pregnancy, for example, Belinda tells Doctor Richardson that she will call her baby Johnny. Her assertion contravenes medical science and its representative, her doctor mentor, who says, "But, Belinda, you... Well, if you want it so much I guess you'll have a boy." Following Silverman, one could argue that in the patrilineal world of Cape Breton (where, when Doctor Peter*son* retires, Doctor Richard*son* replaces him) Belinda wants her child to have the power that her "cultural conditioning" has led her to associate with the male. One could also argue, though, that in an era of song lyrics that presupposed male hegemony ("Mona Lisa, Mona Lisa/Men have named you"), Belinda has crossed gender boundaries by assuming for herself the power of naming. It will hardly be the only power she claims before the picture ends.

In the 29 March 1947 screenplay draft, as Belinda sweats and writhes in labor, Doctor Gray presides and Doctor Richardson attends. In the film, Richardson alone functions as obstetrician, a change that enlarged his part and determined that he would not play nurse to Gray's doctor. Richardson was probably too "feminized" already for studio tastes. He was gentle and genteel; moreover, he was played by Lew Ayres, who rather famously

[12] Kaja Silverman, *The Acoustic Mirror: The Female Voice in Psychoanalysis and Cinema* (Bloomington: Indiana University Press, 1988), 69.

had been the voice of pacifism in *All Quiet on the Western Front* (1930) and a conscientious objector during World War II. "Scenes of *actual child birth*, in fact or in silhouette, are never to be presented," the Production Code read, and, by forcing the producers to minimize the shots of Belinda, the censors maximized the shots of Doctor Richardson. He was the male hand of science, the hero of the picture, the one who, merely assisted by the patient, delivered the baby solo.

Johnny Belinda should never have recovered from the name of the baby, Johnny Belinda, an affront to the patrilineal world of Cape Breton and, along with the posters and publicity and reviews that trumpeted the name, a confirmation of the confusion that nags at gender throughout the text. Both the heroine and the picture nonetheless soldier on. After the arrival of Johnny, for instance, when the farm needs more hands than ever before, the story has Belinda retire to the house to care for her baby and (her shining hair suggests) her appearance She does not wear the new look of postwar fashion, the new look that put women in high heels, narrow toes, wired brassieres, and wide skirts, the new look that restricted movement and comfort.[13] Instead, she wears her best manners: when she has a visitor, she plays Betty Crocker – she dresses like her, *looks* like her – and offers her guest fresh-baked cookies.

Weeks pass. An apparently fragile masculinity propels Locky to visit Johnny, and at the house, as he examines and (*sotto voce*) crows about the robust health of the child, Black slowly senses that the fisherman has raped Belinda and fathered her son. He and Locky come to blows along the edge of a cliff, where Black, pushed, falls to his death. There are no witnesses. Belinda mourns, but, again, soldiers on. And Locky pursues Stella, Doctor Richardson's nurse.

Stella works for the doctor as nurse–housekeeper, a dual role that denoted both the bind of postwar women and a common perception among them that one role (the nurse) was good training for another (the housekeeper as wife). Stella yearns for the doctor. "I gave myself a permanent," she says to him in the 29 March 1947 screenplay. "Very

[13] Susan M. Hartmann, *The Home Front and Beyond: American Women in the 1940s* (Boston: Twayne, 1982), 204. In *Mildred Pierce*, produced by Jerry Wald, who also produced *Johnny Belinda*, Mildred was caught between career and home, between the old look (the working woman) and the new. When the audience sees her on top of a ladder, cleaning a light fixture in the restaurant she will soon open, she wears a masculine-looking flannel shirt, a tight straight skirt, and high heels – the woman "being" (below the waist), the woman "doing" (above), her wardrobe caught in the cultural crosscurrents. The dapper and idle Monte Beragon tries to persuade her to stop working and come to the beach house, and when he complains about her spending too many hours at her job, the narrative offers yet another instance of the shift in gender balance.

dangerous," he responds, aware that she adores him. He brandishes a medical textbook: "a 'permanent wave, improperly administered, may result in the hair breaking off at the roots.' However," he concludes the lecture, using science to destroy her self-esteem, "I suppose there's no harm done – as long as you don't look into a mirror" (57). Undeterred, Stella continues her pursuit by inventing a chest pain. The doctor holds the stethoscope to her chest, no longer covered by her blouse, and she breathes as directed, "so deeply it's a sigh. Shoulders bare above a lacey [sic] slip, she looks rather attractive – but Davidson [later changed to Richardson] has dissected too many females at medical school to be affected by this peaches-and-cream expanse" (60). The nexus of "females" and "cadavers" portends her barrenness, and the valuation (or devaluation) society places on it. Such scenes, as Mary Ann Doane and others have noted, have a long history in American movies, so Hollywood censorship was not the sole reason that this one vanished from the picture. Instead, it may have been cut because the man's sway over the woman was so cruel and so transparent, or because the coolness of the doctor played queerly into the "feminization" of his character.

Though Locky apparently has musk to spare, he weds Stella not only for her inheritance, but also for her fecundity. Soon, however, the relationship founders. "A man wants children," Locky gruffly tells her near the end of the picture, "and I want him [Johnny]. Something in 'ere wants him and by the godfrey I'll have 'im." He needs the child – the boy, Johnny – to prove at least to himself that he can perform sexually, for Stella has not conceived in the twelve or so months they have been wed, and, in the postwar 1940s, when sex succeeds war as a "potent sign of manliness," when the courts begin to view the fetus as a legal entity rather than "a part of the mother," children validate and valorize manhood.[14] Locky's, in other words, was "the problem of male desire."

In the 29 March 1947 screenplay, Locky and Stella turn for redress to the local tribunal on matters domestic, the Ladies' Saturday Club, but the

[14] Froma I. Zeitlin, "On Ravishing Urns: Keats in his Tradition," in Higgins (see note 9), 279. In 1946, as *Johnny Belinda* entered pre-production, a federal district court held that a viable fetus born alive could recover damages in the event of injury. Intended to provide education and medical assistance for children damaged before they were legal persons, *Bombrest v. Kotz* was called "the most spectacular abrupt reversal of a well settled rule in the whole history of the law of torts" (Lawrence J. Nelson, quoted in Susan Bordo, *Unbearable Weight: Feminism, Western Culture, and the Body* [Berkeley: University of California Press, 1993], 87). For fetal-rights advocates, Bordo argues, "pregnant women are not subjects at all (neither under the law nor in the zeitgeist) while fetuses are *super*-subjects. It is as though the subjectivity of the pregnant body were siphoned from it and emptied into fetal life" (88).

script produces the matriarchs only to mock them, once with the "almost grotesque spectacle" the ladies present ("about twenty women squeezed into miniature seats [of a schoolroom], ample bosoms bearing down on desk-tops, posteriors bulging into aisles") (133), and then with their decision to take Johnny from his mother. In the film as released, Locky petitions the town selectmen to declare Belinda unfit so that *her* child may become *his* property. Pacquet chairs the meeting that settles the question. Patrimony was the business of men: the law of the Father ("by the godfrey" was Production Code cant for "by God") authorized the law of the father.

Belinda shoots Locky dead as he tries to "steal" the boy. When the police charge her, though, she will not tell why she has killed her victim. Stella knows, and tells. Her words denote seduction, her sobs connote rape, and both words and sobs silence the "mans/laughter" (Tania Modleski's word) that could doom Belinda. The final sequence has an unmistakable symmetry: the degradation of Belinda McDonald has occurred at the hands of man, and the redemption of Belinda McDonald occurs at the hands of woman. Sisterhood was, of course, a common enough theme in the woman's film of the 1940s: Eve Arden supports Joan Crawford throughout *Mildred Pierce*; Hattie McDaniel, though admittedly a stereotype, treats Claudette Colbert more as friend than employer in *Since You Went Away*; and David Wayne so admires Katharine Hepburn for winning over her maid, her secretary, and her client (Judy Holliday) in *Adam's Rib* that (he says) he "may even go out and become a woman." None of these characters, however, plays so pivotal a role as Stella in *Johnny Belinda*. Stella literally stands up for Belinda and thus dramatizes the female kin bonds that, according to Walsh, accounts for the appeal of the woman's picture.[15] In a story that both champions and fears womanhood, Stella's action represents an important strain of contemporary feminism in postwar America.

Gradually, though, Doctor Richardson steps in to translate the emotionalism of Stella's outburst into the quasi-legalisms the court may use to give Belinda her freedom; the court – not Stella – will have the last word. For good measure Richardson adds that Belinda placed maternal impulses over divine law. The impassioned defense, which tests the bounds of the Production Code ("Law, natural or human, shall not be ridiculed, nor shall sympathy be created for its violation"), wins over the judge whose verdict reminds Nova Scotians (in the 22 August 1947

[15] Tania Modleski, *The Women Who Knew Too Much: Hitchcock and Feminist Theory* (New York: Methuen, 1988); Walsh, *Women's Film*, 110.

screenplay) "that justice in this Dominion will always defend the private citizen against those who would interfere with his rights – and his dignity as a human being" (150A). Though the court harshly judges Locky – a subversion of the charge against Belinda, a subversion that allows rape to be spoken – it also underlines the sexual hierarchy on which the "good order" of Cape Breton is based; after all, males run the court (defense, prosecution, judge, bailiff, jury) and they intend to run the world beyond it.

Though *Johnny Belinda* struggles to make masculinity and femininity as natural and complementary as the flora and fauna of Cape Breton, quotation marks persistently surround "masculinity" and "femininity" as surely as they do the "Cape Breton" of Ft. Bragg and Mendecino. In the denouement, as elsewhere, an aura of gender anxiety and confusion lingers on. When Belinda asks for her baby so that they and Richardson and Aggie can return to the farm and mill (and to the Hollywood happy ending), she signs "Johnny."[16] The meaning, however, appears indeterminate. Has she accepted her "natural" role as mother in the culture? Or – her father dead, her assailant vilified, and her doctor friend bankrupt and broken – has she used that unique coalescence of silence and speech to assert her otherness and her lack, in other words her womanhood, which, according to Julia Kristeva, "disturbs identity, system, order"?[17] *Johnny Belinda* turns, here and throughout, on undecidability.

What contemporary postwar audiences "heard" when *Johnny Belinda* "spoke" depended not only on the audiences' attitudes toward gender and gender roles, but also on the way the audiences read the several texts of the picture. Some audiences, for instance, inescapably read the picture and the heroine against the backdrop of the endless publicity about its star, Jane Wyman. The source of such "news" was the syndicated gossip column and the fan magazine, and its reach was widespread.

Like the romance novel, the fanzine (so called) freed the woman to

16 In the final scene of the play on which the screenwriters based the picture, Belinda says, "John-ny" (Elmer Harris, *Johnny Belinda*, Mimeographed playscript [undated], United Artists Collection, Wisconsin Center for Film and Theatre Research, State Historical Society of Wisconsin, Madison, MSS 99AN Series 1.2, Box 208, Folder 1). In the 29 Mar. 1947 screenplay, as the prosecutor batters Richardson (the putative father of Johnny), suddenly "one single inarticulate outcry pierc[es] the air – a wailing tortured, guttural, protest." Belinda says, "No!!" In the 22 Aug. 1947 shooting script (and also the film) Belinda does not speak.
17 Julia Kristeva, *Powers of Horror: An Essay on Abjection*, trans. Leon S. Roudiez (New York: Columbia University Press, 1982), 4.

serve herself rather than her husband or children; as Janice Radway says, the sheer act of reading was an assertion of independence.[18] Like *Johnny Belinda*, though, the content of the fan magazine was hardly wholly conservative, especially when it featured female stars. On screen, the latter usually portrayed conventional, ordinary, or even mute women, and when (like Katharine Hepburn) they took on an unconventional or independent character, they were often cast against an actor (like Spencer Tracy) whose unabridged masculinity could moderate their high spirits and restore notions of sexual difference. On the other hand, the female star was usually billed above the title, and often, in the woman's film, above her male counterpart. More important, no matter how prosaic, or punished, or "inferior" the character she played, the glamour of the publicity about her accorded her a power and influence that began with fashion and coiffure but, arguably, ended with mores and conduct.

In the case of Jane Wyman and *Johnny Belinda*, the tension between on screen and off was acute. Though Belinda McDonald was apparently meek and mild, "Jane Wyman" was a celebrated and outspoken movie star whose public and private life was increasingly under her own control. And, because her private life became increasingly public during the general release of the picture, her presence in the narrative, like the narrative itself, offers yet another persuasive instance of the undecidability of the film and the postwar American culture that produced it.

Hollywood packaged stars as it packaged movies. Harlow was the "Blonde Bombshell" and Betty Grable the "Million Dollar Legs" and Jane Wyman (no sex goddess even in her early years as a blonde) "the perfect wife." Defined early on less by her talent than her husband, she had wed Ronald Reagan in January 1940. Two years later, a *Photoplay* story on the couple had been called "Love among the Reagans," and, in the war years, the press had lavished attention on her as spouse – on her soldier-husband in service (stationed in the Los Angeles suburbs at "Fort Roach" with the "Culver City Commandos"), on her daughter Maureen (born 1941), on her son Michael (adopted 1945), on her devotion to family and country. The Reagans were the ideal couple when there was no other in Hollywood, when in fact the only one in memory was Douglas Fairbanks and Mary Pickford, whose divorce had torn apart the movie colony.

Mary Pickford based her fame on many roles, Jane Wyman on only one – wife. By 1947, however, when Warner cast her as Belinda McDonald,

[18] Janice Radway, *Reading the Romance: Women, Patriarchy and Popular Literature* (Chapel Hill: University of North Carolina Press, 1984).

her career and her life had undergone a sea change. She had won acclaim in *The Lost Weekend* (1945) and an Academy Award nomination for *The Yearling* (1946), and her producer and Warner cohorts predicted that her work in *Johnny Belinda* would consolidate her success. At home there were fissures. "We wanted children," she told one fan magazine when she and her husband adopted Michael, "but that was to be an incident in the over-all development of our lives together." In other words, like many other women in the postwar years, she would not abandon the workplace for her family. In the aftermath of *The Yearling* and *The Lost Weekend*, pictures she made on loan to other studios, she was renegotiating her Warners contract to reflect her independence as a performer. The contract bound her to twenty pictures over ten years, with her salary escalating handsomely by thirds: $6,666 per week, then $8,333, and finally $10,000, with star billing guaranteed.[19] When enduring stars like Rosalind Russell and Cary Grant were earning on average $15,000, Jane Wyman's salary was an index of her strength.

Since his discharge from service, Reagan had seen his career undergo an eclipse, and, having fewer screen roles than he had had before the war, he immersed himself in the workings of the Screen Actors Guild, the story of which has been recorded in memoirs, biographies, and such recent books as *The Politics of Glamour*. "Without resorting to notes, he reeled off facts and figures with an ease that flabbergasted members of the audience," Hedda Hopper reported after his appearance at a SAG rally in December 1946. According to Sterling Hayden, he was "a one-man battalion." In April 1947, he invited two FBI agents into his living room so that he could provide "information regarding the activities of some members of the Guild who [the Reagans] suspected were carrying on Communist party work."[20] Wyman never had the zeal or even the interest her husband had in political action, though, and by September 1947 SAG politics lay near the core of their marital problems.

Gossip columns and fan magazines (which liked a divorce no less than a honeymoon) told readers that in Autumn 1947 Reagan went north to see Wyman on the set of *Johnny Belinda*. A surviving relic of the visit records the "temperature" of the couple. One evening, on stationery that read

[19] Joe Morella and Edward Z. Epstein, *Jane Wyman: A Biography* (New York: Delacorte, 1985), 89; Jane Wyman, Contract with Warner Bros, 11 Aug. 1947, United Artists Collection, Wisconsin Center for Film and Theatre Research, State Historical Society of Wisconsin, Madison, MSS 99AN Series 1.7, Warner Bros. Contract and Copyright File, Box 38, Folder 221.

[20] David Prindle, *The Politics of Glamour: Ideology and Democracy in the Screen Actors Guild* (Madison: University of Wisconsin Press, 1988), 48, 50.

"Mrs. Ronald Reagan," Reagan recorded in longhand the "minutes" of a SAG board meeting, Reagan (chair) and Wyman and Agnes Moorehead in attendance. (Reagan was by then president and Wyman and Moorehead board members of SAG; Moorehead played Aggie in *Johnny Belinda*.) As the meeting opened, "motion was made, duly seconded & unanimously carried that three martinis should be ordered. (No discussion)." As the meeting continued, Wyman cursed an absent board member. "Discussion was held on this latter subject & ways & means were explored as to how social standing of Miss Wyman could be restored." The group agreed that the absent board member was "a 'shit-heel' in the first place & motion was made, seconded & carried to order 3 more martinis." Then, as Reagan started "yapping and yelping" about being on location, the tongue (and pencil) thickened.

Jane wanted to know what in h--l I was gettin' in a uproar about – I wasn' doin any work. Aggie told her not to change the subject & to lay off I wassa d--n pres. And where in h--l did she get off talking to the d--n pres with all that disrespect. I said lay off my wife thassa woman I love – we decided have 7 more martinis.[21]

The comedy wheezes under the strain of its correspondences to life. The sandpapery character that Moorehead plays in *Johnny Belinda* bosses the character that Wyman plays, just as the character that Wyman plays (a mute) stands about as others argue over her. The charge that "I wasn' doing any work" also struck home. Though once based on many screen parts, his fame – along with his presence on location in northern California – was now increasingly based on only one.

In December 1947, one month after photography on *Johnny Belinda* ended, the Reagans separated. The press announced it, and the gossip columns and movie magazines hollered it; the February 1948 story in *Photoplay* was called "Those Fightin' Reagans." The couple temporarily reconciled, then he moved out in May 1948, the month that *Silver Screen* editorialized against "moody" Jane Wyman, the season that Reagan

[21] "Minutes of Meeting Board of Dir. S.A.G. Tues. Sept. 9 [1947] – 6 P.M," Agnes Moorehead Scrapbook (unpaged), Agnes Moorehead Collection, Wisconsin Center for Film and Theatre Research, State Historical Society of Wisconsin, Madison. On location for *Johnny Belinda* in fall 1947, the cast and crew stayed about eighteen miles away from the town of Fort Bragg, at an inn that was (according to the producer) "a real rough-house place." The company was forever "yapping and yelping about the accommodations," Jerry Wald told another Warner executive (Wald, Letter to Steve Trilling, 5 Sept. 1947, *Johnny Belinda* File, Box 24, Jerry Wald Collection, Special Collections, University Library, University of Southern California, Los Angeles).

quipped, tellingly, "I think I'll name *Johnny Belinda* as the co-respondent."[22]

Johnny Belinda was meanwhile gathering dust in a studio vault. Though the Warners archive nowhere accounts for the delay, Jack Warner (according to Wyman) disliked the picture and would not let director Jean Negulesco edit the final cut.[23] (Negulesco and Warner were not friendly, and though the production was a happy one for Negulesco, it was his last for Warner Bros.) Also, Warners may have had doubts about how to market the picture, since Wyman was not yet a star and television was making hash of the Hollywood marketplace. But neither reason seems compelling when weighed against the cost of keeping a nonproducing million dollar asset in inventory. So one factor – though not the sole factor – may have been Warners' fear that the headlines about Wyman's divorce would adversely affect the reception of her portrayal of a compliant woman, indeed (since Belinda was ostensibly still in her teens) a compliant child-woman.

Whatever the reason, *Johnny Belinda* was released in October 1948. The following year Wyman won an Academy Award for Belinda and a divorce from her husband. In one sense the announcement about the latter was overture to the ruptures and resistances of the 1950s, the era of togetherness that found expression in family vacations, family restaurants, family rooms, family cars, and family films, an era that consecrated *family* as one more response to the lapse of patriarchal control that had occurred in the 1940s, when many women had entered the work place and stayed, when the number of underage girls arrested for sex offenses rose, when prostitution and venereal disease flourished, and when, between 1940 and 1946, the divorce rate more than doubled. Less stigma than fact of life, divorce may have been key; it allowed the woman, publicly, to represent herself *as* herself and not as an accessory of her husband. "She [Wyman] and Reagan engaged in continued arguments on his political views," the *Los Angeles Times* said, reporting on the divorce proceedings. "Despite her lack of interest in his political activities, Miss Wyman continued, Reagan insisted that she attend meetings with him and that she be present during discussions among his friends. But her own ideas, she complained, 'were never considered important.'"[24]

An audience that read Jane Wyman as an icon of postwar feminine independence could also read *Johnny Belinda* against the grain, just as an audience that ignored the "scandal" about Jane Wyman could also read

[22] Lou Cannon, *Reagan* (New York: Putnam's, 1982), 62.   [23] Morella, 128.
[24] Ibid., 128–29.

Belinda McDonald as an icon of postwar feminine submission. Because of the period, because of the star, because of the story, and because of publicity the studio could and (re the divorce) could not hold back, *Johnny Belinda* was a notably porous text.

The gender anxiety and confusion of both the era and the picture notwithstanding, conservative audiences for *Johnny Belinda* would probably not have had doubts about its politics: Johnny Belinda (unlike Michael Reagan) was *not* "an incident" in the development of the life of his mother; rather, he *was* her life. Hollywood often chose to portray marriage as woman's good fortune and childbearing her glory, and, unquestionably, *Johnny Belinda* dilates on the wonder and joy of reproduction. Early on, as she watches the doctor deliver a calf on the McDonalds' farm, Belinda exalts motherhood. "Motionless," the 22 August 1947 screenplay describes Belinda, the audience seeing her for the first time, "holding lamp – but in her face a stirring power of expression – pity – fear – changing mercurially – then suddenly a smile" (17). She shows that her "natural" role was motherhood, her reaction underscored in the action of the doctor, whose "natural" role was the control and "creation" of motherhood. Maternity appears to function as *sine qua non* in *Johnny Belinda*, fertility as quod erat demonstrandum. So extraordinary was the fertility of Belinda that she became pregnant on the basis of one sexual encounter, with one man, Locky. So blessed was the shine of motherhood that Aggie's hostility toward "the dummy" turned into affection and awe when Belinda became pregnant. And so devastating was the barrenness of Stella that, to compensate Locky, she co-operated in "stealin'" Johnny. The theme appears to reach even the margins of the picture. "Spry for a woman had her 'arteries' cut out," one older woman remarks on another she sees at the dance in the mill. Though her cohort whispers the correct word (*ovaries*) in her ear, *ovaries* seem tantamount to *arteries* in the story: in an era of pronatalism, an era when the fertility rate for Caucasian women peaked, when psychologists called "feminists" neurotic, and when women's magazines enshrined the housewife and mother, the loss of the reproductive capacity denoted the loss of the life force.

Reproduction lies near the centre of *Johnny Belinda*, a picture that forcibly ties destiny to female anatomy. Even the 29 March 1947 screenplay, intended for the actors' eyes only, exaggerates the "naturalness" of that assumption. When the pregnant Belinda says that she will have a baby boy, Doctor Richardson smiles, "amused at the primitive directness of her reaction" (91). The word "primitive" shows again that

Johnny was no "incident." If as D'Ann Campbell says, though, the "broad consensus" favored the woman working as the conventional mother or housewife, one wonders what compelled *Johnny Belinda* to enforce the consensus (so called) with such draconian intensity.

The answer lies in part in the culture that produced *Johnny Belinda. He* was man-of-the-house and breadwinner, in literature, films, and the popular press of 1946, and *she* was "naive, dependent, childlike, [and] self-abnegating."[25] Such "propaganda" continued well into 1947 and 1948. In *The Modern Woman: The Lost Sex* (the 1947 best seller) Ferdinand Lundberg and Marynia Farnham blamed the increasing rates of juvenile delinquency, divorce, murder, crime, and alcoholism on married women in the workplace. In the late 1940s, when more and more women went to college and more and more women had jobs beyond the home, many women, for whatever reason, also dropped out of college or exited the work force. They were hardly the "lost," not to the popular press. According to "Most likely to Succeed" in *Good Housekeeping* in June 1948, only months before Warner Bros. released *Johnny Belinda*, "the girl who has a C average in college...has the potentiality of achieving as real a success as, and perhaps a more humanly necessary success than, the girl who is regarded with something like awe by her classmates."[26] Is the apologia for the C average a description, or a prescription? And what happens to the girl with the A average? "What in the world interests women?" *Time* magazine asked in an advertisement pitched to potential advertisers in June 1947, only months before Warners put *Johnny Belinda* into production. "Each week 1,500,000 women, most of them wives and daughters of the 1,800,000 *Time*-reading men, prove they are interested in just about all the news in the world a busy person needs to know." Men were men, and women were...wives and daughters.

More than one year after Doctor Richardson starts tutoring her, Belinda still cannot read (or apparently write) cursive, and once she becomes pregnant, she stops using her bedroom chalkboard. *Johnny Belinda* tends to suggest that she needs only a scant education, passing as she does from one paternal relationship to another, from father to doctor. Finally, though, the hyperbole of procreation and the call of the hearth turns against the picture. As in *The Modern Woman: The Lost Sex*, the rhetoric of overkill in *Johnny Belinda* hints at resistance to the broad consensus and

[25] Maureen Honey, *Creating Rosie the Riveter: Class, Gender, and Propaganda during World War II* (Amherst: University of Massachusetts Press, 1984), 2.
[26] Judith Tarcher, "Most likely to Succeed," *Good Housekeeping*, June 1948, 33+.

raises doubts about the contentment of the postwar domesticated woman; the very end of the picture only nourishes the uncertainty.

As though the writers had sensed the strength of the heroine, the close of the 22 August 1947 shooting script of *Johnny Belinda* had dulled the edge of the heroine's independence and determination by having Doctor Richardson drive the buggy home from the courthouse. "[H]olding reins firmly in one hand, his other goes out to Belinda – takes hers in a warm, strong clasp. As Belinda turns to him, all her love in her eyes, buggy starts" ("152–55").

The ability of a helicopter to fly backwards and gain altitude at the same time was employed in photographing the final scene of "Johnny Belinda." The scene is a traveling shot showing a buggy being driven along the rugged coastline. The camera pulled back and up going out to sea. The buggy reduced further and further in the distance leaving as a final impression only a small segment of earth on which the story was played.   (Press Release)

Only the appearance of those late model automobiles on the fringe of that one shot in Charlottetown would have shown that Warners had set *Johnny Belinda* in the present, and by the end of the picture that brief shot would have been long forgotten. The buggy traveling along a road with no automobiles or utility poles, along with the camera "back and up going out to sea," would ally the end of the picture with the consciousness that opened it and that contextualized the ensuing narrative as male. The fade out, in other words, would ask the audience to "fly backwards" to a preindustrial world when, according to the lyrics of the song that won the Oscar that year, women were women...[27]

As cut and released, however, the coda of *Johnny Belinda* contained strong marks of resistance. The final cut does not use the moony shot ("all her love in her eyes") of Belinda. Instead, set along a horizon on land rather than sea, it shows Belinda and the others in a long shot that stresses the return to the McDonald farm, the farm that Black McDonald has

[27] Warner Bros. Press Release (Untitled), 3 Mar. 1948, *Johnny Belinda*, United Artists Collection, Wisconsin Center for Film and Theatre Research, State Historical Society of Wisconsin, Madison, P68-1989, Microfilm. Written by Jay Livingston and Ray Evans, "Buttons and Bows" was the hit song from *The Paleface* (1948), where Bob Hope sings, "Gimme Eastern trimmin' / where women are women / in high silk hose / and peekaboo clothes / and French perfume / that rocks the room / and I'm all yours / in buttons and bows." Hope plays the dentist (and coward) "Painless" Potter, and Jane Russell plays the lawless Calamity Jane. In the opening reel, when Potter fumbles the reins and harness, Jane drives their covered wagon. Though the sharpshooting Jane twice saves Potter from death, she fumbles the reins and harness in the last reel and goes face down in dirt. The "outlaw" has been tamed, the picture ends.

passed along to Belinda, in a late 1940s version of primogeniture that plainly favors daughters no less than sons. In the buggy, too, the "family" of Doctor Richardson, Belinda, Aggie, and Johnny looks more jerry-built than nuclear or traditional; furthermore, it looks unlikely to solidify the masculinist patterns that elsewhere the film weaves.

As Doctor Richardson says (in the 1 August 1947 shooting script), he was wounded in the war and, afterwards, in love. "It's called 'not being able to readjust oneself'" (16), he confesses to Black McDonald. Though at the close he and Belinda favor the heterosexual couple that populates the fadeout of so many Hollywood pictures, *Johnny Belinda* never suggests that they will marry. Doctor Richardson has lost his moorings in the world, and, during the picture, his practice and his belongings. "Oh, Belinda, don't let me think I've failed again," he once said. As the one acknowledged "feminine" male in the picture and only recently the laughing stock of the town, he once more looks to Belinda for succor. Belinda, then, will be "mother" and "father" to the doctor and Johnny: she will help the doctor readjust, and she will teach Johnny how to farm and how to shoot. She will turn pronatalism inside out, in other words, showing the postwar audience the postwar phenomenon of the capable single mother, the woman who (like Jane Wyman) faces a brave new world without fear.

When the "good order" of patriarchal authority finds itself under siege, as happens in *Johnny Belinda*, as happened in the culture beyond the movie theater, those in control will use all the machinery at hand – from the horror of rape to the exaltation of motherhood – to recover its power. Though *Johnny Belinda* asserts gender borders and reasserts patriarchal authority, it does so with a self-defeating inconsistency. *Box Office* told readers in 1947 that *Johnny Belinda* "will go on the 'must see' list of most women [but that] doesn't mean it is entirely a woman's picture; there's plenty for the males, most especially action, and atmosphere!"[28] The trade paper does not define the "atmosphere" – and perhaps just as well. The crosswinds of the postwar 1940s would probably have made the elaboration as undecidable as *Johnny Belinda* itself.

[28] Warner Bros. Pressbook (undated, unpaged), *Johnny Belinda*, United Artists Collection,

CATHERINE GUNTHER KODAT

Saving Private Property: Steven Spielberg's American DreamWorks

IN A QUIET MOMENT BEFORE THE climactic battle to defend the bridge in *Saving Private Ryan*, the eponymous hero of Steven Spielberg's 1998 film confesses to Tom Hanks's Captain Miller that, try as he may to remember his brothers, he can't see their faces. Since it was the swift and sudden deaths of those three young men that led to the mission to rescue Private Ryan in the first place, we may safely assume that this lapse is meant to signal Something Big. And in fact Captain Miller suggests a solution to Ryan's problem that indirectly confirms its symbolic import: "You've got to think of a context," he replies, and—lest we miss its significance— Spielberg releases a few blows to hammer the point home. Ryan, it turns out, doesn't know what context is ("What's that mean?" he asks), so Miller obligingly provides the image of himself lying on a hammock in his backyard at home, watching his wife prune the rose bushes while wearing his work gloves. Imagining myself lying in the hammock, seeing the rose bushes, the gloves—all that's context, Miller explains, and that's how I'm able to remember my wife. Having now grasped what context is, Ryan responds with the story of his brother Dan's attempted sexual encounter in the Ryan family barn with "Alice Jardine, a girl who took a nosedive from the ugly tree and hit every branch on the way down," an effort that ends with Alice being knocked unconscious and the barn catching fire.[1] "That was it," Ryan concludes. "That was the last time we were together."[2]

As it happens, this scene *is* as important as Spielberg makes it out to be, and not just because of the way it offers a moment of identification for teachers everywhere. (What historian or cultural studies scholar has not discovered that she not only must provide her students with historical context but also must explain the importance of establishing context in the first place? What literature professor has not had appeals to the memory of the Garden answered with tales of family conflagration?) For *Saving Private Ryan* is a film that presumes to provide its own context (I refer, of course, to the framing scenes in the military graveyard near Normandy) and, through the exchange between Private Ryan and Captain Miller, further presumes to school us on the necessity of contextual understanding: charged to remember the dead, we must establish context in order to properly "see their faces." These

REPRESENTATIONS 71 • Summer 2000 © THE REGENTS OF THE UNIVERSITY OF CALIFORNIA
ISSN 0734-6018 pages 77–105. All rights reserved. Send requests for permission to
reprint to Rights and Permissions, University of California Press,
Journals Division, 2000 Center St., Ste. 303, Berkeley, CA 94704-1223.   77

twin gestures offer a near-irresistible challenge to the cultural critic, for they sketch out a framework within which both to view and to assess the film, a framework best expressed as a series of questions: Does *Saving Private Ryan* in fact present us with an appropriate context within which to assess its cultural work? Do we accept the film's definition of context? How do we distinguish *Saving Private Ryan*'s context from its packaging? And is the film indeed as self-conscious about its own context as it manifestly claims to be?

The context Steven Spielberg and his staff at DreamWorks provided for *Saving Private Ryan*, both within the film itself and in interviews during its release, is primarily a memorial one. From the first word of dialogue in the film ("Dad?" the aging Ryan's son exclaims as his father crumples to the ground before Captain Miller's grave) to the last ("Tell me I'm a good man," Ryan asks his wife, who firmly replies, "You are"), *Saving Private Ryan* casts itself as a reverent tribute to our fathers' generation, a gesture Spielberg sought to underline when, upon receiving the 1999 Oscar for Best Director, he thanked his own father, a World War II veteran, "for showing me that there is honor in looking back and respecting the past." (The decision of DreamWorks to wait until the 1999 Memorial Day weekend before releasing *Saving Private Ryan* to video simply underlined the point.) But as the virtually transparent Stars and Stripes that fills the frame of the film's opening and closing shots suggests, this tribute is not without its attendant anxiety; *Saving Private Ryan* may literally wrap itself in the flag, but the substance of that banner appears tissue thin.[3] In fact, the anxiety subtending the film's loudly proclaimed tribute is a necessary corollary of any sustained meditation on the consequences of the Second World War: our fathers' sacrifice didn't simply preserve and protect; it enlarged and transformed. The world that emerged after World War II was dramatically different from the world that went into it, a fact especially present to Americans, since it was World War II that created "the American Century," ushering in a postwar order cementing the United States's position as a superpower and self-ordained leader of the free world.[4] That world order once again is undergoing deep structural transformation; John Gaddis's renaming of the Cold War as "the Long Peace" perhaps offers one window on the contradictions and uncertainties lying just beneath the surface of capitalism's seeming global victory.[5] All of which is to say that any explanation of *Saving Private Ryan* that begins and ends with an appeal to a loosely construed but nevertheless reverent memorial impulse in the last analysis explains nothing at all, for it leaves unasked the question any serious attempt to consider context in the assessment of cultural productions must articulate and, if possible, answer: Why *this* work *now*?

Though I do not agree with the extravagant praise that greeted *Saving Private Ryan* on its release (praise that finally boils down to little more than panegyrics on the wonders of desaturated color and handheld cameras . I do think *Saving Private Ryan* is an important film for the way it simultaneously expresses and seeks to contain the sharp political and economic anxieties peculiar to its moment of production.[6] My task here, then, is to read the context of context in *Saving Private Ryan*, with the aim not of simply offering a "better" reading of that particular film than has appeared heretofore, but of uncovering how the film reads this particular moment of U.S. cultural, political, and economic history. And while it would certainly be possible to proceed by considering the film as a unique manifestation of the anxieties it articulates, it is my conviction that establishing a context for *Saving Private Ryan*—appraising the cultural work it actually does, as opposed to the cultural work that it claims to do—is best approached through an analysis of Spielberg's other recent American history film, *Amistad*. Indeed, I want to argue that, thematically as well as cinematically, *Amistad is* the context for understanding *Saving Private Ryan*, and that both films reveal how the neoconservative values of the Reagan-Bush era have been transmitted, with remarkably little modification, into the neoliberal Clinton years.[7] Recognizing the ways these two films attempt to recruit American history to the tasks of constructing renewed credibility for (and shoring up ideological justification of) continued American global dominance will place us in a position to assess the contemporary anxieties that both films articulate. For in representing past Americans in crisis, these films speak to concerns of a pending American crisis, which may well be, as George Soros recently has put it, the crisis of global capitalism.[8]

The work of the Frankfurt School particularly, and contemporary cultural studies more generally, has helped to establish the commonplace in analyses of historical representations—be they literary, cinematic, pictorial, or historiographic—that all such representations are more about the moments of their production than about the period they purportedly represent: the effort to ground an understanding of consumption in the often contradictory imperatives of production has produced excellent readings of cultural artifacts.[9] So it is not surprising that some version of the notion that historical representations are mainly efforts to work through present obsessions appears in nearly every reading of *Amistad* and *Saving Private Ryan* that has seen print, in both the popular and the scholarly press. To a remarkable degree, however, critics making this point have not moved much beyond the claims DreamWorks itself has made for the films. Thus *Amistad*, a film that, in the odd phrasing of Henry Louis Gates Jr., "reeks of integrity," is cast as a contribution to the work of racial healing in America; *Saving Private Ryan* allegedly forces the draft dodgers of the Vietnam War to consider the possibility that their veteran fathers were better men than they.[10] Failing to move past the public explanations these films offer for themselves has the effect of heightening the sense that *Amistad* and *Saving Private Ryan*, despite their common provenance, are unique and discrete films both ideologically and affectively.[11] In fact, however, *Amistad* and *Saving Private Ryan* are more the same than different; the films articulate similar views of history (as Anthony Hopkins's John Quincy Adams claims in *Amistad*, "Who we are is who we

Saving Private Property: Steven Spielberg's American DreamWorks   79

were"), have similarly ambitious notions of their cultural work, and make similar errors of historical fact. That *Amistad* was roundly castigated for its historical inaccurracies while *Saving Private Ryan* escaped virtually unscathed in this regard certainly tells us something about the role contemporary racial politics has to play in assessing claims to historical fidelity, though that is not the focus of my analysis here.[12] Rather, I want to explore how both *Amistad* and *Saving Private Ryan* attempt to establish their bona fides for the relevance of history to contemporary cultural issues by insisting upon the same specific moment in the U.S. past as the final, transcendent bar at which their claims should be judged. That moment is the Civil War. For *Amistad* the war is the future event, being prepared for in the film's present (that is, the struggle to free the *Amistad* captives), that will finally redeem the past—the war will constitute "the last battle of the American Revolution," as Adams claims in the film, thus ultimately honoring the promissory note that is the Declaration of Independence. In *Saving Private Ryan*, the Civil War represents the righteously glorious past—the other "good war" to free an oppressed people—that not only justifies the present action (generally, World War II; specifically, the mission to save Private Ryan) but ensures ultimate victory.[13] In both films, the Civil War becomes the sine qua non of American historical vindication; invoking the war places *Amistad* and *Saving Private Ryan* on the cinematic and ideological continuum that began with *The Birth of a Nation*.

In examining these two films and the contemporary concerns they indirectly articulate, I turn first to the specific issues of historical fact that *Amistad* and *Saving Private Ryan* misrepresent and, in so misrepresenting, seek to master and manipulate. In the final section of my essay, I explore how this manipulation exposes the contemporary anxieties driving both films, anxieties that account for much, if not all, of their considerable and undeniable emotional power.

In the weeks after its release in December 1997, *Amistad* rapidly became a focus of discussion on the listserves of the nation's historians. One by one, the film's many historical inaccuracies were brought to light; commentary ranged from the minutely particular (for example, how likely would it be to encounter a *draisienne*, the precursor of the bicycle, on the pathways of Culloden Point in 1839?) to the more generally disparaging ("I was bothered by the portrait of Van Buren," one correspondent wrote. "Even his enemies would not have charged him with being almost mentally challenged.")[14] The presence of the Capitol Dome in one shot was widely lamented (a particularly egregious historical error given the wide and fairly recent dissemination, through Ken Burns's PBS epic, of photographs depicting the construction of the dome during the course of the Civil War). More substantive complaints found their way out of the listserves and into print. Spielberg was chastised for grossly misrepresenting attorney Roger Baldwin: In reality an august, learned, and compassionate man with long-standing ties to the abolitionist movement. Baldwin in the film is made out to be a "shady lawyer" with "no sensitivity whatever to the cause" of freeing the *Amistad* captives.[15] Moving from errors of fact to errors of feeling or atmosphere, *Amistad* incorrectly makes it appear that the 1841 Supreme Court ruling in the case marked the beginning of a progress, ever onward and upward, toward abolishing slavery in the United States; as anyone familiar with U.S. racial history knows, the decision was in fact extraordinarily narrow and did nothing to block the infamous Dred Scott decision some sixteen years later.[16]

Somehow, though, the movie's treatment of John Quincy Adams's appearance before the Supreme Court seems to have escaped controversy.[17] As the historical record clearly shows, when Adams made his final arguments before the Supreme Court in the *Amistad* case he spoke for seven hours over the course of two days. Though Adams failed to get a copy of his statement to Richard Peters in time for publication in his *Reports* of the January 1841 term of the Supreme Court, the extremely lengthy defense was published privately by abolitionists later that year. As the historian Howard Jones has pointed out, the fact that Adams's argument does not appear in official records of the Court's proceedings makes it difficult to judge how much of what was later published was actually heard by the Court.[18] What needs to be discussed for my purposes here, however, is not so much the accuracy of the published record, but what the writers involved in DreamWorks's *Amistad* chose to do with that record. In reducing a seven-hour speech to fewer than five minutes, the writers decided to use almost nothing of what Adams wrote about the specifics of the case, preferring instead to focus upon and magnify Adams's rhetorical framing of his remarks (a framing that consisted mainly of a single gesture and two extremely brief comments), so that what in the original speech were little more than passing glances at the Declaration of Independence are made in the film to bear the entire philosophical burden of the defense.[19]

In the published version of his statement, Adams opens by reminding the Court of its duty to uphold disinterested principles of justice—a reminder clearly meant to increase the sting of his enumeration, woven piece by piece into the fabric of his extraordinarily wide-ranging argument, of various underhanded efforts on the part of the executive branch to compromise the independence of the courts in their deliberations in the *Amistad* case.[20] From this opening, Adams moves to his lengthy and detailed discussion of the legal particulars of the case via a brief transition meant to remind the justices that, though the bulk of his speech will take up the intricacies of international maritime treaties, there are other, higher, issues to consider as well:

I know of no law, but one which I am not at liberty to argue before this Court, no law, statute or constitution, no code, no treaty, applicable to the proceedings of the Executive or the Judiciary, except that law (pointing to the copy of the Declaration of Independence, hanging against one of the pillars of the court-room), that law, two copies of which are ever before the eyes of your Honors. I know of no other law that reaches the case of my clients, but the law of Nature and of Nature's God on which our fathers placed our own national existence. The circumstances [of the *Amistad* case] are so peculiar, that no code or treaty has provided for such a case. That law, in its application to my clients, I trust will be the law on which the case will be decided by this Court.[21]

Adams did not return to the Declaration of Independence until the final minutes of the second day of his argument, as he worked his way through an analysis of the 1825 Supreme Court decision in the case of the *Antelope*, which held that the United States was bound to honor the laws of nations sanctioning the slave trade. Adams thundered against Chief Justice John Marshall's decision in that case: "The argument with much hesitation concludes that the African slave trade is *not* contrary to the Law of Nations—but it begins with admitting, also with hesitation, that it is contrary to the law of nature. . . . the cautious and wary manner of stating the moral principle, proclaimed in the Declaration of Independence, as *self-evident truth*, is because the argument is obliged to encounter it with matter of fact. To the *moral principle* the Chief Justice opposes *general usage*—fact against right."[22]

As Jones points out, appeals to the claims of natural law over those of positive law made an appearance before every judge involved in the *Amistad* case; they were mentioned in Baldwin's presentations before the U.S. District and Circuit courts, and, as we see, surfaced again in Adams's summation. Taking the long view, Jones applauds Adams's attempt "to strike a mortal blow at slavery itself by appealing to the natural law principles underlying the Declaration of Independence" (*Mutiny on the Amistad*, 219). But, as he admits in the very next sentence, such an effort had no effect on the Court: Justice Joseph Story "privately expressed amazement at the irrelevance of such a far-reaching argument" (219). In fact, though the Supreme Court ruled in favor of the *Amistad* captives, Judge Story's decision resembled nothing so much as the initial strategy presented by the film's raffish Baldwin: the Africans were free not because they were human beings, and so could not be property, but because they had not become property *legally*.[23] "A major point in the Supreme Court's decision was that slaves *were* property," Jones writes. "No matter how immoral the slave trade and slavery itself, international law required that one nation's decision to legalize either or both deserved recognition by others. . . . To the disdain of antislavery groups, the decision underlined the supremacy of positive law over natural law and revealed how wide the gap between them had grown" (192, 93; emphasis added). In fact, the idea that the decision somehow granted a primacy to natural law—the notion, central to the Declaration of Independence, that all human beings enjoy certain rights that cannot be compromised by any man-made (positive) law—was a creation of the abolitionists' public relations campaign in the months after the decision: "The only impression the public received—and the one the abolitionists repeatedly exalted—was that the Court had set the blacks unequivocally free" (193).

My complaint here is not at all with the historical decision of the abolitionist movement to present the *Amistad* ruling as somewhat more sweeping than it was:

236

such a move seems to me not only understandable but, given the work to be done, completely justifiable. Rather, my concern is with the way Spielberg's film labors to disconnect the appeal to natural law from its home in the Christian abolitionist movement—a movement that, in its strongest lineaments, was widely feared as deeply anti-American, even among those who opposed slavery—and to reattribute it, in a series of moves that climaxes with Adams's performance before the Supreme Court, to traditional American values as embodied in the Founding Fathers.[24] *Amistad* takes special pains to discredit the abolitionist movement, not only through its invidious depictions of Lewis Tappan and Roger Baldwin (as Bertram Wyatt-Brown rightly notes, the film's treatment of the abolitionist Tappan—whose last word in the movie is to claim that the *Amistad* captives would serve the cause of abolition better dead than free—is almost unconscionably cruel; Baldwin, as I've already noted, is simply excised from the abolition movement altogether), but even through its depiction of American antislavery Protestantism itself, which, paired off against the traditional Roman Catholicism of Jeremy Northam's dashing Judge Coglin, comes across as decidedly inferior, and even a bit scary.[25] It is no accident that the extremely affecting scene in which the captive Yamba "reads" the New Testament to Cinqué through biblical illustrations is intercut with shots of Judge Coglin's visit to a church, where he blesses himself with holy water, lights a votive candle, and kneels to recite the Latin confiteor. One of the first things we learn about Judge Coglin—indeed, practically the only thing we need to know about him—is that *his father* was a Catholic. Coglin's appeal to the faith of his fathers in struggling to arrive at the (right) decision in the *Amistad* case does double duty: it discredits the more radical Christian impulses underlying the abolitionist movement and foreshadows John Quincy Adams's appeal to the "faith" of *his* father in his stirring Supreme Court presentation.[26] Thus we are assured that, contrary to what may seem to have been the case, the abolition of slavery was in no way a criticism of the Founding Fathers' values; rather, it was their fulfillment. In this regard, *Amistad* is of a piece with Spielberg's 1980s work, which likewise constructs, as Andrew Britton argues, "a dramatic 'logic' whereby the feelings appropriate to the rejection of the culture are found, once acted through, to conduce to the reproduction of it" ("Blissing Out," 27).

It could be argued that the move to clear the decks of pesky abolitionists who might be seen to take some justifiable credit for the liberation of the Africans was undertaken in a well-intentioned effort to keep the focus on Cinqué and his fellow captives (thus avoiding the *Mississippi Burning* problem of making whites the heroes in a film depicting a struggle for black freedom); this, indeed, would be the explanation that Spielberg himself would find most congenial.[27] This argument is misguided, however, because the fact remains that, despite the tremendous efforts of Djimon Hounsou as Cinqué, and the horrific scenes depicting the Middle Passage, the back-heavy structure of *Amistad* shifts all its emotional and dramatic ballast onto John Quincy Adams. Will he or won't he agree to speak on the Africans' be-

Saving Private Property: Steven Spielberg's American DreamWorks   83

half? And once he decides that he will, what will he say? *Amistad* thus reveals Spielberg's constitutional inability to represent "otherness" in anything approximating a coherent, complex, yet still oppositional position (a difficulty Andrew Britton spotted some thirteen years ago): the film flees to the harbor of its white hero at the first available opportunity.[28]

In latching onto Adams's extremely brief comment, in his actual Supreme Court statement, connecting natural law and the Founding Fathers (natural law is the principle "on which our fathers placed our own national existence"), and inflating it out of all proportion, the *Amistad* writers not only disconnect the appeal to natural law from the abolition movement—they transform Adams's long and legally quite detailed argument into the simple claim that the Supreme Court should free the Africans because it is what our Fathers would have done themselves. The view that the job of "crushing slavery" is little more than unfinished work "the Founding Fathers left to their sons" is briefly articulated early in the film, when Morgan Freeman's Theodore Joadson seeks to convince Adams to take the *Amistad* case. Spielberg waits until the end of the film to return to the point and let Adams drive it home:

> Thomas Jefferson . . . Benjamin Franklin . . . James Madison . . . Alexander Hamilton . . . George Washington . . . John Adams. We have long resisted asking you for guidance. Perhaps we've feared that in doing so we might acknowledge that our individuality, which we so, so revere, is not entirely our own. Perhaps we've feared that an appeal to you might be taken for weakness.
> But we have come to understand, finally, that this is not so. We understand now—we have been made to understand, and to embrace the understanding—that who we are is who we were. We desperately need your strength and wisdom to triumph over our fears, our prejudices, ourselves. Give us the courage to do what is right—and if it means Civil War? Then let it come. And when it does, may it be, finally, the last battle of the American Revolution.

The movie places the source for this appeal to the Fathers in Cinqué's prior decision to tell Adams that, once in court, he will call on his ancestors for aid ("What words did you use to persuade them?" Cinqué later asks Adams, who replies "Yours"), but, as my analysis of Judge Coglin's much earlier appeal to the spirit of *his* father has indicated, this is a feint; it is not Cinqué's ancestors, after all, who helped create the United States, Joadson's "noble invention" that nonetheless has failed to put "self-evident" truths into living practice. Cinqué's ancestors are not on trial here; in a very real way that the film obliquely and uncomfortably registers, it is *America's* Fathers who are being brought before the bar. *Amistad* seeks a way out of this problem by appealing to the primacy of the lofty idealism of the Declaration of Independence over the imperfect reality of the Constitutional Convention, and by then connecting that idealism to the coming cataclysm of the Civil War. In doing so, *Amistad* hopes to construct a convincingly clear, "pro-American" continuity of value in which the Declaration of Independence, the American Revolution, and the Civil War emerge as linked events furthering the cause of human freedom.[29] Such a project elevates the Founding Fathers to the status of G. W. F. Hegel's universal mind, overseeing a surefooted and certain progress to a greater and greater good. And such a vision of American history has, among its possible effects, the power to snuff out any hint that slavery ever was integral to the founding of this nation. It is no small thing, after all, to make the Civil War the last battle of the American Revolution.

But slavery of course *was* integral to the founding of this country, and not only because it was thanks to the enslaved that Americans perfected their understanding of what it meant to be free.[30] Against the Hegelian view of American progress described earlier we should put the Marxist critique of Hegel, especially insofar as that critique works to uncover the relationship between material conditions and freedom (as in the *Grundrisse*, for example). This critique has a particular point for today's United States, where the free movement of capital has been cast not only as a precondition of human freedom but also as its deepest expression. It seems to me that *Amistad* does not just register (if only to attempt to silence) the standing rebuke to U.S. idealism that was constituted in the retention of slavery; it also raises the question of the depth of the contribution slavery made to the emergence of modern capitalism. This question is indeed raised in the film through the bizarre letter the prepubescent Queen Isabella II (played by Anna Paquin) sends to Martin Van Buren:

After all, the business of great countries is to do business. Slavery is a pillar of commerce in the New World. Without it, our good will and excellent trade relations should be imperiled. Without it, we might have been denied the glory of aiding you in your virtuous rebellion against the British. As slave-owning nations, we must together stand firm. Speak the words of humaneness for the masses, but hold tightly to the power that protects them. The power of course is the power of wealth. The Africans must never go free.

Besides having the effect of making the queen sound like a former-day Calvin Coolidge (Coolidge: "The business of America is business"; "Civilization and profits go hand in hand"), this odd little letter renders *Amistad* the invaluable office of articulating the causal connection between the establishment and growth of capitalism (and thus wealth, which the letter not-so-indirectly equates with American sovereignty and freedom) and New World slavery. The existence of such a connection was first claimed by Eric Williams in his 1944 study *Capitalism and Slavery*; hotly debated ever since, the connection has received renewed scholarly attention in Robin Blackburn's *The Making of New World Slavery*.[31] For Williams, "the commercial capitalism of the eighteenth century developed the wealth of Europe by means of slavery and monopoly. But in so doing it helped to create the industrial capitalism of the nineteenth century, which turned round and destroyed the power of commercial capitalism, slavery, and all its works" (210). Blackburn expands upon this view when he writes that

Saving Private Property: Steven Spielberg's American DreamWorks   85

239

slave plantations, and the maritime entrepreneurs who sponsored and serviced them [that is, slave traders], furnished an important intermediary form of economic rationality—notwithstanding their many destructive and inhumane features. Indeed so far as plantation slavery was concerned the point would be, firstly, it embodied some principles of productive rational organization and that, secondly, it did so in such a partial, or even contradictory, manner that it provoked critical reflection, resistance and innovation. (588)

In other words, and following *Grundrisse*, Williams and Blackburn claim that slavery, insofar as it made possible the accumulation of the vast amounts of wealth necessary for industrial investment, created the material conditions whereby slavery itself would wither away as a distinct economic order. However, and again following *Grundrisse*, we should not understand this "self-correcting" dialecticism of capital as a virtue; as the Civil War demonstrated, such transitions are violent and costly, in every sense of that term. On the contrary, Karl Marx saw capital's recourse to repeated terrifying and spasmodic crises as almost unbearably inhumane and the single most convincing evidence that capitalism, as an economic system, would eventually be swept from the earth.[32]

In *Amistad*, then, the withering away of the institution of slavery registers a double crisis in nineteenth-century America: a crisis in the American realization of the full extent of human rights embedded in natural law, and a crisis of capital. It is no accident that the film imagines the two as deeply intertwined; Williams's reading of the history of slavery makes the relationship clear.[33] In fact, a close reading of Williams's study would lead to the conclusion that the appeal to the "higher principles" of natural law works primarily as the ideological fig leaf needed to camouflage the true lineaments of capitalism in crisis.[34] In making this gesture, *Amistad* suggests that the straightest path through any crisis in the capitalist mode of production lies in finding the right overarching narrative; as Adams tells Joadson, "whoever tells the best story wins." In searching for the "best story" with which to frame the crisis in capitalism that marked the end of slavery—a sustained and bloody crisis that resulted largely in "Pyrrhic" victories, tragically incomplete solutions (a savage Civil War and a curtailed Reconstruction, followed by Jim Crow, black peonage, and the rise of the New South), and ongoing human misery—*Amistad* registers the growing fear of another coming crisis and the uncomfortable feeling that we have yet to find the single "best story" to pull us through. To a significant degree, *Saving Private Ryan* presents itself as that story.[35]

In *Saving Private Ryan*, the decision to send a task force behind enemy lines to search for the sole surviving son of an Iowa farming family is made by no less an authority than the Army Chief of Staff General George C. Marshall (played by Harve Presnell). When his officers appear to balk at the idea of such a mission, Marshall pulls a letter out of a book in his study and reads it aloud:

I have been shown in the files of the War Department a statement of the Adjutant General of Massachusetts, that you are the mother of five sons who have died gloriously on the field

240

of battle. I feel how weak and fruitless must be any words of mine which should attempt to beguile you from the grief of a loss so overwhelming. But I cannot refrain from tendering to you the consolation that may be found in the thanks of the Republic they died to save. I pray that our Heavenly Father may assuage the anguish of your bereavement, and leave you only the cherished memory of the loved and lost, and the solemn pride that must be yours, to have laid so costly a sacrifice upon the altar of Freedom.

When Presnell's Marshall announces that the letter is signed by Abraham Lincoln, discussion ends. Mother Ryan will have her consolation; even the words of a president, it is implied, cannot blunt, or justify, the anguish of such catastrophic loss.

The letter Marshall reads in this scene is the Bixby letter, and it is among the most famous Lincoln documents of the Civil War, having drawn nearly as much analysis and commentary as the Gettysburg Address and the Second Inaugural.[36] While the letter has garnered deserved praise for combining heartfelt compassion with direct brevity of expression, it also has drawn considerable notice of a sort not likely to support a cinematic appeal to historic precedent, for nearly everything about the letter is suspect: Lydia Bixby did not lose five sons gloriously in the field of battle; Lincoln may well not have written the letter; and it is certain that any copy of the document purporting to be in Lincoln's hand is a forgery.

The Bixby letter made its first public appearance in the pages of the *Boston Evening Transcript* on 25 November 1864. The letter had an editorial preface in which it was claimed that the indigent Widow Bixby had six sons enlisted in the Union army; five of them were killed in battle, and the sixth was being treated at the Readville Army Hospital. Despite such devastation, the preface continues, "her lonely abode was made cheerful this morning by the receipt of the following letter from President Lincoln."[37] As F. Lauriston Bullard notes in his study, the letter was immediately recognized as a triumph of rhetorical elegance and rapidly reprinted in the *Boston Traveller*, the *Boston Journal*, Horace Greeley's *New York Tribune*, and the *United States Army and Navy Journal*—despite the fact that, just three days after the letter was first printed, a notice appeared in the *Boston Advertiser* announcing that one of the sons was not dead, but captured (*Abraham Lincoln*, 51, 34). In the months and years following the appearance of the letter, a series of investigations (most by curious journalists) established that, of Mrs. Bixby's five (not six) sons, two were killed in action, one was honorably discharged, one deserted, and one was a prisoner of war who may have deserted to the enemy (33–34). Mrs. Bixby herself came in for close scrutiny: though resident in Boston, she was a Virginia native and an "ardent Southern sympathizer" with "little good to say of President Lincoln."[38] At the extreme limit of the move to debunk the Bixby letter, David Rankin Barbee insists that, far from being a poor widow worthy of pity and charity, Lydia Bixby was a liar and a schemer who sought to exploit patriotic feeling during the war for her own personal gain; the mother of "a nest of foul birds," Barbee asserts, she also quite likely was a prostitute.[39]

Efforts to canonize the Bixby letter by disconnecting it from the Bixby family also have run into difficulties.[40] No copy of the letter in Lincoln's hand ever has appeared; a series of facsimiles printed around the turn of the century unquestionably are based on forgeries; and scholars have been unable to establish a single copytext for the letter—in its various incarnations it has appeared sometimes as a single paragraph, sometimes as three paragraphs, and all versions feature widely varying punctuation and capitalization.[41] The long-held suspicion has been that the letter was not written by Lincoln at all, but by his personal secretary John Hay. Bullard's stylistic analysis of 1946, which led him to decide that Lincoln did indeed write the letter, has recently been questioned by the work of Michael Burlingame, who asserts that his research points to the conclusion that "Hay, not Lincoln, is the true author of 'the most beautiful letter ever written.'"[42]

Perhaps not surprisingly, appeals to Mrs. Bixby were popular during the Second World War, and in fact the frequency of those appeals spurred much of the investigative work into the history of the letter that I cite here: Barbee's essay appeared in 1945, Bullard's study in 1946.[43] Still, it is not my claim that screenwriter Robert Rodat and others who contributed to *Saving Private Ryan* should have known all the particulars of the complex case of the Bixby letter, even though it is not possible today to read the letter and not learn *something* of the conflict.[44] Rather, knowing the problems with the Bixby letter serves to heighten our appreciation of the lengths to which the creators of *Saving Private Ryan* were willing to go in order to get Abraham Lincoln into the film. In *Saving Private Ryan*, the appearance of the Bixby letter in General Marshall's hand has the same effect as John Quincy Adams's appeal to the Founding Fathers in *Amistad*: In both cases we are assured that the action being urged is something that our national Fathers themselves would have taken. The work of saving Private Ryan, like the project of freeing the *Amistad* captives, serves the larger task of national vindication by being reduced in both films to a matter of filial piety: Father would approve.

Andrew Britton's 1986 analysis of the "Reaganite entertainment" values of much then-current U.S. cinema singled out this reaffirmation of patriarchy as among the most important aspects of the films' cultural work; the fact that, fourteen years later, we find ourselves wandering in much the same territory perhaps indicates how little the landscape has actually changed.[45] Yet just as *Amistad*'s effort to reduce the history of American slavery to a matter of properly obeying the Father fails to stifle nagging questions about that history's importance to the progress of American freedom through capitalism, so the decision to frame the Pyrrhic rescue of Private Ryan as a means of providing emotional closure to the nationally wounding memory of the Civil War casts unwonted light on larger issues. The rescue scheme, after all, is not the work of Generals Dwight D. Eisenhower, Omar Bradley, or (even) George Patton—it is Marshall's plan, and though *Saving Private Ryan* missed the fiftieth anniversary of D Day by some four years, it was almost perfectly timed to coincide with the fiftieth anniversary of the Marshall Plan for the economic restoration of Europe.[46] The plan made its first public appearance in Marshall's Harvard commencement address of 1947 and was approved by Congress in the spring of 1948.) In its subtle invocation of the Marshall Plan, *Saving Private Ryan* revisits the territory of capitalist crisis that had been broached in *Amistad*. For out of the crisis that was the Second World War, capital was revitalized and transformed: first through the global financial institutions created in the Allies' summit at Bretton Woods in 1944 (the World Bank and the International Monetary Fund), which sought to ensure a stable (and capitalist) postwar economic order, then through the direct infusions of financial assistance to Europe made possible by the Economic Cooperation Act (the Congressional legislation that enacted the Marshall Plan).

On the face of it, this shared concern in both films with transformative crises in the history of capital is striking enough; however, it is the incredible yoking of the Bixby letter with George C. Marshall that sets the terms within which *Saving Private Ryan* realizes this common theme in all its historicity. Invoking the Bixby letter not only conjures up the sentimental vision of a Father's unfulfilled promise to heal his nation: it explicitly connects the Civil War to World War II. Furthermore, choosing to make that connection via the hand of General (later Secretary of State) George C. Marshall pushes the link past the battlefield and into the ensuing peace, so that, as the Civil War lines up with World War II, Southern Reconstruction falls into place next to the work of European restoration.

The immediate, historical justification for the Marshall Plan was the disastrous combined effect of the Treaty of Versailles and the Great Depression, which seemed to work together to create the chaotic economic and political conditions that led to the rise of Adolf Hitler.[47] In *Saving Private Ryan*, however, the appearance of the Bixby letter connects the Marshall Plan to the unfinished work of Southern Reconstruction; if the task of rescuing Private James Ryan is a metonym for the work of saving Europe, saving Europe, in this film, becomes a way for the United States to ensure its future by finally taking care of unfinished business in its past.[48] If in *Amistad* the Civil War became the last battle of the American Revolution, in *Saving Private Ryan* World War II becomes the last battle of the Civil War. Imaginatively transforming the economic restoration of Europe into the long-delayed final chapters of Southern Reconstruction casts America's move to global power through the Marshall Plan as the necessary and natural next step in the unfolding of American destiny, a step that reveals the American promotion of greater human freedom as the creation of free markets and, in so doing, implies that the capitalist order is likewise sanctioned by natural law.

As I will discuss shortly, the film's evocation of the Marshall Plan has particular resonance for Americans struggling to make sense of recent political and economic world affairs. I would like first, however, to explore the racial dimensions of *Saving Private Ryan*'s use of American history via its inflated recycling of the appeals to the Civil War and paternalism initially articulated in *Amistad*. One way to phrase my claim here would be to say that *Saving Private Ryan* is *The Birth of a Nation* without blacks, insofar as Spielberg's film, like D. W. Griffith's epic, seeks to justify the current social order through an appeal to a deeply racialized history that is also thoroughly stage-managed.[49] Indeed, it is precisely by bracketing the contribution of African-Americans to World War II (thus muting the history of the "Double V" campaign)—and by speedily "morphing" James Ryan, his gaze fixed on the dead body of his white father/captain, through the intervening years connecting the (George) Marshall Plan and (Thurgood) Marshall's plan—that *Saving Private Ryan* attempts to pass itself off as a "color-blind" re-birth of a nation.[50] The claim that Spielberg was under no requirement to engage America's racial politics during World War II because there were no blacks in the units crucial to his narrative (the 2d Ranger Battalion, the 29th Infantry Division, and the 101st Airborne) simply begs the question of why Spielberg chose to construct his vision of the war as he did.[51] Griffith's film wrote off the issue of U.S. racism by demonizing blacks in the context of an explicitly racialized subject matter, but Spielberg's subject matter is no less racialized for all its lack of visible African-American bodies. It is a commonplace of World War II history that the irony of using racially segregated troops to fight in the name of freedom from racist fascism was amply present to many Americans. In the waning years of the war, President Harry S. Truman ordered a trial run of an integrated Army unit in the European theater; in 1948, a presidential committee released the report "Freedom to Serve," urging racial integration of the armed forces and outlining steps to achieve that goal; the onset of war in Korea in 1950 saw the first battlefield service of racially integrated U.S. troops. In fact, one of the standard textbooks of African-American history more than implies that World War II, by offering an unprecedented opportunity for white Americans to examine critically their own racial attitudes in the light of Nazi genocide and Japan's occupation of Manchuria, renewed the push for racial justice. Seen in this light, U.S. involvement in World War II is hardly devoid of racial content; indeed, it emerges as an important precursor of the civil rights movement of the 1960s.[52]

Saving Private Ryan cannot allow this history direct expression, however. To do so would too obviously complicate the pledge in *Amistad* that the Civil War would constitute the last battle of the American Revolution (though, as I've already noted, *Saving Private Ryan* is willing to acknowledge that, in other ways, the Civil War is not yet over). Adding a chapter on American racism during the "good war" would also put the film squarely in the path of the tidal wave of World War II nostalgia that had been activated by the anniversary of D Day, had crested during the 1996 presidential elections, and had not yet completely subsided by the time of *Saving Private Ryan*'s release.[53] Charged with telling the "best story" of America's commitment to the furtherance of human freedom, *Saving Private Ryan* opts for a "color-blind" visual strategy to complement its narrative linking of the Civil War and World War II, Reconstruction and the Marshall Plan. Following neoconservative "color-blind" schemes that have reduced racial justice to abstract economic parity, *Saving Private Ryan* works to assure its audience that if blacks do not appear in its narrative of American goodness ("Tell me I'm a good man"), it is because the universalizing effects of free market capitalism—finally liberated in Europe through the good offices of the United States—have rendered racial distinctions unnecessary.[34]

As *Amistad* registers how a crisis in capitalism led to the abolition of slavery, so *Saving Private Ryan* stakes its claim for American freedom in the liberating effects of the rescue of capital engineered by George C. Marshall. But while *Amistad* records a past chapter in the history of slavery, and so counts on its viewers' ability to mark a certain progress between 1841 and 1997. *Saving Private Ryan* cannot find its historical legs so readily, as the dream of an integrated global market that informed the Marshall Plan plunges toward its final realization. Thus the film concludes with the flat-footed assurance that (white) Americans are a good people who have *earned* their considerable perquisites in the current global economic order ("Earn this, James")—no matter how bloody, painful, or ruthless that order may appear.[55]

Though Spielberg and his colleagues at DreamWorks could not have anticipated it, *Saving Private Ryan* opened in theaters across the country as the economic crisis that had begun in Thailand nearly a year earlier reached its Russian climax. The film opened on 24 July 1998; by the second week of August (when gross revenues for *Saving Private Ryan* passed the $100 million mark), the Russian ruble had collapsed.[56] The Cold War "officially" had ended nearly ten years earlier, but the narrative of Russia's economic "meltdown" (the media's term of choice to describe the events) provided the postscript: clearly, the United States had won the war for the hearts and minds of men that had sprung fifty years ago out of the debris of World War II.

There was, of course, more to the story; and on 15 February 1999, the *New York Times* began a four-part series that sought to explain the 1997–98 global financial crisis. Entitled "Global Contagion: A Narrative," the series was not without resemblance to that other narrative of public affairs that had captured the attention of American readers during the summer. Like the Starr report, the *New York Times* series was concerned to uncover just who got screwed, as well as when, where, why, and how it happened. Like the Starr report, the *New York Times* dwelt on issues of responsible limit-setting: under what circumstances might the small and weak enter into a relationship with the rich and powerful? When does intimacy become exploitation? But unlike the Starr report, the *New York Times* determined that, so far as the collapse of the global economic periphery was concerned, Asia, Russia, and Latin America were asking for it.[37]

The *New York Times* comes to this conclusion even though, as the second article in the series makes abundantly clear, the United States had no small role to play in the runaway speculation that fueled the crisis. Reporters Nicholas D. Kristof and David E. Sanger acknowledge that President Clinton's post–Cold War drive for increasingly open markets throughout the world "fostered vulnerabilities that are an underlying cause of the economic crisis that began in Thailand in July 1997, rippled through Asia and Russia, and is now shaking Brazil and Latin America."[58] While the *New York Times* attributes Clinton's program largely to political ambition, a pursuit of a neoliberal agenda that combines a robust investment climate with the appearance of sympathy to social welfare issues, the *Times* also seeks to blunt this assertion through appeals to economic history. Thus, in the same article outlining how Clinton administration policies furthered the crisis, Kristof and Sanger assert that "free movement of capital is nothing new; for it was the norm during most of Western history"; in the first article of the series, they claim that "today's crisis fits neatly into a long history of financial manias and panics. Emerging markets have been risky ever since the 1320s, when England, then a developing country, defaulted on loans to banks in the Italian city-state of Genoa. In the 19th century, states like Mississippi defaulted on debts just as Russia did last year."[59]

As tempting as it is to pause over an appeal to history that likens fourteenth-century England to a modern Third World country and nineteenth-century Mississippi to post-Soviet Russia, I want only to note that, despite this effort to mute the scope and nature of the crisis, Kristof acknowledges, in the final installment of the series, that "today's global economic upheaval may be a landmark crisis of the post–Cold War era."[60] This is precisely the conclusion that the financier George Soros arrived at some five months earlier in his hastily published anatomy of the crisis in contemporary global capitalism, and it is this possibility—that "American values" have won the Cold War only to lose an economically overheated peace—that haunts the narrativization of crisis in *Saving Private Ryan*.

The Crisis of Global Capitalism has been hard for economists to take seriously, but the book is useful as a symptom, doing us the favor of articulating a gnawing fear that the current rapid economic expansion will conclude in a similarly dramatic contraction.[61] The edge of the fear appears to have subsided in the United States, largely because U.S. markets seem to have emerged relatively unscathed from the yearlong financial disaster. But even as the *New York Times*, for example, declares the worst of the danger passed, it also features articles describing how globalization has compounded the gap between rich and poor, along with others predicting a coming recession.[62] As uncertainty and anxiety rise, analysts and members of the media have turned to the past for examples of successful crisis management. And the favorite model by far is the Marshall Plan—what Charles L. Mee Jr. termed the "Pax Americana."[63]

On the face of it, the call for a new Marshall Plan makes little sense, for, as Secretary of the Treasury Lawrence H. Summers has pointed out, "the Cold War rationale for economic integration—that it was a necessary ingredient of building a power base to fight global communism—has been removed."[64] A claim could be made that the newfound popularity of the Marshall Plan in the waning months of 1998 owed its existence, in no small degree, to Spielberg's decision to conjoin the trimly uniformed, dignified presence of Harve Presnell's George C. Marshall with the stirring words of the Bixby letter. Evidence for this view appears to strengthen when we connect that voice and image with the simultaneously unfolding events in the Balkans, where Slobodan Milosevic's pursuit of "ethnic cleansing" in Kosovo prompted a wholesale mass media appropriation of the World War II narrative.[65] And, in fact, the war in Kosovo ended with an agreement that was widely described as a Marshall Plan for the Balkans, a plan aimed, like its predecessor, not only at rebuilding the war-damaged economies of several neighboring nations but also at radically transforming one particular nation's political and economic regime.[66]

Even before the onset of the war in Kosovo, however, Soros's demand for a new Marshall Plan to manage the global economy reiterated the appeal to military history that had been articulated, during the summer of the Russian financial disaster, by *Saving Private Ryan*—an appeal picked up and echoed in the 28 March 1999 cover story of the *New York Times Sunday Magazine*, where journalist Thomas L. Friedman called upon the United States to assume its responsibilities as the "enforcer" of the new economic order. "The hidden hand of the market will never work without a hidden fist," Friedman writes. "McDonald's cannot flourish without McDonnell Douglas, the builder of the F-15. And the hidden fist that keeps the world safe for Silicon Valley's technologies is called the United States Army, Air Force, Navy and Marine Corps."[67] George Soros wants to rewrite the Marshall Plan, but Thomas Friedman is busy rewriting "The American Century," Henry Luce's vision of America's rise to world power thanks to "things in this country which are infinitely precious and especially American—a love of freedom, a feeling for the equality of opportunity, a tradition of self-reliance and independence and also of cooperation" ("American Century," 65). Luce's primary aim was to get a deeply isolationist United States into World War II, and his capitalism accordingly came rather thickly swaddled in Freedom and Justice; for Friedman, on the other hand, capitalism has matured to the degree that it can now simply *stand for* Freedom and Justice.

In his analysis of the 1996 film *Independence Day*, Michael Rogin notes that the movie "serves American power in the name of attacking it."[68] It might be too much to say that *Amistad* and *Saving Private Ryan* attack American power in the name of serving it, but the films certainly cannot be reduced to the pro-American "context" DreamWorks sought to provide for them upon their release. Indeed, when read together, the two films emerge as interlocked phenomena in which the contradictions of freedom in capital (and capital as freedom) emerge in all their stubborn irresolution: *Amistad* may deeply wish to cast the emergence of a postslavery capitalism as completely liberating, but the "color-blind" *Saving Private Ryan* tacitly reminds us that integrated markets aren't the same thing as integrated societies. In this regard, the films indicate how little Spielberg's work has actually changed, despite the much-vaunted "turn" to history as serious drama; as Andrew Britton noted (speaking to the particular case of *Raiders of the Lost Ark*), Spielberg's films "actually have to give form to the anxieties they address, even as they work to dissi-

Saving Private Property: Steven Spielberg's American DreamWorks   93

247

pate them" ("Blissing Out," 20). This formal compulsion results in "a latent discrepancy . . . between the kinds of reassurance the films provide and the kinds of uncertainty the audience actually feels" (20). Thus Spielberg gambles with the possibility that *Saving Private Ryan* ultimately conveys not the nobility and necessity of sacrificing many for the sake of one, but rather the grotesque, repellent wastefulness of a salvation that has been so constituted.

In Spielberg's film, Private Ryan's story about his brother Dan's escapade with Alice Jardine is played for a few laughs and a lot of sentiment: what high-spirited young men, we're asked to think; what a pity that they're gone. But the exchange between Private Ryan and the mournful Captain Miller has been not about the lost brothers as such, but about memory and context. In Spielberg's view, memory plus context equals history; and history, both *Amistad* and *Saving Private Ryan* strive to make us understand, is what makes us who we are today. However, if we are willing to see history as something more than a vindication of the current ideological order, attending to the context of context in *Saving Private Ryan* might lead thoughtful viewers to come away with a different reading of the scene: We may tell ourselves that we're trying to return to a remembered life in the Garden, but maybe what we're really doing is fighting to get our own piece of the action before everything goes up in flames.

Notes

In writing this essay, I've been the beneficiary of innumerable conversations and e-mail exchanges. Thanks to Thomas A. Bass, Mark Eaton, Richard Godden, Maurice Isserman, Elizabeth J. Jensen, Doran Larson, Patricia O'Neill, and Noel Polk for early important criticism, and to the editors of *Representations*, especially Carol J. Clover and Michael Rogin, for helping me rethink and sharpen my conclusions. Thanks also to Robert L. Paquette, who freely shared with me materials he had amassed while working on his own *Amistad* essay. Finally, I must acknowledge the superb assistance of the reference librarians and the interlibrary loan staff at the Daniel Burke Library of Hamilton College; their help was indispensable.

1. As Daniel Gross notes. Matt Damon, who plays Private James Ryan, seems to have a penchant for mentioning scholars in his speeches: Besides Alice Jardine (professor of Romance Languages and Women's Studies at Harvard), the sociologist Howard Zinn and University of New Hampshire English professor Rachel Trubowitz have found themselves named in Damon's films. See Daniel Gross, "Go Ask Alice," *Lingua Franca* 8, no. 7 (October 1998): 15.
2. Steven Spielberg, director. *Saving Private Ryan*, produced by Steven Spielberg, Ian Bryce,

Mark Gordon, and Gary Levinsohn DreamWorks Pictures and Paramount Pictures. Los Angeles, 1998 .

3. My thanks to John T. Matthews for this point.

4. As is well known, the phrase "the American Century" comes from Henry R. Luce's essay of the same name, first published in the 17 February 1941 issue of his *Life* magazine and later released in a book with commentaries, Henry R. Luce, *The American Century* (New York, 1941). Subsequent citations will be to the *Life* article and will appear parenthetically in the text.

5. John Gaddis, *The Long Peace: Inquiries into the History of the Cold War* (New York, 1987).

6. Indeed, the acclaim for Spielberg's rendering of D Day is reminiscent of nothing so much as the praise that greeted Ernest Hemingway's rendering of Caporetto in *A Farewell to Arms*. In both cases, technical realism is mistaken for historical accuracy.

7. The political unconscious of U.S. cinema became remarkably more political and less unconscious during the Reagan-Bush years, as Reagan's own pregovernment life in Hollywood prompted a heightened interest in the cultural work of film. See, for example, Alan Nadel, *Flatlining on the Field of Dreams: Cultural Narratives in the Films of President Reagan's America* (New Brunswick, N.J., 1997), and Andrew Britton's prescient "Blissing Out: The Politics of Reaganite Entertainment," *Movie* 31/32 (Winter 1986): 1–42. Subsequent citations will appear parenthetically in the text. While Britton's interest lies less in analyzing Spielberg's work than in describing a certain type of cinema (the "Reaganite entertainment" of the title , his analysis of Spielberg's 1980s films (particularly *E. T.* and the Indiana Jones movies) is devastatingly accurate and, for the post–*Schindler's List* reader, remarkable for its ability to anticipate the continuity of values subtending both the earlier "popcorn" movies and the more recent "serious" work.

8. George Soros, *The Crisis of Global Capitalism: Open Society Endangered* (New York, 1998). Subsequent citations will appear parenthetically in the text.

I should make clear that my discussions of both past and anticipated crises in capitalism are *not* meant to indicate an impending, final demise of the capitalist system. On the contrary, and following Karl Marx's *Grundrisse* (of which I will have more to say later), by "crisis" I mean to indicate the primary engine by which capital readies itself for its next incarnation its "new and improved" version, as it were). When, later in this essay, I write of fears of an impending crisis in contemporary capitalism, then, I am not claiming that "the end is near." Rather, I hope to draw attention to the ongoing, and not insignificant, costs of what at the close of the century seems to have emerged as *the* global economic order, and to the ways in which *Amistad* and *Saving Private Ryan* simultaneously eulogize and register anxieties about that order. For an excellent discussion of capitalism and crisis that offers a much more detailed reading of recent American history than I manage here, see Richard Godden, "Fordism: From Desire to Destruction (an Historical Interlude ," in his *Fictions of Capital: The American Novel from James to Mailer* (Cambridge, 1990).

9. See, for example, Robert Brent Toplin, *History by Hollywood: The Use and Abuse of the American Past* (Urbana, Ill., 1996 : and George Lipsitz, *Time Passages: Collective Memory and American Popular Culture* (Minneapolis, 1990).

10. The extracinematic ambitions of *Amistad*—of course an aspect of the "spin" on the film provided by DreamWorks even before its release—have been accepted as contextual fact regardless of the critic's political agenda; conservative writers sneered at what was perceived to be the bleeding heart on the film's sleeve, while liberal critics praised its

good intentions. For an example of the former, see John Simon's review, "Souls at Sea," *National Review* 49, no. 25 (31 December 1997): 56–57, in which he terms *Amistad* "poster art for the delectation of knee-jerk liberals" (56); for the latter, see Stanley Kauffmann's article, "Of Human Bondage," *New Republic*, 22 December 1997, 24–25; *Amistad*, he writes, "seems to stand free, like a strong sculpture" (25). For Henry Louis Gates's quotation, see *Amistad: A Celebration of the Film by Steven Spielberg* (New York, 1998), 42; Gates was one of eleven cultural and historical consultants retained by DreamWorks during the filming of *Amistad*.

For one example of *Saving Private Ryan*'s patriotic effect, see Anthony Lane, "The Current Cinema: Soldiering On," *New Yorker* 74, no. 22 (3 August 1998), 79: "I was practically standing on my seat and yelling at Tom Hanks to kill more Germans, and then, when he had finished killing Germans, to kill more Germans. If anything, the heroism of *Saving Private Ryan* is all the more startling for not being rigged or haloed; it seems to bloom out of the shapeless dreck of fighting like a madman for your life." Of course, *Saving Private Ryan* can also be read in tandem with another millenarian paean to fathers, Tom Brokaw's *The Greatest Generation* (New York, 1998). In his meditation on the public reaction to *Saving Private Ryan*, John Gregory Dunne wryly terms this overall phenomenon "Generational Flagellation Lite"; John Gregory Dunne, "Virtual Patriotism," *New Yorker* 74, no. 35 (16 November 1998), 101.

11.	Besides a common director, the films share the same cinematographer (Janusz Kaminski), the same editor (Michael Kahn), and the same composer (John Williams). This team has worked together on only one other film: *Schindler's List*.

I would like briefly to gloss one reading of Spielberg's dramatic work that would treat *Schindler's List* (1993), *Amistad* (1997), and *Saving Private Ryan* (1998) as a trilogy and thus would explore ideological and epistemological questions of historical representation in mass culture in greater depth and detail than I manage here. Certainly the films share a thematic question—What is the worth of human life?—and a common approach to that theme: in all three films, human worth is articulated almost entirely in the terms of capital (as Oskar Schindler puts it, "If I had made more money I could have saved more lives"). Taken together, the three films also present an oddly regressive economy of salvation: First, one man saves one thousand people; then, three men (or five, if one decides to include Cinqué and Lewis Tappan) save forty-three people; finally, eight men save one man.

One way to approach the films as a group would be to consider how they offer themselves as imaginative prostheses meant to patch the gap between history and memory. (On this gap, see Pierre Nora, "Between Memory and History: Les lieux de mémoire," *Representations* 26 [Spring 1989]: 7–25.) The films could be read as an effort to compensate for the "fundamental collapse of memory" that Nora sees as product of "mass culture on a global scale" (7). Such a reading would pursue a dialectical (or homeopathic?) analysis; in other words, it would explore how the films claim to amend a situation they in fact have helped create. Because my interest here is in Spielberg's appeals to a specifically American history for an imagined American audience, however, I have chosen not to discuss *Schindler's List* in anything more than a tangential manner, even though the film has spurred much of the finest recent criticism of Spielberg's work. See, for example, Geoffrey Hartman, "The Cinema Animal," *Salmagundi* 106–7 (Spring–Summer 1995): 127–45; and Miriam Bratu Hansen, "*Schindler's List* is Not *Shoah*: The Second Commandment, Popular Modernism, and Public Memory," *Critical Inquiry* 22

Winter 1996 : 292–312. Hansen's detection of the links between *Schindler's List* and *The Birth of a Nation* parallels my recognition of the connections between D. W. Griffith's epic and *Saving Private Ryan*. Yosefa Loshitzky's collection *Spielberg's Holocaust: Critical Perspectives on* Schindler's List (Bloomington, Ind., 1997), reprints the Hansen and Hartman essays and offers additional views of the film, by no means all of them negative.

12. *Amistad's* distortions of historical fact were attacked by historians across the political spectrum. For representative examples see Eric Foner's condemnation of the movie, "Hollywood Invades the Classroom," *New York Times*, 20 December 1997, A13; and Robert L. Paquette's critique, "From History to Hollywood: The Voyage of 'La Amistad,' " *New Criterion* 16, no. 7 (March 1998): 74–78. Bertram Wyatt-Brown's review, "Amistad," *Journal of American History* 85, no. 3 (December 1998): 1174–76, is rather unique in its willingness to forgive the film's historical lapses for the sake of its "remarkable intensity" (1174), though so far as I can tell he is the only historian to dwell on the film's bizarre treatment of abolitionism, a problem I pursue in some detail here.

Certainly one reading of Steven Spielberg's decision to hire Stephen E. Ambrose as paid (and prominently displayed) historical consultant to *Saving Private Ryan* would cast it as an effort to forestall the savaging that greeted *Amistad*, an effort that seems largely to have worked (Dunne hints as much; Dunne, "Virtual Patriotism," 98). What little criticism there was of *Saving Private Ryan* during its theatrical release dwelled more on its pretension to set a new standard for realism in war films; Jeanine Basinger and Louis Menand both rightly note that *Saving Private Ryan* is, on the contrary, utterly conventional. See Jeanine Basinger, "Translating War: The Combat Film Genre and *Saving Private Ryan*," *Perspectives* (American Historical Association Newsletter) 36, no. 7 (October 1998): 1, 43–47; and Louis Menand, "Jerry Don't Surf," *New York Review of Books* 45, no. 14 (24 September 1998), 7–8. Tom Carson's essay takes the criticisms of Menand and Basinger a step further, and deeper into the realm of ideology critique, when it dismisses *Saving Private Ryan* as "one of the most mindlessly adulatory war movies of all time—one that treats combat as horrific, but only on the way to making it sublime, and calls the result the ultimate tribute to our national character while egging us on to live up to it"; Tom Carson, "And the Leni Riefenstahl Award for Rabid Nationalism Goes to: *Saving Private Ryan*," *Esquire* 131, no. 3 (March 1999), 77. It is worth emphasizing that Carson's blistering attack appeared well after the conclusion of *Saving Private Ryan's* U.S. theatrical run, and so had no effect on the film's financial performance; attacks on *Amistad*, however, appeared almost immediately after the film's release and served largely to increase the likelihood that potential moviegoers would jump ship for *Titanic*.

Basinger, Menand, and Carson aside, detailed criticism of historical accuracy in *Saving Private Ryan* for the most part failed to move beyond the rather narrow confines of H-WAR, the listserve for military history maintained by Michigan State University's H-NET. The one exception I've been able to discover is Michael Marino's article on the *Film and History* Web site, "Bloody but Not History: What's Wrong with *Saving Private Ryan*"; http://h-net2.msu.edu/~filmhis/ryan.html. Marino lists several errors of historical fact in the film (noting that most of these errors seem attributable to a desire on Spielberg's part "to portray the odds facing the Americans as far longer than they actually were") and concludes that *Saving Private Ryan* "rather than being an accurate historical depiction of World War II is little more than another in a long line of outlandish war movies that disregards facts and reality in favor of dramatic effect."

13. In his effort to discern the contemporary context for *Saving Private Ryan*, Jacob Weisberg notes that "the suggestion that America's main goal [in World War II] was to save Jews from Hitler is the revisionist product of a post-Holocaust consciousness"; Jacob Weisberg, "Bombs and Blockbusters: World War II Nostalgia at the Movies Is Blurring the Picture of Kosovo," *New York Times Sunday Magazine*, 11 April 1999, 18. I agree and would add that, to the extent that it does not need to make this revisionist claim explicit, *Saving Private Ryan* is a product of post–*Schindler's List* consciousness.

14. A particularly active list in discussions of the film was SLAVERY, the listserve for historians of U.S. slavery operated out of the University of Houston. The archives of the listserve are available at http://listserv.uh.edu/archives/slavery.html. As of April 1999, SLAVERY had 374 subscribers.

15. Paquette makes the point about the film's misrepresentation of Roger Baldwin (in his "From History to Hollywood," 76–77); the quotations are from *Amistad: A Celebration*, 44, 45.

16. This is Foner's point; see note 12.

17. In fact Sean Wilentz praises the film's "forceful portrayal of one of the aging Adams's finest moments," calling *Amistad* a "big, persuasive rendering of history" despite its flaws; Sean Wilentz, "The Mandarin and the Rebel," *New Republic*, 22 December 1997, 25, 32. Be that as it may, and the history of rhetoric certainly demonstrates that bigness and persuasiveness are not contingent on accuracy), I cannot second Wilentz's enthusiasm for the film's representation of the abolitionist movement.

18. For Adams's Supreme Court statement, see John Quincy Adams, *Argument in the Case of United States vs. Cinque*, (1841; reprint, New York, 1969). This is a reprint of the document published in 1841 by S. W. Benedict of New York; Adams's statement runs to some 135 closely printed pages. For Howard Jones's discussion of Adams's argument and its publication history, see his *Mutiny on the Amistad* (New York, 1987), 175–88 for the argument, 250 n. 17 for its publication history; Jones's work is the standard reference on the history of the *Amistad* case; citations hereafter will appear parethetically in the text.

19. Steven Spielberg, director, *Amistad*, produced by Steven Spielberg, Debbie Allen, and Colin Wilson (DreamWorks Pictures and HBO Pictures, Los Angeles, 1997).

20. Martin Van Buren did indeed interfere in the *Amistad* case—though not at all in the manner depicted in the film. The substitution of U.S. District Court Judge Andrew T. Judson with a presumably more politically manipulable (and certainly more handsome) Roman Catholic upstart is utter fiction. Rather than single and impeachment-worthy, Van Buren's actual sins in the case are multiple and, taken individually, somewhat small-scale (though cumulatively, as Jones points out, they add up to something quite serious), and so are too complex to go into here. Jones, *Mutiny on the Amistad*, remains the best single source.

21. Adams, *Argument*, 8–9: parenthetical description of Adams's gesture toward the Declaration of Independence in the original.

22. Ibid., 116–17; emphases in original.

23. In fact, the Supreme Court decision held that Antonio, the *Amistad*'s cabin boy and a slave owned by Captain Ramón Ferrer, who was killed in the uprising, should be returned to Ferrer's widow in Cuba. Lewis Tappan and other abolitionists helped the youth flee to Montreal; Jones, *Mutiny on the Amistad*, 199–200.

24. By "anti-American" I am thinking, of course, of the constitutional critique embodied in the abolitionism of William Lloyd Garrison, and the eventual break Garrison's politics precipitated with Frederick Douglass.

25. "As founder and chief spokesman for the *Amistad* Committee, [Tappan] wrote and managed all publicity, raised the funds, and supervised the prisoners' needs. Tappan set legal policy, initiated the Cuban slave owners' arrest for slave trading [an action attributed to Judge Coglin in the film], and enlisted all attorneys, including ex-president John Quincy Adams. His dedication cost him much anguish. Tappan's Manhattan store was slipping into bankruptcy.... Meantime, his daughter Eliza was dying of tuberculosis. Tappan did not accompany the body to the gravesite in Brookline. His *Amistad* Committee was staging a fund raiser: he felt obliged to attend"; Wyatt-Brown, "Amistad," 1175.

26. It is also possible that the upright, young, attractive, Roman Catholic Judge Coglin appears in *Amistad* in order to protect DreamWorks from charges of promoting anti-Catholic feeling: Were he not in the film, the only Catholics depicted would be the slave traders José Ruiz and Pedro Montes, and "her Catholic Majesty" Queen Isabella II, all clearly on the wrong side of the slavery issue.

Though I am primarily interested in how *Amistad* registers the twinned historical crises in slavery and capital, I should point out that the film also speaks to the current abortion debate. *Amistad*'s engagement with contemporary politics of reproduction is admittedly fragmented and faint, but Spielberg's decision to cast then-retired Supreme Court Justice Harry Blackmun in the role of Supreme Court Justice Joseph Story raises the connection, since Justice Blackmun, a 1970 Nixon appointee to the court, was best known as the author of *Roe v. Wade*. Insofar as Spielberg wants to cast the *Amistad* decision as an unvarnished blow for freedom, it would seem that linking Judge Blackmun to Judge Story makes a similarly elevated claim for the court's 1973 abortion decision. *Amistad*'s narrative alignment of abolition and pro-choice politics, no matter how submerged, thus also may account for Spielberg's care with the film's Catholics.

27. "Spielberg, [producer Debbie] Allen, and [screenwriter David] Franzoni ... agreed on what kind of script they *didn't* want. 'Many movies that deal with slavery are unintentionally racist,' Franzoni says. 'The typical slant in this sort of film is to have the poor, chained black man arrive in the presence of the white guy, who has a good soul and fights the good fight to liberate the black man'"; *Amistad: A Celebration*, 38.

28. "Representations of Otherness in Spielberg's work are always visibly afflicted by this contradiction: the Other can never be an alternative to the dominant norms in that they're sacrosanct, but nor can it subserve a convinced endorsement of them, in that the films are well aware of what, in practice, the norms are like. The problem is very much less embarrassing, naturally, in those cases where the Other is Evil [i.e., in *Jaws*, *Poltergeist, Raiders of the Lost Ark*] ... When the Other is Good, however, the incoherence and pusillanimousness of the Spielberg thematic is blatantly exposed as the film attempts to reconcile the felt need to flee or disrupt America with the desire to believe that nothing is wrong with it"; Britton, "Blissing Out," 36. The effort to effect this reconciliation is precisely the problem in *Amistad*.

29. Of course, as Michael Rogin has pointed out, making the Declaration of Independence the founding document in this chain is not without its problems (and this was the case even before the November 1998 "news" that Thomas Jefferson was the father of children born to his slave Sally Hemings). See, for example, Michael Rogin, "Two Declara-

tions of Independence: The Contaminated Origins of American National Culture," in his *Blackface, White Noise: Jewish Immigrants in the Hollywood Melting Pot* (Berkeley, 1996); and his essay that further develops this theme, "Two Declarations of Independence," in the collection *Race and Representation: Affirmative Action*, ed. Robert Post and Michael Rogin (New York, 1998). Briefly, Rogin's close reading of the Declaration reveals "a Janus-faced legacy to the new nation—the logic on the one hand that the equality to which white men were naturally born could be extended to women and slaves, and the foundation on the other of white freedom on black servitude"; Michael Rogin, "Two Declarations," 76.

30. For the relationship between slavery and freedom, see David Brion Davis's two studies, *The Problem of Slavery in Western Culture* (Ithaca, N.Y., 1966), and *The Problem of Slavery in the Age of Revolution, 1770–1823* (Ithaca, N.Y., 1975); and Orlando Patterson, *Freedom in the Making of Western Culture* (New York, 1991).

31. Eric Williams, *Capitalism and Slavery* 1944; reprint, Chapel Hill, 1994); Robin Blackburn, *The Making of New World Slavery: From the Baroque to the Modern, 1492–1800* (London, 1997). Subsequent citations from both works will appear parethetically in the text.

32. "Beyond a certain point, the development of the powers of production becomes a barrier for capital. . . . When it has reached this point, capital. i.e., wage labour, enters into the same relation towards the development of social wealth and of the forces of production as the guild system, serfdom, slavery; and is necessarily stripped off as a fetter. . . . The growing incompatibility between the productive development of society and its hitherto existing relations of production expresses itself in bitter contradictions, crises, spasms. The violent destruction of capital, not by relations external to it, but rather as a condition of its self-preservation, is the most striking form in which advice is given it to be gone and give room to a higher state of social production"; Karl Marx, *Grundrisse*, trans. Martin Nicolaus (New York, 1993), 749–50.

33. Along with Queen Isabella's letter, John Calhoun's tirade at the White House dinner also works to make this connection explicit in the film.

34. "*The political and moral ideas of the age are to be examined in the very closest relation to the economic development.* Politics and morals in the abstract make no sense. We find . . . statesmen and publicists defending slavery today, abusing slavery tomorrow, defending slavery the day after. Today they are imperialist, the next day anti-imperialist, and equally pro-imperialist a generation after. And always with the same vehemence. The defense or attack is always on the high moral or political plane. The thing defended or attacked is always something you can touch and see, to be measured in pounds sterling or pounds avoirdupois, in dollars and cents, yards, feet and inches. This is not a crime. It is a fact. It is understandable at the time. But historians, writing a hundred years after, have no excuse for continuing to wrap the real interests in confusion. Even the great mass movements, and the antislavery mass movement was one of the greatest of these, show a curious affinity with the rise and development of new interests and the necessity of the destruction of the old"; Williams, *Capitalism and Slavery*, 211; emphasis in original.

35. The "Pyrrhic" victory is Jones's description of the *Amistad* decision; Jones, *Mutiny on the Amistad*, 194.

36. The text of the Bixby letter is published in *The Collected Works of Abraham Lincoln*, ed. Roy P. Basler (New Brunswick, N.J., 1953). 8:116–17. Lest we miss the importance of this letter to *Saving Private Ryan*, it is read aloud once more—again in the voice of Harve

Presnell as Gen. George C. Marshall—near the end of the film, the second time as a quotation within the letter sent to Mrs. Ryan informing her of the impending return of her son.

37. F. Lauriston Bullard. *Abraham Lincoln and The Widow Bixby* (New Brunswick, N.J., 1946), 51. Subsequent citations will appear parenthetically in the text.

38. Michael Burlingame. "New Light on the Bixby Letter," *Journal of the Abraham Lincoln Association* 16 (1995 : 60.

39. David Rankin Barbee. "The Plain Truth about the Bixby Letter," *Tyler's Quarterly Historical and Genealogical Magazine* 26 (January 1945): 162.

40. Bullard is representative here: "The errors of fact on which the letter is based have nothing to do with the case. We may regret these errors and we may wonder how they can be explained, but they do not alter the intrinsic worth and beauty of the letter," which is such as to "ease the pain and uplift the hearts of war-stricken mothers in all generations"; Bullard, *Abraham Lincoln*, 3, 142.

41. See ibid., 146 n. 19, for a lengthy description of textual variants. Burlingame notes that, given Mrs. Bixby's political sympathies, it is more than likely that she simply threw the letter away; Burlingame, "New Light," 60.

42. Burlingame, "New Light," 71. "Gifted and versatile though John Hay was, we do not think that the young man, twenty-six years old in 1864, could have written the letter to Mrs. Bixby. He had not suffered enough. He could not, and did not, feel the burden of fratricidal conflict as did the man who suffered with and for the people of both the South and the North"; Bullard, *Abraham Lincoln*, 134.

43. The case of Mrs. Bixby—as it was represented in the letter, not in the critiques of the letter—was especially popular for reporters covering the Sullivan disaster: On 13 November 1942, the five Sullivan brothers of Waterloo, Iowa, were killed when their ship, USS *Juneau*, sank during one of the Guadalcanal engagements. Their mother, Alleta Sullivan, first was compared to Mrs. Bixby by the local paper, the *Waterloo Daily Courier*, this comparison soon was disseminated widely by the national wire services. See, for example, the Associated Press story "Mother of 5 Boys Lost in War Still Hopes It's a Mistake," Washington *Sunday Star*, 17 January 1943, A10.

The Sullivan tragedy was the subject of Lloyd Bacon's 1944 Hollywood film *The Fighting Sullivans*, in many ways as much a precursor text for Spielberg's movie as the more often cited *The Longest Day* (Darryl F. Zanuck, 1962); in fact, the Sullivan brothers are explicitly named in *Saving Private Ryan* during the scene in Marshall's office that closes with the Bixby letter. In his 1999 Academy Award speech, Spielberg singled out the Sullivan family for special thanks, as well as the Niland family. In July 1944 Sgt. Frederick Niland of Tonawanda, N.Y., was returned home from Europe after his three oldest brothers were reported lost in action. Two were killed in the Normandy invasion; the third, shot down over Burma, spent the war in a Japanese POW camp and eventually was liberated by British troops. The Niland case, largely as it has been recounted in Stephen E. Ambrose's World War II histories *Band of Brothers* and *D-Day*, was widely reported to be the greatest single inspiration for *Saving Private Ryan*. In both of those histories, Ambrose mistakenly reports that all three brothers were killed and that Mrs. Niland received her three War Department telegrams on the same day; see Stephen E. Ambrose, *Band of Brothers* (New York, 1992), 103; and Stephen E. Ambrose, *D-Day* (New York, 1994), 316. A small irony of *Saving Private Ryan* was that it took the release of the film to correct the historical record, as journalists covering the movie sought out and interviewed surviving members of the Niland family. For representative news stories, see Tom Buckham, "New Movie Partially Based on Area Family's Story," *Buffalo News*, 22 June 1998, C1; and Bob St. John, "Family History Like Something out of a Movie," *Dallas Morning News*, 22 August 1998, A31.

44. An effort to establish the exact wording of the letter alone would bring the matter to the writers' attention: in the *Collected Works of Abraham Lincoln*, the footnote outlining the controversy over the Bixby letter is longer than the letter itself. See Basler, *Collected Works of Abraham Lincoln*, 8:116–17.

45. "Whatever one's position on this issue may be, it seems to me that 'patriarchy' is very much the term to describe what gets reaffirmed in Reaganite entertainment: with unremitting insistence and stridency, it is the status and function of the father and their inheritance by the son that are at stake"; Britton, "Blissing Out." 24. Britton makes this observation with Spielberg's work particularly in mind: "*E. T.* . . . remains the ultimate Reaganite movie about patriarchy" (27). Michael Rogin makes a similar point in his reading of *Amistad*: "Like the Moynihan Report on the Negro Family and the Million Man March, and from Africa to the American founders to God, *Amistad* consists of fathers, fathers, fathers, all the way down"; Michael Rogin. "Spielberg's List," *New Left Review* 230 (July–August 1998): 155.

46. The film oddly echoes one of the semisecret scandals of George Patton's German campaign: a decision to send a task force to liberate a POW camp at Hammelburg where his son-in-law, John Waters, was a prisoner. Patton's biographer, Carlo D'Este, reports that the task force raid "turned into a bloody fiasco when [the men] were surrounded by elements of at least three German divisions and chopped to pieces in a series of desperate fire fights. . . . Of the 294 men who started the raid, all but one were listed as missing in action"; Carlo D'Este, *Patton: A Genius for War* New York, 1995), 716. The task force was led by Captain Abraham Baum, who survived to receive a Distinguished Service Cross. When Patton visited his bedside, Baum remarked, " 'You know, sir, it's difficult for me to believe that you would have sent us on that mission just to rescue one man' " (718). Needless to say, this episode does not appear in Franklin J. Schaffner's film *Patton* (1970).

47. For a reading of the Marshall Plan that discusses its meshing of economic and political security issues, see Michael Hogan, *The Marshall Plan: America, Britain, and the Reconstruction of Western Europe, 1947–1952* (Cambridge, 1987). I do not have space here for a thorough analysis of the motivations behind the Marshall Plan—largely because those motivations are the subject of an ongoing dispute among historians, centering on the sincerity of the United States's invitation to the Soviet Union to join the plan. Some historians claim that the United States was sincere, others that the Marshall Plan was always imagined as a way of undermining Soviet economic stability and thus indirectly recruiting Western Europe to the fight against Communism; certainly, the Marshall Plan worked remarkably well with other U.S. strategies of Soviet containment. It is not clear to me why these two views should be seen as mutually exclusive, however. The economist Charles P. Kindleberger claims that the United States was willing to allow Soviet participation, but also that there was "a sigh of relief when Molotov refused to play"; Charles P. Kindleberger, *Marshall Plan Days* (Boston. 1987), 95. It was quite clear even before Congress passed the act that the Soviet Union would not participate in the plan nor allow its client states to participate; see, for example, the 11 June 1947 *Pravda Ukraine* article quoted in Forrest C. Pogue's biography of Marshall, which condemns

Marshall's speech as "evidence of even wider plans of American reaction. of a new stage in Washington's campaign against forces of world democracy and progress. . . . From retail purchase of several European countries. Washington has conceived [a] design of wholesale purchase of [the] whole European continent"; Forrest C. Pogue, *George C. Marshall. Statesman: 1945–1959* (New York, 1987), 220.

48. Cartoonish French peasants and Nazi soldiers aside, *Saving Private Ryan* is remarkable for the way it casts Europe as little more than a backdrop for the ongoing American historical narrative. This is exactly the point that the historian (and World War II veteran) Herbert Aptheker makes when he notes *Saving Private Ryan's* "failure to convey any sense of the reality of Hitlerism's monstrosity. . . . This, I suppose. would conflict with Washington's postwar policy of alliance with the forces—and even personalities—responsible for the infinite horror those forces created"; Herbert Aptheker, *Perspectives* (American Historical Association Newsletter), 37, no. 5 (May 1999): 51. The idea that American destiny plays itself out on the stage of Europe is also, of course, the argument subtending Luce's "The American Century."

49. For a brilliant reading of Griffith's epic that explores links among national identity formation, racism, and father-worship, see Michael Rogin, "'The Sword Became a Flashing Vision': D. W. Griffith's *The Birth of a Nation*," *Representations* 9 (Winter 1985): 150–95. I say that *Saving Private Ryan* is *The Birth of a Nation* without blacks, but of course, in a real way, *The Birth of a Nation* has no blacks, either.

50. For one account of the struggle of African-American servicemen against discrimination ("Double V" referred to their campaign for a "double victory" in the fight against tyranny at home as well as abroad), see Lawrence P. Scott, *Double V: The Civil Rights Struggle of the Tuskegee Airmen* (East Lansing, Mich., 1994). The time-lapsed aging of James Ryan is all the more remarkable for the way it makes explicit—in a film that purports to be about the importance of history—the premise that only *certain* history is worth remembering (or, to use the film's terms, contextualizing).

51. The logs of H-WAR are instructive in this instance: correspondents seeking to defend the film against charges that it is historically inaccurate or incomplete repeatedly claim that *Saving Private Ryan*. as a work of art. answers to a higher authority than pedantic insistence on historical accuracy will allow. On the other hand, correspondents seeking to dismiss concerns about the film's remarkable racial (and sexual) homogeneity argue that historical fidelity requires nothing less. For the H-WAR discussion logs, see http://www.h-net.msu.edu/logs.

52. The textbook is John Hope Franklin's *From Slavery to Freedom: A History of African Americans*, 7th ed. (New York, 1994). Franklin mentions the experiment in integrated service during World War II on 441–42; the description of the steps leading to integration in the armed forces appears on 462; the passage outlining the importance of the war and the immediate postwar period to the growing civil rights movement is on 461.

53. For a reading of the ongoing political usefulness of World War II nostalgia, see Michael Rogin. *Independence Day, or How I Learned to Stop Worrying and Love the Enola Gay* (London, 1998): "It was [the] failure of Cold War victory to breathe new life into the United States that had intensified World War II nostalgia in the first place. From this perspective, then, the ideal America lay back across the great divide opened up by Hiroshima, and World War II was on the far side" (17).

54. I have written elsewhere about how the economic underpinnings of neoconservative "color-blind" discourse make themselves felt in contemporary cultural production and

Saving Private Property: Steven Spielberg's American DreamWorks 103

reception. See Catherine Gunther Kodat, "Confusion in a Dream Deferred: Teaching *A Raisin in the Sun,*" *Studies in the Literary Imagination* 31, no. 1 (Spring 1998): 149–64, which contrasts Lorraine Hansberry's play with the film *Jerry Maguire* (Cameron Crowe, 1996). For one discussion of the logic underlying the emergence of "color-blind" policies, see Michael Omi and Howard Winant, *Racial Formation in the United States: From the 1960s to the 1990s,* 2d ed. (New York, 1994), especially chap. 7, "Race and Reaction." As Michael Rogin notes in his analysis of *Independence Day,* contemporary World War II nostalgia casts the segregated "multiethnic" World War II platoon as the finest example of U.S. pluralism, a move that, of course, operates "in the name of multiculturalism but against its actual contemporary exemplars"; Rogin, *Independence Day,* 13. *Saving Private Ryan* demonstrates a breathtaking impatience with the meager "multiethnicity" of its own platoon (one Jew, one Italian, one "hillbilly"), killing off six of its eight members in the name of one white Iowa farmboy.

55. Hogan's analysis of the Marshall Plan stresses the importance of global market integration as a U.S. postwar ideal; see, for example, Hogan, *Marshall Plan,* 428–29, 438. For the ongoing usefulness of racism, sexism, and nationalism to the "universalizing" work of capitalism, see Etienne Balibar and Immanuel Wallerstein, *Race, Nation, Class: Ambiguous Identities* (London, 1991), especially Wallerstein's essay, "The Ideological Tensions of Capitalism: Universalism versus Racism and Sexism," 29–36.

56. Budget data for *Saving Private Ryan* from the Internet Movie Database (http://us.imdb.com). The film cost $70 million.

57. See, for example, the sexually suggestive headline over the "jump" of the second story in the series: "How U.S. Wooed an Already Yielding Asia to Let Cash Flow In," *New York Times,* 16 February 1999, A10.

58. Nicholas D. Kristof and David E. Sanger, "How U.S. Wooed Asia to Let Cash Flow In," *New York Times,* 16 February 1999, A1, A10–11.

59. Ibid., A10; Nicholas D. Kristof and Edward Wyatt, "Who Went Under in the World's Sea of Cash," *New York Times,* 15 February 1999, A1, A10–11.

60. Nicholas D. Kristof, "World Ills Are Obvious, the Cures Much Less So," *New York Times,* 18 February 1999, A1, A10–11.

61. See, for example, the review of Soros's book by Robert M. Solow, "The Amateur," *The New Republic,* 8 February 1999, 28–31.

62. For the claim that the global crisis has passed, see David E. Sanger and Mark Landler, "Asian Rebound Derails Reform as Many Suffer," *New York Times,* 12 July 1999, A1. For a description of how globalization has widened further the gap between the world's richest and poorest nations, see Judith Miller, "Globalization Widens Rich-Poor Gap, U.N. Report Says," *New York Times,* 13 July 1999, A8. For a somewhat tongue-in-cheek description of the indicators of economic slump, see Jennifer Cohen, "How to Tell the End Is Near," *New York Times Sunday Magazine,* 25 July 1999, 17. While the article's intent is humorous, it begins with the claim that "most economists say that a recession will eventually hit, but few agree about when or even how to figure it out."

63. Charles L. Mee Jr., *The Marshall Plan: The Launching of the Pax Americana* (New York, 1984). Both George Soros and Lawrence H. Summers, Secretary of the U.S. Department Treasury, recently have singled out the Marshall Plan for special attention. See Soros, *Crisis of Global Capitalism,* 218, and Lawrence H. Summers, "Distinguished Lecture on Economics in Government: Reflections on Managing Global Integration," *Journal of Economic Perspectives* 13, no. 2 (Spring 1999): 17.

64. Summers, "Distinguished Lecture," 17.

65. Jacob Weisberg's *New York Times Sunday Magazine* article notes that "even in its first days, the conflict [in Kosovo] presented itself as a miniaturized and modernized version of what we've seen on the screen [in *Saving Private Ryan*]. Early reports were peppered with distinctly Spielbergian plot lines and references. . . . But the most significant connection may be the way World War II creates a rationale for involvement in Kosovo. Many people, both inside and outside the Clinton Administration, have drawn the parallel: once again we're fighting alongside our allies to stop an expansionist power and forestall the mass murder of an ethnic minority. In the analogy, Milosevic is a low-rent Hitler; his ethnic cleansing, a B-movie Holocaust"; Weisberg, "Bombs and Blockbusters," 17-18.

66. See Katharine Q. Seelye, "World Leaders Join in a Drive to Aid Balkans," *New York Times*, 31 July 1999, A3. That the Balkan aid plan revisits Cold War strategies of capital development and political containment becomes even more clear in the description of what has been proposed for Serbia under Slobodan Milosevic: "The United States pledged $10 million to 'promote democracy' in Serbia. The money will go to the democratic opposition to Milosevic and to encircle Serbia with a ring of transmitters for the Voice of America and Radio Free Europe to counter Milosevic's state-run propaganda machine" (A3). The notion that the Balkans needed a Marshall Plan first was articulated clearly in a 21 April 1999 *New York Times* article, "Allies Seek a Way to Promote Prosperity in Restive Balkans," also by Katharine Q. Seelye (this article also links the "new" Marshall Plan, by way of a "floater" headline, to "The Reconstruction"). In that article, Clinton remarks that, "We should try to do for Southeastern Europe what we helped to do for Western Europe after World War II." Seelye continues, "Clinton has been careful to avoid describing the rebuilding as a modern-day Marshall Plan. . . . but officials said that the Clinton administration and the European Union are nonetheless striving for a thematic vision comparable to that of the Marshall Plan to signal the west's intentions of bringing long-term stability to the region" (A12). Nothing in my extremely brief discussion of the war in Kosovo should be construed as a defense, in any form, of Milosevic's regime; I simply mean to point out the reluctance of the mass media to treat events in the Balkans as anything more than World War II, the Sequel.

67. Thomas L. Friedman, "A Manifesto for the Fast World," *New York Times Sunday Magazine*, 28 March 1999. 96. The article is adapted from Thomas L. Friedman, *The Lexus and the Olive Tree* (New York, 1999).

68. Rogin, *Independence Day*, 40.

Saving Private Property: Steven Spielberg's American DreamWorks 105

Culture, Power, and *Mission to Moscow:* Film and Soviet-American Relations during World War II

Todd Bennett

For suggestions on how to use this article in the United States history survey course, see our "Teaching the *JAH*" Web site supplement at <http://www.indiana.edu/~jah/teaching>.

Following a sumptuous feast (and copious amounts of vodka), the guests, gathered around a banquet table deep within the Kremlin's walls in May 1943, toasted Soviet-American friendship. Premier Joseph V. Stalin and Foreign Minister Vyacheslav M. Molotov praised the Grand Alliance. Anastas I. Mikoyan, the Soviet commissar for foreign trade, Lavrenty P. Beria, the head of the People's Commissariat of Internal Affairs (Narodnyi Kommissariat Vnutrennykh Del, NKVD), and Maxim Litvinov, the Soviet ambassador to the United States, offered toasts, and the Anglo-Americans present—including the British ambassador to Moscow, Adm. William H. Standley, the reigning United States representative, and Joseph E. Davies, Washington's former ambassador—reciprocated. The American emissary from 1936 to 1938, Davies was there because President Franklin D. Roosevelt had sent him to arrange an introductory summit with Stalin, a meeting at which Roosevelt was sure all outstanding Soviet-American differences could be ironed out. Although Davies' presence was unusual, thus far the evening had been little different from similar receptions held by Soviet leaders for their Allied comrades during World War II. On this occasion, however, the former ambassador had brought with him a movie that both he and Roosevelt hoped would convince the Soviet dictator to eschew separate peace negotiations with Adolf Hitler and to remain within the tenuous Big Three

Todd Bennett is visiting assistant professor of history at the University of Nevada, Reno. Along with William W. Stueck Jr. and John E. Moser, thanks go to Walter L. Hixson and the other *Journal of American History* referees, who chose to remain anonymous, for reading earlier drafts and offering invaluable criticism. The Franklin and Eleanor Roosevelt Institute and the University of Georgia's Department of History and Center for Humanities and Arts provided generous financial support. The author also acknowledges the Franklin D. Roosevelt Library's staff, Madeline F. Matz of the Library of Congress, Barbara Hall of the Academy of Motion Picture Arts and Sciences, Noelle R. Carter of the Warner Bros. Archives, Richard Wiggers, and Galina Al'bertovna Kuznetsova of the State Archive of the Russian Federation for their help in facilitating research.
 Readers may contact Bennett at <mbenn@arches.uga.edu>.

partnership. After the toasts were complete, Stalin, a great enthusiast for Hollywood film, asked his guests to repair to his private Kremlin theater where they were to watch *Mission to Moscow,* an American-made pro-Soviet picture based upon Davies' diplomatic career. As the lights dimmed and the projector rolled, all waited for the marshal's reaction.[1]

Among the most infamous movies in American history, *Mission to Moscow* has drawn attention—and fire—from contemporaries and scholars alike. Since its release critics, investigators for the House Committee on Un-American Activities, and some scholars have charged that Communist Party of the United States (CPUSA) members, abetted by the sympathetic Roosevelt administration, infiltrated the project, producing a piece of Communist propaganda. With more detachment, other historians have detailed the picture's production history, arguing that it was a well-intentioned, if overzealous and unsuccessful, attempt by FDR, Davies, Warner Bros. Studios, and the official United States wartime propaganda agency, the Office of War Information (OWI), to counter Americans' distrust of their socialist and allegedly totalitarian Soviet ally.[2]

Mission to Moscow, as its Kremlin exhibition suggests, was of more than domestic consequence. It was an integral, but until now overlooked, cinematic component of Roosevelt's Soviet diplomacy. That so-called grand design aimed to hasten victory and to construct a stable peace by wooing Stalin and the Soviet Union. To support that strategy, the White House pursued such measures as *Mission to Moscow,* designed to build a popular consensus for a pro-Soviet foreign policy by impressing upon Americans the view that the Soviet Union was a normal and dependable state. Abroad, FDR took the unprecedented step of integrating the docudrama into the fabric of diplomatic negotiation, where it was one of several means used to convince Stalin that the United States wanted to cooperate in war and in peace. By helping affirm the Soviet premier's conviction that a continued, if temporary and conditional, Big Three entente offered the best means for achieving Moscow's immediate interests, the film helped solidify the Grand Alliance at a particularly tenuous moment. To prepare the Soviet public for that continued tack, Stalin himself authorized the theatrical distribution of *Mission to Moscow,* one of the first American

[1] William H. Standley to Secretary of State, telegram, May 25, 1943, Russia: July 1942–1943 Folder, box 49, President's Secretary's File, Franklin D. Roosevelt Papers (Franklin D. Roosevelt Library, Hyde Park, N.Y.); *Mission to Moscow,* dir. Michael Curtiz (Warner Bros., 1943).

[2] U.S. Congress, House, Committee on Un-American Activities, *Hearings regarding the Communist Infiltration of the Motion Picture Industry,* 80 Cong., 1 sess., Oct. 20, 1947, pp. 9–11, 32–39; Kenneth Lloyd Billingsley, *Hollywood Party: How Communism Seduced the American Film Industry in the 1930s and 1940s* (Rocklin, 1998), 90; John Earl Haynes and Harvey Klehr, *Venona: Decoding Soviet Espionage in America* (New Haven, 1999), 196–201. For a directly contrary view, see Larry Ceplair and Steven Englund, *The Inquisition in Hollywood: Politics in the Film Community, 1930–1960* (Garden City, 1980), 186, 198. David Culbert, "Our Awkward Ally: *Mission to Moscow* (1943)," in *American History/American Film: Interpreting the Hollywood Image,* ed. John E. O'Connor and Martin A. Jackson (New York, 1979), 122–45; David Culbert, "Introduction: The Feature Film as Official Propaganda," in *Mission to Moscow,* ed. David Culbert (Madison, 1980), 11–41; Clayton R. Koppes and Gregory D. Black, *Hollywood Goes to War: How Politics, Profits, and Propaganda Shaped World War II Movies* (New York, 1987), 189–209; Bernard F. Dick, *The Star-Spangled Screen: The American World War II Film* (Lexington, Ky., 1987), 158–59; Thomas Doherty, *Projections of War: Hollywood, American Culture, and World War II* (New York, 1993), 144.

movies seen by popular Soviet viewers in well over a decade. Since it also contained imagery favorable to the United States and capitalism and lay at the cutting edge of an Allied cultural penetration of the Soviet Union, the movie provided the United States a rare voice with which to speak to Soviet audiences. In light of that fact, neither the film nor Roosevelt's approach was as "naïve" as critics have claimed.[3]

A broader view of *Mission to Moscow*'s diplomatic history makes it apparent that it—certainly more than any other American film and perhaps more than any other American cultural artifact figuring in a diplomatic context—illuminates the elusive linkages between culture and power. To connect the two in the framework of international relations, some recent scholars have deconstructed such texts as diplomatic reportage, showing how concepts of gender and race shaped policy formulation.[4] Others have traced the impact of domestic culture on foreign policy or the interaction of divergent cultural systems on a global stage. Still others have focused on cultural transmission, demonstrating that United States policy makers often attempted to promote national interests by exporting American ideas, media, and commodities. By adopting such approaches and, especially, by using empirical evidence, scholars draw convincing associations between culture and power.[5]

Based upon multiarchival research, this study of *Mission to Moscow* touches upon broad issues by exploring the construction of domestic support for foreign

[3] Frederick W. Marks III, *Wind over Sand: The Diplomacy of Franklin Roosevelt* (Athens, Ga., 1988), 169; Amos Perlmutter, *FDR and Stalin: A Not So Grand Alliance, 1943–1945* (Columbia, Mo., 1993), 215, 217. Franklin D. Roosevelt's defenders include Robert Dallek, *Franklin D. Roosevelt and American Foreign Policy, 1932–1945* (New York, 1995), 533–34; John Lewis Gaddis, *Strategies of Containment: A Critical Appraisal of Postwar American National Security Policy* (New York, 1982), 3–16; and Warren F. Kimball, *The Juggler: Franklin Roosevelt as Wartime Statesman* (Princeton, 1991), 8, 14, 185, 198–200.

[4] Frank Costigliola, "'Unceasing Pressure for Penetration': Gender, Pathology, and Emotion in George Kennan's Formation of the Cold War," *Journal of American History*, 83 (March 1997), 1309–39; Frank Costigliola, "The Nuclear Family: Tropes of Gender and Pathology in the Western Alliance," *Diplomatic History*, 21 (Spring 1997), 163–83; Joan Wallach Scott, *Gender and the Politics of History* (New York, 1988), 42–49. On the emerging cultural turn in the history of international relations, see Michael H. Hunt, "The Long Crisis in U.S. Diplomatic History: Coming to Closure," *Diplomatic History*, 16 (Winter 1992), 126–27. I employ "culture" to denote a widely shared collection of beliefs, customs, and artifacts, along with the means, including the mass media, by which they are organized, contested, and transmitted. See Akira Iriye, "Culture," *Journal of American History*, 77 (June 1990), 100; and Chandra Mukerji and Michael Schudson, "Introduction," in *Rethinking Popular Culture: Contemporary Perspectives in Cultural Studies*, ed. Chandra Mukerji and Michael Schudson (Berkeley, 1991), 3. Here "power" means a nation's ability to get other nations or peoples to do or want what it wants. Joseph S. Nye Jr., *Bound to Lead: The Changing Nature of American Power* (New York, 1990), 31.

[5] Akira Iriye, "Culture and Power: International Relations as Intercultural Relations," *Diplomatic History*, 3 (Spring 1979), 115–28; Michael H. Hunt, *Ideology and U.S. Foreign Policy* (New Haven, 1987); Akira Iriye, "Culture and International History," in *Explaining the History of American Foreign Relations*, ed. Michael J. Hogan and Thomas G. Paterson (Cambridge, Eng., 1991), 221–22; Frank Costigliola, *Awkward Dominion: American Political, Economic, and Cultural Relations with Europe, 1919–1933* (Ithaca, 1984); Frank A. Ninkovich, *The Diplomacy of Ideas: U.S. Foreign Policy and Cultural Relations, 1938–1950* (Cambridge, Eng., 1981); Emily S. Rosenberg, *Spreading the American Dream: American Economic and Cultural Expansion, 1890–1945* (New York, 1982); Emily S. Rosenberg, "Cultural Interactions," in *Encyclopedia of the United States in the Twentieth Century*, ed. Stanley I. Kutler (4 vols., New York, 1996), II, 695–716; Walter L. Hixson, *Parting the Curtain: Propaganda, Culture, and the Cold War, 1945–1961* (New York, 1997); Richard H. Pells, *Not like Us: How Europeans Have Loved, Hated, and Transformed American Culture since World War II* (New York, 1997). Such approaches have been criticized for failing to establish convincing associations between national interests and culture using empirical evidence. See Robert Buzzanco, "Where's the Beef? Culture without Power in the Study of U.S. Foreign Relations," *Diplomatic History*, 24 (Fall 2000), 623–32.

policy, exemplifying the transmission and reception of ideals across national boundaries, and expanding our understanding of the possible geopolitical applications of culture. As the uses made of the film indicate, culture and statecraft were connected at intra- and extrasystemic (that is, domestic and international) levels. On the home front, the White House, the OWI, and Davies all exerted influence on the movie during its production, shaping it to persuade American viewers and to create a stable popular consensus for foreign policies that, statesmen believed, would enhance American security and strength. Although the filmmakers Harry M. Warner and Jack L. Warner were Roosevelt supporters and committed New Deal liberals, they were businessmen reluctant to sacrifice entertainment for a political message that was assumed to be anathema at the box office. It was only through a corporatist bargain that industrialists lent their cooperation in exchange for domestic and international financial considerations. Corporatism, as Michael J. Hogan and other historians have argued, involved the cooperation of elites from the public and private spheres to ensure political stability and economic profitability. Taking place at such nodes of contact as regulatory bodies and trade associations, that collaboration often manifested itself in joint campaigns to expand overseas markets. Like other Hollywood movies, *Mission to Moscow* was a commodity traded in the international marketplace. As such, the film promoted domestic prosperity by generating favorable trade balances and by acting as a salesman for other national products depicted on screen. Although it generated only token distribution proceeds in the Soviet Union, the movie helped open the potentially lucrative Soviet market to other Hollywood products. Once circulating as a form of international currency, culture—cinematic and otherwise—also sold nations and their ways of life. As they did with *Mission to Moscow*, filmmakers exported idealized versions of American life, thereby attempting to sway foreign audiences through the "soft power" of attraction.[6]

While Roosevelt's and Davies' original intentions were to entice Stalin through expressions of collaboration with, and enthusiasm for, the Soviet experiment, the intended messages were not always those received. The multiple, often contradictory, and occasionally counterproductive meanings derived from *Mission to Moscow* both at home and abroad demonstrated policy makers' inability to control film as an instrument of diplomacy. Once the American product was released in the Soviet Union, its rationalizations for the Great Terror and the Nazi-Soviet Pact reinforced the Stalinist regime's domestic ideological strength. Conversely, in *Mission to Moscow* and other American movies subsequently circulated, popular Soviet viewers gleaned

[6] For a discussion of the internal and external connections between culture and foreign policy, see Leslie A. White, *The Concept of Cultural Systems: A Key to Understanding Tribes and Nations* (New York, 1975), 20–21. On corporatism and corporatist cooperation between Washington and Hollywood, see Michael J. Hogan, "Corporatism," in *Explaining the History of American Foreign Relations*, ed. Hogan and Paterson, 227, 230; Ian Jarvie, *Hollywood's Overseas Campaign: The North Atlantic Movie Trade, 1920–1950* (Cambridge, Eng., 1992), 16–17, 319–20, 324, 326, 354; Rosenberg, *Spreading the American Dream*, 7–8, 202–6, 230; and Rosenberg, "Cultural Interactions," 695. Nye, *Bound to Lead*, 31–32, 267n11; Joseph S. Nye Jr. and William A. Owens, "America's Information Edge," *Foreign Affairs*, 75 (March/April 1996), 20–23.

visual confirmation of the superior standard of living enjoyed by Americans, information that—both United States and Soviet policy makers believed—undermined confidence in the leadership of the Communist Party of the Soviet Union (CPSU).[7] In the United States the movie was unpopular despite officials' hopes. It failed to inspire pro-Soviet thinking and, worse, stirred a minor backlash. In those divergent settings, *Mission to Moscow* became an object for contestation between Washington and American moviegoers and filmmakers, between supporters and opponents of Roosevelt's foreign policies, and between America and the Kremlin for Soviet citizens' hearts and minds.

In the United States, the White House struggled against a rich tradition of anti-communist and anti-Soviet attitudes to craft a popular consensus for its pro-Soviet foreign policies. Following Japan's attack on Pearl Harbor in December 1941, Americans found themselves allied with the Soviet Union, a nation they held in extraordinarily low regard. Most criticized the Soviet Union's socialist system and alleged that its government was totalitarian. Earlier, those charges had gained greater credence when news of the purges and of the Nazi-Soviet Pact of August 1939 reached American shores. Stalin's terror led some, including the liberal philosopher John Dewey, to compare his internal repression to that practiced by Hitler. The mutual nonaggression treaty, according to *Collier's* magazine and others, removed "all doubt, except in the minds of incurable dreamers, that there is any real difference between Communism and Fascism." Many argued that the two totalitarian states subordinated the individual to the mass, used dictatorial methods or violence to stifle personal liberty and democracy at home, and were inherently expansionistic. Although the Soviets' stubborn resistance to the German invasion after the breakup of the totalitarian coalition in June 1941 and their co-belligerency with the United States six months later purified them in the minds of many, Americans were still suspicious. In June 1942 a poll conducted by the Office of Public Opinion Research, a private organization headquartered at Princeton University, indicated that only 41 percent of respondents professed faith that the Soviets could be trusted to cooperate with the United States once victory was achieved. Although by August 1942 that figure would reach 51 percent (a high-water mark until the war's final year), it paled in comparison to the percentage who believed in the good

[7] On responses to American culture in the Eastern bloc and elsewhere, see Rob Kroes, Robert W. Rydell, and Doeko F. J. Bosscher, eds., *Cultural Transmissions and Receptions: American Mass Culture in Europe* (Amsterdam, 1993), ix, 302–3, 305; Richard F. Kuisel, *Seducing the French: The Dilemma of Americanization* (Berkeley, 1993), 3; Pells, *Not like Us*, xiv–xv; Reinhold Wagnleitner, *Coca-Colonization and the Cold War: The Cultural Mission of the United States in Austria after the Second World War*, trans. Diana M. Wolf (Chapel Hill, 1994), xi–xiii; Daniel Deudney and G. John Ikenberry, "Who Won the Cold War?," *Foreign Policy*, 87 (Summer 1992), 133–36; Gale Stokes, *The Walls Came Tumbling Down: The Collapse of Communism in Eastern Europe* (New York, 1993), 24–25; Frank Costigliola, "'Mixed Up' and 'Contact': Culture and Emotion among the Allies in the Second World War," *International History Review*, 20 (Dec. 1998), 792, 794–95; and Hixson, *Parting the Curtain*, xii, 51, 165–67, 228. For a literature review, see Jessica C. E. Gienow-Hecht, "Shame on US? Academics, Cultural Transfer, and the Cold War—A Critical Review," *Diplomatic History*, 24 (Summer 2000), 465–94.

faith of the nation's two other major allies—Britain (72 percent) and China (88 percent).[8]

In late spring 1942 such data concerned Roosevelt. The president, who paid careful attention to opinion polls, was fresh from a meeting with Molotov during which he had promised the opening of a second front that year. The chief executive suspected, however, that an invasion might not be possible in 1942, and he consequently feared that the Soviets either would not survive or would again make a separate pact with Berlin, enabling Hitler to turn his full might westward. Because FDR regarded the Soviet Union's survival and continued participation in the Grand Alliance as crucial ingredients for victory, he reasoned that the United States might have to take measures—perhaps increased Lend-Lease aid or even recognition of expanded Soviet postwar borders—to retain Soviet amity. But Congress, where anticommunist sentiment was acute, held Lend-Lease's purse strings. If FDR were to accede to Moscow's territorial demands, he believed, a public backlash would surely ensue, especially among Polish Americans, Catholics, conservatives, and American nationalists. Since in 1942 the maintenance of domestic unity, which he considered indispensable for an effective prosecution of the war, was among his priorities, Roosevelt was eager to improve public views of the Soviet Union.[9]

In mid-1942 Davies presented him with a proposal for doing so. The two had known each other since World War I, when Davies, a Wisconsin native, Democratic activist, and millionaire, had met and befriended Roosevelt, then serving as assistant secretary of the navy. Davies managed part of FDR's 1932 campaign and contributed heavily to his reelection effort, and in late 1936 the president rewarded him by appointing him ambassador to the Soviet Union. Although Roosevelt hoped that Davies' pro-Soviet attitudes would help reenergize bilateral relations, during his service in Moscow (from early 1937 to mid-1938), Davies failed to improve ties. He did succeed in forging a rapport with many of his Soviet counterparts, however, and his diplomatic experiences formed the basis of a book, *Mission to Moscow.* With FDR's blessing, Davies wrote it to "get better public acceptance for aid to Russia which was vital to the Christian front, and to the Boss [Roosevelt] in his magnificent crusade." Despite its pro-Soviet leanings, the book, which appeared just weeks after the attack on Pearl Harbor, was a huge success. It quickly sold over seven hundred thousand copies in hardcover and paperback editions and was serialized in the *New York Times Magazine.* Either Davies or Jack and Harry Warner, co-presidents of Warner Bros. Studios, came up with the idea of turning the bestseller into a com-

[8] "Imperialism 1939 Model," *Collier's,* Oct. 28, 1939, p. 74; Hadley Cantril, ed., *Public Opinion, 1935–1946* (Princeton, 1951), 370. On the intellectual currency of "totalitarianism," see Les K. Adler and Thomas G. Paterson, "Red Fascism: The Merger of Nazi Germany and Soviet Russia in the American Image of Totalitarianism, 1930s–1950s," *American Historical Review,* 75 (April 1970), 1050; and Abbot Gleason, *Totalitarianism: The Inner History of the Cold War* (New York, 1995), 31–32, 43–44, 47–50.

[9] Dallek, *Franklin D. Roosevelt and American Foreign Policy,* 337–44, 350–51, 360; Edward M. Bennett, *Franklin D. Roosevelt and the Search for Victory: American-Soviet Relations, 1939–1945* (Wilmington, 1990), 55; John Lewis Gaddis, *Russia, the Soviet Union, and the United States: An Interpretive History* (New York, 1990), 150. On Franklin D. Roosevelt's earlier identification of the Soviet Union as a key to victory, see Waldo Heinrichs, *Threshold of War: Franklin D. Roosevelt and American Entry into World War II* (New York, 1989), 105, 141, 145.

mercial movie. Before proceeding, however, the newly successful author solicited and obtained Roosevelt's approval. Thereafter, through regular White House meetings with Davies in July, October, and November 1942, the president kept abreast of the film's progress. As it neared completion in early March 1943, Davies again went to the Oval Office, where he found Roosevelt "very much interested in hearing about the picture."[10]

Production began in early July 1942 after Warner Bros. had contracted with Davies, who retained the right to approve the screenplay and final print. The former ambassador was clear about the messages "his" film should convey. To Stephen Early, FDR's press secretary, he wrote, "it is vital we should understand" the Soviets and "have confidence in the integrity and honesty of . . . their desire to preserve future peace." Moreover, ever since his days in Moscow, Davies had voiced a belief that Stalinist Russia was undergoing a thermidorian reaction. Incentives given to unusually productive individual workers, cultural conservatism, the purge of Old Bolsheviks, and, later, collaboration with fascist Germany misled him into thinking that the Soviet Union was gradually jettisoning its Bolshevist ideals, embracing authoritarian capitalism, and becoming more like the United States. In 1937, Davies wrote, "theoretical communists, when clothed with responsibility," had been "compelled to resort to the elementals of human nature." To the wealthy capitalist, those "elementals of human nature" included self-interest and a desire for material comfort.[11]

During production Davies regularly invoked his contractual rights and the president's name, under whose authority filmmakers assumed he marched. Upon reading an early version of the script in September 1942, he promptly sent twenty-four single-spaced pages of comments to the startled producer and director, Robert Buckner and Michael Curtiz. Traveling to the Los Angeles area, Davies and his wife were on the set almost daily, from November 1942 through mid-January 1943, making suggestions to filmmakers and reporting to the White House. As a result, Davies had a direct hand in shaping the movie's prologue and its depictions of the purges, the Nazi-Soviet Pact, and Moscow's invasion of Finland.[12]

But Davies' and Roosevelt's were not the only hands shaping *Mission to Moscow*. Known as the "Roosevelt studio" and led by friends of the president and committed reformers, Warner Bros. had championed on screen both FDR's New Deal and his increasingly pro-Allied and interventionist foreign policies before Pearl Harbor. In part, genuine patriotism, as Jack Warner claimed, motivated the executives. But

[10] Joseph E. Davies to Lowell Mellett, Dec. 31, 1941, Davies File, box 11, Lowell Mellett Papers (Roosevelt Library). See Elizabeth Kimball MacLean, "Joseph E. Davies and Soviet-American Relations, 1941–43," *Diplomatic History,* 4 (Winter 1980), 73–75. Davies to Jack L. Warner, March 4, 1943, Scrapbook File, *Mission to Moscow* Collection (Warner Bros. Archives, School of Cinema-Television, University of Southern California, Los Angeles, Calif.); [Marvin McIntyre], memo, July 23, 1942, President's Personal File 1381, Roosevelt Papers; Culbert, "Introduction," 13, 16–17, 25.

[11] Davies to Stephen T. Early, Jan. 6, 1943, Davies File, box 3, Stephen T. Early Papers (Roosevelt Library); Eduard Mark, "October or Thermidor? Interpretations of Stalinism and the Perception of Soviet Foreign Policy in the United States, 1927–1947," *American Historical Review,* 94 (Oct. 1989), 938–41, 946–47.

[12] Joseph Davies Diary, Nov. 23, 1942, in *Mission to Moscow,* ed. Culbert, 251.

because, like other industrialists, he and his brother were in the movie business to make money and not to educate, they needed financial inducements to make diplomatically charged films. A large portion of that incentive arrived just before American intervention when the White House, at the Warners' urging, protected the industry from domestic antitrust litigation, insuring Hollywood's domestic profitability and making executives more amenable to the administration's publicity needs. In July 1939, at the request of small producers and independent theater owners, the Justice Department had charged the major studios—which dominated production, distribution, and exhibition—with violating the Sherman Antitrust Act. The Justice Department's suit portended financial ruin by threatening to force the studios to divest themselves of their distribution and exhibition arms. The Warners, along with Will H. Hays, president of Hollywood's trade association, the Motion Picture Producers and Distributors Association (MPPDA), beseeched the president and his confidant, Secretary of Commerce Harry L. Hopkins, for relief. By mid-1940 Hopkins intervened and persuaded the Justice Department to issue a consent decree permitting the industry to remain intact while discontinuing some of its unfair trading practices. In exchange for the White House's help, the trade periodical *Variety* reported, Hollywood pledged to lend cinematic support to the administration's domestic and foreign policies. Soon afterward, Lowell Mellett, the head of an official information agency created by Roosevelt in 1939 (the Office of Government Reports) and the administration's main contact with Hollywood, lent greater credence to such assumptions when he informed the president that an "effective plan" for securing filmmakers' cooperation was "being developed." Roosevelt sent a note, which was read during the 1941 Academy Awards ceremony, thanking the industry for its help. To FDR, Mellett privately added, "the motion picture industry is pretty well living up to its offers of cooperation. Practically everything being shown on the screen . . . that touches on our national purpose is of the right sort." Just one month after acquiring the rights to *Mission to Moscow,* a film designed to satisfy their internationalist patron in the White House, the Warners offered their "services and experience in the motion picture field" to the administration.[13]

The United States intervention in World War II helped coalesce Hollywood's client-patron relationship with Washington, forming a corporatist arrangement with international overtones that had a direct bearing on *Mission to Moscow.* Because the demands of total war required a concerted propaganda effort, in June 1942 the president consolidated several poorly coordinated information agencies into a newly created Office of War Information (OWI). Charged with explaining the United States

[13] Mellett for Roosevelt, memo, Dec. 23, 1940, White House—1940 File, box 5, Mellett Papers; Richard W. Steele, *Propaganda in an Open Society: The Roosevelt Administration and the Media, 1933–1941* (Westport, 1985), 155–58, 160–62. On the relationship of Harry M. Warner and Jack L. Warner with the Roosevelt administration, see Harry M. Warner to Roosevelt, Sept. 5, 1939, Official File 73, box 4, Roosevelt Papers; Nicholas John Cull, *Selling War: The British Propaganda Campaign against American "Neutrality" in World War II* (New York, 1995), 51–52, 108, 112–13, 137; and Nick Roddick, *A New Deal in Entertainment: Warner Brothers in the 1930s* (London, 1983), 65. Mellett for Roosevelt, draft memo, [1941], White House—1941 File, box 5, Mellett Papers. On the Warners' offer, see Marvin McIntyre for Roosevelt, memo, Aug. 14, 1942, Official File 73, box 5, Roosevelt Papers.

war effort to audiences at home and abroad, the bureau worked with the mass media to publicize official information themes. Initially, the OWI's Domestic Operations Branch, Bureau of Motion Pictures (domestic BMP), enjoyed little success because it had authority only to "advise" Hollywood regarding official propaganda themes and had virtually no power over filmmakers, who were reluctant to spice entertainment with political messages that turned customers away. By late 1942–early 1943, however, official propagandists had gained the leverage necessary to shape Hollywood's production. Mellett had created a Los Angeles branch of the OWI's Overseas Operations Branch, Bureau of Motion Pictures, led by Ulric Bell, the former head of the interventionist pressure group Fight for Freedom. Under Roosevelt's executive order permitting the OWI to conduct foreign information programs, Bell's bureau, in conjunction with the Office of Censorship, had authority to determine which commercial films received export licenses. Since the industry reportedly realized up to half its gross revenues overseas, the OWI's promotion (or lack thereof) of Hollywood's foreign markets, which grew as Allied forces liberated areas from Axis control, enabled it to inject movies with propaganda themes while avoiding charges of domestic censorship.[14]

Official publicists used their growing strength to craft Hollywood's presentation of the allies of the United States. Along with its better-known campaigns to fire domestic support for the nation's war effort, rationing, and home front unity, the OWI articulated a "united nations" theme, which strove to overcome inter-Allied differences about ideology, former international policies, and future geopolitical objectives. This was particularly important when the Grand Alliance first coalesced and German propaganda portrayed it as hopelessly fractured due to the inclusion of the Soviet Union. The campaign claimed that the United States could not win the war alone. It required the assistance of its allies, including most prominently Great Britain and the Soviet Union, which, although diverse, were all fighting for freedom from the Axis, whose eventual defeat would produce a better and more democratic future. In June 1942 a government information manual distributed to all Hollywood studios insisted, "we must understand and know more about our Allies" by counteracting "unity-destroying lies about England and Russia."[15]

Because both FDR and other United States opinion makers portrayed the war as a movement for the global extension of freedom, democracy, and regulated capitalism, the Soviet Union presented a particular problem. Performing intellectual gymnastics, publicists responded by generally avoiding the sensitive issues of socialism and Stalin, rationalizing past Soviet behavior, suggesting the Soviet Union was evolving into a less revolutionary state, and focusing on the heroic wartime efforts of the Russian people. Nelson Poynter, the chief of the domestic BMP, cautioned

[14] Koppes and Black, *Hollywood Goes to War,* 56–60, 80–81, 105, 108–9, 112. For a discussion of the administration's intercession on the industry's behalf in the United Kingdom, see Jarvie, *Hollywood's Overseas Campaign,* 351–60, 368–72.
[15] *Government Information Manual for the Motion Picture Industry,* June 8, 1942, Manual Material— Hollywood Office File, box 1438, Records of Mellett, Bureau of Motion Pictures, Domestic Operations Branch, Records of the Office of War Information, RG 208 (National Archives, College Park, Md.).

filmmakers that although "we Americans reject Communism . . . *we do not reject our Russian Ally.*" There was a sense among movie executives that the American public would in fact reject productions about their Soviet ally. Just before work began on *Mission to Moscow,* the first pro-Soviet feature film of the war years, the dearth of such movies led Poynter to implore studios to "give us a *Mrs. Miniver* [a well-received 1942 pro-British production] of China or Russia, making clear our common interest with the Russians or Chinese in this struggle."[16]

By reviewing scripts and prints, owi propagandists exercised authority over *Mission to Moscow,* insuring that it promoted the "united nations" theme. Poynter praised the film for emphasizing the Soviet Union's supposed interwar support for collective security and for demonstrating that "Russians are an honest people trying to do an honest job with about the same total objectives as the people of the United States." Poynter met with Davies to remind him and Warner Bros. executives of opinion surveys showing that many Americans feared Moscow would either sign a separate peace with Berlin or fail to adhere to its postwar treaty obligations. To counter such pessimism, he advised the project's principals to offer explanations for the Nazi-Soviet Pact and the Red Army's invasion of Finland.[17]

After reading the final script, in November 1942 the owi expressed its hope that *Mission to Moscow* would "make one of the most remarkable pictures of this war" and "a very great contribution to the war information program." It would "be a most convincing means of helping Americans to understand their Russian allies. Because it is a true story told by a man who cannot possibly be accused of Communistic leanings, it will be doubly reassuring to Americans." Along with emphasizing Soviet support for collective security, the story

> *presents the Russian people most sympathetically.* Every effort has been made to show that Russians and Americans are not so very different after all. The Russians are shown to eat well and live comfortably—which will be a surprise to many Americans. The leaders of both countries desire peace and both possess a blunt honesty of address and purpose. Both peoples have great respect for education and achievement.
>
> One of the best services performed by this picture is the presentation of Russian leaders, not as wild-eyed madmen, but as far-seeing, earnest, responsible statesmen. It is pointed out that essentially it is none of our business how they keep house—what we want to know is what kind of neighbors they will make in case of fire. They have proved very good neighbors, and this picture will help to explain why, as well as to encourage faith in the feasibility of post-war cooperation.[18]

Government information specialists were equally enthusiastic about the com-

[16] *Ibid.*; "Worksheet," [1942], Propaganda File, box 213, Harry L. Hopkins Papers (Roosevelt Library); *Mrs. Miniver,* dir. William Wyler (MGM, 1942); *Variety,* June 17, 1942, p. 1.

[17] Nelson Poynter to Robert Buckner, memo, Dec. 3, 1942, Poynter File, box 16, Mellett Papers; "Notes re. Rushes on 'Mission to Moscow,'" Jan. 6, 1943, *Mission to Moscow* File, box 3521, Motion Picture Reviews and Analyses, Motion Picture Division, Los Angeles Office, Overseas Operations Branch, Office of War Information Records; Nelson Poynter, "Weekly Log of Activities," Dec. 26, 1942–Jan. 2, 1943, Weekly Log File, box 3510, Records of the Chief, Los Angeles Office, *ibid.*

[18] Script reviews, Nov. 28, 30, 1942, Reviews and Activities Reports File, box 1439, Mellett Records, Bureau of Motion Pictures, Domestic Operations Branch, *ibid.*

pleted print. Judging it "a magnificent contribution" to wartime propaganda, the OWI believed the picture would "do much to bring understanding of Soviet international policy in the past years and dispel the fears which many honest persons have felt with regard to our alliance with Russia." That was particularly so since "the possibility for the friendly alliance of the Capitalist United States and the Socialist Russia is shown to be firmly rooted in the mutual desire for peace of the two great countries."[19]

Completed in late April 1943, the film was, in the words of Buckner, the film's producer, "an expedient lie for political purposes, glossily covering up important facts with full or partial knowledge of their false presentation." It whitewashed the purges, rationalized Moscow's participation in the Nazi-Soviet Pact and its invasion of Finland, and portrayed the Soviet Union as a nontotalitarian state that was moving toward the American model and was committed to internationalism. Following a prologue, in which the real Davies assured American audiences he was no Communist, his character (portrayed by actor Walter Huston) traveled to the Soviet Union in 1937 at Roosevelt's request. There, according to the movie, citizens were well fed and happy, the NKVD "protected" people, and a consumer economy was emerging. In one scene, which was added at the last minute at the Davies family's insistence, Mrs. Davies (played by Ann Harding) visited the "USSR Cosmetic Factory" run by Polina Molotov, the foreign minister's spouse. Commenting on the shop's attractive window display of perfumes and beauty products that resembled something one might find on Fifth Avenue in New York City, Marjorie Davies expressed surprise that such luxury goods were available in the Soviet Union. Madame Molotov, whom the New York Times found "suspiciously" aristocratic and "Elizabeth Ardenish," replied that the Soviets had "discovered that feminine beauty was not a luxury." Through such scenes, according to Life magazine, the Soviets were "made to look and act like residents of Kansas City, and the American standard of living appears to prevail throughout the Soviet Union."[20]

If Americans' perceptions of Stalinist Russia were to be altered, however, it was essential that Mission to Moscow present the purge victims as being guilty of treason. Here Joseph Davies' influence proved critical. As they had in the book Mission to Moscow, the meaning of the purges and the defendants' guilt or innocence had remained ambiguous throughout early screenplays. Insisting that the defendants' complicity be made explicit, Davies reportedly threatened to compensate the Warner brothers one million dollars for money thus far spent on the project and to leave Burbank with the negatives of the unfinished picture if filmmakers failed to do so. The Warners relented, and the final version clearly identified Nikolai Bukharin, Marshal M. Tukhachevskii, Karl Radek, and others as saboteurs and traitors who

[19] Feature review, April 28, 1943, Mission to Moscow File, box 3521, Motion Picture Reviews and Analyses, Motion Picture Division, Los Angeles Office, Overseas Operations Branch, ibid.
[20] Robert Buckner to David Culbert, Jan. 1, 14, 1978, in Mission to Moscow, ed. Culbert, 254; New York Times, May 9, 1943, sec. 2, p. 3; "'Mission to Moscow': Davies Movie Whitewashes Russia," Life, May 10, 1943, p. 39. Polina Molotov was in fact commissar of the Soviet cosmetic industry. Vladislav Zubok and Constantine Pleshakov, Inside the Kremlin's Cold War: From Stalin to Khrushchev (Cambridge, Mass., 1996), 80.

had participated in a plot, directed from abroad by Leon Trotsky in conjunction with Japan and Nazi Germany, to soften up the Soviet Union in advance of a foreign invasion that would topple the Stalinist government. Although the real Davies privately acknowledged the fatuousness of such a scenario, during the Moscow show trial scenes his character informed the audience, "Based on twenty years' trial practice, I'd be inclined to believe these confessions."[21] *Mission to Moscow* thereby tried to assure Americans that the purges, far from being Stalin's bloodthirsty assaults on innocent victims, were necessary to eliminate quasi-fascist fifth columnists.

Finally, the production justified Moscow's prewar diplomacy and aggression, presenting the Soviet Union as a bellwether of internationalism. It privileged Maxim Litvinov's prewar collective security efforts in the League of Nations. In a key scene, the cinematic Davies visited Stalin (portrayed by Manart Kippen), who expressed his desire for an antifascist alliance with the Western democracies. But the Soviet Union, he informed the ambassador in a veiled reference to the Western appeasement of Hitler at Munich in 1938, would not "be put in the position of pulling other people's chestnuts out of the fire. Either we must be able to rely on our mutual guarantees with the other democracies or . . . well, we may be forced to protect ourselves in another way." The Soviet Union, *Mission to Moscow* instructed audiences, thus had cooperated with Berlin from August 1939 to June 1941 only because it had to protect itself once it was abandoned by Britain and France. In addition, claiming that he was privy to secret information, Davies insisted filmmakers justify the Soviet Union's invasion of Finland in winter 1939–1940, an action heavily criticized in the United States. As a result, the movie ultimately suggested that Stalin had ordered the Red Army's advance only because Finland's government was collaborating with Hitler and had resisted the Soviet Union's preinvasion requests to occupy "defensive" positions on Finnish soil.[22]

Premiering in American theaters on April 30, 1943, *Mission to Moscow*, which some dubbed "Submission to Moscow," stirred a storm of criticism despite Warner's lavish half-million-dollar advertising budget. A few defended the picture. Believing that it would facilitate a military victory by solidifying the Grand Alliance, such conservative nationalist groups as local American Legion councils offered their endorsements. On the other end of the political spectrum, the CPUSA's the *Daily Worker* and Jack McManus of the left-leaning periodical *PM* praised "the first clean break with Hollywood's persistent policy of silence or deceit about the Soviet Union." While bemoaning *Mission to Moscow*'s counterproductive lack of objectivity and historical fidelity, most film critics, including Bosley Crowther of the *New*

---

[21] On Joseph E. Davies' influence and private views, see *Foreign Relations of the United States, 1943* (6 vols., Washington, 1963–1965), III, 504–5; and Culbert, "Introduction," 24.

[22] Culbert, "Introduction," 21, 23–24. The movie's explanation for the Nazi-Soviet Pact was the one voiced by Moscow and the Communist Party of the Soviet Union. Nikolai Sivachev and Nikolai N. Yakovlev, *Russia and the United States*, trans. Olga Adler Titelbaum (Chicago, 1979), 122–23. This rationale fails to note that in dealing with Berlin, the Kremlin sought territory in the Baltics and eastern Poland. Steven Merritt Miner, *Between Churchill and Stalin: The Soviet Union, Great Britain, and the Origins of the Grand Alliance* (Chapel Hill, 1988), 3–6.

York Times and Dwight Whitney of the *San Francisco Chronicle,* and some liberals conceded that its alliance-building intentions were laudable. According to the *New Yorker,*

> If the greater part of the public is startled by the information it offers and is sympathetic to its message, it is a good picture. If it attracts the notice of high social circles and in some way allays congressional anxieties about Russia as an ally, it is a good picture . . . because those congressional anxieties need allaying, and quick. There is a perilous likelihood, however, that because it is a very top-heavy flimsy affair, the film will fail to achieve the important ends it should.[23]

Other liberals and leftists were more disturbed by the movie's departures from both the historical record and Davies' own book in rationalizing the purges and Moscow's international behavior. Dwight Macdonald, editor of the *Partisan Review,* circulated a letter protesting the film that was also signed by Max Eastman, James T. Farrell, Sidney Hook, Alfred Kazin, A. Philip Randolph, and Norman Thomas. Although pleased with the picture's criticism of conservative isolationists and its portrayal of the Soviet Union's staunch fight against Nazism, the *Nation*'s James Agee claimed *Mission to Moscow* was

> A mishmash: of Stalinism with journalism with opportunism with shaky experimentalism with mesmerism with onanism, all mosaicked into a remarkable portrait of what the makers of the film think that the American public should think the Soviet Union is like—a great glad two-million-dollar bowl of canned borscht, eminently approvable by the Institute of Good Housekeeping.[24]

Manny Farber of the *New Republic* declared himself "ready to vote for the booby prize" because *Mission to Moscow* had made "up its own facts" and mindlessly praised the Soviet Union. Henry R. Luce's *Life* magazine, normally a bastion of liberal internationalism that only weeks earlier had dedicated its cover to Stalin, claimed the "U.S.S.R., its leaders and its foreign policies are whitewashed to a degree far exceeding Davies' book." Such historical inaccuracies led the liberal intellectuals Suzanne La Follette and John Dewey, both of whom had earlier participated in an independent inquiry into the Moscow trials' charges, to claim in an influential letter written to the *New York Times* that the movie was "the first instance in our country of totalitarian propaganda for mass consumption."[25]

The harshest criticisms came from an odd assortment including the non-Stalinist

[23] Eugene Lyons, "Memo on Movie Reviewers," *American Mercury,* 56 (July 1943), 81; Koppes and Black, *Hollywood Goes to War,* 207–8; David Lardner, "Repercussions Would Help," *New Yorker,* May 8, 1943, pp. 58–59; *New York Times,* May 9, 1943, sec. 2, p. 3; *San Francisco Chronicle,* June 12, 1943, Scrapbook File, *Mission to Moscow* Collection.

[24] James Agee, "Films," *Nation,* May 22, 1943, p. 749; Herman Shumlin et al. to Walter White, June 1, 1943, in *Mission to Moscow,* ed. Culbert, 257.

[25] Manny Farber, "Mishmash," *New Republic,* May 10, 1943, p. 636; "'Mission to Moscow,'" p. 39; *New York Times,* May 9, 1943, sec. 4, p. 8. For a challenge to the charges made by John Dewey and Suzanne La Follette, see *New York Times,* May 16, 1943, sec. 4, p. 12. For Dewey's critique of propaganda, see Brett Gary, "Modernity's Challenge to Democracy: The Lippmann-Dewey Debate," in *Cultural Transmissions and Receptions,* ed. Kroes, Rydell, and Bosscher, 43.

Left, Catholics, and the far Right. Calling the film "grotesque," the Marxist Eugene Lyons claimed that "Stalin-Worship" had reached new heights. Trotskyites in Los Angeles and New York held mass rallies protesting the production's claim that the exiled Bolshevik had engineered a conspiracy against the Soviet Union. Noting that the Warner Bros. movie avoided the issue of religion, Philip T. Hartung of the Catholic periodical *Commonweal* called it "obviously one-sided" and "straight propaganda." In a letter to that publication, one reader expressed a widely held view when he wrote, "of course, from a military standpoint, we are happy to have Russia as our ally. . . . but it is hardly necessary that we should also love Stalin, his judicial and political system and his international diplomacy; nor are we obliged, because of our military alliance, to encourage the spreading of communist propaganda."[26]

Similarly, such diehard anticommunists as Rep. Marion T. Bennett, a Republican from Missouri, charged that Hollywood had "lost its head and gone completely overboard in its attempt to make Communism look good. Our temporary military alliance with Russia must not make us forget that, except insofar as treatment of Jews is concerned, there is no difference between Communism and nazi-ism as it affects the common man." Such sentiments led some congressional Republicans, including Sen. Robert A. Taft, a Republican from Ohio, to call for an investigation of movie propaganda and the administration's links with Hollywood.[27]

General audiences did not care for *Mission to Moscow*, which they regarded as a boring film or an example of Communist propaganda. In January 1944 *Variety* ranked the film only eighty-fourth out of the year's top ninety-five films in box office gross. Warner Bros., which spent a slightly higher than normal $1.5 million on production, lost about $600,000 on the project. Orville F. Grahame of Worcester, Massachusetts, expressed his displeasure to the studio:

> I regret the liberties you have taken with truth in . . . *Mission to Moscow*. It is unfortunate that a film on Moscow should have to be in accord with the traditional attitude of American Communists and hew to their line. The American people admire the Russian people and their fight, and perhaps even the realism of their leaders. But we admire most our own attitudes towards life and truth.

W. F. Flowers of Encino, California, sardonically began,

> Allow me to congratulate you on a very open faced piece of communistic propaganda. I believe you have done a good job from the standpoint of propaganda work, but a work that is going to backfire . . . on Warner Bros. I am convinced that a great many people will do as my family are going to do and . . . attend theatres only where Warner Bros. films are *not* being shown.

---

[26] Eugene Lyons, "The Progress of Stalin-Worship," *American Mercury,* 56 (June 1943), 693–97; "Trotskyists Protest 'Mission to Moscow' Film," press release, [1943], Scrapbook File, *Mission to Moscow* Collection; Philip T. Hartung, "Hollywood's Mission," *Commonweal,* May 21, 1943, p. 125; Nathan D. Shapiro, "Mission to Moscow," *ibid.,* June 4, 1943, p. 168.
[27] *Congressional Record,* 78 Cong., 1 sess., May 24, 1943, p. A2570; *New York Herald Tribune,* Oct. 10, 1943, Propaganda File (microfilm: reel 8), Motion Picture Association of America General Correspondence (Margaret Herrick Library, Academy of Motion Picture Arts and Sciences, Beverly Hills, Calif.).

And with a hint of xenophobia (the Warner brothers were Jewish and Harry was born in Poland), Alice McCarthy of Jackson Heights, New York, wrote, "As a *native-born* American citizen, I am hereby submitting a violent protest against your propaganda film 'Mission to Moscow.'" She continued, "Why such films are not considered subversive is far beyond me and a sign of ill omen and, further beyond me, is why you don't go to Russia and stay there."[28]

All told, these responses and criticisms suggest that elite and popular audiences generally rejected *Mission to Moscow,* which did little to increase, and may have actually decreased, domestic support for both the Soviet Union and Roosevelt's accommodationist policy. Just weeks before the film's release, a Gallup Poll indicated that 44 percent of Americans, the lowest figure since the previous July, believed the Soviets would cooperate with the United States once the war was finished. Following the movie's premiere, that number increased only slightly to 47 percent, where it would remain until early 1945.[29] Given the generally critical reception of the film, that small improvement probably had more to do with the Red Army's integral role in defeating Nazi Germany than with *Mission to Moscow.*

Just prior to the film's unsuccessful domestic premiere, Davies took a copy to Roosevelt, which the two viewed in the White House's makeshift theater. At the time, the war, the Soviet Union, and Moscow's geopolitical intentions preoccupied the chief executive. His concerns about the Grand Alliance's cohesiveness ran much deeper than they had been the previous summer. Following the Red Army's watershed victory at Stalingrad, the Office of Strategic Services, the wartime American intelligence bureau, learned that Moscow, disenchanted with the still-absent second front and desirous of obtaining international recognition of its distended 1941 borders, was conducting secret peace talks with Berlin. This was crushing news to FDR, for a separate Soviet-German peace would enable Hitler to concentrate his remaining forces in western Europe, thereby making Anglo-American military operations and victory there much more difficult and costly. Along with the impending Anglo-American invasion of Italy, Stalingrad brought other considerations to the fore. First, with American military planners expecting the ultimate war with Japan to result in heavy United States casualties, Roosevelt desired eventual Soviet intervention in the Pacific theater. Second, it was now clear that the Red Army had the initiative on the eastern front, opening the possibility that through future offensives it would soon occupy portions of eastern Europe. While FDR was willing to concede a Soviet sphere of influence, such a development might inflame American opinion. He hoped to work with the Soviet dictator and to persuade him to take those attitudes into account by either limiting expansion or holding plebiscites, which would soothe the American electorate by giving the appearance of democracy and self-determination. Finally, although his plans for an international peace-keeping system

[28] Orville F. Grahame to Warner Brothers, May 10, 1943, Scrapbook File, *Mission to Moscow* Collection; Culbert, "Introduction," 34; W. F. Flowers to Warner Bros. Studios, May 21, 1943, Scrapbook File, *Mission to Moscow* Collection; Alice McCarthy to Warner Bros. Studios, May 18, 1943, *ibid.*
[29] George H. Gallup, *The Gallup Poll: Public Opinion, 1935–1971* (3 vols., New York, 1972), I, 382, 419, 492.

were still vague, the commander in chief believed that a stable peace was simply not possible without Soviet participation.[30]

Combined, these considerations further stimulated Roosevelt's "grand design" of accommodating Stalin, who, he reasoned, was not ideologically incapable of cooperating with the Western democracies. Because he had concluded that insecurity, rather than socialist thinking, drove the Soviets to isolate themselves and seek a territorial buffer, FDR believed that an atmosphere of trust had to be built between Stalin and Western leaders that would assure him he had nothing to fear. At their Casablanca Conference in January 1943, FDR and British prime minister Winston S. Churchill tried to allay Soviet concerns about a separate capitalist peace by announcing their commitment to an unconditional, indivisible German surrender. Reflecting the administration's renewed drive for cooperation with Moscow, in spring 1943 the OWI numbered among its major foreign propaganda goals preventing "the allies [from] making a separate peace," diminishing inter-Allied "frictions" that could "impede the successful co-ordinated prosecution of the war," and maintaining "an atmosphere of cordial co-operation beyond the immediate crisis of the war." Roosevelt, however, was unsatisfied. Confident in his own powers of persuasion, he felt that if only he could meet face-to-face with Stalin, the two could forge a personal relationship and eliminate any outstanding differences. For almost a year he had tried to arrange a summit, but the Soviet premier had demurred, claiming the need to be near the front. Roosevelt believed Davies, whose optimism about the Soviet Union and bilateral relations had earned him a benign reputation among Soviet leaders, could persuade Stalin. He decided to send the ex-ambassador on a second "mission" to Moscow. FDR instructed Davies to let the Soviet dictator know that "there should be no differences now to divide the allied strength against Hitler" and that the United States was "on the level—had no axes to grind, and [was] concerned first with winning the war."[31]

It was in this context that *Mission to Moscow* became an integral part of both Davies' diplomatic undertaking and the foreign half of Roosevelt's Soviet policy. Standley, then the United States ambassador to Moscow, Secretary of State Cordell Hull, and the president had learned that Stalin was a movie enthusiast. Both before and during the war, the marshal, usually accompanied by Molotov, regularly screened Western-made pictures in the private theater he had had installed near his Kremlin quarters. During the terror, after reportedly signing 3,187 execution orders, the two

[30] For discussions of FDR's thinking, see Bennett, *Franklin D. Roosevelt and the Search for Victory*, 88; Dallek, *Franklin D. Roosevelt and American Foreign Policy*, 379–82; and Gaddis, *Russia, the Soviet Union, and the United States*, 153–60. On Soviet-German peace talks and their implications for American policymakers, see Vojtech Mastny, *Russia's Road to the Cold War: Diplomacy, Warfare, and the Politics of Communism, 1941–1945* (New York, 1979), 73–80, 84–85; and John Lewis Gaddis, *The United States and the Origins of the Cold War, 1941–1947* (New York, 1972), 73.

[31] George Taylor, "The Potentialities of Psychological Warfare," March 29, 1943, Washington Office File, box 125, Correspondence with Government Agencies, Office of Policy Coordination, Director of Overseas Operations, Office of War Information Records; Gaddis, *Russia, the Soviet Union, and the United States*, 153–59; Gaddis, *United States and the Origins of the Cold War*, 64–65; MacLean, "Joseph E. Davies and Soviet-American Relations," 85–86; Bennett, *Franklin D. Roosevelt and the Search for Victory*, 88.

settled down for an evening's entertainment filled with Hollywood productions. In the Soviet Union, Stalin, who not only enjoyed Hollywood's output but also sensed its communicative powers, permitted select Soviet filmmakers to watch American movies and to draw upon them in their own creations. The end results were Stalinist movies that incorporated stars, characteristically American happy endings, and elements from Hollywood westerns and musicals to make the requisite socialist propaganda more palatable to popular viewers. The premier was deeply involved in Soviet motion picture production. He censored prints before their public release, occasionally revised scripts, and at night oftentimes called frightened directors with "suggestions" for plot or title changes. According to Peter Kenez, a leading authority on Soviet film, Stalin became somewhat obsessed with cinema. In part that was because, unlike the real world, the fictional one depicted on screen was highly susceptible to manipulation and, thereby, to the full attainment of ideal outcomes. As he withdrew into the make-believe world, Stalin lost some touch with reality "in the sense of seeing actual factories, collective farms, villages, and even streets of Moscow." And "more and more his view of the world was determined by what he saw on the screen."[32]

Although Roosevelt and Davies did not know the full extent of Stalin's enthusiasm, after previewing *Mission to Moscow* they hatched a plan. The ex-ambassador was to take the movie to Moscow and there to exhibit it for Stalin, Molotov, and other leading Soviet policy makers. By showing it to the Soviet dictator, they hoped to entertain him and put him in a pliable mood. But they had deeper goals, believing that the movie's plot and the fact that it was privately made and broadly distributed in the United States would serve as further proof of American sincerity and willingness to collaborate. In short, they introduced *Mission to Moscow* into the diplomatic realm, where they hoped it would act as an agent of "soft power" in persuading Stalin to remain with the alliance. As the historian David Culbert has noted, it was among "the few examples one can point to of Roosevelt's being able to show Stalin that America had experienced a change of heart and that friendship and understanding were the new watchwords of the day."[33]

Three days after his May 20, 1943, arrival on an airplane emblazoned with the words "Mission to Moscow," Davies went to the Kremlin, where Stalin had arranged the farewell feast in his honor. Davies most likely took this precious opportunity to provide Stalin with evidence of the American people's revised attitudes about the Soviet Union. Before leaving the United States, Davies had asked Poynter

[32] Peter Kenez, *Cinema and Soviet Society, 1917–1953* (Cambridge, Eng., 1992), 148. On Joseph Stalin's interest in film and Hollywood's influence on Soviet cinema, see Zubok and Pleshakov, *Inside the Kremlin's Cold War,* 82; Dmitri Volkogonov, *Stalin: Triumph and Tragedy,* trans. Harold Shukman (New York, 1991), 127, 131; Richard Taylor, "Red Stars, Positive Heroes, and Personality Cults," in *Stalinism and Soviet Cinema,* ed. Richard Taylor and Derek Spring (London, 1993), 76–77; Maya Turovskaya, "1930s and 1940s: Cinema in Context," *ibid.,* 237; Denise J. Youngblood, "'Americanitis': The *Amerikanshchina* in Soviet Cinema," *Journal of Popular Film & Television,* 19 (Winter 1992), 151–52; and Denise J. Youngblood, *Movies for the Masses: Popular Cinema and Soviet Society* (Cambridge, Eng., 1992), 174. Chairman of the Council of People's Commissars of the Soviet Union and the United States Ambassador to the Soviet Union, memo of conversation, April 23, 1942, in Ministerstvo Inostrannykh Del SSSR (Soviet Union Ministry of Foreign Affairs), *Sovetsko-Amerikanskie otnosheniia vo vremia Velikoi Otechestvennoi Voiny, 1941–1945: Dokumenty i materialy* (Soviet-American relations during the Great Patriotic War, 1941–1945: Documents and materials) (2 vols., Moscow, 1984), I, 171.
[33] Culbert, "Our Awkward Ally," 136–37.

to provide him with an inventory of Hollywood movies about Soviet Russia then in production. The domestic BMP chief promptly responded with information about *The North Star, Song of Russia,* and *Three Russian Girls*—all forthcoming Hollywood features with pro-Soviet messages. Poynter suggested to Davies that he inform Soviet leaders of the significance "that private companies, *not just United States government,* films are being made to interpret Russia to the American people."[34] It was improbable that Davies missed this opportunity to interject the cinematic evidence of decreasing anti-Soviet attitudes collected by Poynter.

After retiring to the Kremlin's private movie theater, Davies and Standley—accompanied by Molotov, Beria, Mikoyan, Litvinov, and Red Army marshal Kliment E. Voroshilov—tried to decipher the marshal's response. Opinions differed. Standley, who had submitted his resignation only a month earlier, was increasingly critical of Roosevelt's Soviet policy. He also resented the fact that the chief executive had gone around him in dispatching Davies, who, he believed, was encroaching not only upon his diplomatic turf but also upon his pet project. With the approval of both the State Department and the OWI, the former United States Navy public relations officer had launched a motion picture information program the previous summer. Including only official newreels and informative short films, it sought to improve bilateral relations by informing Soviet leaders about the United States, thereby lessening their distrust. The reigning ambassador's hostility fueled his critique of the diplomatic use of the movie. After meeting Davies at the Moscow airport, Standley privately expressed his disdain for a trip that he deemed a mere publicity stunt. "To send a man 30,000 miles around the world using an American Army plane, a crew of nine men, gas and oil, the prestige of the U.S. Government, and the entire facilities of the American Embassy in Moscow to advertise and increase the box office receipts for Mr. Davies' movie doesn't sit so very well," he wrote his wife. In a memorandum later given to FDR by Hull, Standley reported the Soviet leadership had received the film "with rather glum curiousity." He

> doubted if the Hollywood treatment of events described in Davies' book met with the general approval of the Russians. They successfully refrained from favorable comment while the film was being shown but Stalin was heard to grunt once or twice. The glaring discrepancies must have provoked considerable resentment among the Soviet officials present. Its abject flattery of everything Russian and the ill-advised introduction of unpleasant events in Soviet internal history that I am inclined to think the Kremlin would prefer to forget makes me believe that the Russians will not desire to give publicity to the film at least in its present form. In any event I feel that the film will not contribute to better understanding between the two countries.[35]

---

[34] Poynter to Davies, memo, May 8, 1943, Poynter File, box 16, Mellett Papers; *The North Star,* dir. Lewis Milestone (Goldwyn Pictures, 1943); *Song of Russia,* dir. Gregory Ratoff (MGM, 1943); *Three Russian Girls,* dir. Fedor Ozep and Henry Kesler (United Artists, 1944).

[35] William H. Standley and Arthur A. Ageton, *Admiral Ambassador to Russia* (Chicago, 1955), 380. Several diplomatic and propaganda historians have briefly mentioned the film's Kremlin exhibition, including Gaddis, *United States and the Origins of the Cold War,* 44–45; William Taubman, *Stalin's American Policy: Entente to Détente to Cold War* (New York, 1982), 59; Culbert, "Our Awkward Ally," 136–37; and Culbert, "Introduction," 36–37. Standley to Secretary of State, telegram, May 25, 1943, Russia: July 1942–1943 Folder, box 49, President's Secretary's File, Roosevelt Papers; Cordell Hull for Roosevelt, memo, May 27, 1943, *ibid.*

Davies held a very different view. He wrote Harry Warner, telling him of "the favorable and even enthusiastic comments by some of the living characters portrayed in the film. . . . The Marshal [Stalin] and Premier Molotov were generous in their praise of the picture." At the end of his journey, he informed the president that the Soviets "feel kindly toward us" and that the "mission here could not have been more satisfactory."[36]

Davies was right. His reporting clouded by growing bitterness, Standley erred in thinking that Soviet elites would neither like nor release *Mission to Moscow* because it dredged up the purges. In fact, the opposite was true. A foreign capitalist film's justification for the Nazi-Soviet Pact and its insistence that the purge victims had been guilty were made-to-order domestic propaganda that only lent credence to previous explanations offered by party opinion makers. That realization helped lead Stalin to approve *Mission to Moscow*'s release to the Soviet public, making it one of the first American movies to receive general distribution in well over a decade. However, the production's unintentional provision of ideological support to the Stalinist regime not only exposed a weakness in Roosevelt's approach, it also demonstrated the inability of American policy makers to control culture's uses and meanings once it passed from their hands into the international marketplace. According to a correspondent for the *New York Times* who attended the July 27, 1943, Moscow premiere, Muscovites watched the trial scenes with "intense interest."[37]

That said, in spring 1943, when Washington was trying to forge a stable peace and win the war, FDR's integration of *Mission to Moscow* into his personal diplomacy paid dividends by helping coalesce the alliance. Although neither Roosevelt's appeals nor *Mission to Moscow* could persuade Stalin to reconsider either his core values or his national security agenda, they—along with the collapse of Soviet-German peace talks, intelligence reports, and other bits of information—helped convince him that a temporary and conditional entente was feasible. The dictator had been persuaded that continued Big Three collaboration offered the best means for achieving Moscow's immediate geopolitical interests. Given that the Soviet Union had sustained heavy wartime damage and was in no condition to challenge the Anglo-Americans, Moscow needed the Allies' assistance in attaining German neutralization and reparations, Allied financial assistance to fuel domestic reconstruction, an enduring peace that would give the Kremlin breathing space to retool, and its *sine qua non* of a security ring in eastern Europe. As a gesture of friendship, Stalin timed the dissolution of the Comintern, which had been criticized in the United States for allegedly fomenting revolution there, to coincide with Davies' visit. More important, despite learning in June that there would be no second front in 1943, he remained within the coalition and fulfilled a pledge

---

[36] Davies to Warner, May 24, 1943, in *Mission to Moscow*, ed. Culbert, 261; *Foreign Relations of the United States, 1943*, III, 657.

[37] *New York Times*, July 28, 1943, sec. 1, p. 18. Critics have argued that both Roosevelt's Soviet policy and the film fostered a belief in the Kremlin that the United States would acquiesce to any action, thus encouraging its postwar expansion in eastern Europe and elsewhere. Taubman, *Stalin's American Policy*, 39, 59; Mastny, *Russia's Road to the Cold War*, 84–85.

made during Davies' trip by meeting with Roosevelt and Churchill in Tehran at the first Big Three summit in November.[38]

With its plentiful imagery of collective security and Soviet-American friendship, *Mission to Moscow* enabled the Kremlin to prepare the Soviet people for that continued diplomatic tack. At the insistence of Stalin, the version of the film released to the Soviet public retained its pro-alliance and internationalist flavors. Although they eliminated a minor scene suggesting that the NKVD had bugged the American embassy, in a departure from both pre- and postwar policy, censors kept others favorably portraying Roosevelt, Davies, and other liberal internationalist Americans and their efforts to work with Stalinist Russia. Soviet audiences heard Davies, in his subtitled prefatory remarks, say that "unity, mutual understanding, confidence in each other was necessary to win the war. It is still more necessary to win the peace, for there can be no durable peace without an agreement among those nations who have won the war that they will project that peace, and maintain that peace, and protect that peace." Sequences in which Litvinov's character, before the League of Nations, and Stalin's character, during his meeting with Davies, enunciated their hopes for great-power cooperation also remained. Censors retained depictions of Soviet and American citizens freely interacting within the Soviet Union's borders. When the Davies' limousine stopped in front of Polina Molotov's cosmetics factory, several Soviet boys rushed to it, admiring both the modern automobile and its prominently displayed American flags. Soviet viewers also saw Ambassador Davies, his wife, and their daughter enjoying warm personal relationships with leading Soviet citizens, including Stalin, Molotov, Ambassador Litvinov and his family, and a fictional Red Army officer.[39]

Official reactions, most of which were closely monitored by the CPSU, indicated that in ruling circles *Mission to Moscow* was received as an expression of Soviet-American condominium. Although like others Ivan G. Bol'shakov, head of the Soviet film monopoly, the Council of People's Commissars' Committee on Cinematography Affairs (Komitet po Delam Kinematografii, KDK), privately found its ste-

[38] On Moscow's mid–1943 foreign policy, see Taubman, *Stalin's American Policy*, 38–40, 74–75; Robert C. Tucker, *Stalin in Power: The Revolution from Above, 1928–1941* (New York, 1990), 233–35; Zubok and Pleshakov, *Inside the Kremlin's Cold War*, 6, 12, 26–35; Vladimir O. Pechatnov, *The Big Three after World War II: New Documents on Soviet Thinking about Post-War Relations with the United States and Great Britain*, Cold War International History Project, Working Paper no. 13 (Washington, 1995), 5–6, 8–9, 16–17; Vojtech Mastny, *The Cold War and Soviet Insecurity: The Stalin Years* (New York, 1996), 6, 21, 23; and Volkogonov, *Stalin*, 484–86. Although the Kremlin did abolish the Comintern in May 1943, the Party Central Committee's Department of International Information clandestinely continued to direct the worldwide Communist movement. See Kevin McDermott and Jeremy Agnew, *The Comintern: A History of International Communism from Lenin to Stalin* (New York, 1997), 204–11. On the Kremlin's fear of the secret Anglo-American project to develop atomic weapons, see David Holloway, *Stalin and the Bomb: The Soviet Union and Atomic Energy, 1939–1956* (New Haven, 1994), 84, 96, 364–65, 368.

[39] *New York Times*, July 28, 1943, sec. 1, p. 18. On negative pre- and postwar presentations of capitalists and the United States in Soviet culture, see *Tsirk'* (The circus), dir. Grigorii Aleksandrov (Mosfil'm, 1936); Vsesoiuznyi Gosudarstvennyi Fond Kinofil'mov (All-Union State Film Foundation), *Sovetskie khudozhestvennyi fil'my: Annotirovannyi katalog* (Soviet feature films: An annotated catalog) (3 vols., Moscow, 1961), 1, 487–88; J. D. Parks, *Culture, Conflict, and Coexistence: American-Soviet Cultural Relations, 1917–1958* (Jefferson, 1983), 121–22; Turovskaya, "1930s and 1940s," 47.

reotypical displays of "enormous samovars, bearded men, dancing gopaks, sledges decorated with flowers and the like" laughable and "naïve," the press offered public praise. According to the Soviet newspapers *Komsomol'skaia Pravda, Vechernaia Moskva,* and *Izvestiia,* the movie, which played in at least six separate Moscow theaters, was "an act of friendly gratitude towards the Soviet Union and the Red Army." In *Pravda* reviewer N. Sergeev approvingly noted that *Mission to Moscow*'s aim was "to promote mutual understanding and [to] strengthen the bonds between two great countries." Moscow's approval of the picture's message reached a peak in early 1944, when Vladimir Dekanozov, an NKVD agent assigned to the Soviet Ministry of Foreign Affairs (Ministerstvo Inostrannykh Del, MID), informed the American embassy that his government wanted to confer official awards on *Mission to Moscow*'s producers for their work in strengthening bilateral ties.[40]

While popular viewers in the Soviet Union also welcomed the American picture's expressions of political goodwill, some clandestinely derived alternative interpretations that neither American nor Soviet elites intended to communicate. As they did, *Mission to Moscow* emerged as an engine of American influence. Those popular interpretations exemplified the inability of propagandists, even Stalinist opinion makers, to regulate the multiplicity of public meanings made from cultural artifacts.[41]

Frederick C. Barghoorn, a junior officer stationed at the American embassy in Moscow, spoke with several Soviet citizens, all of whom said that *Mission to Moscow*'s depictions of the standard of living in the Soviet Union were "funny." To Soviet viewers unaccustomed to personal comforts, plentiful necessities, and consumer goods, the window display at the "USSR Cosmetic Factory," the ubiquity of food and modern automobiles, and the well-dressed American and Soviet citizens depicted in the movie were all "fantastically luxurious." Rather than simply dismissing the American production as hopelessly parochial, however, Barghoorn's contacts confided that such scenes revealed to them the expectations of its original American audience, who enjoyed higher standards of living. For Barghoorn that view was confirmed when, sometime after the war on a flight from Tbilisi to Moscow, he struck up a conversation with a well-educated and relatively wealthy Georgian woman. The wife of a Red Army officer, she confessed to having watched such American movies as *Mission to Moscow,* but she had found them "depressing" because they so clearly contrasted the material quality of life in the Soviet Union with that in the United States. In light of those revelations, other Soviet reactions made more sense. Stefan Sharff, a Moscow correspondent for the *New York Times,* reported that Mus-

[40] The British embassy in Moscow monitored the Soviet press. See "Monthly Report on the Distribution of British Films in the USSR," July 1943, document N 5651/9/38, FO 371/36921, Foreign Office Records (Public Record Office, Kew, Eng.). On official Soviet commendations, see W. Averell Harriman to Secretary of State, telegram, Jan. 22, 1944, 861.4061 Motion Pictures/79, Records of the Department of State, RG 59 (National Archives).
[41] On the popular deconstruction and then reassembly of American culture at home and abroad, see Rob Kroes, "Americanisation: What Are We Talking About?," in *Cultural Transmissions and Receptions,* ed. Kroes, Rydell, and Bosscher, 303; and John Fiske, *Understanding Popular Culture* (Boston, 1989), 5, 11, 15, 19–20, 25, 36, 44, 103–6, 126. Distinctions between popular and elite responses are made by Richard Pells, "Who's Afraid of Steven Spielberg?," *Diplomatic History,* 24 (Summer 2000), 500–501.

covites were "amused" by a scene showing Tania Litvinov, the ambassador's daughter, and other Russians "ice skating in an Alpine resort atmosphere." While American and Soviet policy makers had sought to use the production to build bilateral ties, in the unique context of Stalinist Russia many viewers had disassembled *Mission to Moscow,* taking from it imagery of capitalist life-styles that both fulfilled their own desires and, according to Barghoorn, provided a basis for quiet opposition to the Kremlin. Although unforeseen by Roosevelt, Davies, or the OWI, such interpretations worked to Washington's long-term advantage.[42]

Soviet viewers were especially eager to seize upon *Mission to Moscow* because it was one of the first Hollywood movies to play in the Soviet Union in nearly a generation. During the relatively liberal 1920s, American films had been extremely popular in the Soviet Union, in 1927 accounting for almost 59 percent of all those exhibited there. Stalin's rise to power, however, was accompanied by a cultural revolution, which beginning in 1928 sought to build "socialism in one country" and a socialist consciousness among the masses by cleansing national culture of foreign and bourgeois influence. Among other things, the campaign targeted Hollywood films as the CPSU's Central Committee purged film libraries of foreign pictures, suppressed domestic productions deemed too Western, and, more important, erected an import ban on foreign movies.[43]

In late 1942, following a decade in which American cinema was absent from the Soviet Union, Standley had launched attempts to overcome that cultural barrier, which he and Soviet experts in Washington believed bred xenophobia and both ignorance about and hostility toward the United States. With the nations allied, Soviet cultural authorities were also interested, if only hesitatingly, in expanding cultural and informational contacts with the United States and Great Britain. Since it was recognized that the populace was more likely to defend family, home, Mother Russia, and the Eastern Orthodox Church than socialism, for the duration of the wartime emergency the Kremlin loosened social restrictions, muting ideological themes and permitting public displays of Russian nationalism and religious iconography. Given party propagandists' need to fire domestic morale by informing Soviet citizens about their international antifascist comrades, this temporary liberalization also included the limited dissemination of Allied information and culture. Furthermore, the German invasion, which resulted in the loss of a studio at Kiev and the relocation of other parts of the movie industry either beyond the Ural Mountains or to Central Asia, had gravely weakened a Soviet motion picture industry that even before the hostilities had succeeded in meeting only 20 to 30 percent of its production quotas. Because party propagandists in the Central Committee's Propaganda and Agitation Administration (Upravlenie Propagandy i Agitatsii, UPA) were thus less able to stoke morale by entertaining the masses and conveying war information

---

[42] *New York Times,* July 28, 1943, sec. 1, p. 18; Frederick C. Barghoorn, *The Soviet Image of the United States: A Study in Distortion* (1950; Port Washington, 1969), 229, 242.

[43] Youngblood, *Movies for the Masses,* 6–7, 19–20, 31–34; Kenez, *Cinema and Soviet Society,* 133–34. Other forms of American popular culture, including jazz, were also suppressed. See S. Frederick Starr, *Red and Hot: The Fate of Jazz in the Soviet Union, 1917–1980* (New York, 1983).

to them, this development impaired the Soviet war effort and stimulated interest in obtaining both supplements to domestic production and cinematic technical assistance from the United States.[44]

After a Moscow conference on Allied film held in summer 1942 at which Bol'shakov indicated the Soviet Union's nascent openness, Standley organized a program sending official United States newsreels and short documentaries to the Soviet capital. To Hull and Roosevelt the ambassador expressed his belief "that much could be accomplished in the development of good will and understanding between the United States and the USSR by making available technical, educational and propaganda . . . films to the Russians." Once Washington indicated its approval, these productions seeped into Stalinist Russia. Standley's program aimed to build Soviet-American comity by countering criticism of the second front's absence through publicity about Lend-Lease aid to the Soviet Union and Anglo-American military activities in North Africa, Italy, and the Pacific. Upon the films' arrival in Moscow, the United States embassy organized demonstrations for, and loaned copies to, the Kremlin, MID, All-Union Society for Cultural Relations with Foreign Countries (Vsesoiuznoe Obshchestvo Kul'turnykh Sviazei s Zagranitsei, VOKS), KDK, the military, and the Soviet Information Bureau (Sovinformburo). On occasion, Bol'shakov's committee edited portions of American newsreels into its own serial, *Soiuzkinozhurnal* (All-Union newsreel), which was widely circulated among popular Soviet audiences.[45]

For some time, Ambassador Standley had tried to leaven his program with Hollywood pictures. The war, defined by FDR and the OWI as a crusade for freedom and democracy, had rekindled Standley's faith in the American way. Eager to share and propagate that outlook, he believed that Hollywood movies were powerful communicators of American cultural influence. That was particularly true in the Soviet

[44] On Soviet domestic wartime propaganda, see John Barber and Mark Harrison, *The Soviet Home Front, 1941–1945: A Social and Economic History of the USSR in World War II* (London, 1991), 68–79; Mikhail N. Narinsky, "The Soviet Union: The Great Patriotic War?," in *Allies at War: The Soviet, American, and British Experience, 1939–1945*, ed. David Reynolds, Warren F. Kimball, and A. O. Chubarian (New York, 1994), 271, 273; and Sergei Drobashenko and Peter Kenez, "Film Propaganda in the Soviet Union, 1941–1945: Two Views," in *Film and Radio Propaganda in World War II*, ed. K. R. M. Short (Knoxville, 1983), 96. For discussions of wartime shortages and imports of foreign information, see *ibid.*, 96, 111; R. N. Iurenev, "Kinoiskusstvo voennykh let" (Film art during the war years), in *Sovetskaia kul'tura v gody Velikoi Otechestvennoi Voiny* (Soviet culture during the Great Patriotic War), ed. M. P. Kim (Moscow, 1976), 236; and Kenez, *Cinema and Soviet Society*, 105–7, 130–32, 134, 137, 140–44, 186–88, 192–93. For Soviet industrialists' views on the United States, see Joan Hoff Wilson, *Ideology and Economics: U.S. Relations with the Soviet Union, 1918–1933* (Columbia, Mo., 1974), 8–9.

[45] Standley to Hull and Roosevelt, telegram, Aug. 23, 1942, 861.4061 Motion Pictures/15, State Department Records. On the Moscow conference on Allied film and Soviet expressions of openness, see Ivan G. Bol'shakov, speech, "American and English Films," Aug. 21, 1942, fond 5283, opis' 14, delo 122, list 129, Records of the All-Union Society for Cultural Relations with Foreign Countries (Vsesoiuznoe Obshchestvo Kul'turnykh Sviazei s Zagranitsei, VOKS) (State Archive of the Russian Federation, Moscow); and "Moscow Conference on American and British Cinema," Aug. 21–22, 1942, Vladimir I. Bazykin File, box 1432, Mellett Records, Bureau of Motion Pictures, Domestic Operations Branch, Office of War Information Records; Division of European Affairs, memo, Aug. 27, 1942, 861.4061 Motion Pictures/15, State Department Records; D. W. Spring, "Soviet Newsreel and the Great Patriotic War," in *Propaganda, Politics, and Film, 1918–45*, ed. Nicholas Pronay and D. W. Spring (London, 1982), 280, 284–86. For brief discussions of the program, see Parks, *Culture, Conflict, and Coexistence*, 84–86; and Hixson, *Parting the Curtain*, 6.

Union, where the wartime cultural liberalization offered unprecedented informational opportunities but Soviet law, although sporadically enforced, still technically criminalized personal contact with foreigners. Finding "the conditions of the common people" in the Soviet Union to be "very low," Standley wanted to improve their lot by teaching them "about America and Americans, about our ideals, our standards, the way we think, the way we live, [and] our wants and needs in this modern world." Meanwhile, Assistant Secretary of State Adolf A. Berle Jr. informed foreign missions of the State Department's belief that commercial movies could promote American power abroad by generating foreign trade surpluses, by acting as salesmen for other American products, and, most important, by projecting "a picture of this nation, its culture, its institutions, [and] its method of dealing with social problems which may be invaluable from the political, cultural, and commercial point of view." Responding to Berle's circular, W. Averell Harriman, who in October 1943 replaced Standley as ambassador, agreed that popular cinema was important as a "vehicle for publicizing the American point of view and as a cultural instrument, especially in the Soviet Union."[46]

Before permanently leaving his post, Standley briefly returned to Washington, where he obtained approval from Hull, Roosevelt, and the head of owi's Overseas Operations Branch, Robert Sherwood, to incorporate Hollywood productions into his motion picture information program. Despite strenuous efforts by the ambassador and his cultural attaché Young, by May 1943 only a handful of the program's feature films had reached the Soviet Union, and none had appeared in public theaters there. Frustrated, Standley concluded, "it is well known that the Soviet Government has long followed a policy of giving the Soviet people a minimum of information concerning foreign countries and in my opinion any radical departure from that policy in the near future is unlikely."[47]

With those rare exceptions when *Soiuzkinozhurnal* did incorporate United States newsreel footage, before *Mission to Moscow*'s release American statesmen had succeeded in communicating with only a very thin veneer of Soviet elites using official motion pictures. Stalin's decision to permit *Mission to Moscow*'s general distribution changed that. Responding to this signal of openness from above, the previously reluctant Andrei N. Andrievsky, head of Soiuzintorgkino, the Soviet agency in charge of foreign film trade, signed an agreement with the American embassy codifying the bilateral exchange of nontheatrical shorts and newsreels.

[46] Standley and Ageton, *Admiral Ambassador to Russia*, 244; Costigliola, "'Mixed Up' and 'Contact,'" 797. On Americans' newfound cultural confidence, see Robert Dallek, *The American Style of Foreign Policy: Cultural Politics and Foreign Affairs* (New York, 1983), 125–26, 134–37, 150; Tony Smith, *America's Mission: The United States and the Worldwide Struggle for Democracy in the Twentieth Century* (Princeton, 1994), 114; Warren Susman, "Introduction," in *Culture and Commitment, 1929–1945*, ed. Warren Susman (New York, 1973), 9–16, 20, 23; Adolf A. Berle Jr., "American Motion Pictures in the Postwar World," telegram, Feb. 22, 1944, 800.4061 Motion Pictures/409A, State Department Records; Harriman to Secretary of State, "American Motion Pictures in the Postwar World," telegram, April 13, 1944, 800.4061 Motion Pictures/458, *ibid.*
[47] Standley for Secretary of State, "Report on the Exchange of Information between the United States and the Soviet Union," telegram, April 7, 1943, 861.4061 Motion Pictures/45, State Department Records; Standley and Ageton, *Admiral Ambassador to Russia*, 306, 315; Standley Diary, n.d., Correspondence—John Young/Will H. Hays File, box 17, William H. Standley Papers (Doheny Library, University of Southern California, Los Angeles).

Heartened by Stalin's decision and Andrievsky's reversal, Standley dispatched Young to secure Hollywood's participation. Although it was cooperating with Washington's efforts to build domestic support for the Grand Alliance, the American motion picture industry had been hesitant to provide the Moscow embassy with feature films because it saw no compelling financial interest in doing so. Since 1932 MPPDA members—including the eight major studios: Warner Bros., Loew's Inc.'s Metro-Goldwyn-Mayer (MGM), Twentieth Century–Fox, Paramount, Radio-Keith-Orpheum (RKO), Columbia, Universal, and United Artists—had sold nary a picture in the Soviet Union. To add insult to injury, when the Red Army had invaded Poland, Romania, and the Baltic states in 1939, the Soviets had appropriated hundreds of the industry's copyrighted movies, and executives saw little point in again risking their intellectual properties in a closed market.[48]

Their reticence quickly disappeared when Young informed the MPPDA president, Will H. Hays, and other industry leaders that the Kremlin had sanctioned *Mission to Moscow*'s release and that Soiuzintorgkino was interested in purchasing its distribution rights for around $25,000. Once they also learned that the Soviet industry had been virtually destroyed by the war and that British competitors were making inroads into the burgeoning market, Hays and managers from the MPPDA companies recognized that they had a unique opportunity to recapture a long-lost, but once profitable, market and to satisfy their corporatist patron, the Roosevelt administration. Fox's Murray Silverstone wrote to George R. Canty, the head of the State Department's Telecommunications Division, "it would be a great achievement if our industry were permitted to open offices and operate directly in Russia. . . . I hope this will be more than a pious thought." Hays had received assurances that the administration, which had protected the industry from domestic antitrust litigation and was then promoting its overseas market interests, was "very much interested in facilitating the distribution of suitable American films in the Soviet Union." Hays encouraged the studios to provide Young with an initial supply of forty-eight features and thirty-seven theatrical shorts. Once feature films arrived in the Soviet Union, the United States embassy hosted premieres and then loaned copies to Bol'shakov's KDK and Andrievsky's Soiuzintorgkino. While Bol'shakov and Andrievsky decided whether to contract for their distribution rights, they circulated the movies among an "approved list," including Stalin, Molotov, the MID, VOKS, the military, Sovinformburo, and various party-controlled actors' and artists' clubs. As a result, the United States embassy estimated that even before their public exhibition, most Hollywood pic-

[48] Andrei N. Andrievsky for Solomon A. Lozovksii, "Agreement," Aug. 30, 1943, fond 13, opis' 5, papka 14, delo 246, listy 2–3, Secretariat of Vice-Commissar for Foreign Affairs, Solomon A. Lozovskii (Sekretariat Zam. Narkoma Inostrannykh Del Solomon A. Lozovskogo) (Archive of the Foreign Policy of the Russian Federation, Moscow); Vassily Zarubin, memo, Oct. 4, 1943, fond 13, opis' 5, papka 14, delo 246, list 7, *ibid.* On Poland, see A. M. Loew to Hull, Oct. 10, 1939, 840.6 General, London, Records of the Foreign Service Posts of the Department of State, RG 84 (National Archives); and letter for Harold L. Smith, Dec. 13, 1939, Poland File (reel 5), Motion Picture Association of America General Correspondence.

tures had played before audiences of at least twelve thousand intellectuals and Soviet state, military, and party elites.[49]

Following a rigorous selection process involving the KDK, the UPA, and ultimately Stalin, during the war years Soiuzintorgkino purchased the public distribution rights to almost two dozen pictures for prices ranging from $25,000 to $50,000 each. Although compared with receipts generated in other markets such fees were quite small, movie industrialists hoped that the initial sales would eventually lead to larger revenues. As had *Mission to Moscow*, several of the American movies seen by popular Soviet viewers conveyed pro-Soviet sentiments. The majority, however, presented the United States as a prosperous, free, and amusing country. By detailing what one reviewer called the Horatio "Algeresque" tale of Thomas A. Edison's mythical rise from obscurity to world renown as an inventor, MGM's *Edison, the Man*, suggested that the American dream was alive and well, permitting citizens to rise up and achieve prosperity by dint only of their hard work. The Jack Benny comedy *Charley's Aunt* and the Sonja Henie musical *Sun Valley Serenade* conveyed the sense that the good life of personal fulfillment and entertainment was available to most Americans, who also had the means and leisure time to pursue it. Like *Sun Valley Serenade*, other pictures, including the Deanna Durbin musical *His Butler's Sister*, *Appointment for Love* starring Charles Boyer, and Columbia's *The Men in Her Life*, were set in such relatively opulent surroundings as upper-middle-class urban apartments, the estates of Broadway playwrights, or winter resorts. As had *Mission to Moscow*, those films, while entertaining Soviet audiences, empowered them to compare celluloid westerners' standards of living with their own. One American review of *Sun Valley Serenade*, for instance, noted that its presentation of people enjoying "luxuries in one of the world's most magnificent Winter resorts" was a "visual delight" and a "poor man's substitute" for actually being there.[50]

United States and Soviet officials felt that the overall effect of Hollywood movies, which by all accounts were both popular and effective in communicating ideal versions of the American way of life, was a corrosion of the Kremlin's ideological

---

[49] Murray Silverstone to George R. Canty, Jan. 30, 1945, 861.4061 Motion Pictures/1-3045, State Department Records; "Sales of American Films to Soviet Russia," memo, June 16, 1943, Foreign Relations—Russia File (reel 10), Motion Picture Association of America General Correspondence; Hays to John G. Bryson, June 15, 1943, *ibid.*; Breckinridge Long to Hays, June 28, 1943, Correspondence—John Young/Will H. Hays File, box 17, Standley Papers. For the embassy's estimation, see George F. Kennan, "Motion Picture Program for U.S.S.R.," telegram, Feb. 18, 1946, 840.6 Motion Pictures, Moscow, Records of the Foreign Service Posts of the Department of State.

[50] For American-made pro-Soviet movies receiving general circulation, see *The North Star; Song of Russia;* and *The Battle of Russia,* dir. Frank Capra and Anatole Litvak (U.S. Army Special Service Division, 1943). The lone exception to positive portrayals of American life was *The Little Foxes,* a "socially conscious" picture based upon a screenplay by the leftist writer Lillian Hellman that criticized a turn-of-the-century southern family's greed. See *The Little Foxes,* dir. William Wyler (RKO, 1941). Kennan, "Motion Picture Program for U.S.S.R."; *New York Times,* June 7, 1940, sec. 1, p. 27; *Edison, the Man,* dir. Clarence Brown (MGM, 1940); *Charley's Aunt,* dir. Archie Mayo (Twentieth Century–Fox, 1941); *Sun Valley Serenade,* dir. H. Bruce Humberstone (Twentieth Century–Fox, 1941); *His Butler's Sister,* dir. Frank Borzage (Universal Pictures, 1943); *Appointment for Love,* dir. William A. Seiter (Universal Pictures, 1941); *The Men in Her Life,* dir. Gregory Ratoff (Columbia Pictures, 1941); *New York Times,* Sept. 6, 1941, sec. 1, p. 20; *The American Film Institute Catalog of Motion Pictures Produced in the United States* (23 vols., Berkeley, 1993–1999), F3, 564–65; F4, 92–93, 403–4, 1049–50, 1527–28, 2378–79.

monopoly. The United States embassy reported that commercial films were "particularly in demand" and that one of its Soviet employees had repeatedly been "offered bribes by various organizations desirous of borrowing pictures." Convinced that interest had been stirred in American films and "in our country," Ambassador Harriman lauded movies' success in reaching the "opinion forming audience in Moscow." After gauging the effects of *Mission to Moscow* and other productions, American diplomats praised their mass appeal. They believed that in conjunction with Washington's broader informational program, movies had demonstrated the superior American standard of living to many Soviet viewers. Edward Ames, a junior officer assigned to the United States embassy in Moscow, claimed that because of the CPSU's prewar regimentation of domestic cultural life, the Soviet Union had experienced almost complete cultural isolation, producing xenophobia and a populace incapable of comprehending its poor living conditions. Cinematic information had changed that, he argued, leading some to "acquire a great craving for things foreign, [to] go to the American movies, and [to] attempt to do things as they are done abroad." American films had made "it possible for the Russians to get an idea of how people in other countries looked, dressed and acted. Admitting the inadequacies of the Hollywood film as a picture of American life, still the movie has been a great eye-opener."[51]

By the latter stages of World War II, the United States had established an informational and cultural beachhead in the Soviet Union. His concerns dispelled by American displays, cinematic and otherwise, of pro-Soviet attitudes, in late 1943 Molotov had reversed course and acceded to the establishment of an OWI outpost in Moscow. Thereafter, the bureau informed "the Russian people about American life, American culture, [and] America's part in the war" by providing Soviet news authorities with United States press reports and photographs, arranging radio contacts, distributing two specially made magazines and an official information bulletin, and maintaining a reference library open to the public. From 1942 through 1945, America's communicative power grew as officials distributed over one hundred and fifty newsreels, around fifty official short documentaries, and approximately seventy-three feature films, two dozen of which were seen by broad Soviet audiences. While at first glance that latter figure seemed insignificant, it was a noteworthy threat to the decrepit Soviet motion picture industry, which in 1944 produced only twenty-five features and in 1945 a record low of nineteen.[52]

[51] Kennan, "Motion Picture Program for U.S.S.R"; Harriman, "American Motion Pictures in the Postwar World"; Harriman to Secretary of State, telegram, Nov. 6, 1945, 861.4061 Motion Pictures/11-645, State Department Records; Edward Ames, "Cultural Lags in the Soviet Union," Oct. 27, 1945, 842 Cultural Relations, Moscow, Records of the Foreign Service Posts of the Department of State; Barghoorn, *Soviet Image of the United States*, 242.

[52] Samuel Spewack for Robert Sherwood, telegram, Nov. 16, 1943, Moscow Cables File, box 829, Office of Policy Coordination, Director of Overseas Operations, Office of War Information Records; "The O.W.I. and the U.S.S.R.," n.d., O.W.I. and the U.S.S.R. File, box 1716, Records of the Chief, Liaison Office, Overseas Operations Branch, *ibid.*; Vsesoiuznyi Gosudarstvennyi Fond Kinofil'mov, *Sovetskie khudozhestvennye fil'my*, III appendices, 15–23; Kennan to Secretary of State, Dec. 14, 1945, 840.6 Motion Pictures, Moscow, Records of the Foreign Service Posts of the Department of State; Drobashenko and Kenez, "Film Propaganda," 96.

Soviet authorities, who in summer 1944 began to withdraw from cinematic contacts, were cognizant of American movies' ideological and economic powers. The retreat first manifested itself when, despite earlier assurances from Bol'shakov and Stalin, the KDK refused to include newsreel footage of the D day invasion in *Soiuzkinozhurnal*. Although earlier plans had called for the purchase of fifteen Hollywood features that year, in August 1944 the committee informed American diplomats that it was under new orders to contract only for the explicitly pro-Soviet *Song of Russia* and those portraying "American life and society in an unflattering light." According to Andrievsky, Soviet cultural authorities pulled back because in just over a year, audiences had acquired "a taste" for Hollywood movies, enabling those products to recapture a sizable share of the domestic market and imperil the native industry. More important, by demonstrating the higher American standard of living and empowering Soviet viewers to compare it with their own, Hollywood had begun to compete with the party for viewers' hearts and minds. In June 1944 the Soiuzintorgkino chief explained to an OWI representative, "films contrary to Russian ideology were not acceptable, no matter how good technically they might be." It soon became clear that Moscow's disengagement was an initial step in a much broader cultural cleansing, which was reminiscent of the earlier Stalinist cultural revolution and a direct response to the wartime influx of Allied movies and other cultural forms. By early 1946 Andrei A. Zhdanov, the party's chief ideologue and head of the UPA, directed a campaign that purged the national culture of bourgeois and alien influence, reduced Soviet contacts with the outside world, and formed an intellectual basis for the postwar extension of socialism to eastern Europe.[53]

Perceiving the sharply diverging responses by official and popular Soviet groups to foreign cultural stimuli, by the war's end American statesmen gained an increasing appreciation of "soft power." As Ames's analysis suggests, American culture had penetrated so deeply that some State Department experts detected a growing, and exploitable, gulf separating the Soviet people from the Kremlin. Barghoorn, calling ordinary citizens the party's "Achilles Heel," claimed that the United States had emerged as a popular, but still subterranean, symbol of opposition to authoritarian rule. Not long after the war's conclusion, George F. Kennan, who had returned to the Moscow embassy in 1944, argued in his influential "long telegram" that "never since the termination of civil war have [the] mass of Russian people been emotionally farther removed from [the] doctrines of [the] Communist Party than they are today." Rather than succumbing to CPSU propaganda, the Soviet public was "remarkably resistant in the stronghold of its innermost thoughts." In a separate

[53] Harriman to Secretary of State, telegram, Aug. 25, 1944, 861.4061 Motion Pictures/8-2544, State Department Records; Parks, *Culture, Conflict, and Coexistence*, 96; Melby to Ferdinand Kuhn and Robert Riskin, telegram, June 24, 1944, Foreign Relations—Russia File (reel 10), Motion Picture Association of America General Correspondence; "All-Soviet Union Communist Party Central Committee Propaganda and Agitation Administration Meeting Regarding the Film Question," minutes, April 26, 1946, fond 17, opis' 125, delo 378, listy 5-6 All-Union Communist Party Central Committee (Tsentral'nyi Komitet, VKP) (Russian State Archive of Socio-Political History, Moscow); Parks, *Culture, Conflict, and Coexistence*, 116-18; Zubok and Pleshakov, *Inside the Kremlin's Cold War*, 123-25.

lengthy "cinematic telegram," the architect of containment claimed the wartime introduction of Hollywood movies had helped expose that divide and contended that, despite the party's renewed ban, Washington should continue sending movies to Moscow. There, they could project an ideal "exposition of American life" and counteract the growing sense, fostered by CPSU propaganda, that the Soviet people were "surrounded by enemies, that they are in the midst of a crisis, which must culminate in war with the capitalist west and that they must therefore sacrifice their personal well-being and material enjoyment for the furthering of Soviet might and power." Such sentiments would not have been inconsistent with those of Roosevelt, who had a deep faith in liberal Americanism and throughout the war supported OWI programs that spread that ideology abroad. Confident that overseas audiences would be attracted to the high American standard of living and to the entertaining American mass media, Roosevelt proposed the creation of so-called free zones of information in Europe designed to promote United States, and to limit Soviet, influence.[54]

Kennan's recommendations, which guided policy regarding the Soviet Union for the next several years, led the State Department to incorporate Hollywood into its Cold War cultural offensive and to promote the industry's sales in the Soviet Union. Because the Soviet movie industry continually failed to meet production quotas, by early 1947 the CPSU relented somewhat and permitted the distribution of limited numbers of Hollywood movies. During the coldest days of the Cold War, America had rare cinematic voices with which to speak to Soviet audiences. While not large, Hollywood's sales, which during World War II totaled from $600,000 to $1.2 million and in the late forties equaled roughly $1 million, would not have been possible without diplomats' intervention. Promising to uphold his end of the corporatist bargain that had begun to coalesce eight years earlier, in 1948 Eric Johnston, then head of the MPPDA's successor, the Motion Picture Association of America, assured foreign policy makers that no "films which could be used to portray the United States of America in an unfavorable light would be" sold to the Soviets.[55]

Mission to Moscow had facilitated the reintroduction of American movies into the Soviet Union and their integration into Washington's wartime and Cold War cultural offensives. At home, the picture was the result of an intricate and corporatist web of power relationships constructed by Roosevelt, Davies, OWI propagandists, and movie industrialists who hoped that the film would undergird American might abroad by silencing anticommunism and by cultivating a domestic consensus for the administration's pro-Soviet policy. They failed, however, as most domestic viewers either remained unconvinced or rejected *Mission to Moscow*'s unentertaining, pro-

[54] *Foreign Relations of the United States, 1946* (11 vols., Washington, 1969–1972), VI, 698, 707; Barghoorn, *Soviet Image of the United States*, xiii, 229–30. Kennan reiterated his views in George Kennan, "The Sources of Soviet Conduct," *Foreign Affairs*, 25 (July 1947), 577; and Kennan to Freeman Matthews, undelivered letter, 1945, Writings and Publications (1934–1949) File, box 23, George Kennan Papers (Seeley G. Mudd Manuscript Library, Princeton University, Princeton, N.J.); Kennan, "Motion Picture Program for U.S.S.R."; Kimball, *Juggler*, 10, 18–19, 102, 182, 186–87, 191, 198.
[55] Moscow embassy to Secretary of State, airgram, Sept. 21, 1948, 861.4061 Motion Pictures/9-2148, State Department Records; Dean Acheson to Moscow embassy, telegram, April 11, 1947, 861.4061 Motion Pictures/4-1147, *ibid.*

Soviet, and overtly propagandistic character. But this cultural artifact had another, unprecedented application to statecraft. When FDR and Davies used it to persuade Stalin of the Grand Alliance's strength, they integrated *Mission to Moscow* into the process of diplomatic negotiation, making it an instrument for achieving geopolitical power. Once the Kremlin took the unanticipated step of releasing the film to the Soviet public, an entirely new set of forces was unleashed, some beyond Washington's control or expectations. Although in its Soviet context the picture helped legitimate the Stalinist regime, as Soviet viewers teased out its enticing imagery of the good life in the capitalist United States, *Mission to Moscow* emerged as a weapon of "soft power." More important, its public release opened the previously closed Soviet Union to legions of Hollywood movies. While generating foreign revenues and threatening the Soviet industry, those pictures augmented *Mission to Moscow*'s ideological influence by championing an American prosperity that stood in stark contrast to Soviet audiences' experiences.

The Holocaust in American Popular Culture

ALVIN H. ROSENFELD

If we are what we eat, as the current jingle would have it, we are also what we see and hear and otherwise absorb in our daily lives. Ingestions, both culinary and cultural, do help to define us, shape us, and constitute more than a little of body and mind.

In the present essay I want to reflect on the condition of the public body in its increasingly frequent exposure to popular images of the Holocaust. The eye and ear remain hungry for visual and mental representations of the Hitler period and apparently are far from being sated. What accounts for this hunger for the horrible? How is it being stimulated and fed? And how is the public responding to the variety of Holocaust images put before it by the popular media?

In attempting to answer these questions I want to focus on television, movies, popular literature, and popular parlance. Taken together these comprise a sizable part of popular culture, by which I refer chiefly to those forms of common taste and recreation that occupy the non-working hours of great numbers of Americans.

Television is primary and, with respect to present concerns, one turns first to a review of the NBC docudrama *Holocaust*. During the time of its initial showing in the spring of 1978 there was a heated debate about the value of the program. It ran over four consecutive evenings, took up some nine-and-a-half hours of prime-time broadcasting, and apparently reached over 100 million viewers in America alone (the overseas audiences were also to be large.)

What is it they saw? A program that was advertised as being "only a story" but one "that really happened." The story was occasionally gripping but more often than not overly sentimentalized, at times compelling but also painfully synthetic. At its best it was a partial approximation of "the real thing" — no more than that. Did the story behind the "story" come through, one wonders? Apparently some measure of historical truth was communicated, not so much and certainly not in the way that an historian would prefer, and yet, for all the compromises that were made, something more than just easy entertainment did register on the millions.

The NBC *Holocaust* program was shown again on American television in 1980, not to so large an audience as the first time but nevertheless once more to many millions. And since that showing there have been a

ALVIN H. ROSENFELD *is Professor of English and Director of Jewish Studies at Indiana University.*

number of related programs, among them a new version of *The Diary of Anne Frank*; a dramatization of Fania Fenelon's *Playing for Time*; *Kitty*, the story of a survivor of Auschwitz who returns to the camp years after her liberation and recounts to her son the horrors of incarceration; *We Were German Jews*, another story of a survivor's return, this time by a German Jewish couple to thier lost homeland; a three-hour television adaptation of John Hersey's *The Wall*, filmed in Poland in 1980 (a fact that necessitated some heavy compromises in the historical depictions of the Warsaw Ghetto uprising and of Polish-Jewish relations); *The Hunter and The Hunted*, an Australian-made program devoted to the work of Simon Wiesenthal and Beate and Serge Klarsfeld in tracking down Nazi war-criminals; a dramatization of Hitler's last days entitled *The Bunker*; and, most recently, *Inside the Third Reich*, a five-hour television remake of Albert Speer's memoirs. There have been other productions as well, some of them of a documentary nature (such as the *World at War* series), others of a more dramatic kind (such as Arthur Miller's *Incident at Vichy*).

Is it possible to generalize about the frequency, effectiveness, or impact of these TV programs on the Holocaust? While there is very little hard information to offer, one can set forth these impressions: (1) It is not the case that American viewers are being "saturated" with television broadcasting on the Holocaust; there have been several programs and there will be more, but their number is tiny and does not begin even remotely to challenge the broadcasting time devoted to soap operas, quiz programs, domestic comedies, sex-and-violence fantasies, and the like. (2) As television programming goes, the Holocaust shows are probably a couple of degrees higher in quality than most other shows. This is not to suggest that they are good or even good enough; they are not, but given the commercial patterns of American TV production and the very low level of common entertainment nightly offered to the millions, the Holocaust-related programs, for all of their artificiality and sentimentality, are better than most. (3) As for impact, it is undeniable that in one manner or another very large numbers of people are being educated about the Holocaust via television. It is probable, in fact, that to millions who have never read a book of any kind on the subject, the Holocaust is now somehow more

53

291

"real"; whether it is real as a part of historical consciousness and not just as dramatic and visual spectacle, though, it is impossible to know; nor can one know how deep and how permanent an impact these shows have on the masses who watch them. It is probably the case that for many the NBC *Holocaust* and, more recently, *Kitty* were not regarded so much as recreational viewing as they were taken as acts of conscience and lessons in historical and moral education; if so, then in many cases the impact has been more than superficial. (4) Finally, and perhaps most importantly of all, what image of the Jews is being transmitted and absorbed via television programs on the Holocaust? Overwhelmingly, one fears, it is an image of the Jew as victim, of a person cruelly set upon, perpetually persecuted and oppressed, done unto death. NBC's *Holocaust* relieved this image artificially by showing some flamboyant scenes of Jewish armed resistance; some of the other programs highlight examples of moral resistance; for the most part, though, the paramount image that is communicated is that of the Jew as sufferer, an image not untruthful to Jewish history in its most tragic dimension but also not balanced by counter-images of the Jew from the broader contexts of Jewish history.

As for television image-making of the Nazis, it may be evolving in the direction of more "sympathetic" understanding. If one is to judge on the basis of *Inside the Third Reich*, the major portraits are those of human frailty and its entrapments by the power and allure of the Hitler period. Sympathy is bound to flow in that direction, as it generally did for the actor who played Albert Speer, who showed his man to be handsome, intelligent, clean-cut, sensitive, a bit too ambitious perhaps but not very far removed in feeling or action from the common run of talented and enterprising humanity. The inclination, in other words, is to see the Nazi as a fallen Everyman, an attitude that at certain touching moments of *Inside the Third Reich* applied to the portrayal of Hitler as well.

These portraits should give us pause. There is nothing to be gained from demonizing the Nazis, and by making them exceptional creatures, placing their actions beyond the measure of human understanding or judgment. The Holocaust did not take place on some transcendental plane, after all, but within the glare of human history: it needs to be grasped within historical dimensions. If, on the other hand, the tendency continues to reduce the worst of the Nazi murderers to the familiar level of the man next door — weak, perhaps, but not exceptionally wicked; venal and vulnerable, no doubt, but otherwise hardly to be distinguished from you or me — something worse than mere banalization will have been accomplished. The bumbling Nazi caricatures of *Hogan's Heroes* are just that, and not many viewers of that popular afternoon and early evening show will be fooled into believing that the real men who served Hitler were in fact such comic buffoons. *Inside the*

Third Reich, though, was ostensibly aiming to achieve verisimilitude, and its distortions and failures are accordingly much more serious in shaping and misshaping our sense of history.

As everyone now recognizes, television is today the most influential single force in American popular culture. The images one sees in one's living room night after night directly influence one's general image of reality, and even influence the apperceiving powers of imagination itself. Since the tendency of TV image-making is to project generally superficial, one-dimensional characters, one's overall grasp of human character runs the risk of being reduced to cartoon shapes. NBC's *Holocaust*, praised by some as a significant tool of mass education, condemned by others as a soap-opera version of history, projected such simplistic shapes, although at its best it did so in a fashion somewhat less blatant than in most television fare. *Kitty*, produced in England and focusing exclusive attention on a Holocaust survivor, was far less synthetic and offered a kind of personal witness to history that compelled more serious reflection. The act of testimony at the heart of *Kitty* convinced by its directness, its candor, its obvious lack of extra dramatization. The program's single largest failing, and it is a large one indeed, is that it hardly ever mentioned the word "Jew," an omission that renders understanding of the Holocaust woefully incomplete.

As for *Inside the Third Reich*, it is one more graphic illustration of the appeal of the Speer legend, according to which good men get themselves involved with evil almost against their will and then manage to extricate themselves and rejoin the family of man as if the bad times had never happened or were somebody else's fault. In some very general sense, therefore, to be "inside" the Third Reich is to be inside the human skin, which covers us all more or less in the same way. Accusation, judgment, blame tend to fall away once one begins to recognize the ordinary dimensions of this man's failings, which are, after all, not so far removed from one's own.

To what degree is popular understanding of the Holocaust rounded out by the other popular arts? With respect to our concerns, cinema runs a close second to television as a central source of image-making and mass information, and recreational reading a more distant third. Popular music and illustration need hardly be touched upon here. Popular parlance, while not generically analogous to any of the above, is nevertheless highly revealing and a proper part of our concern, for it indicates with an unsettling directness just how the language of the Holocaust is being assimilated and reemployed by those to whom it is being transmitted by the media.

A comprehensive filmography of Holocaust-related

films will list today more than 300 titles. These include both documentary and theatrical films, some of them shorts but a significant number of them full-length. While many of the most important of these films have been produced abroad, all are readily available and frequently shown in the United States. They are shown, moreover, not only in the large movie houses of the major cities but in churches, synagogues, and community centers, on college campuses, and in secondary schools around the country. Some are also shown on television. In the fall of 1979, for instance, one of the TV channels in New York broadcast a month-long series of film programs commemorating the outbreak of World War II, a practice that has since been repeated elsewhere. Some 13 films were shown over a period of three weeks, dramatizing the experiences of victims and survivors and generally driving home the massiveness of destruction brought on by the war. As part of the Days of Commemoration in the spring of 1981 and 1982, numerous films relating to the Jewish tragedy were likewise carried by television stations around the country. And in mid-June, 1981, PBS broadcast from Israel some of the proceedings of the World Gathering of Holocaust Survivors taking place in Jerusalem.

As a result, it is no longer the case that the film version of *The Diary of Anne Frank* is the only visual version of the Holocaust that people know. A great many people — the figures once more will run up into the tens of millions — have seen *Night and Fog, The Garden of the Finzi-Continis, The Shop on Main Street, The Sorrow and the Pity, The 81st Blow*, and other films of a high order of cinematic quality. America has experienced nothing similar to the *Hitler Welle* of Germany in recent years, but the better known German films, including some of the Nazi propaganda films (*Triumph of the Will* most prominently), are also shown. *The Tin Drum* recently enjoyed a good deal of popularity, although most people probably left the theater wondering what it was about. Syberberg's *Hitler* has been shown in New York and debated by critics in the better periodicals, but the film is too long and too complex for popular taste and probably will not be seen by the mass audiences that have viewed the films mentioned above or such others as *Cabaret, Voyage of the Damned, The Pawnbroker*, or *Das Boot*.

The impact of these films is once more difficult to gauge, but at the least one can say that they keep memory of the war years alive. They tend to do so in a highly stylized manner, shaping their images according to the dictates of artistic sensibility and not necessarily historical sense. Accordingly, one cannot reasonably appeal to most films on the Holocaust for documentary evidence or even, in most cases, for approximate historical truth, for apart from such efforts as *Night and Fog* and *The 81st Blow* they do not attempt to record so much as to interpret. Even these last two films, relying as they do overwhelmingly on documentation, interpret selectively, as all art must.

What we confront here, then, is a large and diverse body of visual narrative centering in the war years and projecting a powerful, albeit highly selective, interpretation of historical extremity. On the most superficial level, these films implant in their viewers images of horror that shock the mind and offend sensibility; at their most effective, they also direct sympathy and help to guide understanding; at their most manipulative and irresponsible, they distort and demean. As with the TV programs on the Holocaust, there are examples of each tendency, and there is little certainty that in the future the most serious filmmakers will prevail. What we do know is that while the Holocaust films are not an adequate replacement of historical knowledge, they are, at their best, now part of its most graphic and indispensable illustration. Very large numbers of people will see them, most of whom, one hopes, will come away chastened by a surer sense of just how bad bad can be. Others, predictably, will use such films to nurture private fantasies of cruelty, some to the point of encouraging their meanest instincts, namely those that allow them to play at being Nazis.

In turning from film to literature one turns in two different ways, to a serious body of fiction, poetry, drama, and essayistic writing that demands the most careful scrutiny, and to popular, or "pulp," writing that is critically far less demanding. Inasmuch as I have dealt with the former in a recent book,* I shall pass it by and briefly review the more transient literature. I refer to the kind of book, its covers almost always swastika-adorned, that one finds on the popular book racks of drugstores, supermarkets, airports, and the like. There are a great many of these, written for the most part formulaically, and making their appeal to tastes of the most superficial kind. They have titles like *The Nightmare, The Wolf, Rogue Male, The Man Who Killed Hitler, The Führer Seed, Lord of the Swastika*, etc., and they combine ingredients of mystery, torture, debased sexuality, gothic horror, and the like. It is not clear who reads these books, or why, but apparently there is an audience for them. Is it, one wonders, the same audience that collects imitation Nazi jewelery, buys World War II memorabilia, favors the most violent of the hard rock and punk rock groups, fantasizes joining the toughest of the motorcycle gangs?

Consider the following blurb from the cover of one of these recently published books, this one entitled *Masquerade* and billed as "a sensuous, opulent novel of love and evil":

Before the darkness of Nazi terror, they were engaged in the dazzling rituals of love and desire.

Alexander and Marie Therese. He, an incredibly handsome golden youth, born of a lovely English

* *A Double Dying: Reflections on Holocaust Literature* (Indiana University Press, 1980).

293

woman and a titled German, growing to irresistible manhood in a world of privilege and perversity. She, a princess that was everything that Vienna wanted in a woman — beautiful, aristocratic, sophisticated, and as amoral as she was insatiable in her sensuality.

And into the lives of these two captivating and corrupting creatures came Livingston, the young Englishman who fell under their enchanting spell as he learned of love and lust, evil and intrigue, in a Europe shadowed by the rising Nazi menace.

This thrillingly romantic novel about the intoxication of the flesh and dangerous choices for the spirit indelibly captures a time and a place that will never exist again.
. . .

One need not read this book in its entirety, or the dozens of others like it currently available to the American reading public, to realize what this novel is up to. The whole purpose of books such as these is imaginatively to recreate the spirit of "that time and that place," to carry over into the lives of ordinary people the perverse excitement of the extraordinary. For this purpose Nazism is invoked as a stimulant to a heightened sensuality, a link with passions coveted but denied the average man and woman. The terror of Nazism, in other words, is a temptation into a new order of romance, one imagined to be infinitely more passionate than normal bedroom experience. Follow the black boot and the whip into a new kind of bliss, one so intense, so hints the lure of this romance, that it may almost kill you. The impulse is not primarily political but erotic, although the eroticism invoked is one whose political implications are the familiar ones of Fascism. Given what goes on in America it might be more accurate to call it "pop Fascism," an indulgence as prankish as it is tasteless, an erotic projection more freakish than fearsome.

This particular kind of fun has a musical counterpart in the currently popular, British-inspired punk rock, a new form of musical frenzy whose violent style has spilled over into the world of fashion and social manner. According to a *Newsweek* report (June 20, 1977):

though punks pierce their cheeks with safety pins and wear swastikas, the purpose is more visual than political. "They like the Nazi things because they are interesting decorations," explains Vivienne Westwood, whose "Seditionaries" boutique in London features punk fashions. Adds Gina Stevenson, a pink-haired San Francisco hairdresser: "This is our aggression. Everything's been done and this is the only way of doing something new to shock people."

The names of the musical groups are themselves intended to shock — names like "The Dictators" and "Kiss" with the double "ss" at the end of "Kiss" printed in the runic characters of the Nazis. The names of some of the performers — Sid Vicious and Johnny Rotten — are likewise intended to broadcast a message that is threatening and ominous. On the face of it these names and this rough style carry us to another social world altogether from that of the bored and beautiful "Alexander and Marie Therese," but the latter are really just

the more aristocratic side of the same vulgar fantasy, one that makes of cruelty a new and socially acceptable form of sadistic delight.

The appeal of pulp literature and punk rock is to those who readily indulge the so-called "lower class" pleasures, although both books and music have been taken up and embraced by numbers of people in the middle class, who typically look below themselves to find new and more exotic ways of excitement. This style of social and erotic debasement traditionally belongs more to the British than the Americans, and if one really wants to indulge such tastes, England is still the place to go. For there, according to the Alternative Holiday Catalogue, one can, for 30 British pounds a day, "vacation" in a Nazi-style camp, "complete with barbed wire, searchlights, watch towers, and fifty guards in SS uniforms." So far this idea of Auschwitz-as-theme-park has remained on the other side of the Atlantic, but there are some activities in American popular culture that begin almost to rival it.

As bizarre as it may seem, for instance, there is a comic side to pop Fascism, as exemplified by the following "jokes" from an issue of *The National Lampoon* (August, 1971):

From "Children's Letters to the Gestapo":
Dear Heinrich Himmler:
How do you get all those people into your oven? We can hardly get a pot roast into ours.

Dear Mr. Himmler:
Please don't get rid of all the kikes because I like to fly them except when the string breaks or they get tangled in a tree.

Dear Mr. Himmler:
I am Rolfe. I am 8. When I grow up I want to kill Sheenys and wear big boots like the Fuehrer.

As follow-up, *The National Lampoon* offers in one of its 1982 special numbers a collection of "Hitler's Favorite Cartoons," none of which has anything to do with Hitler himself or dates from the Nazi period. One would not suspect as much from the bright red cover, though, which features a stylized version of the German Führer. The point, if there is any, is that pop Fascism is catchy and, in today's America, also funny, in a slanted and crazy way.

A version of the same sick humor was featured in a mock menu at a Cincinnati high school awhile back, listing such offerings as "Beans Anne Frank," "Holocaust and cheese," "Fruit Jews," "Straight Jews," and advertising free swastika patches. Thus the joke goes on, sustained by a perverse desire to twist gross historical pain into trite and malicious gags.

At this point, admittedly a low one, we leave behind the more "artful" dimensions of American popular culture and descend several degrees to touch the raw nerve of demotic expression. The descent is ugly but well worth taking, for what it reveals — in terms unmediated by the conventional forms of the television, film, and pulp literature industries — is something of the effect of mass communication on those who absorb their words, sights, and sounds. There is no exact scientific measure by which we can know precisely how people respond to the images and ideas put before them on a daily basis, but what goes in by way of popular stimuli eventually comes out as popular expression, and a scrutiny of common, everyday speech that invokes the vocabulary of the Hitler period can provide insights into how the Holocaust is beginning to register on those to whom its images are broadcast by the media.

Such emphases as these inevitably carry us to the border regions of genre study — to jokes, cartoons, curses, and beyond — to more primitive expressions of verbal and physical aggression. The restraints established by art forms drop away in these instances, and more elemental layers of feeling are exposed, often in a highly theatrical manner. As an example, consider the following brief story from the student newspaper of a large Midwestern university:

HITLER'S BIRTHDAY CELEBRATED AS COMIC RELEASE FOR STUDENT

"I'm going to scare a lot of people," said freshman Mindy Madorin about her party Sunday in the lounge of Teter Wissler IV commemorating the birthday of Adolph Hitler.

For Madorin, herself Jewish, the party was a personal response to the Holocaust prompted by Hitler during World War II. "Charlie Chaplin was Jewish. Most of the comedians that have dealt with this kind of thing are Jewish. Mel Brooks, Woody Allen and Lenny Bruce are Jewish. I am Jewish," she said. "This is something you can look at unemotionally. We can laugh about it or cry about it. In laughing, you remember, you accept and you release the tension."

Large red posters with black swastikas, portraits of Hitler and signs proclaiming "Juden Verboten" adorned the walls of the lounge and halls of Wissler IV.

A special shrine to Hitler featuring a hand-penciled portrait of the Nazi leader, a four-foot-long picture of a troop rally and candles was placed on one side of the lounge. Music by Richard Wagner was played. . . .

The incident is altogether bizarre, but it should probably be regarded more as a neo-dadaist's prank than as a political act. The fact that the prankster was in this instance a Jew adds to the scandal, but it is precisely scandal, with all of its attendant publicity, that Mindy Madorin undoubtedly set out to create in the first place. If she could have attracted the same kind of attention by climbing a flag pole or riding nude across campus on a horse, one imagines she would have done so. The fact that she passed up these more conventional opportunities to shock and chose to celebrate Hitler, though, should not be passed over too quickly, for her choice confirms the notion that a Holocaust-inspired "humor" is now "in" and can be indulged without fear of social penalties. To Madorin, in other words, a party is a party is a party, and

if Hitler can add to the good times, why not invite him in?

Roger Frisbee, a student at another university, also had Hitler in mind, but he was up to more serious business, for which he armed himself and got himself fittingly costumed in Nazi regalia. His story is no less perverse than the preceding one, but inasmuch as it begins to show a descent into the next and more deadly stage of campus Nazi fun and games, it is worth citing in some detail:

STUDENT SHOOTING JEWISH COED WITH BEE-BEE GUN, CALLS IT PRANK

A University of Maryland sophomore was convicted of assault and battery and possession of a deadly weapon on the school's property, when he shot a bee-bee gun at a Jewish student while shouting "Heil Hitler" and "Yawoel Mein Feuhrer [sic]."

In court, Roger L. Frisbee, 19, sought to persuade the judge that there was no anti-Semitic intent involved in the incident, which took place on the morning of May 10 while Abbe Kannarek was using the telephone in the dormitory hall in which both lived.

Even Frisbee's attire was as a Hitlerite. He wore black trousers and coat, and a black tie, with a white shirt.

There were witnesses to the attack, which saw Abbe being shot in the legs five times. He then aimed the gun at her face, and when she shouted he did not pull the trigger, which required a cocking of the firing mechanism after each shot. Miss Kannarek, 21, of Los Altos, Ca., is the granddaughter of a Holocaust survivor.

When Frisbee told Judge Joseph F. Casula that it was all a practical joke and he didn't know that his target was Jewish, the judge responded that he wasn't being tried for anti-Semitism, but for assault and battery.

There have been other incidents of anti-Semitism on the university campus. In addition to a swastika daubing, an underground newspaper whose most recent issue was circulated on Hitler's birthday, May 20, chose Frisbee as its Man of the Month, and suggested that he use a flamethrower instead of a bee-bee gun.

It is a truism in comic routines that what begins as imprecation ends as a fake punch in the nose, but the "comedy" in this instance ran beyond its controls and seems almost to have ended in a homicide. Did the student get caught in his costume and forget his lines, or did he don his Hitler suit in the first place in order to feel at liberty to attack? Whichever way, it is evident that flirtations with Fascism, whether intended as a gag or not, can excite the fantasy levels of those who so indulge themselves beyond "play-acting" and towards actual performance. In the unpredictable and often undisciplined realm of popular expression, therefore, the lines of restraint separating words and deeds are vulnerable and can easily give way to raw and aggressive abuse.

Something of this sort occurred at a football game at another American university in the winter of 1981, a contest that began innocently enough but before long began to take on features of open warfare. The game was an intramural contest between two fraternities, one

295

made up predominantly of Jews, the other Gentile. The passions of both players and their fans get heated up at these matches, and it is common enough for some pretty rough verbal aggression to accompany the rough play on the field, but no one on this campus could recall a parallel to what happened this time. To be brief about it, the cheers called out by the fans of the non-Jewish fraternity took a turn beyond vulgarity to assume the most ugly kind of assault. Not just "Kill those bums," a refrain one typically hears at the games, but "Kill the Jews." And "Remember Auschwitz." "Remember the gas chambers." "Burn them in the ovens." These chants were not confined to one or two people who called them out and then ran away but were taken up by numbers of people on the sidelines and sustained for some time. It was the most glaring anti-Semitic incident that one could recall in many years on this campus.

The question, of course, is why did it occur at all? And what does it occurrence signify? The answers, as I was able to gather them during an evening at the fraternity house in question, are both unsettling and reassuring. Reassuring because, for all of its extreme ugliness, the incident was not, in fact, the work of hardened Jew-haters or ideological proto-Nazis. Most of the people involved claimed they hardly knew Jews and did not harbor any hatred of them. Why, then, their violent verbal attacks against the Jewish players? Not for religious reasons and not owing to any deeply-held political ideology, but, and this is the unsettling dimension, just because the Jewish players were *there*, opposed to them in an important game that both sides wanted to win. If part of the strategy of winning meant unnerving the opposition by turning them into Jewish victims, then so be it. After the game they could all make up. After all, the fraternity fellows didn't really intend to offend the Jews, just to beat them at football.

Beat them at any cost, I asked, even if that meant linking hands with Hitler? When I talked to the students that evening about Hitler and his Holocaust of the Jews, they felt properly ashamed and genuinely contrite. *That far*, they said, they didn't intend to go. Why, then, did they do it? Why did they use the language of Hitler to curse the Jews back into the ovens of Auschwitz? They didn't mean to, they said. It's just that the Jews were there, the language of Jew-hatred was also there, and the two came together, as it were — a violence foreordained by the ready availability of the rhetoric of anti-Jewish violence.

For the most part, they are to be taken at their word. Incidents of this kind have occurred elsewhere, against a Brandeis University sports team awhile back and against high-school teams with heavy Jewish representation. While some of this activity may be of the prankish sort described earlier, some of it is meaner and more deadly in its intentions. All of its draws upon the easy circulation of Holocaust language and Holocaust-related images, the ready availability of the words and

pictures of Jewish victimization. These words and pictures are beginning to release some ugly passions as well, and are doing so in a climate of feeling no longer bound by the earlier historical shock and moral disgrace of the Holocaust. Certain taboos seem to be in the process of falling, and with their fall it becomes easier to lapse into the former habits of anti-Jewish feeling.

As of this writing, the matter has not reached alarming proportions in America. At the same time, it is necessary to recognize that transmission of knowledge of the Holocaust, for all its value, has an ugly and possibly uncontrollable underside to it, one whose popular resonance can take the kind of obscene turn noted above. The vulgarization and trivialization of the Holocaust take from the dead whatever sanctity and protection historical memory properly bestows upon them. Moreover, it makes of their death an incentive to the indulgence of perverse passions, the most hostile of which will be directed against the living descendants of the dead — today's Jews — who then become, in imagination if not in fact, tomorrow's victims. Something of this sort is taking place today, and is doing so within a context sufficiently fraught with economic anxiety and social and political unease to cause concern.

One would not want to say that a new Holocaust is on its way, but at the same time it is clear that echoes of the old one have not altogether left us; if anything, they seem to be growing louder and more persistent. The signs and symbols of Jewish victimization are in fairly wide circulation, and by the very nature of their presence among us some of the ugliest passions of the past are reviving as well. These passions are encoded in the rhetoric and iconography of the Third Reich and are now ready at hand for those who want to reactivate them and tease Hitler's demons back into our lives.

The most shocking example of such a revival appeared not long ago in the upper reaches of American political power. I refer to Gordon Liddy, whose autobiography, *Will* (1980), records his plan to set up a covert intelligence and terror operation to carry out some of the nastier work of the Nixon reelection campaign:

> Diamond was our counterdemonstration plan. At the time, we still expected the [Republican] convention to be held in San Diego. I proposed to identify protest leaders, kidnap them, drug them and hold them in Mexico until after the convention was over, then release them unharmed. The sudden disappearances, which I labeled on the chart in the original German, *Nacht und Nebel* (Night and Fog), would strike fear into the hearts of the leftist guerrillas [as would] a team slated to carry out the plan as a "Special Action Group." When John Mitchell asked "What's that?" I knew that Mitchell, a Naval officer in World War II, would get the message if I translated the English "Special Action Group" into German. It was a gross exaggeration, but it made my point. "An *Einsatzgruppe*, General," I said, inadvertently

using a hard G for the word General and turning it too into German. "These men include professional killers who have accounted between them for twenty-two dead so far, including two hanged from a beam in a garage."

Liddy's *Nacht und Nebel* scheme seems a cut from popular films on the Nazi period. Fortunately, it failed to materialize; nonetheless Liddy has gone on to win a large success for himself in the aftermath of his failures. Indeed, he has become something of a minor pop-hero, one who likes quoting Nietzsche on television talk-shows and who can command several thousand dollars a night on the lecture circuit for affecting attitudes of extreme loyalty to his master, an extreme disdain for most others, a resolute will, and a steely defiance. The fact that Liddy's Nazi imitations have won him as much popular success as they have should confirm one's worst suspicions about how the Holocaust presently resonates through American popular culture at its most unin-

formed, a culture that always has enjoyed the adulation of villians.

So long as our villains are confined to the movie houses or the boxing ring they can do relatively little harm, but once they begin to take on a political dimension or, as in Liddy's case, once they are able to gain direct access to political power, villainy enters a new and more menacing phase. In an age when the large screen is capable of producing our political leaders and the smaller one in every American home serves to keep their images before us on a daily basis, the last thing we want to see are people in power who dream up real-life replays of *Nacht und Nebel*. It is bad enough that such dreams have become a commonplace of our popular culture. Were they now to radically overleap the confines of imagination and infiltrate politics in an energetic way, the results would be fearful to contemplate. ■

Sea of Galilee

ISIDORE CENTURY

and you would trade it all
trade it all
to lie beneath a tall palm tree
at an orange lilac sunset
watching the spangled blue
Smyrna Kingfisher skim
above its silver, shimmering twin
in the purpled waters below
its journey into night.

where gray bearded fishing boats
anchored deep, light
ancestral lamps of brass
whose red and amber glass
keep an ancient watch
over travelers in the night;
- and before going to sleep,
you set out nets full of dreams.

My Father's Hands

ISIDORE CENTURY

even now,
knowing my skin,
knowing my skin is raw
from his untouchings
knowing his hands were frozen
by his fathers untouchings
knowing a gravestone
stands between us
like a wall between his room and mine

even now,
his calloused hands
reach towards me
from a graveyard of lost childhoods
asking
for my hands.

59

297

The Political Lessons of Two World War II Novels: A Review Essay

MICHAEL MANDELBAUM

Forty years ago this September World War II began. The memory of this greatest of all human conflicts has reached a kind of middle age. It is no longer green. The leaders of the warring nations have long since passed from the scene. The world that the war made is disappearing. New issues, even entirely new nations, have arisen. The memoirs have all, or almost all, been written.

But the war is not wholly remote from us. Its survivors are still numerous. Its history is not yet of interest solely for the purposes of scholarly dissection. If World War II is no longer what the Vietnam War, whose wounds have not yet healed, still is, neither has it quite become World War I, which enflamed European passions for decades afterward but now matters only to historians.

World War II is the subject of a 1900-page, two-volume work by the novelist Herman Wouk, which falls somewhere between fiction and history.[1] Since both have been best sellers, it is likely that more Americans have learned about, or remembered, the war through Wouk's account than from any other single source in the last decade. The literary form that he has chosen—he calls it a "historical romance"—is well suited to the portrayal of those things that seem, in retrospect, most important about the war: its scope, the leaders who conducted it, its effects on ordinary people, the great naval struggle for control of the Pacific, and the Holocaust. The books' central characters, an American naval officer named Victor "Pug" Henry and his family, are fictional. The

[1] Herman Wouk, *The Winds of War* (Boston: Little, Brown, 1971) and *War and Remembrance* (Boston: Little, Brown, 1978).

MICHAEL MANDELBAUM is associate professor of government and research associate of the Center for Science and International Affairs at Harvard University. He is the author of *The Nuclear Question: The United States and Nuclear Weapons, 1946–76*.

Political Science Quarterly   Volume 94   Number 3   Fall 1979   515

events in which they are caught up, however, are real and are described in scrupulous detail with impressive fidelity to the historical record. The first volume, *The Winds of War*, carries the Henrys from the invasion of Poland to Pearl Harbor; the second, *War and Remembrance*, from Pearl Harbor to Hiroshima.

. A memorandum he writes from Berlin, where he is posted as naval attaché in 1939, predicting the Nazi-Soviet Pact brings Victor Henry to the attention of Franklin D. Roosevelt. As a special presidential envoy, he comes to meet Hitler, Stalin, Churchill, and even Mussolini. He is present at the summit meetings off Nova Scotia in 1940 and in Teheran in 1943. He is in London during the Battle of Britain; accompanies the Harriman-Beaverbrook mission to Moscow in 1941; and, in Russia again, tours the front in 1944. His naval service brings him to Pearl Harbor on the morrow of the Japanese attack, and he takes part in the battles of Midway, Guadalcanal, and Leyte Gulf. Along the way he comes in contact with people working on the Manhattan Project. And what little he misses, members of his family see: Poland under attack, the campaign in North Africa, the fall of Singapore, and, most vividly and terribly, Auschwitz.

The ordinary person who is privy to extraordinary men and events is a familiar literary device. Upton Sinclair's Lanny Budd rubs shoulders with the high and the mighty. More recently in Gore Vidal's *Burr*, the narrator, Charlie Schuyler, serves as Aaron Burr's amanuensis and meets, or hears Burr's firsthand accounts of, the leading personalities of the American Revolution. Schuyler is simply an observer; the Henrys are caught up in events. And they are more concrete and fully drawn characters than the family that plays an important part in another recent amalgam of fiction and history, E.L. Doctorow's *Ragtime*.

Literary critics have given higher marks as works of fiction to *Burr* and *Ragtime* than to Wouk's opus, which they have fixed firmly in the category of "middlebrow" writing. (The book's prominence on national best-seller lists has no doubt reinforced this general opinion.) If literary critics have on the whole been reserved in their enthusiasm for *The Winds of War* and *War and Remembrance*, historians have simply ignored them. They do not qualify as works of history at all.

Wouk's aim, however, was to create something that was neither purely fictional nor straightforwardly historical. His intention, he says in the foreword to the second volume, is for the reader to "remember what happened in the worst world catastrophe." To this task his hybrid literary genre turns out to be singularly appropriate.

It was a global war. The unity of the planet in our age of instantaneous worldwide communication and daily transcontinental jet transportation seems a commonplace. The war of 1939 to 1945 was, however, the first time that all the land masses and oceans of the globe were the stage of a single enterprise. World War I spread from Europe to the Middle East. World War II engulfed Africa, East and South Asia, and the South Pacific as well.

Conventional histories of the war find it difficult to tie together these far-flung theaters. Wouk successfully integrates them. Victor Henry himself is a unifying thread; as Roosevelt's personal envoy he shuttles around the world. The United States Navy is another: Henry and his sons—the elder, Warren, a carrier pilot; the younger, Byron, a submariner—see action in both the Atlantic and the Pacific.

A special invention of the two novels brings home the scope of the war with particular force. The narrative is interspersed with chapters from the war memoirs of a member of the German General Staff named Armin von Roon, which Victor Henry has translated into English during his retirement. Although Roon is a fictional character, his memoir, *World Empire Lost*, is based on actual postwar writings of German officers. For Roon, the war's global dimension offered opportunities that could have changed history. The two principal theaters of operation might have become linked, and if they had been, the course of the war might have been different, but because of German and Japanese decisions they never were.

In the fall of 1941 the Japanese might, for example, have struck Siberia rather than Hawaii. Coming on the heels of the German onslaught, this might have finished the Soviet Union. Another turning point came in early 1942. After Pearl Harbor and Barbarossa, Axis strength stood at high tide. Japan had pinned the United States back in the western Pacific; Hitler's legions were at the gates of Moscow. Had the Germans held their eastern lines and turned their full attention to North Africa and the Middle East, and had the Japanese swept south, through India to the Persian Gulf, together they might have crushed the tottering British Empire, in Roon's words, "like a nutcracker," linked up in the Middle East with its huge reserves of oil, and then turned on their principal foes, the United States and the Soviet Union, with greater strength than they ultimately mustered.[2] Plans for such strategic thrusts were floating around both the German and the Japanese high commands. But they chose differently. Both turned east: the Japanese toward Midway, the Germans toward Stalingrad, decisive battles that they would lose and that would mark the beginning of the end of their thrusts for world empire.

Wouk's two books give more vivid pictures of the principal leaders of the war than military and political history could. Fiction is better than history at showing "how it really was" where matters of human character are concerned. And the characters of national leaders were crucial during World War II. A few men held their nations' destinies more firmly in their hands than at any time since the defeat of Napoleon. "It all boils down to Hitler's impulses nowadays" Wouk has Roosevelt say of European affairs in 1940.[3] Roosevelt himself became the arbiter of American policy after Pearl Harbor; Churchill dominated his war cabinet and thus British policy; and Stalin, as absolute a ruler as Hitler, like his German

[2] *War and Remembrance*, p. 210.
[3] *The Winds of War*, p. 579.

counterpart not only made the major Soviet strategic decisions himself—often seemingly without any consultations—but also controlled day-to-day operations in the field, sometimes conferring hourly with his generals.

War during the nineteenth century, and between 1914 and 1918, was war by committee. World War II was a war of the warlords. Victor Henry meets them all. The Hitler he encounters is a study in contrast. On one occasion he is shy, pasty-faced, and unprepossessing. The American finds him wholly ordinary, "all the Germans rolled into one."[4] In an unguarded moment he is even clumsy and waiflike. It is as if he were returning the compliment of "The Great Dictator" by imitating Charlie Chaplin's "Little Tramp." On another occasion, however, Hitler is a powerful, raging orator, pouring out venom against his enemies. His magnetic appeal is all too apparent. Far from a "half-crazy, half-comical gangster," Henry tells Roosevelt, Hitler is "a very able man."[5]

Henry glimpses Stalin at a Kremlin reception, and later, as a personal emissary of Harry Hopkins, has a private meeting with him. Short, with a noticeably pock-marked face, immaculately dressed, the Soviet dictator says little. When he does speak, however, the attention he commands from the other Russians present makes clear his enormous power. He can be emphatic, and eloquent when he chooses, such as on the need for a second front in Europe.

Churchill is a jolly, fussy, playful Toby jug of a man, but with an iron determination to beat Hitler that gleams through the light banter and cigar smoke with which he surrounds himself.

Franklin Roosevelt is the subject of the fullest, richest portrait of the four. Victor Henry finds a sugary coating covering a hard nut; a cheery, casual, slightly comic aristocratic veneer masking cunning and purpose. Wouk is no revisionist. His Roosevelt does not conduct foreign policy haphazardly, without clear direction. He is as determined to defeat Hitler as is Churchill, but is acutely wary of the fickleness of American public opinion and resolved not to race too far ahead of his countrymen.

Where the warlords led between 1939 and 1945, millions followed. No one was untouched by the war, not even Americans, who were the safest of all the belligerents from its ravages. The virtue of historical fiction is precisely its capacity to show how great events affect ordinary people. The most famous example is the classic from which Wouk has drawn at least indirect inspiration, Tolstoy's *War and Peace*.

The lives of the Henry family form the counterpoint to the overarching theme of the world at war. Wouk is less artful at romance than he is at history. He is a workmanlike, even accomplished, novelist, but he is hardly to be compared to Tolstoy. The axes of the domestic subplot are the romantic entanglements of Victor Henry with Pamela Tudsbury, an English woman twenty years his junior and the daughter of a peripatetic journalist whom she accompanies as he covers the war, and of Byron Henry with Natalie Jastrow, a Jewish Radcliffe graduate

[4] Ibid., p. 301.
[5] Ibid.

and the niece of Aaron Jastrow, an American historian living in Italy who is patterned after Bernard Berenson. The two romances are conducted throughout the war and across the continents and oceans. Both result in marriage—"Pug" and Pamela near the end of the war, Byron and Natalie at the outset. Neither is an altogether plausible match. The second, especially, seems to be included as much to bear the weight of the historical theme as for its own sake: Natalie and Aaron are trapped in Europe as the Germans conquer it and share the fate of the continent's Jews.

Neither, however, are the matches wholly implausible. The war did forge hasty, unlikely liaisons, even as it dissolved marriages and families. And one effect of the war on ordinary people Wouk portrays uncommonly well. The death of Victor Henry's son Warren, who is shot down at Midway, is superbly rendered. It is a powerful reminder of the price of war.

If the central wartime experience of national leaders is the making of great decisions, that of ordinary men is combat. Accounts of combat come in two varieties. Most military histories chart the overall pattern of battles, like running accounts of chess games. They afford a commander's eye view of things. All too rarely is what the man under fire sees and feels recorded. Wouk describes combat from both points of view and for each of the two very different main theaters of World War II.

The war in Europe was a war of the nations, a brutal death struggle on land among peoples, above all the Russians and the Germans, who hated each other deeply. Roon's memoir gives a German commander's perspective on the European war, and the narrative provides glimpses of some of its crucial moments from ground level. Byron Henry finds himself in Poland when the Germans attack in September 1939. Victor Henry rides along on an RAF night raid over Berlin in 1940. He tours the Russian front in 1941, coming under fire outside Moscow, and walks through the rubble of Stalingrad and the ghost town that Leningrad has become three years later.

The war in the Pacific was mainly a naval war, and a war of the professionals. Wouk furnishes glimpses of the principal American naval commanders, Nimitz, Spruance, and Halsey. He gives splendid descriptions of the Battle of Midway, the turning point of the Pacific campaign and perhaps the most important naval engagement of the twentieth century, and of the Battle of Leyte Gulf, which had a less decisive impact on the course of the war but was, by the number of ships involved, a bigger battle.

He gives too a sailor's eye view of all three kinds of naval warfare. Warren Henry pilots a dive bomber against Japanese aircraft carriers off Midway. The heavy cruiser that Victor Henry commands is sunk by a Japanese torpedo in the Battle of Tassaforanga. Byron Henry's submarine sinks a freighter and later a troop ship, and is itself badly damaged by a depth charge and forced into desperate, and ultimately successful, evasive maneuvers. All are vividly portrayed.

The naval war in the Pacific is perhaps the part of Wouk's tale that is most decisively part of the past and least connected with the events of our own day.

303

Like the war in Europe, it was the greatest of its kind, measured by the men and material involved, that has ever been fought. Unlike the war in Europe, it is probably the last of its kind that ever will be fought. Tanks, infantry, and supporting aircraft have clashed frequently since 1945. Since the end of World War II there has, however, been no combat between aircraft carriers. It is unlikely that there ever will be. The march of technology has overtaken them.

A foreshadowing of the carrier's probable fate occurs at the end of *The Winds of War*, when Victor Henry flies to Pearl Harbor to fulfill his lifelong dream by assuming command of the battleship, only to find that his ship has been smashed beyond repair by Japanese planes. He had disdained carriers, believing that the heavy-armored battleship, with its booming guns, would remain the heart of the modern fleet. As he gazes on the wreckage in Pearl Harbor he realizes that in this, "the one crucial judgment of his profession," he has been wrong.[6] The war in the Pacific, he recognizes instantly, will be principally a carrier war, with battleships serving as escorts or spectators.

In another major naval conflict carriers would likely meet the same fate that awaited battleships in 1941. Today's models are far larger and carry much more airborne firepower than their World War II ancestors. But they are perilously vulnerable to air power launched from long distances away. In the battle of Midway that Wouk describes, American B-17 bombers fly sorties against the Japanese carriers; but the height at which they must operate degrades their accuracy to the point that the bombs fall harmlessly into the sea. Today, with television and computer-guided bombs, with missiles that can be launched with pinpoint accuracy against targets halfway around the world, the descendants of those bombers would probably not miss.

History, as well as military history, comes in two varieties. Traditionally it has taken a narrative form. Wouk's historical romance is simply traditional history, with fictional characters added to depict the lives of the Indians in addition to the policies of chiefs about which historians have always written. More recently professional historians have turned from description to analysis, from narrative to argument. Their emphasis has shifted from showing what happened to trying to explain why. There is an argument running through Wouk's opus, which, with the course of the war and the fate of the Henry family, stands as its third major theme.

It centers on the German question. Why did the Germans do it? Why did they cause so much trouble? Why, especially, did they behave in such brutal, aggressive fashion? These questions arise again and again, and Wouk has different characters give different answers. Together they make for a symposium on the central puzzle of the twentieth century.

There is the geopolitical explanation. According to Roon, Germany did what great nations always do: it made a bid for world power. There are cultural explanations: one person describes the Third Reich as romanticism gone berserk; another emphasizes the peculiar rigidity of the German character. There is the

---

[6] Ibid., p. 839.

political explanation: Germany as a nation thrown into turmoil by the Great Depression and succumbing to the extremism that is "the universal tuberculosis of modern society."[7] There is a historical explanation. Aaron Jastrow at first sees Hitler as another of the great conquerors set upon the European stage to serve as an agent of history's sweeping purpose, in this case the destruction of the petty, obsolete, cumbersome political units into which Europeans have been divided, leading to the unification of the continent.

The heart of the German question is the fate of the Jews under the Third Reich. World War II was really three conflicts: the battle between Germany and the Soviet Union, with Britain and the United States playing secondary but crucial parts, for control of Europe; the struggle between Japan and the United States for mastery of the Pacific; and the unequal conquest between the Nazis and Europe's defenseless Jews. Wouk describes this terrible slaughter from beginning to end; from the Nuremberg Laws, which cause a Jewish merchant to seek out Victor Henry in Berlin in 1939 and ask the American to rent his house, to Auschwitz, where one of Aaron Jastrow's Polish relatives is sent as a laborer and where Aaron and Natalie finally arrive in early 1945.

No doubt a fully adequate appreciation of Auschwitz is impossible to convey in print. By portraying the German officials as well as the victims, by describing day-to-day existence in the camp based on such records as there are and on the memoirs of survivors, however, Wouk does bring what he calls the "sinister red stain on all mankind" to a kind of grim life.[8]

The description of the war against the Jews gives the two books their enduring message, a message that neither plain fiction nor standard history could convey as forcefully. It is not the only, nor perhaps the primary, message that the author intends. His theme, he says in the foreword to *War and Remembrance*, is the obsolescence of organized human conflict: "either war is finished or we are."[9] The last scene of *War and Remembrance* is Hiroshima.

Auschwitz, however, leaves a more powerful impression. Historians of World War I, and now of the Vietnam War, have tended to investigate each war's origins as a way of asking why each conflict was fought. In retrospect neither seems to have been worth fighting. World War II raises no such question. It was a war that had to be fought because it was a war against evil. That is the enduring lesson that it has to teach.

In contrast to Auschwitz stands Victor Henry himself. If he is flawed as a fictional creation it is because he is too tough, too down to earth, too much what his wife Rhoda calls him, "something simple and almost obsolete . . . a patriot."[10] He is too much what he is because he is a symbol—of the basic decency and strength, of Americans and America, that stopped Hitler and saved the world from barbarism. He is the expression of the fact that, for Americans as

---

[7] *War and Remembrance*, p. 610.
[8] Ibid., p. 726.
[9] Ibid., p. 973.
[10] *The Winds of War*, p. 230.

well as for Englishmen, World War II was our finest hour. The world has been a far better place because the war was fought and won, and American power, which has been put to uses that have seemed less than noble in the years since, helped to win it. His elder son, Victor Henry writes to the younger one, "died in a right and great cause."[11] Forty years later, that is something worth remembering.

[11] *War and Remembrance*, p. 1022.

Copyright Acknowledgments

Reprinted with permission.

Frederic Krome. "*The True Glory* and the Failure of Anglo-American Film Propaganda in the Second World War." *Journal of Contemporary History* (January 1998): 21–34. Reprinted by permission of Sage Publications Ltd. Copyright © Sage Publications Ltd. 1998.

Leonard J. Leff. "Hollywood and the Holocaust: Remembering *The Pawnbroker*." *American Jewish History* 84 (1996): 353–376. Reprinted with the permission of the Johns Hopkins University Press.

——. "What in the World Interests Women? Hollywood, Postwar America, and *Johnny Belinda*." *Journal of American Studies* (December 1997): 385–405. Reprinted with the permission of Cambridge University Press.

Frank Manchell. "A Reel Witness: Steven Speilberg's Representation of the Holocaust in *Schindler's List*." *The Journal of Modern History* (March 1995): 83–100. Reprinted with the permission of the University of Chicago Press, publisher.

Michael Mandelbaum. "The Political Lessons of Two World War II Novels: A Review Essay." *Political Science Quarterly* (Fall 1979): 515–522. Reprinted with the permission of the author and the Academy of Political Science.

Susan D. Moeller. "Pictures of the Enemy: Fifty Years of Images of Japan in the American Press, 1941–92." *Journal of American Culture* (Spring 1996): 29–42. Reprinted with the permission of the Popular Press.

Alvin H. Rosenfield. "The Holocaust in American Popular Culture." *Midstream* (June/July 1983): 53–59. Reprinted with the permission of the Theodor Herzl Foundation, Inc.

Peter L. Valenti. "The Cultural Hero in the World War II Fantasy Film." *Journal of Popular Film and Television* (1979): 310–321. Reprinted with the permission of Heldref Publications.

For Product Safety Concerns and Information please contact our EU
representative GPSR@taylorandfrancis.com
Taylor & Francis Verlag GmbH, Kaufingerstraße 24, 80331 München, Germany

* 9 7 8 0 4 1 5 9 4 0 3 9 9 *